Portland Community College Libraries

SCARLETT DOESN'T LIVE HERE ANYMORE

Scarlett doesn't live here Anymore

Southern Women in the Civil War Era

LAURA F. EDWARDS

UNIVERSITY OF ILLINOIS PRESS / URBANA AND CHICAGO

Library of Congress Cataloging-in-Publication Data
Edwards, Laura F.
Scarlett doesn't live here anymore : Southern women in the Civil War era /
Laura F. Edwards.
p.   cm.
Includes bibliographical references and index.
ISBN 0-252-02568-7 (alk. paper)
1. United States—History—Civil War, 1861–1865—Women.
2. United States—History—Civil War, 1861–1865—Social aspects.
3. Women—Confederate States of America—Social conditions.
4. Confederate States of America—Social conditions.
5. Women—Southern States—History—19th century.
I. Title.
E628.E39   2000
973.7'13'082—dc21   99-050422

C 5 4 3 2 1

FOR THE WOMEN IN MY FAMILY:
Josephine Johnson Rennich
Sandra Rennich Edwards
Marion Rennich Griffith
Frances Marian Edwards

Contents

*A*CKNOWLEDGMENTS

*M*Y biggest debt is to all the historians working in southern history, particularly those writing about southern women. Their work literally made the book possible. This group of scholars also has provided advice to me over the years. Many have commented on conference papers and other pieces that have eventually made their way into this book: Vikki Bynum, David Cecelski, Peter Coclanis, Pete Daniel, Kirsten Fischer, Glenda Gilmore, Jim Grossman, Jacquelyn Hall, Nancy Hewitt, Karen Leathem, and Tim Tyson. Others outside the field—including Jan Reiff, Michael Bellesiles, and Giovanna Benadusi—have been equally generous with their time and their insights. Noralee Frankel read the entire manuscript, and her comments were greatly appreciated. Laurie Weakley and Edward Estock have put up with me for weeks at a time while I did research in North Carolina, and they still insist that I am welcome to come back. Sheila Cohen, Samantha Holtkamp, Jessica Millward, Chelsea Neel, and Ana Varela-Lago all provided exceptionally thorough and extremely timely research assistance at various points. The ideas and friendship of all these people have been enormously important to this book and to me.

I was fortunate to have two excellent readers at the press. One of these readers, Peter Bardaglio, went above and beyond the call of duty: he read the manuscript twice, and each time his suggestions were invaluable. The readers, along with Anne Scott, who commented on a preliminary draft, made this a much better book. Karen Hewitt's advice and enthusiasm have been vital to this project. She has been the most supportive editor I have ever encountered—and that has been absolutely crucial to me. Many thanks also to Jane Mohraz, who copyedited the manuscript.

Financial support for this project came from a number of sources: a postdoctoral fellowship at the Smithsonian Institution's National Museum of American History, a research fellowship through UCLA's Center for American Politics and Public Policy, and leaves from the History Department at the University of South Florida and the History Department at UCLA.

Finally there is John, and he already knows what he has meant in all this.

Scarlett Doesn't Live Here Anymore

Introduction

THE Civil War and Reconstruction still grip our national imagination. A country at war with itself, hundreds of thousands dead on the bat-
tlefield, the collapse of slavery, and the promise of freedom: history leaps
out of the textbooks and becomes theater, complete with villains and heroes, grand intentions and tragic losses. In the hands of historians who focus on military and political battles, however, the period has become a history of men, specifically white, propertied men. To be sure, both popular
histories and traditional academic scholarship have always included exceptional women—such as those, white and black, who left the slave South and
became abolitionists or those who had access to the inner circles of the
Confederate government during the Civil War. But the bulk of southern
women generally played a supporting role in a history largely directed by
white, propertied men. It was men who debated the issues leading up to the
fatal conflict, decided to take the nation into war, spilled their blood in the
ensuing battles, officially ended the hostilities, and then battled once again
over Reconstruction. Most women seemed marginal to the period's key
events and became invisible in many history books and courses.

A new generation of historians, however, has broadened its focus to include social conflicts generated by the war and its aftermath. The work of
these historians has centered on a wider range of people, including all women
as well as African American and poor white men. The scholarship in southern
women's history has been particularly dynamic. In the past fifteen years, it
has grown from a small outpost in the subfield of southern history into a

field of its own, complete with its own professional organization (Southern Association for Women Historians) and a triennial national conference.[1]

Southern women—white and black, rich and poor—are the primary focus of this book. Although books and articles on them now line the shelves of university libraries, this work has not yet filtered into the classroom, popular histories, and even traditional academic work on battles and politics. One goal of this book is to bring together the growing literature on southern women and to make it accessible to a wider audience. Another is to show how the inclusion of women in the history of the nineteenth-century South changes our understanding of the Civil War and Reconstruction.

As recent work reveals, colorful military campaigns and stirring public pronouncements only set the stage for another war that was equally compelling. Confederate leaders fought the North to preserve their social order, but the resulting upheaval undermined it by inflaming existing tensions and opening up new questions in the South. The result was an internal conflict over the nature of southern society. Households, fields, country lanes, and city streets became battlefields as southerners faced off in conflicts that extended through Confederate surrender and beyond the official end of Reconstruction.

This war was not conducted through easily identifiable organizational structures, written statements, and recognized leaders. Nor was it defined by such simple dichotomies as North and South, Union and Confederate, Republican and Democrat. Rather, this war was woven into the very fabric of life. Each thread held many others in place, locating different individuals in specific positions within the dense web that was southern society. As the individual threads grew thin with the strain of war and then broke with the impact of emancipation, the cloth itself began to disintegrate. Released from the bonds that had held them, some men and women eagerly began piecing together their lives and their communities in new ways. Others reacted with fear and anger as the strands that had anchored them fell away.

Southern women played key roles in this war. In fact, it is difficult to separate the war of men from the one that involved women because the Civil War and emancipation shattered the region's households and political institutions with the same blow. In the legal and political structure of the slave South, the household was more than a place of residence or a self-contained nuclear family. Its physical borders extended beyond the four walls of the main house to the outbuildings and the fields. Most of the work of southern society took place here: the production of cash crops, food, and clothing as well as the daily round of household chores and child care. Household heads— masters, husbands, and fathers—oversaw these many operations and presided over a range of dependents, who included African American slaves as well as white women and children.

By structuring relationships within and outside its borders, the household stood at the juncture between private and public life. Men and women acquired specific rights through relationships within households as husbands and wives, parents and children, masters and slaves. When they stepped across their thresholds, they carried these rights with them. Wives, for instance, faced limitations in property ownership. Beyond that, they could not keep their wages, make contracts, or claim parental rights over their children. As property themselves, slaves suffered even greater restrictions. They could not even contract a legally recognized marriage, let alone claim the prerogatives of husbands or even the more limited rights of wives.

Husbands and masters thus controlled the labor, property, children, and bodies of their wives and slaves. In the case of slaves, masters exercised absolute power, with rights to buy and sell and even to end life itself. Although household heads lost some formal control toward the end of the antebellum period, their power was still considerable. In return, they were required to maintain and protect all their dependents. But there were no guidelines mandating the level of support. Nor did wives and slaves find it easy to challenge their husbands' and masters' decisions in this regard.

Who were the household heads and dependents? Both the law and southern social conventions assumed that household heads were adult, white, propertied males. According to the dominant ideology of the time, only this particular group of people possessed the capacity for reason and self-control necessary to manage households, take responsibility for dependents, and make decisions about the public good. White women and all African Americans were thought to require protection and guidance because they lacked these qualities. Technically, free black women and men as well as white women could be household heads, but few were. Dependency was defined as part of all white women's and African Americans' natural makeup. By this logic, their status as wives and slaves was a necessary accommodation to the human condition.

Not all white men were considered fully independent either. They actually claimed power on their ability to fulfill the duties of household head, not on the basis of their race and sex alone. Property was crucial to the task. Without it, even white men found it difficult to maintain households and often found themselves working for other men in conditions that smacked of dependency. Nevertheless, all propertyless white men still possessed the potential to head their own households. In this sense, their position was always different from that of women and African Americans, who could step into the role of household head but could never *be* household heads in the same way as free white men.

The Civil War and emancipation shook antebellum southern households to their foundations, shattering relations within the households and outside them. No longer slaves, African American men could, theoretically, assume the same roles and the same rights as free white men. In taking on the role of household head, freedmen could also conceivably claim the authority to govern their dependents and, by extension, the power to participate in public life. Freedwomen, who now faced the legal restrictions of coverture, would find it as difficult as other free women to claim and perform all the duties and rights of household heads, but they could demand the privileges that came with their new legal status as dependent wives and daughters.

At the same time, the economic upheaval of war and its aftermath stripped many common white families of their property. With their land, livestock, and tools went these men's ability to maintain their own households and provide for dependents. The implications reached beyond their households. As economic independence slipped from common white men's grasp, their exclusive claims to public power also began to collapse.

Many former slaveholders managed to hold onto their land. But it had much less value, because slavery had provided the labor that made land profitable. Without these profits, their class standing deteriorated, and their hold on political leadership gave way.

These economic changes for white men meant changes for white women, who still derived their class status through that of their male relatives. The abolition of slavery called the position of all women into question in other ways as well. Without the institution that grounded racial difference, what now distinguished white men and women from black men and women? Further, if the domestic relation of slavery could be dissolved, what was so sacred about the other domestic relations, such as marriage?

In the nineteenth-century South, domestic relations were inseparably connected to civil and political rights. From this perspective, it is impossible to understand the Civil War's military campaigns and Reconstruction's political contests without understanding the home front, where the actions of women were as central as those of men in fights over the South's social order. From this perspective, women's history and men's history are not separate. They are part of the same story.

Women were politically active long before women's clubs and political organizations began advocating temperance, women's rights, social reform, and suffrage. To be sure, the agenda of women in the earlier part of the century was different from that of later women reformers and women today.

Nor did these women measure up by later standards of political activism. They did not necessarily demand individual rights or contest their subordination to men. But they did actively participate in key conflicts over the economic status of their households, justice for their families, and the shape of southern society generally. If those are not political issues, then what are?

The book is divided into three sections: Before, During, and After. Because the conflicts of the Civil War and Reconstruction were so deeply rooted in the antebellum period, it is necessary to begin the story there. Few southern women, as we learn in this section, were belles like Scarlett and Melanie in either the novel or the movie version of *Gone with the Wind*.[2] They were a diverse group, who occupied very different positions in southern society, had very different experiences, and possessed very different interests. They also had very different levels of commitment to the existing social order.

The next section deals specifically with the war years. It examines the effect of the war on women and the ways that women shaped its course and outcome. Here, again, *Gone with the Wind* fails as a historical model. Diehard loyal Confederate women were harder to find than either the movie or the book indicates. They were there, but the South was also filled with women who were reluctant supporters and outright opponents of the Confederate cause.

The final section turns to the postwar years. Here *Gone with the Wind* provides some important historical clues. As both the book and the movie suggest, women took an active a part in reconstructing southern society after the Civil War. Some hoped to resurrect the past, while others set off in new directions. But there were many more alternatives than either the book or the movie implies. Southerners battled over a range of issues—the terms of wage work, racial etiquette, the rights of former slaves, the status of former slaveholders, the position of common whites, and the standards of womanhood and manhood. Few of these issues would be resolved through institutional politics. Most remained unresolved when national political leaders abandoned the project of Reconstruction in 1876. Instead, ordinary southern women and men shouldered the daily work of Reconstruction. For better or worse, it was they who remade southern society.

This book is a synthetic, interpretive work that rests on scholarship in southern women's history. As with any book of this kind, the biggest debt is to the work of these other scholars. Recent work in the field has unearthed new material and has reinterpreted old sources in new ways. As a result, we now know much more about a much wider range of southern women than anyone thought possible just fifteen years ago. Historians of southern women have also been conceptually innovative. They had to be. Of all the women in the United States, women in this region were assumed to be the most downtrodden and the least interesting as historical subjects. Historians in the field have had to rethink central issues and assumptions in southern history generally to make southern women visible and to make a case for their historical importance.

This book covers key debates about southern women and southern history. Readers, however, will not always find full reference to historiographical debates in the text. Those who want to know more about the historians associated with particular historical perspectives or the literature on a given issue should consult the endnotes.

This book also relies on existing literature for factual information. Despite the recent flowering of work in nineteenth-century southern women's history, there are significant gaps in the scholarship. Common white women remain understudied generally, as do African American women during the Civil War and Reconstruction. Where the literature became thin, I turned to traditional social and political histories of the period. Even when these studies did not mention women or contained only scattered references to them, they still had valuable information about issues and events that affected and involved women. I then took the existing analyses and reworked them to make women visible.

This book thus combines scholarship on southern women with more traditional (male-centered) social and political history of the South and primary research from various archives. As my handling of the material suggests, this book does not simply summarize the existing scholarship. In synthesizing, I have interpreted. In some instances, I worked my own archival research into the analysis. I have also relied heavily on ideas developed elsewhere in my own work.

One of the book's goals is to capture the richness and diversity of southern women's lives, but diversity and complexity can translate into narrative chaos. To avoid chaos, I have made some strategic decisions about presentation. This work includes African American women, middling and poor white women, and wealthy white women in one narrative. It also addresses issues of gender, race, and class simultaneously. The book does not include *all* southern women, however. It leaves out Indian women. It also leaves out women in ethnic and religious minorities—German, Italian, Irish, French, and Creole southerners as well as Jews, Quakers, and Catholics. Nor, by extension, does the book include ethnicity or religion as analytical categories as thoroughly as it does gender, race, and class.[3]

The book also sacrifices geographic coverage to address other complexities in women's lives. The analysis focuses on the eleven states that seceded from the Union to form the Confederacy. It leaves out border states, such as Kentucky, Maryland, Delaware, and Missouri, all of which took very interesting, very different historical trajectories, particularly during and after the Civil War.

Not all the Confederate states receive equal coverage, nor do all the distinct geographic areas within these states—such as low country, Piedmont, and up-country or farms and cities. Of course, geography played an important role in shaping women's lives, and I do discuss these issues. But I decided to center the analysis on the stories of particular women rather than generalizations about women in different regions. After all, what better way to make women visible than to center the narrative on them? Doing so allows readers to get to know individuals, to read their words, to confront the contradictions in their lives, and to see the challenges they faced. But it also means less space for comprehensive, geographic coverage.

Whenever possible, I have tried to follow the lives of individual women over time. This is easiest to do with wealthy white women, who were more likely than their less prosperous neighbors to leave extensive diaries and letter collections. Four wealthy white women appear in the book: Gertrude Clanton Thomas, Kate Stone, Marion Singleton Deveaux, and, to a lesser extent, Marion's sister, Angelica Singleton Van Buren. (Yes, *those* Van Burens: Angelica married Martin Van Buren's son and served as White House hostess during Van Buren's presidency.) None of these women were "typical." Nor do they necessarily represent the range of planter-class women. They all lived in the Deep South and were members of the most elite southern families. Nonetheless, their lives highlight the diversity of experience among this group of women. Their lives also provide insights into the changes planter-class women faced over the course of the nineteenth century. In the case of Kate Stone and Gertrude Thomas, their lives are also more accessible. Those who wish to find out more about them can read their published diaries.

African American women and common white women are more difficult to follow over time. The chapter on enslaved women focuses on the life of a Harriet Jacobs, who escaped to the North and left a narrative of her life. (Although I refer to Jacobs by her real name, I have used the fictionalized names for the other characters who appear in her account.) The yeoman and poor white women in Walker County, Alabama, appear in all three sections.

I chose them partly because there is a particularly rich collection of sources that provide detailed information about their lives before, during, and after the war. They also provide revealing glimpses into the experiences of this group of southerners in particularly vivid ways.

For the most part, however, I was unable to follow particular common white and African American women over time in the same way that I did wealthy white women. Nonetheless, I do integrate their voices and experiences into the narrative. They sent letters to their governors and appeared in court cases and government reports. Some caught a journalist's eye or annoyed a wealthy neighbor enough for him or her to make note of it. These moments provide insight into the general situation faced by many others.

The question of how to identify women in the text has been a difficult issue, because their last names change over time with marriage. To identify Marion Singleton Deveaux Converse by her last name would mean that she would have three different designations in the text (and she dropped Converse in her later life). But to call women by their first names and men by their last names suggests a lack of respect that is contrary to the goals of this text. As a compromise, I decided to use first names for both the men and the women in cases such as Marion's. I use last names for women whose names did not change during the course of the narrative, although I sometimes refer to them by their first names so they will not be confused with other family members.

Much has been done. Much more remains to be done. I see this work as a beginning, not an end. I hope those who read it will continue to think about southern women as they study U.S. history. I also hope a few will be inspired to continue the work of recovering these women's lives, putting them back into history, and then rethinking the history of the region.

Part One

Before

The myth of moonlight and magnolias still shapes our ideas about the lives of southern women before the Civil War. If anyone lived this life, it was Marion Singleton Deveaux and Gertrude Clanton Thomas. Marion was the daughter of a wealthy South Carolina slaveholder, who went to boarding school in Philadelphia, ordered her clothes from New York, summered at fashionable resorts, and moved among the South's most powerful families. Material comfort also surrounded Gertrude, a daughter of one of the wealthiest men in Georgia.[1]

The magnolias' seductive scent and the moonlight's soft focus tend to obscure the diversity of southern women and to blur the sharp edges of their lives. Behind the inviting languor of the mythic South lay chattel slavery. Slaves grew the cotton, tobacco, sugar, and rice that generated the wealth of such families as Marion's and Gertrude's. They also did all the cleaning and cooking that made southern hospitality so legendary.

For such enslaved women as Harriet Jacobs, the South was anything but hospitable. She started work as a house servant in Edenton, North Carolina, while still a child. In her early teens, she began dodging her master's sexual advances and her mistress's physical threats. Determined to escape, she spent seven years hiding in a cramped attic before she found an opportunity to go North.[2]

Southern hospitality also meant different things to the vast majority of southern white women. They rarely saw columned piazzas, mint juleps, or wide hoopskirts. Like the women of poor to modest means who lived in the red clay hills of Walker County, Alabama, they raised large families, kept food in their children's stomachs and clothes on their backs, and worked in the fields when necessary.[3]

Even the lives of planter-class women had a more gritty side. All the luxury that surrounded Marion Singleton Deveaux, for instance, could not spare her from the deaths of her first husband and two of her children or an abusive second marriage that finally ended in a painful, humiliating separation.

The South itself was a large, diverse region. The upper South states of Virginia, North Carolina, and Tennessee began to develop mixed economies during the antebellum period. All three had thriving plantation districts: on the rich flatlands in the western half of Tennessee and below the fall line on the eastern coast of Virginia and North Carolina. The economies of these states were not based just on plantation production. Instead, commerce and manufacturing mixed with agriculture. In Virginia, for instance, where exhausted land and competition from western states made slave labor less profitable, some slaveholders began to sell slaves to the lower South. Here, as well as in North Carolina and Tennessee, it was also common for slaveholders to hire out slaves rather than work them on their own land.

The lower South, by contrast, was more dependent on agriculture. Although the economy began expanding and commercializing by the 1850s, cotton was still king, along with its royal retainers, rice and sugar. The plantations on the Sea Islands of South Carolina and Georgia covered hundreds of acres. So did those that lay along the Mississippi River and on the rich, dark lands of the "Black Belt," in Georgia, Alabama, and Mississippi.

The Southwest's potential had only just begun to be tapped during the antebellum period. At the beginning of the Civil War, parts of Alabama, Mississippi, Arkansas, and Texas were still newly settled frontiers. Even for the wealthy, conditions on the southwestern frontier could be spartan, even crude. Here, life was much more like William Faulkner's *Absalom, Absalom,* where the slaveholder Thomas Sutpen lived in a cabin with his slaves, than like *Gone with the Wind.*

Geography carved up every southern state into distinct areas as well. The fall line in Virginia, North Carolina, and South Carolina separated the eastern plantation districts from the Piedmont. The East's high concentration of slaveholders and slaves contrasted with the Piedmont's mix of commercial enterprises, large plantations, and yeoman farms. Slaveholders and slaves could also be found in large numbers in the tobacco belt, which reached through the middle of Virginia and into north-central North Carolina. As the Piedmont gave way to the Appalachian Mountains, the land became poorer, farms smaller, and slaves scarcer.

Tennessee and Georgia were mirror images of states along the eastern seaboard, with the Piedmont flanked by the mountainous up-country in the East and plantations in western Tennessee and southern Georgia. Alabama, Mississippi, Arkansas, and Louisiana were divided in half, with slaveholders and slaves on the plantations of the rich bottomlands in the South and along the Mississippi River. White yeoman families clustered on the smaller farms in the hills to the north.

Within this diverse region, women's lives varied so much that it is misleading to speak of them as a uniform group. Race and class further complicated the picture. The class position of free women, white and black, depended primarily on their husbands. When married, women surrendered their property and wages to their husbands according to the laws of coverture. In some states, the laws were changed in the 1850s to ease these restrictions somewhat. Nonetheless, wives never controlled property in the same way that their husbands did. If women remained unmarried, they were economically vulnerable. Since women were presumed to be wives who would not need to support themselves, few jobs paid women a living wage. If widowed or single women had their own property, managing it or conducting business was no easy proposition.

The same laws that placed all wives in a similar position of subordination to their husbands also distinguished among them. Coverture linked free women's economic and social position directly to that of their husbands. As a result, the conditions of free women's lives differed widely: from the wives of laborers with no property at all to those of wealthy planters with vast acres and hundreds of slaves.

Slave women occupied a different class position altogether. The laws did not recognize them as wives because slaves could not contract legal marriages, even though they did form unions recognized as marriages within their own communities. Slave women, then, were not bound by the laws of coverture, nor did they derive their class position through their husbands. They answered instead to the laws of slavery, which recognized them as slaves, not as women at all.

A woman's racial status was both distinct from and connected to her class standing. Most southern states defined race in biological terms, as the degree of separation from African parentage or the amount of "African blood." While many white southerners subscribed to the belief that any amount of "African blood" classified a person as black, such a measure was impossible to apply. Instead, states generally adopted rules specifying a certain percentage—such as one-eighth or one-sixteenth. Even this sharp legal line blurred in practice because race was not a simple biological trait. Some people who had always lived as white and were considered as such by their communities actually had African American relatives. Similarly, a few people who grew up in black communities "passed" as white. Others who could "pass" chose not to do so. For these people, racial status was determined by something more than skin color. It also depended on the willingness and ability to meet the social and cultural standards of "whiteness."[4]

This is not to say that race was only a matter of individual preference. Free black southerners knew the burden of imposed racial restrictions only too well. Southern law assumed that all blacks were slaves and that all whites were free. Southerners who appeared to be of African descent had to produce documentation proving their free status, while those who looked white did not. These assumptions undercut the legal status of free blacks in other ways as well. Southern states denied free blacks full civil and political rights on the basis that race made them more similar to slaves than to free citizens. Because they had no masters to provide supervision, the responsibility fell to the state instead—or so the logic went. These legal restraints reinforced and combined with widespread racial prejudice to place free blacks on the margins of southern society. All white women consequently enjoyed legal rights and social privileges that no black woman ever could.

Although race and class combined with gender to place southern women in different social spaces, these spaces were neither entirely static nor completely predetermined. Family, kin, personal reputation, and social context all merged with gender, race, and class to shape what particular women could do in particular circumstances. Within these boundaries, moreover, southern women fashioned their own positive identities as women. They created strong social bonds to sustain themselves in difficult times. They developed powerful social critiques to make sense of their lives and to give them hope for the future. They also continually pushed at the edges of their allotted social spaces, challenging the barriers imposed on them from the outside.

There were, however, limits. Few women thought of demolishing and then reconstructing southern society on their own. Such a project would be extremely difficult for any group of southern women to undertake, even if they had wanted to, given their inability to control property, raise capital, and pass the necessary laws. If they initiated work outside the proper channels, the price would have been too high and may well have resulted in severe disciplinary measures. Most southern women therefore worked within existing structures as they tried to make their living spaces more habitable.

1   *Privilege and Its Price*

MARION Singleton married her first husband, Robert Deveaux, in 1835. They moved to his South Carolina plantation, had several children, and lived happily until Robert's death in the 1840s. Until then, Marion's privilege had cushioned her like a protective cocoon.

Then she married Augustus L. Converse. Augustus was sanctimonious, short-tempered, and domineering—a volatile mix that Marion ultimately found impossible to negotiate. The crisis came in December 1854. Marion had been sleeping with one of her daughters to shield herself from Augustus, but he managed to lock her in his bedroom. During the ensuing argument, he reached for his gun and loaded it. Fearing for her life, she leaped out of the window and onto the piazza ten feet below, where a crowd of slaves had gathered to watch. That night, the slaves sheltered Marion in their quarters. But as slaves, they could do little to counter Augustus's authority and were severely punished for what they did do. Legally, there was little anyone could do, since the law gave husbands authority to "discipline" their wives. Even a neighboring white planter refused to intervene. Marion failed to escape the next confrontation and endured a prolonged beating. Soon after, she fled and sought shelter with her own family.[1]

As Marion's second marriage revealed, her racial and class privilege had a price. That price was subordination to fathers and husbands. The positions of wives and slaves were so closely tied together that marriage and slavery were inseparable in the legal, religious, and political ideology of the South. To challenge the authority of husbands was to challenge the authority of masters, who were often the same people. As Augustus later argued in the couple's separation suit, Marion's refusal to submit to his orders had undermined his position to the point where the slaves began to revolt as well.[2]

The institutional connection between slavery and marriage reveals a great deal about the power structure of southern society. It can also mislead by downplaying the vast differences in the lives of slaves and planter-class women, casting both groups as the abject subjects of masters and husbands. White slaveholding women had more resources at their disposal than slaves did. They used the privileges that came with their racial and class position to exercise some control over their lives. Therein lay the central contradiction of these women's lives, however: the privileges that gave them power as members of the white, planter class also defined their subordination as women.

～

Historians usually define the planter class as those who owned twenty or more slaves. Also included in this group are those who had substantial assets and maintained close ties with the slaveholding elite, even though they may not have owned many slaves themselves. The planter class exercised influence over southern society disproportionate to its size. White slaveholding households formed a minority in southern society. Although the number of slaveholders increased during the antebellum period, their proportion relative to all white households declined from 36 percent in 1850 to 26 percent in 1860. Most of these households owned only one or two slaves. Those owning twenty or more slaves formed just 12 percent of all slaveholding households in 1860. Fewer still owned a hundred or more.[3]

It was not just slaveownership that defined the planter class. This leaves out wealthy southerners who lived in towns and cities. Urban slaveholders might retain only a few domestic servants. They were also likely to hire slaves rather than own them outright. Superficially, urban southerners resembled the northern middle class. The men held professional jobs as lawyers, merchants, bankers, and teachers. The wives devoted most of their time to domestic chores and child care. The children attended school. These families lived in large but unostentatious homes tucked along city streets. In some ways, the world of the plantation South seemed far away.

Yet many wealthy urban southerners had strong social and economic ties to the planter class. Marion's family, for instance, had relatives in Richmond, Virginia; Columbia and Charleston, South Carolina; and Washington, D.C. All those in the Singleton family's network moved comfortably between city and plantation. Slavery supported various family members in different ways, but their social status was the same, regardless of where they lived.[4]

The material conditions of the planter class also varied. The Singletons lived in a grand, columned house similar to Tara. So did Gertrude Clanton's family, which lived near Augusta, Georgia. They were the exception rather than the rule, though.

Geographic mobility determined living conditions to a certain extent. Many slaveholding families were continually on the move in search of more fertile lands and better economic opportunities. The homes of those living in the newly settled Southwest were much less impressive than those in more established areas of the East. Those in the East with no intention of relocating their plantations were also a restless bunch. Planters in South Carolina, Georgia, and Florida regularly decamped to escape the sweltering heat and deadly diseases that descended during the summer months. Those in the more moderate, healthy areas also spent a great deal of time away from home.[5]

Even in the East, few slaveholders' residences resembled the movie set of *Gone with the Wind* or what we might consider gracious living today. These homes were lavish by the standards of *their* time, not ours. Many of those who could afford to drape their homes in luxury chose not to do so. After all, the plantation's primary purpose was production. Of all the buildings that made up plantations, the residence was the least central to this process. It did serve the important function of symbolizing the family's authority and status, but slaveholders did not have to do much to distinguish their homes from the shanties and cabins of poorer whites and slaves.

Despite all the differences in their immediate surroundings, there were certain common threads in the lives of planter-class women. It was not so much material standards, place of residence, or even numbers of slaves as it was certain shared experiences and assumptions that defined the planter class. These commonalities framed planter-class women's view of southern society and defined their place within it.[6]

Both wealth and the presence of slaves meant that girls in the slaveholding class enjoyed a great deal of freedom during their childhoods. Of course, they did have their studies, but girls' schooling could be spotty, particularly in the early part of the nineteenth century. It usually ended altogether when they reached their midteens. With few chores or other responsibilities, the rest of the day was unstructured and given over to various amusements. Gertrude Clanton slept late, read novels, wrote in her diary, and daydreamed—"building castles in the air," as she called it.[7]

Marion Singleton and her younger sister, Angelica, probably occupied themselves similarly, although their parents seem to have emphasized music and sewing more that Gertrude's parents did. Angelica was particularly fas-

cinated by clothing, an interest that continued into adulthood. She routinely devoted large portions of her correspondence to describing colors, fabrics,
and fashions, sometimes to the exclusion of all else and to the exasperation
of her family. Although Gertrude detested sewing, she shared Angelica's interest in clothes. As a girl, she took great care with her wardrobe and changed
several times a day. Other girls ignored such feminine niceties and played the
tomboy, roaming their families' plantations on foot or horseback.[8]

Parents began emphasizing discipline as their daughters approached their
teens to prepare them for their future roles as wives, mothers, and mistresses of their own households. At this point, many girls left home for the more
structured routine of boarding or day schools. Gertrude spent two years at
Wesleyan Female College in Macon, Georgia. Marion and Angelica first
went to a day school in Columbia, South Carolina, and then attended Mrs.
Greland's Philadelphia boarding school, a popular establishment among
some southern planters. Early in the century, such institutions were sparsely attended. The curriculum was also sparse, focusing primarily on dancing, needlework, painting, and music. As southern parents began following national trends and embracing more rigorous standards of female
education, attendance increased and the curriculum changed to include
history, science, mathematics, literature, and classical languages.[9]

Like many other planter parents, the Singletons followed their daughters' academic progress with great interest. They wrote often, asking questions and offering advice about Marion's and Angelica's studies. Academic
study, however, never completely replaced training in social skills. The Singletons expected their girls to cultivate the personal refinement that marked
accomplished women of their class. Submission to authority and the development of self-discipline were essential. The Singletons were constantly
reminding Marion and Angelica to "conduct yourselves with the greatest
propriety," "apply yourselves diligently to your improvement," and "submit
entirely to the will and wishes of Mrs. Greland."[10]

Marion and Angelica would need both discipline and fortitude to fill
the contradictory demands of a wife and slave mistress. Women of their class
were, simultaneously, to submit to their husbands, maintain the authority
necessary to oversee house slaves, and conform to their class's strict standards
of womanhood. The Singletons were therefore well advised to repeat their
instructions on these points.

Frequent repetition was necessary because young women in the planter
class were accustomed to having their own way. Even if not particularly
rebellious, they did not surrender the freedoms of their youth easily. Gertrude, who habitually skipped classes and spent many a late night talking

with her friends, seems to have devoted far more time to socializing than to studying. Both Marion and Angelica also let their studies slide and knowingly defied school rules on occasion, eliciting sharp words from their parents. The bark, however, was usually worse than the bite. Marion and Angelica never received any serious punishment for their offenses. Neither did Gertrude.[11]

Parents could dismiss such minor transgressions because school was not the only or even the most important means of preparing daughters for their future roles. Religion and extended family networks also played crucial roles. Young women in the planter class often embraced religion with fervor in their midteens. While in college, Gertrude and her classmates read the Bible, held prayer meetings, and waited for conversion, an experience marked by characteristic spasms, shouts of joy, and a sense of spiritual peace. In the process, they gradually reorganized their individual identities and their worldview around the religious tenets of the South's particular brand of Evangelical Protestantism.[12]

Faith did provide support and comfort for women as the trials of adulthood took their toll, but it also reinforced women's subordination to the men of their class and their commitment to slavery. Although Evangelical southern Protestants believed that everyone was spiritually equal in the eyes of the Lord, the same did not hold true for matters of this world. God stood at the head of the Christian household, just as white men presided over their earthly ones. White women, like slaves, were supposed to realize their spiritual mission through cheerful obedience to the authority of white men. As members of the slaveholding class, they were also to share in the privileges and responsibilities of overseeing African Americans. This social order, the South's ministers assured their congregations, was not just natural but divinely ordained. Any change would bring down the wrath of God. Teenage girls like Gertrude accepted their place, equating religious salvation with the ability to fill their appointed social role as wives of slaveholders.[13]

A dense web of family ties eased young women's passage into adulthood. Extended families served as a vital social and economic support system. In a time when illness and early death were common, when commerce operated through personal connections, and when no public safety net assisted individuals who fell on hard times, even the wealthiest slaveholders leaned heavily on their families.[14]

Men and women in the southern planter class carefully integrated their children into these family networks at an early age. One of the few chores expected of children was writing to kin. Later, they visited with relatives for extended periods of time. Even when young girls were away from home, they were never far from family. Always under the watchful eyes of grandparents, aunts, uncles, and cousins, Marion and Angelica were rarely unsupervised or even alone. The girls lived with relatives in Columbia, South Carolina, while they attended day school. They also had family near Mrs. Greland's school in Philadelphia. Marion and Angelica hardly saw their parents at all while they attended Mrs. Greland's school. They spent their holidays with kin, instead. Mrs. Singleton expected the relatives to treat her daughters as "their own children." They did, reinforcing the values of Marion's and Angelica's parents and shielding them from alternative ways of thinking about the place of women and the social relations of the slaveholding South.[15]

Growing to adulthood in the constant presence of kin also discouraged girls from seeing themselves as independent individuals. Instead, they forged their identities through family relationships, as daughters, nieces, mothers, wives, aunts, and cousins. As we will see, such ties supported as well as constrained. The relationships that Marion and Angelica established as school girls would carry them through the rest of their lives. As adults, women could mobilize family networks, just as Marion would do when her marriage to Augustus Converse began to disintegrate.[16]

In their mid- to late teens, young women "came out" as belles, an intensely exciting and anxious time. It began with a dramatic physical makeover, as girls abandoned the braids and short skirts of their school days for the long, full dresses and elegant hair styles of adult women. Then came the dizzying whirl of parties designed to match them up with suitable young men. Parents oversaw the process with great care. Many sent away as far as New York or Paris for their daughters' new gowns. Then they arranged for debuts in such cities as Richmond, Charleston, or Washington, where the best families and most likely young men socialized. Marion and Angelica both debuted in Richmond. Thereafter, they toured the eastern seaboard, visiting relatives and attending social functions. Young women like Marion, who was shy and preferred staying at home, suffered through this time in their lives. Others, like the pretty and vivacious Angelica, thrived on the attention and all the trappings of society—the fashion, gossip, dinner parties, music, dancing, and travel.[17]

Even those belles who reveled in such frivolities knew that they were engaged in serious business, though. The choice of a husband was crucial to their future. It was also critical to the future of the belle's whole family, because marriage solidified social and economic networks. While allowing daughters some latitude in choosing their husbands, parents depended on highly structured social rituals to nudge them in the right direction. Friends and relatives organized events and served as escorts. When couples did pair off, it was only for brief periods of time. They never strayed far from the larger group. Only certain young men received invitations, and families kept close tabs on them, exchanging information about personal character, family background, and economic prospects. If flaws were found, invitations were denied.[18]

A few young women did follow their hearts and married men their parents deemed unsuitable, but these matches often served as warnings. Gertrude, like many young planter-class women, was smitten with the idea of romantic love until she visited a cousin who had married for love and ended up living in a small cabin with a dirt floor. Gertrude was appalled. Love alone, she decided, was not enough. She also wanted respectability, social status, financial security, and mastery tempered by compassion. Gertrude thought she saw all these things in Jefferson Thomas, who combined "such moral qualitys, such an affectionate heart, with just such a master will as suits my woman's nature, for true to my sex, I delight *in looking up* and love to feel my woman's weakness protected by man's superior strength." Unfortunately, this kind of masculine authority often excluded the kind of loving companionship that Gertrude and many other young women also craved.[19]

The first few years following marriage could be difficult. During this time, young women began assuming the burdens that came with their racial and class position. Managing a house was no easy task, given the amount and variety of work it took to keep one functioning smoothly. It was also work for which many young women in the planter class were completely unprepared, because they had no direct experience in basic domestic skills. Of course, slaves actually did the cooking, cleaning, gardening, washing, child care, and much of the sewing, but mistresses were expected to oversee all these operations. Even with skilled and cooperative slaves, many young wives were completely overwhelmed.[20]

Gertrude was so busy that she did not write in her journal for more than two years after her marriage. "I have not been keeping a Journal since I have been housekeeping but intend endeavouring to persevere in this undertaking," she wrote when she did return to writing. She still had difficulty finding the time, though. "My domestic affairs in which I take quite an interest," she sighed, echoing the lament of many more experienced mistresses, "cause me to have few leisure moments."[21]

Few slaves accepted the idea that their sole function was to make their mistresses' lives more leisurely. Of all mistresses' domestic responsibilities, slave management proved the most perplexing and frustrating. It was particularly difficult for young wives to establish their position with slaves who were older and more skilled, but the job did not necessarily become easier as mistresses grew in years and knowledge. They could never command the same authority as masters. They exercised power through their relationships with the men in their families, not in their own right. To complicate matters, they dealt with slaves on a more personal level than masters, who often worked through overseers. Jealousy muddied the waters further. Some mistresses had to work with the same slaves their husbands, fathers, or sons had forced into sexual relations. This combination of factors produced simmering tensions that occasionally boiled over into open conflict.[22]

Mistresses did develop strong emotional ties to certain slaves and often acted on these slaves' behalf, giving them more food, more clothes, and more privileges generally. These ties, however, were fraught with difficulties as well. Mistresses usually saw the relationships in extremely one-sided terms. They expected their favorite slaves to identify completely with their own concerns and desires and refused to acknowledge that slaves had separate lives and interests. Disappointment was inevitable. When it came, mistresses felt not just inconvenienced but personally betrayed. Not surprisingly, they reserved the sharpest words and most bruising blows for the very slaves about whom they professed to care so much. "I have had so many trials with her," Gertrude complained of Isabella, her son's nurse and an accomplished seamstress. "[Y]et it is strange that to this girl I have a feeling amounting nearer to attachment than to any servant I ever met with in my life." She nonetheless delivered a series of punishments designed to break Isabella's will. When these efforts failed, Gertrude sold her to a speculator.[23]

Slaveholding mistresses complained regularly about the burdens slavery imposed on them and the difficulties of controlling unruly slaves. Complaints about slavery were not the same thing as opposition to the institution or support for racial equality, however. To be sure, some planter-class women did do more than gripe. Some advocated abolition in the early decades of the nineteenth century. Revolutionary idealism and its condemnation of all forms of absolute authority prompted southerners as well as northerners to question the legitimacy and the wisdom of holding people in perpetual bondage. Some southerners also opposed slavery on the basis of deeply held religious convictions.

The most famous white female abolitionists from the South were Angelina and Sarah Grimké, who left their native South Carolina to become outspoken political activists in the North. There were women abolitionists—other than slaves—in the South as well, although most were far less radical than the Grimké sisters. White women in Virginia supported the American Colonization Society (ACS), an organization devoted to freeing slaves and resettling them in Africa. Yet, like so many white abolitionists of this period, particularly those in the South, the female supporters of the ACS tended to emphasize slavery's negative effects on the nation and on white slaveholders. The effects on African Americans were of secondary importance. Their desire to send freed slaves to Africa underscores their aversion to African Americans as well as to slavery. Nor did they consider the wishes of freed blacks, many of whom had no desire to leave their homes and families.[24]

As sectional conflict heated up and southerners came to see abolitionism as a direct political threat, antislavery organizations disbanded. Those who refused to observe the ban were hounded out of the region. Pockets of abolitionists still remained, and a few slaveholding women held onto their abolitionist principles, but they were a tiny minority, particularly in the decades leading up to the war.[25]

Planter-class women continued to complain about slaves and slavery. Gertrude criticized the way slavery encouraged sexual license among white men and ruined family life by allowing them unrestricted access to black women. She was not alone. Other planter-class women also wondered whether the disadvantages of slaveholding outweighed the benefits. Most, however, supported the institution of slavery, even as they took pot shots at it. Fewer still doubted the subordination of blacks to whites. To do so would be to question the entire structure of southern society. As much as planter-class women might be inconvenienced or even offended by slavery, they also knew that it supported their social position and all the privileges that went with it.[26]

Young wives had to learn to live with their husbands as well as their slaves. Of course, each relationship was different, ranging from close and loving to detached and even abusive. Marion's first marriage to Robert Deveaux approached the ideal. Deeply devoted, they enjoyed each other's company and worked together as a team in financial and family matters. But the power differential romanticized by a youthful Gertrude, who reveled in the idea of "looking up" to her future husband, did not always produce happy results. In the first years of her marriage, Gertrude found her beloved Jeff to be emotionally distant, often treating her with indifference and sometimes closing her out altogether. As the historian Nell Painter has suggested, Gertrude discovered and then struggled with the knowledge of Jeff's long-time relationship with a female slave. Although deeply disappointed, Gertrude ultimately altered her expectations without questioning either Jeff or the marriage.[27]

Marion's second marriage was far more problematic. Augustus Converse expected to be the master of his household in the fullest meaning of that term, assuming exclusive control over the family finances and insisting that

Marion and her daughters carry out his wishes without question. Although extreme, Augustus was well within his legal and customary rights. Husbands could allow their wives the freedom to make decisions about their own lives and family matters. Some, like Robert Deveaux, did. But they could just as easily refuse.[28]

The law reinforced husbands' power by making it difficult for women to escape abusive marriages. In the first decades of the nineteenth century, southern states still required a special legislative act to obtain a divorce. Even after the laws were relaxed, divorces were not easy to obtain. In most southern states, the marital tie could be completely severed only in a few extreme circumstances—adultery combined with abandonment on the part of either party, adultery on the part of the wife, and impotence. Abandonment and extreme cruelty were grounds only for a divorce from bed and board, a less complete separation in which the couple ceased living together but were not allowed to remarry. Women also had the most to lose in divorce, since they rarely received alimony and usually lost custody of their children. The liberalization of divorce laws did not necessarily work in the interests of wives. In fact, the changes tended to benefit husbands trying to rid themselves of inconvenient wives as much as wives fleeing physically and emotionally abusive husbands.[29]

Yet husbands did face certain limits. Slaveholding society directed both husbands and masters to wrap their raw power in velvet gloves. In theory, they were to earn their dependents' respect, compel their obedience by cultivating loyalty and affection, and use brute force only as a last resort. If anything, members of the planter class held husbands to these standards more than they did masters because they were so deeply invested in seeing marriage as a relationship of mutual affection.[30]

Of course, theory did not always match practice. Still, men who flagrantly defied social expectations did risk public censure, as Augustus Converse discovered. South Carolina, where Augustus and Marion lived, did not allow for divorce at all, even in the limited way that other southern states did. Couples there could, however, draw up legal separations to divide family assets and make the other arrangements necessary for them to live apart. In 1854, Marion initiated such a suit. During the proceedings, Augustus did nothing to ingratiate himself to the presiding judge. First he admitted using emotional and physical force to bend Marion to his will and dismissed these incidents by arrogantly insisting on the propriety of his actions. Then he offended the judge's sensibilities even more by divulging sexually suggestive details.[31]

The judge summarized Augustus's defense as "revolting": "I could not forbear to express my indignation at the indecent exposure which the deft. has made of himself, and his family & the manner in which has held himself & them up [as] a spectacle for vulgar curiosity & deversion." In other states, where divorce was allowed, judges responded similarly to cases where female claimants established their own virtue and where their husbands' abuse of power was so obviously out of line with accepted standards. Even as legal reprimands stripped individual patriarchs of their power, they did not necessarily undermine the principle of patriarchal rule. If anything, punishing particularly egregious offenders upheld the legitimacy of the system by making it appear as if wronged wives had a benevolent defender in the patriarchal state.[32]

Planter-class women's lives, however, were not confined to their relationships with their husbands. The demands of motherhood framed women's lives during their childbearing years. Bringing a new baby into the world produced strong, often conflicting emotions in women. The high rates of still births, infant mortality, and death during childbirth made motherhood an extremely difficult, potentially tragic experience. Some women also recoiled from the heavy responsibilities of yet another child and the resulting limits on their own lives. Speaking of her second pregnancy, Gertrude admitted that the "knowledge causes no exhilarating feelings neither do I regret it." Pregnancy plunged other women into deep depression. Gertrude's experience with this baby suggests why. Just six months later, she was in mourning: "Within a few weeks past I have become a Mother, and last night . . . the little treasure which had been loaned me *for so short a time,* winged its flight to the God who gave it." "Now," she wrote, "I do indeed begin to know what are the trials of life."[33]

Yet, as Gertrude's great sorrow suggests, women welcomed new children with genuine joy as well. Slaveholding society held up motherhood as a woman's highest mission, emphasizing her role in providing numerous (preferably male) heirs to sustain the family line. While accepting this view, slaveholding women also derived deep satisfaction from motherhood for their own reasons. They enjoyed raising their children and watched them grow to adulthood with evident pride as well as a sense of personal accomplishment. Mothers also retained close ties with their adult children, particularly their daughters, relying on them for companionship and support.[34]

Children formed the most immediate links in much wider social networks that, as we have already seen, dated back to women's own childhoods. Slaveholding women's mobility was limited, since they could not travel alone and their husbands generally made decisions about where they could go and when they could leave home. But neither were they completely isolated within their homes. Before the demands of childbearing, unmarried women and young wives spent a great deal of time in other people's houses. After marriage, they often lived with kin before moving to their own households. When at home, women kept up a voluminous correspondence, even with the demands of children and housekeeping. They also received a constant round of visitors. Neighbors came to spend a day or an afternoon. Relatives and close friends stayed for weeks or even months. Some slaveholding women were alone so rarely that they made special note of such times in their diaries and letters. As their children grew older, women spent more time away from home, traveling great distances and visiting relatives and friends for lengthy periods.[35]

Women in the sparsely settled sections of the southwestern frontier found it difficult to keep up these networks, particularly in the early stages of settlement. Many women resisted their husbands' decisions to move west because it would cut them off from their family ties. Once there, women's sense of loneliness and isolation could be profound. But kin networks soon formed again on the frontier, as transportation improved, the countryside filled up, new migrants settled near other family members, and family-based commercial practices appeared.[36]

It was not just the company of family that planter-class women valued. They relied on their kin to get them through difficult times. Mothers or other close female relatives attended slaveholding women at childbirth. They reappeared during times of illness and death. They shopped and sewed for one another, sent delicacies from their gardens, worked in one another's houses, and provided advice and support in times of trouble. Women's ties with their male relatives were different but nonetheless close. Affection and responsibility led many fathers, brothers, and uncles to offer advice, loans, and other forms of direct assistance to their female relatives.[37]

Women also used their families to blunt their husbands' power. Some women went visiting to escape troubled marriages. Women also invited relatives and friends into their own homes to moderate their husbands' behavior or to protect themselves. Marion, for instance, did both. She visited relatives when Augustus got abusive. She also slept in her daughter's room because she knew her husband would be less likely to confront her when she was not alone.[38]

Ultimately Marion's sizable, influential family stepped in to discipline Augustus. Close contact meant that many family members witnessed Augustus's violent outbursts and his heavy-handed efforts to gain control of her property. They spread the news to other relatives who were close to Marion. Together, these family members advised her and occasionally intervened to ease mounting tensions in the marriage. When their efforts to reform Augustus and protect Marion proved unsatisfactory, they urged her to obtain a legal separation, and they threw their considerable weight behind her during the proceedings. Afterward, they sealed Augustus's fate by ensuring his banishment from society. Then they closed ranks around Marion and her daughters, shielding them from criticism and openly championing their cause. Marion was unusually fortunate. Other families left their daughters, sisters, nieces, and cousins to suffer alone.[39]

Family ties were not the only way slaveholding women's world extended beyond their houses. Some wrote and published their work. Some were active in charitable organizations, acting on the idea that they, as women, had a unique responsibility to ease the pain of those less fortunate and to repair social rifts. Some even took an interest in partisan politics. Southern Whigs, in particular, cultivated women's support. Although "Whig women" could not vote, they supported the party by displaying campaign symbols, participating in partisan events, and influencing their menfolk.[40]

Nonetheless, the assumption that male household heads were the proper representatives of their wives and other domestic dependents kept many planter-class women out of public reform. So did a hierarchical social structure that encouraged these women to identify themselves in terms of their class, race, and families instead of focusing on their commonalities with other women.

While Angelica was visiting in Richmond, for example, her aunt Sally dragged her to a fair to raise money for orphans. Never one to miss a social occasion, Angelica was decidedly unenthusiastic about this one. The weather "was bad enough to have kept anybody at home less bent than Aunt Sally was on contributing & on making me contribute my $5." To make matters worse, she added, "everything was sold, except what was so ugly a purchaser could not be found, but spend my money I must so I selected the *last horrible* apron I could find for little Mary Mac, a mat for Aunt Sally, Lamp, a Basket, & a cruet. . . . And then I came home heartily tired of the whole affair."[41] Angelica saw this event as another social duty, although it is unclear to whom she felt the most obligated—her aunt Sally, the society women who put on the event, or the orphans.

As Angelica's comments suggest, female solidarity did not come naturally to women of the planter class. Only later, after southern surrender, emancipation, and the resulting social and economic changes, would women like Angelica claim their own distinctive public voice as women who represented distinctively women's issues.

As a result, slaveholding women's benevolent and political work was limited in size and scope, particularly compared with that in the North. Most tended to remain in their appointed feminine role, ministering to their slaves and their poor neighbors and perhaps giving some time to a local church group. They did so without questioning their own subordination to the men of their class, let alone the racial and class hierarchies that legitimized slavery and the marginalization of many poor white southerners.

Just because these women did not see themselves as working for progressive social reform or women's issues does not mean that their actions did not have political effects. Planter-class women tended to maintain these social hierarchies when dispensing aid and engaging in public work. Often, charitable events looked like fashionable social gatherings, with impressive guest lists and lavish entertainment. When elite women had contact with the poor, they played Lady Bountiful, affirming their own privileged place in the social structure and the recipients' dependence on the goodwill of their social betters.[42]

The demands of property could also propel women of the planter class beyond their households. To be sure, slaveholding society considered property and business the province of men. Like most women in her class, Gertrude knew virtually nothing of her husband's handling of the property her father gave them, let alone his other business affairs. But others, such as Marion, did. Marion kept an eye on her father's plantation during his frequent absences. Although the overseer continued to manage the day-to-day operations, she assumed some of her father's supervisory duties, checking on the crops, repairs to the house, and other work on the plantation.[43]

Some planter-class women did control property and even owned it outright. Wealthy families willed sizable estates to wives and daughters throughout the antebellum period. They also appointed widows as guardians of property that would eventually be passed down to the children. Marion assumed this role after her first husband died, managing the property until her children came of age. After her father died, she became the owner of two plantations and several hundred slaves. Although she relied on her brothers, who lived nearby, to assist in legal and financial matters, she continued to manage one of the plantations herself. Other women did the same. Some enjoyed the independence.[44]

Families often went to great lengths to protect their female relatives' property from husbands through separate estates, marriage contracts, and wills. A separate estate was an established legal device that shielded a married woman's property from her husband by giving it over to a male guardian. Separate estates were obtained through equity courts, legal forums that were parallel to, but distinct from, common-law courts and their strict adherence to coverture. Marriage contracts could achieve the same results that separate estates did. So could tightly worded codicils in wills that specified how property could be used and placed restrictions on ownership. But these measures were available only to those with resources, since parties had to pay substantial fees to initiate suits and had to do all the paper work involved in drawing up and filing marriage contracts and wills. In fact, equity courts had been abolished in the North after the Revolution because they were perceived as allowing the privileged to dodge laws everyone else had to obey.[45]

Southern states also began to loosen the legal restrictions that kept married women from owning property. In 1839, Mississippi was the first state in the nation to pass a married woman's property act. Other states on the southwestern frontier soon followed suit, although states along the Atlantic seaboard did not do so until after the Civil War.[46]

Property brought the mantle of power within planter-class women's reach. The fit, however, was never perfect. The changes in property laws were not intended to make women equal to men. Instead, women usually managed property and conducted business affairs in the traditional role of "deputy husband," filling in as representatives of their male relatives' authority to look after the family's property and business affairs. Even so, husbands were not always eager to entrust their property to their wives and often appointed other men as executors of their estates. When wealthy families willed property to their daughters, they wanted to keep assets within the maternal family line and out of the hands of their husbands. They did not intend to set up women in an independent position of power comparable with that of men. Daughters were expected to act as caretakers, using the money for their maintenance and then passing it on to their children.[47]

Even married women's property acts were not designed with women's individual interests in mind. Passed in the aftermath of the panic of 1837, they were designed to protect their families' property from creditors. These laws did take women into account in the sense that lawmakers wanted to shield them from devastating swings in the economy and from their husbands' unwise business decisions. But the idea of equalizing the power differential between men and women did not enter into the debate at all.[48]

Property ownership could also be difficult for women and threatening to others. For these reasons, most planter-class women did not seek it. Nor did they always relish the responsibility when it devolved on them. Marion's property, for instance, became extremely problematic when she married Augustus Converse. While she had extensive holdings, Augustus claimed only the income he earned as an Episcopal minister. He did not even own the modest parsonage where he had been living. The situation infuriated him. He later explained that "if he did become unamicable," it was because Marion assumed "entire command" of the plantation where they made their home together, "supposing" that "all his rights as husband were subordinate to her claim." He "at last informed her that rather than be goaded by a constant reference to his position with regard to the property, and to be perpetually harrassed with a constant repetition from her, that this was her land, these her negroes, and her horses &c., he would remove to the parsonage where at least he could be master of his own house."[49]

According to Marion, she eventually gave him legal control over much of her property in a vain effort to avoid conflict. In the face of similar pressures from individual men and society at large, other women found it equally difficult to maintain control over their holdings, let alone claim the power that men did through property ownership.[50]

Slaveholding women's subordination to the men of their class entailed both burdens and privileges. The burdens compromised women's ability to manage property, slaves, their children, and even their own lives. Nonetheless, slaveholding women still held considerable power because of their race and class. Even if they could not command the same authority that propertied masters had, they benefited from slave labor and their families' other property.

These resources enabled slaveholding women to control crucial aspects of their own lives in ways that other southern women could not. Marion's separation underscores her racial and class privilege as well as her subordination as a woman. Without her wealth, social position, kin ties, and white skin, she never could have imagined conducting such a lawsuit. The slaves who witnessed Marion's marital conflicts and tried to help her had even less control over their own domestic lives. The law did not recognize their marriages and allowed planters to break up their families at any point for any reason. Poor free women also had fewer options than Marion had. Even if they could afford the necessary legal fees or live comfortably without a husband, they found it difficult to play the part of the wronged but worthy wife in need of the court's chivalrous protection.

In all these ways, Marion's separation suggests the limits of slaveholding women's willingness to question and alter the existing social structure. She tried to make her own life more comfortable. To do so, she challenged the power of a particular man, not the entire system. Similarly, Gertrude criticized the inconveniences of slavery, not her right to the labor of black people. In their resistance, planter-class women actually reinforced the very system that subordinated them. To do otherwise would have been extremely difficult, but these women also had good reason to lend their support to the existing social structure. If they suffered under it, they were also among its chief beneficiaries. On the eve of the Civil War, they stood among its most vocal supporters.

2 · The Myth of Male Independence

FREDERICK Law Olmsted, a northern abolitionist and popular writer who would later design New York City's Central Park, was appalled at the housekeeping standards in the southern backcountry. The houses where he stayed "swarmed with vermin." That was only the first of many failings. "I slept in a room with others," he wrote, "in a bed which stank, supplied with but one sheet, if with any; I washed with utensils common to the whole household; I found no garden, no flowers, no fruit, no tea, no cream, no sugar, no bread [except for corn pone which, to Olmsted, did not qualify as bread]; . . . no curtains, no lifting windows . . . no couch—if one reclined in the family room it was on the bare floor—for there were no car-pets or mats." His hosts were not even poor. They were respectable white yeoman farm families that owned their land and even a few slaves. Imagine what Olmsted might have endured if he had stayed with propertyless white southerners.[1]

Of course, Olmsted was arguing a particular point. He intended to demonstrate the superiority of the North's free labor system by showing how slavery lowered the moral and material standards of everyone in the region. Still, his description provides a glimpse at another South, one far removed from the world inhabited by such women as Marion Singleton Deveaux and Gertrude Clanton Thomas. This was the South of wage laborers and yeoman farm families. It was also the South that the vast majority of free women, white and black, called home.

These women suffered the same legal restrictions as planter-class women. They experienced these restrictions very differently, however, because the law placed them under the dominion of their male relatives, whose social and economic positions were not the same as those of planter-class men.[2]

Most white southern males were yeomen—those who worked their own land and sometimes owned a few slaves as well. Some yeoman families combined farming with a trade, such as blacksmithing, tanning, or coopering. What defined the yeomanry, however, was not farming per se but the ownership of sufficient land or tools to direct their own labor instead of working for someone else.

During the early nineteenth century when land was plentiful and cheap, most white southern families could reasonably expect to attain yeoman status. Propertyless whites were usually young people just starting out, who rented farms or worked for wages until they were able to purchase land or marry someone who could. Opportunities narrowed as the midcentury approached and economic transformations already underway in the North began to reach into the South. The change was most evident in the well-established and heavily settled states along the eastern seaboard. In Davidson County, North Carolina, for instance, 31 percent of the household heads were either tenant farmers or laborers in 1850. In nearby Randolph County, the figure was 44 percent. The percentages declined by 1860 but only because out-migration was so high among the propertyless.[3]

These settlers slowly pushed the southern frontier westward, hoping for better opportunities there. The residents of Walker County, Alabama, traveled a common route, beginning in North or South Carolina, then stopping in Georgia before settling in Alabama, Mississippi, or Texas. Many, however, searched in vain, since much of the best farmland had already been bought by speculators and was priced beyond their reach. Poor white southerners either made do with the rocky, red clay hills of the up-country or moved on. Still, slavery slowed the changes that drove people off their own farms and into tenancy and wage labor. Most white southerners therefore continued to think of propertylessness as a temporary stage in the life cycle rather than as a permanent state.[4]

The situation was always different for free blacks. There were some economically successful free blacks. Some even owned slaves. The majority, however, were forced down to the lowest rungs of the economic ladder through formal and informal restrictions that kept them out of most skilled trades and curtailed their ability to acquire and control property. There, the effects of increasing economic stratification hit particularly hard.[5]

Criticism of free southern women came from within as well as outside the South. Women and men of the slaveholding class looked down their noses at women from both yeoman and propertyless families because of the sharp class distinctions they drew. If women from yeoman households were a class apart, propertyless white women and free black women were beyond contempt, ranking so low that many slaveholders did not even include them in the same category as other women. Such assumptions found expression not just in disdainful comments but also in the region's governing structures. Free black women lived under a distinct code of laws that placed them on the margins of southern society. In theory, propertyless white women were entitled to the same legal rights as other white women. In practice, however, both groups were often treated as "lewd," "vicious," and "common prostitutes."[6]

Free black and white women did not accept such negative portrayals or such lowly positions in southern society. Instead, they adhered to their own standards of womanhood. They also used their values and their networks to negotiate their way through an often hostile world, to blunt assertions of male power in their own households and communities, and to maintain the economic and social status of their families.

~

As Frederick Law Olmsted correctly observed, the finer points of domesticity were lost on many free southerners, even those in prosperous yeoman families. What he did not understand was that the southerners he stayed with valued independence more than material possessions, fine houses, and the other trappings of middle-class respectability. Yeoman families practiced what historians have called safety-first agriculture. They grew market crops, such as cotton and tobacco, but they did not produce solely for the market. Instead, they focused on providing a subsistence for themselves and steered clear of debt and other encumbrances. Cash crops were used only to purchase land and other items that yeoman families could not make themselves or obtain through trade.[7]

The goal was independence, defined as men's possession of sufficient land, tools, or skills to establish a household and maintain control over their own and their families' labor. Not all free men succeeded. Propertyless white men were not considered independent in the same way that propertied men were because they surrendered mastery over their own lives to their employers and could not support their own households. In the political ideology of the time, propertied white men's independence translated directly into civil and political rights. Such men were thought to require public power to protect their property and their dependents' interests. Many southern states limited propertyless white men's voting privileges precisely because they had no dependents to represent and no property to protect.[8]

Free black men were pushed even lower on the scale of independence. Even if they had property, they did not have the privileges that free whites enjoyed and that defined independent status. They lacked the civil and political rights necessary to control their own labor, property, and households. Most southern states required all free blacks to have white guardians, as if they were not really able to manage their own lives. In fact, free blacks were legally considered slaves, unless they could prove otherwise.[9]

Propertyless white and free black women shared their menfolk's lack of status. Sometimes, they lived without men at all. Free black women, in particular, frequently headed their own households. Some historians have seen free black women's propensity to remain unmarried as a conscious choice to avoid the legal subordination of marriage. Others, however, insist that their marital status says far more about the constraints on their lives. The law prohibited free black women from marrying enslaved men or white men. That left only free black men, of which there were few. Marriage was preferable, these historians argue, because it provided support in an uncertain world. That support, however, could have a price. Some work suggests that free black men's desire to be recognized as free men may have led them to play the patriarch at home with as much bluster as any white man.[10]

Poverty, combined with the lack of male protection in a society that assumed women would be represented by men, made the lives of all poor, single women precarious. Whether white or black, poor women who headed their own households barely made ends meet. They lived and worked under the dirtiest, hardest conditions. They were regularly hauled into court for various offenses. They could expect little protection if raped or sexually assaulted. They could lose their children to court-ordered apprenticeships if they lived alone. They also risked losing their freedom through involuntary internment and forced labor in local poorhouses.[11]

Racial bias added to free black women's load. Ironically, property ownership provides a measure of their marginality. They controlled a greater share of the wealth in their families and communities than did white women. As the historian Suzanne Lebsock has found, a third of all free black real estate owners in Petersburg, Virginia, were women in 1810. By 1860, the figure had risen to about 46 percent. In that year, the value of land owned by free black women was greater than that owned by men. Other historians have found similar statistics elsewhere in the South. That free black women owned that much property is a remarkable accomplishment. Yet the situation ultimately says more about the powerlessness of free black men than it does about the power of free black women. Free black women were more often placed in the position of supporting themselves than free white women were.[12]

Free black women were therefore poorer than poor white women. They had fewer occupational options. They were paid less. Their children were more likely to be taken from them. They were more likely to wind up in court and more likely to lose their cases. Everything they owned could be taken from them at any time. Eliza Gallie's life, for instance, ran aground over a few cabbages. Accused of stealing them from a white neighbor's garden, she was convicted and sentenced to twenty lashes at the public whipping post. She also spent a considerable sum on legal fees, which may have caused even more long-term damage than the whipping. Fanny Mason was even less fortunate. Local authorities in North Carolina jailed her because "she has nothing to show that she is free and from her appearance we think she must be a slave."[13]

By contrast, white women in yeoman families had easier lives. The privileges of yeoman independence were not equally distributed among all family members, though. As the socially acknowledged representatives of their households, only free men could claim independent status in their own names.[14]

Nonetheless, white women in yeoman families shared in the benefits of their households' independent status and lent their support and their labor to achieving it. They had no intention of trying to meet either Olmsted's domestic standards or those of the southern slaveholders, however. The increasingly elaborate homes favored by Olmsted and the North's emerging middle class rested on an economic calculus different from that of most southern households. Not only did middle-class northerners sell more of what they produced to obtain the funds necessary for consumer items, but also women surrendered their role as producers to focus more time on their homes and their children. In the South, fine houses and generous entertaining (by antebellum standards) were marks of class standing that wealthy women had to maintain, regardless of their individual preferences.[15]

While many free women and their families hoped to move up the economic ladder into the planter class, others dismissed the material standards of wealthy slaveholders as frivolous, if not dangerously decadent. This is not to say that free women did not covet creature comforts—a tasty confection, finely ground wheat flour, clean white sheets, a soft featherbed, or a brightly colored dress. But, like their menfolk, many free southern women were unwilling to remake their families' economic strategies completely. Instead, they prided themselves on their resourcefulness in helping preserve the economic independence of their households. For them, this was the ultimate measure of their domestic success.[16]

Their communities thought so as well. Although independence was the possession of white propertied men, they did not pretend it was the product of their efforts alone. Yeomen readily admitted that their position rested on the collective labor of everyone in the household, particularly their womenfolk. In fact, the cherished independence of the South's free white men looks very different when viewed from within southern households. From this perspective, men's independence was dependent on the productive and reproductive labor of women.[17]

Men took responsibility for acquiring and producing key raw materials, such as land, cotton, tobacco, livestock, and the two staples of the southern diet, corn and hogs. But it was women who transformed many of these raw materials into usable goods to be traded or consumed by the family: they tended the garden and preserved its bounty; they milked, collected eggs, and made butter; they prepared meat for the smokehouse; and they turned all these basic food items into daily meals. Women also sewed their families' clothes and linens. Those with the resources to afford spinning wheels and looms spun and wove cloth.

In all these ways, women contributed directly to their families' economic well-being. Producing food and clothing at home eased dependence on the market, the instability of which could wreak havoc on a family's fortunes. In good years, families sold surplus eggs, milk, and cloth along with the cash crop. They used the proceeds to purchase land or items not produced at home, such as a team of mules, a plow, or milk cows. In years when the cash crop failed, women's contributions to the domestic economy were crucial in getting their households through the winter without going into debt.[18]

The poorer the family, the more women's work expanded beyond their houses. Men may have taken responsibility for the crops, but women in poor tenant and landowning households regularly worked in the fields to make up for the labor of slaves and hired hands that their families could not afford. Women's presence in the fields served as a class barometer in the rural South, distinguishing the poor from those of modest means.[19]

The residents of Walker County, Alabama, affirmed such distinctions when they filed to reclaim property taken by the Union army during the war. The white yeoman households in this Union stronghold all faced similar wartime hardships, but preexisting economic differences among the residents remained and were partly reflected in the work women performed. Aramitta Guttery, whose father, Lucius C. Miller, was a physician and owned land and some slaves, claimed that she could not judge the amount or value of the corn, smoked meat, fodder, livestock, and other provisions the Union troops had taken. "[B]eing a woman," she testified, I "am no judge of such articles and have no means by which I am able to judge the quanti-

Women in an up-country family in Cedar Mountain, Virginia, at work in a domestic setting. (Courtesy of the Library of Congress)

ty." Rebecca Hisaw, whose husband could afford hired help even during the hardest years of the war, claimed that she was not a "competant judge of the amount" of corn, bacon, and fodder taken. "[A]ll I know," she insisted, was "they took all that we had." Other women from the settlement's more comfortable families testified similarly.[20]

Just one mile away from Aramitta Guttery and Lucius C. Miller, Sarah Guttery worked regularly in the fields, before, during, and after the war. She and other poor women like her could give federal officials the exact amount and value of the crops and livestock they had lost because they were directly involved in all aspects of farm production. "I killed that winter 13 hogs," claimed Nancy Beard, a widow of limited means with seven children. "They weighed about 125 or 130 lbs each." Sarah Boshell knew that she had a hundred bushels of corn because she purchased part and "raised" the rest "myself." When asked her occupation, Catherine Bowen stated that a "part of the time I was working in the farm and the balance about my house." Other women simply identified themselves as in the "farming business."[21]

Federal officials clearly found it difficult to believe that women were so actively engaged in farm work. They demanded to know whether they had been rehearsed by male relatives—a question never put to the men. To be sure, some women may have been prepped to buttress their families' claims. The hardships of war also meant that more women than usual tended the fields and ran farms on their own. But they and other women elsewhere in the South could successfully step into this role because they were already so familiar with the work.

Sometimes women's work moved beyond their family's houses and fields altogether. Wage work, like field work, revealed women's economic standing. With few exceptions, the only women who hired out for wages were either wives and daughters from the poorest families or widowed or unmarried women who had to support themselves. Everyone in poor households was expected to contribute to the family's economic well-being. If their families did not have fields in which to work, poor women worked for wages.[22]

Their numbers were not negligible. Census figures regularly underestimated the extent of women's paid employment. They did not include occasional, irregular waged labor that women were likely to do or paid work, such as sewing, that they did in their homes. Still, in five of the future Confederate states, 10 percent of all white women worked for wages by 1860. The figures were higher for free black women. As a group, they were generally far poorer and far more likely to have to support themselves than white women were. In Petersburg, Virginia, for instance, 53.6 percent of all free black women aged fourteen and over worked for wages in 1860.[23]

Unfortunately, there were few occupations open to women in the South. All free women labored under the weight of gender proscriptions that assigned them roles as wives and mothers in households headed by men. Because they were never expected to be the primary economic providers in their families, they endured lower wages, fewer occupational options, and far more supervision on the job than their male counterparts did. These conditions then created a self-fulfilling prophesy, making it nearly impossible for women to support themselves. Women with social polish and some education could find work as governesses and private tutors in planter-class families, but the pay was low and the working conditions could be demeaning and isolating.

Instead of living as glorified servants under other families' roofs, some women preferred to open their own shops, boardinghouses, or day schools. Some were fashionable establishments that catered to the elite. Such a business, however, required financial resources and social connections.

Far more common was the store Harriet Ann Page ran out of her house in New Orleans. When her husband began drinking, gambling, and carousing and stopped supporting her, Harriet "borrowed a hammer and saw and put my shelves and counter up with my own hands." Then she "bought such things as were necessary to stock my little shop" and opened up for business. Other women ran "disorderly houses," which offered some combination of drinking, gambling, and prostitution.[24]

Even Harriet's store or a "disorderly house" was beyond the reach of most poor women who had to support themselves and their families. Elizabeth Dare, a white woman who lived in Greensboro, North Carolina, worked as a seamstress in her home after her husband deserted her and her infant son in 1822. As she admitted when she filed for a formal separation four years later, her earnings were so low that "by her unremitting industry she is barely able to procure a decent support." Other women, white and black, pieced together a subsistence through field work, washing, sewing, and domestic service. Toward the end of the antebellum period, they also began working in tobacco factories and cotton mills.[25]

Young children could be an economic burden before they were old enough to work, particularly for single women. As children grew older, however, they became economic assets. Sarah Guttery, who lived on her father's farm with her two children, did field work while her son was young. As Sarah's mother later explained, "After he got old enough to do good work," Sarah "quit hard work in the field . . . except she would pick out cotton, but mostly work in the house spinning and weaving." The pattern was common in many poor families, with adult women leaving the fields and paid employment as their children grew older or their families acquired slaves.[26]

One of free women's major contributions to their households' economic standing was producing and rearing large families. Free southern women bore more children than their northern counterparts. The birthrate declined in the nation as a whole during the antebellum period, from an average of 7.04 children per woman of childbearing age in 1800 to 5.40 in 1850. Free southern women, however, continued to pull up these figures, averaging closer to seven children throughout the period. About 10 to 20 percent of these children died before reaching their fifth birthdays. Still, infant mortality rates were higher in some northern states than they were in the South.[27]

The main reason the birthrate remained so high was that children were a financial asset in the nineteenth-century South. A household's economic viability depended on the amount of labor it could command. Over time, large households were far more successful in maintaining and expanding their landholdings, livestock, and other farm equipment than smaller ones were. For those who could not afford slave labor or hired help, children literally meant the difference between poverty and the cherished independence that came with economic prosperity. Even propertyless families benefited from children, who could contribute economically to the family through wage work.[28]

Of course, free women did not view motherhood as merely a matter of producing field hands for the family farm. The emotional and physical burdens of frequent pregnancies, difficult births, constant nursing, and high infant mortality rates weighed heavily on all women in the antebellum South, regardless of race or class. Understandably, women in propertyless and yeoman families viewed motherhood with the same mixed feelings as women of the slaveholding class: the danger to their own lives and the sorrow of losing a child were always close at hand.[29]

Free women also valued their relationships with their children, though. Sarah Guttery, for instance, paid an extremely high price to keep her daughter and son, neither of whose fathers she married. These two men apparently had no intention of contributing to Sarah's or their children's support. Sarah clearly had no desire to pursue the issue on her own or through the courts. She also had no inclination to apprentice or hire out her children. Instead, in her mother's words, Sarah "proposed to raise [them] herself." It was not a decision that Sarah made lightly. She knew that she would have to work hard to support them, for her parents were poor and unable to feed three extra mouths, but it was a price she was willing to pay to keep her children.[30]

For women like Sarah and for those in more conventional households, children provided important links in larger social networks. Daughters and sons relieved the isolation of rural life, which fell particularly hard on married women of childbearing age. Their daily round of domestic chores and child care kept them tied to their homes. By contrast, men's chores required periods of heavy labor followed by inactivity that left time for regular socializing. Gender conventions more often kept women at home as well. Not only did men have more freedom to travel on their own, but also they had greater access to public places and events, such as country stores, elections, and militia musters.[31]

When children grew to adulthood and married, they widened the circle of kin. The white families in Walker County, Alabama, followed a pattern similar throughout the South. Sons and daughters married nearby neighbors and then settled close to their parents' farms to create tightly knit networks of related households. In these communities, the boundaries between households were fluid. Young unmarried men and women in Walker County worked in houses and on the farms of their older relatives. Mothers past childbearing age stayed for extended periods with their daughters to help with new babies. Older widowed women moved in with their daughters or sons. These ties not only provided companionship but also cushioned the insecurities that men and women both experienced in the rural South.

Such networks were particularly important for women, who were far more vulnerable, economically and socially, than men.[32]

Culture and religion instructed girls in their future duties from an early age. Toward the end of the antebellum period, some states did start free public school systems. For the most part, however, education was not readily available to most white southerners. It was even less accessible to free blacks. Some girls did attend subscription schools, but more often they received an informal education at home. Most got little or no instruction at all, as high illiteracy rates indicate. It was not just lack of access that kept girls from school. Many southerners thought reading, writing, and arithmetic were unnecessary for women, who would spend their lives bearing children and working on the farm. Others considered education pointless because they believed all women incapable of rational thought. A significant number thought education was a waste of time generally.[33]

Instead, girls apprenticed at their mothers' sides, acquiring a different kind of knowledge. Cooking with inconsistent ingredients and without recipes over an open fire; sewing and knitting without patterns; making soap from ashes and lard; washing and ironing without ruining the clothes; preserving seeds and then tending to the needs of different plants in the garden; putting up fruit and vegetables for the winter; treating the illnesses and injuries that threatened life in a time of no antibiotics; dealing with childbirth; caring for babies and young children; harvesting, hoeing, and doing other field work all required specialized knowledge that could be acquired only through experience.

Girls began their training early, since all children were expected to begin contributing economically to the household as soon as they were old enough. Even toddlers helped by watching the younger babies and doing small chores. As girls grew older and more adept, they took on more physically demanding and complex housekeeping tasks and, if their families were poor, work in the fields.[34]

After marriage, young women continued their training, honing their skills and adding new ones learned from older women. Marriage did not serve as the same kind of cultural milestone for free women of poor to modest backgrounds that it did for women in the slaveholding class. Worked into the daily routine and celebrated simply, if at all, marriage simply moved free women from their fathers' households to their husbands' households, from the role of dependent daughters to that of dependent wives. Wives, of course, had more authority in their households. But, in many respects, the two positions were similar, and the work was much the same.[35]

In addition to domestic skills, girls learned subordination to male authority while working with their mothers. The Evangelical Protestant churches that most free southerners attended, if they went to church, underscored the lesson. For adolescent girls, religious conversion was a significant rite of passage in which they symbolically subordinated themselves to the will of God and were accepted as members of their churches. The doctrine they struggled with and sought to internalize was similar to that held by their slaveholding neighbors: men headed their earthly households, just as God headed his heavenly one; women, children, and slaves served both masters. As Evangelical ministers and writers insisted, productive domestic labor was a necessary complement to cheerful subordination. Women needed to do both to fulfill the role laid out for them by their heavenly master.[36]

The disciplinary hearings held by many Evangelical Protestant churches rigorously enforced this womanly ideal. Church members were charged with keeping a close eye on one another to make sure that no one strayed too far from the fold. Those in the congregation of the Beaufort, South Carolina, Primitive Baptist Church, for instance, considered it their "duty to watch over one anothers actions, and conversation and when need requires to warn rebuke, Exhort, and intreat in all humility and brotherly love, meekness and long suffering, with the same affection to all that love our Lord Jesus Christ."[37]

Free women were disciplined for a variety of offenses—committing adultery, having children outside of marriage, quarreling with their husbands and neighbors, deserting their husbands, neglecting their domestic duties, and slandering their neighbors' reputations. All undermined male authority by challenging the position of individual male household heads and, in a larger sense, the very structure of the household itself.[38]

Quarreling and gossiping were also problematic, although the threat was more subtle. In an oral culture, people's standing in the community depended on what was said about them—"rumor" and "common report," to use the terminology of the time. Personal reputation, in turn, affected credit, economic prospects, and social ties in the community. For women to insert themselves into this public discussion and redirect it was to subvert men's control over public power. Verbal displays of anger also ran counter to the deferential stance women were supposed to assume. In Georgia, Rachel Dunn's congregation charged her with using "improper language" in her dispute with Mr. Sharp. "If she could kill Mr. Sharp," she was reported to have said, "she would be willing to land in the bottomless pit of eternity." She later recanted and was forgiven.[39]

Although subordinate, women were not completely powerless. Successfully meeting their domestic and familial responsibilities brought women respect in their communities. They could then transform this respect into social power that allowed them to bypass or at least soften some of the law's and their own culture's more onerous restrictions. Not every woman, for instance, who deserted her husband, committed adultery, or bore children out of wedlock was equally stigmatized.[40]

Some were like Sarah Guttery, whose reputation for hard work, attention to familial responsibilities, and good relations with her neighbors outweighed her youthful sexual transgressions and her two illegitimate children. Her father, a Baptist preacher, let her stay on the family farm after the birth of her first child, although her brothers did "complain some about" the situation. She continued to live there even after she gave birth to her second child. But the agreement was that Sarah could stay only as long as her labor covered the support of her and her children. She worked hard to fulfill her obligations, performing heavy field work until her son, Henry, could take her place and then doing spinning, weaving, and other domestic chores required for her own children's and her extended family's subsistence.[41]

Sarah's diligence earned her the respect of her family and community. Her neighbor L. C. Miller noted that "when she was a small young woman, she bore the character of being a little fast." Since then, however, "she has had the reputation of being an honest woman." Most important, "she always works and is considered a very industrious woman." Mary Romme concurred, revealing the relative unimportance attached to Sarah's two illegitimate births: "She has always bore a good name as long as I have known her. Never heard anything against her except about the two children."[42]

Elsewhere, women who left their husbands or filed for divorce received similar reprieves, rebuilding or maintaining their standing because they fulfilled their own communities' womanly ideal so well. By contrast, the slaveholding class placed much more emphasis on women's sexual virtue, allowing women much less leeway for missteps like those of Sarah Guttery.[43]

Free women also relied on neighbors and kin to curb their husbands' assertions of authority, as Westley Rhodes of North Carolina discovered. Rhodes, who had long "indulged himself in the habits of intemperance and abuse to his wife," beat her "in a most cruel manner" one night in 1823. Mrs. Rhodes "fled to her father's house" for protection. After hearing the story, her mother immediately marched back to Westley, "reprimanded him for his conduct," and "perhaps struck him with a tobacco stem which she had picked up on the road." By this time, Mrs. Rhodes's grandfather had appeared at the house, apparently to get his two cents in as well. Infuriated and outnumbered, Westley lunged at the old man with a knife. In so doing, he only widened the scope of community involvement in his domestic affairs and undermined whatever sympathy he might have claimed.[44]

Neighbors and kin assisted women against their husbands only under certain conditions, though. Not only did the woman have to maintain her own good standing in the community, but also others had to acknowledge her husband's dereliction of duty. Westley Rhodes, for instance, was known in the community for drinking in excess and abusing his wife without reason. If neighbors and kin thought that the woman had "deserved" punishment, they would refuse to intervene. They left those women who neglected their work or overtly defied male authority to the "discipline" of their husbands.[45]

Women often nudged the process along, using oral networks and the lack of domestic privacy to publicize their husbands' transgressions and to generate support for themselves. Community members would have known that Westley drank excessively because he did so in the company of other men, but they would not know that he beat his wife unless she made them aware of the situation herself, as she did the night she fled to her father's house for protection. Women, then, could appeal to the community to reprimand wayward household heads. But in doing so, they appealed to a larger system of patriarchal social relations and thus affirmed the basic principle of women's subordination to men.[46]

This feminine ideal, however, did not govern the lives of all free southern women in equal measure. Poverty meant that many women, particularly free black women, were born on the fringes of free southern society. Other women dropped out—or were pushed out—of respectable families when sexual liaisons left them pregnant and unmarried or romance resulted in marrying beneath their economic and social status.[47]

With neither the constraints nor the securities provided by propertied male-headed households, free black and poor white women stretched the womanly standards of respectable society or disregarded them altogether. These women traveled alone, supported themselves, "took up" with men, spoke their minds, and even engaged in physical combat on occasion. Some participated in a biracial subculture, where men and women of both races drank, gambled, traded, fought, and loved across the color line. When they did so, it was not in open defiance of elite conventions. It was because such behavior was accepted among the poor people with whom they lived and was essential for their survival.[48]

Such were the experiences of the women who drifted in and out of Edward Isham's life. A white man born into a propertyless Georgia family in the 1820s and executed for murder in North Carolina in 1860, Isham dictated his life story to his lawyer, David Schenck, shortly before his death. Isham clearly embellished his brawling, drinking, and womanizing exploits (it was physically impossible for him to have drunk as much liquor as he claimed and to have lived to tell the tale), but the way he described his relations with women is still revealing. Mary was Isham's first wife. As he described it, "I saw her and she and I agreed to run off and we did so, her name was Mary, she was 20 yrs old and very pretty." She moved in with his mother, while he left to find work and a house. During that time, the two women supported themselves.

Isham did fill the role of provider for a brief time, when he "got money enough to bring my mother and Mary up" to his rented farm, where he "raised one crop." But he soon took to fighting again and had to leave to avoid retaliation and arrest. He was gone for some months, perhaps over a year. Although he did visit when he passed through the county, Isham did not make regular contributions to Mary's or his mother's support. On one visit, he "found there was something wrong with Mary, she did not treat me kindly and I became jealous." As it turned out, Mary had become involved with another man, one who was around more, even if he was not a better provider. Later, she married yet another man, Hiram Brown.[49]

In some ways, Mary's life differed only in degree from those of poor women generally. Sarah Guttery had started down a similar path early in her life, and she was not the only one to do so. Left to protect and provide for themselves, poor women formed relationships with men as need and desire dictated, sometimes "taking up" informally, sometimes living in the relationship of husband and wife without legal marriage, sometimes marrying legally, and occasionally separating without legally divorcing. They appeared regularly in the local court records for fighting, engaging in petty theft, fornicating, committing adultery, having a child out of wedlock, and frequenting the "disorderly" houses, where most of the drinking and fighting took place and where many sexual liaisons were formed.

Poor women participated in this alternative culture to varying degrees. Sarah abandoned the "fast" ways of her youth and returned to respectable society by filling the role laid out for her there. Perhaps Mary did so as well when she married Hiram Brown. But other poor women did not. Their choices were few, and, as Sarah's experience suggests, the price of respectability was high. For some, it would never be worth the cost. Even Sarah's hard-won status did not entitle her to the same social position or privileges that elite slaveholding women had.

White women like Sarah Guttery confronted the Civil War with this knowledge. In Walker County, many of these white women and their families opposed the war from the outset. Elsewhere, Union sentiment was not as strong, and white women willingly sent their menfolk to fight for the Confederacy. As the war dragged on, however, they had second thoughts. Many of these women ultimately denounced the Confederate effort as a rich man's war and a poor man's fight.

Many free black women were even less enthusiastic about the Confederacy. To be sure, the resulting destabilization did not necessarily work in favor of free blacks. Some free blacks feared the collapse of slavery would undermine their own fragile status by eliminating the institution that distinguished them from other black southerners. Restrictive legislation passed at the beginning of the war confirmed their worst fears. Others would eventually side with slaves, seeing in the war an opportunity to create a more equitable society.

3 The Dilemmas of Womanhood in Slavery

𝓗ARRIET Jacobs was an exceptional woman by any measure. In 1850, she emerged from the attic of her grandmother's house in New Bern, North Carolina, where she had remained hidden for over seven years. A few days later, she boarded a boat and sailed north. There, she joined her two children, whom she had already managed to spirit out of slavery.

Jacobs went to excruciating lengths to free herself and her children. The attic where she stayed was unheated, unventilated, unlit, and so small that she could not even stand upright. Jacobs had to remain completely silent during the day, for fear a visitor in the house or passerby on the street would discover her hiding place. She could exchange hushed whispers at night with her grandmother and brother, the only two people who knew where she was. Most difficult of all, she could not let her children know of her presence, because they were young and might inadvertently reveal her whereabouts. Despite the physical and emotional toll, Jacobs did not think twice about the sacrifice. She had suffered much more in slavery, had seen others endure far worse than she, and could not abide the thought of subjecting her children to such an experience.

Even Jacobs's determination was not enough to break slavery's bonds, though. She also needed resources and leverage, which most other slave women did not have. Her grandmother was a free woman with strong ties among both whites and blacks in New Bern, and Jacobs herself had powerful friends of both races who helped in her own and her children's escape. She was also lucky enough to live in an urban area near the ocean, which made it possible for her go into hiding and then obtain transportation north.

For all these reasons, Harriet Jacobs was hardly typical of most slave women, but the account she left of her life in slavery reveals the burdens all slave women endured. It also unveils the countless ways that slave women resisted the role imposed on them, created strong families and communities, and maintained their own sense of themselves as women. In so doing, they challenged the logic of the slave system, which saw them only as slaves, not as women.

~

On the eve of the Civil War, 33 percent of the South's inhabitants were slaves. The system that enslaved them was unique to the southern United States. English common law provided the legal foundation for the British colonies in North America, although individual colonies did alter significant portions to suit their particular religious and social missions. One of the most dramatic departures came in the South with the development of chattel slavery.

Slavery actually developed out of the laws relating to servants, a category that included most unskilled laborers. In the early decades of settlement, the position of African "slaves" resembled that of English indentured servants. Indentured servitude, the dominant form of labor in the southern colonies' early years, was the most servile form of labor allowed in common law. Indentured servants, who entered into extended labor contracts to obtain passage to the colonies, were "unfree" in the sense that masters obtained not just the servants' labor but also control over their lives for the duration of the contract. Servants could not leave their masters' employ. They were to submit entirely to their masters' orders and discipline. They could not marry and form their own households. They could even be sold to another master while under contract.

English indentured servants' period of servitude, however, was limited. African slaves often served for life. Still, in the early years of settlement, some Africans did obtain their freedom after a serving a period of years, and slavery was not initially a status that children inherited from their parents. Racial lines were not as rigidly drawn as they would be later, when all people of African descent were presumed to be slaves.

Southern planters, however, began to draw these lines very quickly. They needed a steady labor supply that was more easily exploited than indentured servants, who could rely on rights granted them as English citizens. They therefore pushed the outer boundaries of traditional servitude to new limits and then shoved all people of African descent into these repressive spaces. English indentured servitude also declined, thus reinforcing the associations of white skin with freedom and black skin with servitude. By the late 1600s, lawmakers in the southern colonies had created chattel slavery. It was applicable only to people of African descent and Native Americans. Unlike other unfree laborers, slaves were classified as mere property and subject to permanent enslavement, inheritable by their children.[1]

These same basic assumptions defined slavery in the nineteenth century. Southern states did drop some of the harsher physical punishments common in the colonial period, such as branding and other forms of mutilation. Many states also extended common-law procedural protections in criminal cases. For the most part, however, slaves could not claim the civil rights that free white citizens enjoyed. Of course, no domestic dependent—wives, children, or slaves—could legally act as independent individuals in the same way free white men could. But the law did grant them rights that slaves did not have.

Legally, slaves were property. They could be sold at any time. They could not own property themselves or enter into any contracts, including the marriage contract. Anything that slaves used or produced, including their children, belonged to their masters. Physically tied to their owners' households, they could not leave without written permission and could be physically punished if they could not produce it. They were prohibited from reading and writing and, by the nineteenth century, limited in their ability to meet in groups unsupervised by whites. Barred from initiating criminal or civil suits, slaves could not charge anyone else with assault or claim compensation for injuries they suffered. The law granted masters the right to "discipline" slaves as they saw fit, only stepping in when punishment resulted in death. If another person assaulted a slave, the law considered it a crime against the owner. Sexual assault was not a crime at all, since slaves had no legally recognized power to give or withhold consent.[2]

Of course, defining people as inert property created a contradiction that the law could never fully contain. Southern lawmakers, for instance, hesitantly recognized slaves as something more than chattel by forbidding masters to kill them. They also had to accommodate the fact that slaves had wills of their own. Most notably, masters were not held responsible for criminal acts committed by their slaves, who had to answer for their crimes just as free whites did. The similarities ended there, though, for slaves often faced harsher penalties than whites. They were also restricted in their defense since they could not testify against whites. Silencing slaves, the law refused to acknowledge them as fully human individuals who could speak and act for themselves.[3]

The law, however, reveals only so much. It described the boundaries of the slave system, not the full substance of slaves' lives. Although slaves could never completely escape the constraints imposed on them, they did build places of refuge in the form of communities, families, and strong individual identities. In some ways, it was easier for slaves on large plantations to build their own communities. Field workers, who lived in quarters away from the prying eyes and endless orders of their masters and overseers, had the most opportunity for socializing with one another. Some historians have found that slaves preferred field work to domestic service in plantation households for this reason. Ironically, then, the concentration of slaveholding that accentuated class differences among whites worked to the benefit of slaves. In 1860, 48 percent of all slaves lived on plantations with twenty or more slaves, and 68 percent lived on plantations with ten or more slaves. Only 32 percent lived with ten or fewer slaves.[4]

Even those slaves on small farms and in cities were not completely isolated. To be sure, it was more difficult to maintain social ties. In cities, where slaves often had more discretion over their time and more freedom of movement, they had to find spaces to gather. That could be difficult, given the restrictions on unsupervised travel and meetings. Still, slaves managed to visit, worship, marry, and have children with other slaves and free blacks who lived nearby. Jacobs's family, who lived in the town of New Bern, had connections with free blacks and slaves all over the area.[5]

Some historians have argued that the success of families and communities in meeting slaves' emotional needs ultimately encouraged accommodation and undermined the possibility of overt, organized resistance. Opposition does not always take the form of bloody revolts, though. As slaves knew only too well, such efforts would likely end in death and had little chance of success even then. Instead, they engaged in forms of daily resistance that were less dramatic but still subversive. Such acts were rooted in a vibrant culture that gave slaves alternate ways of understanding themselves and sustained a powerful critique of antebellum southern society.[6]

Slave families rested on the economic fortunes and personal caprices of their owners. It was an extremely precarious foundation. Slaveholders did encourage family ties to some extent. After all, they had a vested interest in encouraging relationships that produced more slaves. Some took a more paternalistic stance, presiding over marriage ceremonies and even throwing wedding parties for favored slaves.

Still, most whites tended to view slave marriages with condescension, certain that slaves were childlike, morally inferior, and thus incapable of marital fidelity. Gertrude Thomas, for instance, wondered how Lurany, one of her family's slaves, could "reconcile her great professions of religion with the sin of having children constantly without a husband?" Her comment ignored the power that slaveholders held over slave families, which they could break up at will. Slaveholders regularly did so through sale and by moving slaves around on their properties.[7]

Slaveholders could also require slaves to obtain their permission before marrying. It was not always granted. When Harriet Jacobs wanted to marry a free black man, the only romantic love of her life, her master, Mr. Flint, forbid it. As it turned out, he did so because he wanted Jacobs for himself.[8]

Working against the odds, slaves managed to construct families both strong enough and flexible enough to withstand the instabilities of the slave system. The nature of slave families has been the subject of much debate. Rejecting the long-held assumption that slavery destroyed family life among African Americans, scholars in the 1970s and 1980s marshaled impressive evidence showing that slaves preferred long-term, monogamous relationships and nuclear families, although they were not always able to maintain them in practice. On large plantations where there were many slaves and sale was infrequent, these scholars argued, families tended to revolve around a husband, wife, and their children. Even on smaller and less stable plantations, men and women sought out such ties and went to great lengths to sustain them.

Recently, however, new work has begun to revise this view. These historians maintain that extended kin ties and mother-child relationships were far more important to slaves. Even when slaves married and lived as husband and wife with their children, these families had different meanings than they did for white southerners.[9]

Slaves' marriages, considered binding in their own communities, followed an internally consistent set of cultural rules often lost on slaveholders like Gertrude. Despite the importance placed on long-term relationships, slaves did not elevate the integrity of marital ties above the interests of the parties involved or the larger community. They believed that harmonious relationships, not the sanctity of the institution of marriage, promoted the larger good. Marriages were celebrated formally and informally, but it was the substance of the relationship and community recognition of it that constituted a marriage. The community recognized a couple as husband and wife when they took on certain responsibilities for each other. The woman washed, cleaned, cooked, and tended the house, while the man publicly acknowledged his connection to her and her children and contributed to their maintenance in whatever way he could.

This understanding of marriage meant that slaves considered voluntary separation an acceptable way to resolve marital conflicts—a position not unlike that of many poor southern whites. Both men and women could sever the marital bonds if their partners abandoned their responsibilities or otherwise mistreated them. Neighbors and family members could also step in and censure a couple, particularly if their relationship had disintegrated to the point where it jeopardized existing ties. Promiscuity that upset family ties, for instance, was different from either short-term sexual liaisons or serial monogamy that did not, although promiscuity in general was more tolerated in men than in women.

Slaves also allowed for short-term relationships and sexual liaisons outside marriage under certain circumstances. Unlike Gertrude, for instance, Lurany probably saw no conflict between her "great professions of religion" and "the sin of having children constantly without a husband." She may have been involved in a series of monogamous relationships, recognized as valid "marriages" by her fellow slaves. Or she may have had short-term encounters with men that resulted in "outside" children. Either way, she remained squarely within her own community's mores.[10]

Focusing only on couples and their children, as historians have often done, artificially isolates them from the larger community. No matter how strong, individual nuclear families could not weather the vagaries of the slave system alone. Necessity also combined with African cultural patterns, making extended kin and community networks central to slaves' lives. When Jacobs's parents died while she was still a child, her grandmother, aunt, and uncles filled the gap. They provided food and clothes that her master did not, dispensed advice, and tried to shield her from physical harm to the best of their abilities.

The untimely deaths of Jacobs's parents only magnified the role that her extended family and the larger community would have assumed anyway. Parents were often separated from their children through sale. Even when they lived together, work kept parents from their children for most of the day. Other slaves regularly stepped in to nurture and supervise the young. Jacobs depended on her relatives to help with her own children, who lived with her grandmother before and after she went into hiding.[11]

By contrast, the laws governing white southerners' domestic relations did precisely the opposite. Southern law gave fathers exclusive rights to their children and enforced this arrangement by stigmatizing children born to unmarried women. As we have seen, social practice altered the meaning of the law. Wealthy white families relied on extended kin ties in raising their children, and poor whites could be tolerant of unmarried mothers and their children. Slaves, however, went further. As Lurany's experience suggests, neither "outside" children nor their mothers suffered disgrace in the slave community. Jacobs also bore two "outside" children without sacrificing her reputation or social standing in her own community. Following cultural conventions common in Africa, slaves generally tolerated pregnancy in young unmarried women and did not view it as a barrier to entering into a long-term relationship with another man at a later point. Moreover, the emphasis on extended family and community ties meant that all mothers and children were more dependent on the support of neighbors and kin than on individual men. In this context, children without fathers and mothers without husbands seemed less problematic.[12]

Circles of kin expanded and contracted according to desire and necessity, giving them the flexibility to bend under the stress of the slave system without ever breaking completely. Jacobs's grandmother, for instance, presided over a far-flung network of slaves and free blacks who moved in and out of one another's lives, offering support when they could and receiving it when they could not. It was also through such acts that kin ties were built. Slaves recognized people as mothers, fathers, sisters, brothers, grandmothers, grandfathers, aunts, uncles, nieces, nephews, and cousins even if they were not actually related to them by blood. They understood kin in the same way as marriage: as a social relationship defined by mutual affection and shared responsibilities. Women like Jacobs's grandmother often stood at the center of such networks. Acknowledged leaders because of their age and position, these women carefully tended the fragile threads that bound their families and communities together.[13]

White observers never fully appreciated these extended family networks. Even sympathetic northern abolitionists insisted that the slave system utterly destroyed slaves' sense of family and morality by encouraging them to engage in promiscuous sexual behavior. Harriet Beecher Stowe provided one of the most famous examples of this argument in *Uncle Tom's Cabin*, where slavery demolished every family it touched. Harriet Jacobs, however, defended her respectability and the value she placed on her family to dubious northerners. As she pointed out, slave women had few alternatives in a context where marriage was not legally recognized, where slaves had no parental rights, and where masters could demand the sexual services of female slaves at will.[14]

Although supportive, slave families and communities were neither completely egalitarian nor wholly harmonious. Slaves structured relations between husbands and wives differently than southern law or their white masters and mistresses did. That did not mean that slaves considered men and women to be equal, however. They still acknowledged their own brand of gender difference that placed husbands above wives and children in the home and men above women in the community at large. Despite—or perhaps because of—the importance placed on community ties, conflicts broke out regularly, as couples, neighbors, and kin quarreled over issues both petty and profound.[15]

Still, families and communities blunted slavery's sharp edge, providing crucial support and an alternate social space where slaves could drop the mask of servitude. There, slaves could laugh and cry over life's joys and sorrows, express their frustrations and their hopes for the future, and work together to undermine the worst indignities of the slave system. They worshipped together. They sang and danced. They told tales like those of Br'er Rabbit, the wily trickster who upended existing social relations by outsmarting those in power. They reclaimed their own labor, directing it toward the benefit of their loved ones. Or they just grabbed a moment to sit back, chat, and do nothing at all. By allowing enslaved people to see themselves as something other than simply slaves, families and communities nurtured a strong tradition of resistance.[16]

So did religion. Masters encouraged religion among slaves for their own reasons. In services overseen by masters, the text usually centered on the biblical injunction for servants to obey their masters. Jacobs describes one such sermon by the "pious Mr. Pike." "Hearken, ye servants!" he intoned, "Give strict heed unto my words. You are rebellious sinners. . . . Instead of serving your masters faithfully, which is pleasing in the sight of your heavenly Master, you are idle, and shirk your work. . . . Although your masters may not find you out, God sees you; and he will punish you. . . . If you disobey your earthly master, you offend your heavenly Master. . . . When you go from here, don't stop at the corners of the streets to talk, but go directly home, and let your master and mistress see that you have come." The slave audience, according to Jacobs, "went home, highly amused at brother Pike's gospel teaching."[17]

Other slaves suffered through similar services without accepting the message either. Instead, they embraced the most liberating aspects of Evangelical Protestantism and suffused it with their own African religious traditions. The result was a powerful mix. The importance attached to Moses, a central religious figure for slaves, is suggestive. It is easy to see why slaves identified with Moses, who led his own people out of bondage. It is also easy to see why masters liked to ignore this particular biblical story. Moses was even more subversive than masters imagined, because he was not just a distant historical figure to slaves. They saw him through the lens of African religious traditions that fused this world with the afterlife, blurring the boundaries between past, present, and future. Moses thus assumed an immediacy in slaves' lives as a potential leader and a moral critic. He appeared in spirituals to relieve them of their burdens and to lead them to the promised land, which symbolized freedom in both the afterlife and this world. Justice would ultimately prevail, for when Moses let his people go, their masters would also be punished.[18]

Sheltered in their own communities, slaves and ex-slaves often remembered childhood as a period of relative freedom. In some ways it was, particularly compared with what they would later experience. Although youth did not exempt children from supervision, their care was a low priority for busy masters and mistresses. Generally, they were expected to do light chores and keep out of trouble. Otherwise children could spend their time playing and exploring, sometimes in the company of their young white masters and mistresses.[19]

The main reason that slaves remembered their early years so positively was that they were as yet unaware of their status. "I was so fondly shielded," Harriet Jacobs remembered, "that I never dreamed I was a piece of merchandise." When she was six, her mother died. "And then, for the first time, I learned, by the talk around me, that I was a slave." Even so, Jacobs still did not realize the full import of her position because her mistress was so kind. She even taught Jacobs to read. Only after this mistress died a few years later—when Jacobs became the property of her mistress's sister, Mrs. Flint, and began working full-time as a domestic servant in the Flint household—did she begin to understand.[20]

Painfully aware of their children's status, slave mothers harbored no illusions about childhood. Even with the expectation of community involvement in childrearing, the mother-child bond was very strong among slaves. Some historians have argued that slaves invested this relationship with more social importance than the tie between husbands and wives.[21]

Such devotion was not easy for slave women, who had to squeeze motherhood into an already exhausting work schedule, over which they had little control. Jacobs was fortunate enough to have her grandmother to look after her children while she worked at the Flint's house. But at one point, Flint banished Jacobs and her daughter, a toddler, to an outlying plantation in retaliation for Jacobs's continued rejection of him. There Jacobs faced the conflicting demands of slavery and motherhood that so many other mothers juggled on a regular basis. On the first day, Jacobs was working in the big house and could hear her daughter crying just outside, but she could not leave her assigned duties to go to the child. Her mistress's wishes came before the needs of her own children. Just as her own grandmother had been unable to protect Jacobs from Flint, so Jacobs was unable to protect her own daughter.[22]

Despite the difficulties, mothers tried to shield their children from slavery's hardships. They worked evenings and Sundays in their own garden plots to supplement their families' meager rations and sat up long into the night to sew, mend, and quilt. As much as they might want to, however, mothers could not protect their children completely. Even if possible, it would have been dangerous. Children who grew up unaware of the deference and subordination that whites expected of them risked severe punishment and even death.[23]

These were bitter lessons that mothers as well as children found difficult to swallow. Not only did Jacobs hate the idea that her children would be forced to act as slaves, but also she feared that they would internalize the expectations and begin to think themselves inferior. She ultimately resolved the problem by getting her children out of slavery altogether. This was hardly an option for most slave mothers, who had no choice but to teach their children how to get along in the system as best they could.

The realization of slavery's limits often coincided with the commencement of full-time labor. From then on, enslaved children would be expected to labor for the benefit of their white masters and mistresses and to maintain a subservient attitude toward whites generally. From that point, they would have little say about the kinds of work they did for most of the day.[24]

In assigning chores, slaveowners cast aside the gender conventions they so carefully observed among themselves. Their primary concern lay in keeping their plantations productive, not in maintaining rigid gender distinctions among their slaves. Just as important, white slaveholders considered their own gender roles inapplicable to slaves, whom they placed in a category fundamentally different from elite white men and women. Many slave women thus performed hard, physical labor alongside their menfolk from sunup to sundown, through bone-chilling winters and sweltering summers. In many areas, the majority of field laborers were actually women.[25]

The ideology of gender difference, however, was too central to slaveholders' social vision for them to abandon the practice completely. Although gender distinctions did not take the same form they did among slaveholding men and women, they still served as a central organizing principle on southern plantations. Planters often assigned men and women different tasks in the field. Women, for instance, hoed, while men plowed. In some areas, slave men and women also worked in segregated gangs. Slave men, however, generally held supervisory positions, such as gang leaders and drivers. They were also trained for artisanal positions, such as blacksmithing, carpentry, and coopering. Women did the bulk of the domestic work in the plantation household, cooking, washing, ironing, cleaning, and sewing for their mistresses.[26]

Although slaveholders did value black women's childbearing capacity, they tended to devalue all their other domestic labor as menial work. It required no less skill than the artisanal work that men did, but domestic labor did not result in the same freedom and privileges that male artisans enjoyed. The same devaluation of domestic chores also led some planters to require women to complete set amounts of spinning or weaving in addition to their field labor each week. Following suit, many historians still label slave women's domestic positions, even highly specialized ones, as "unskilled."[27]

Slaveowners also influenced the division of labor in slave communities by dumping the responsibility for taking care of children, cooking, cleaning, washing, mending, and sewing in the laps of slave women. Sometimes the expectations were overt, as with the mandatory spinning and weaving assignments, the Saturday afternoons when women were supposed to perform domestic chores, and the gifts and reduced work loads to encourage them to bear and rear large numbers of children. Planters also took advantage of women's domestic skills, giving raw supplies to families with the expectation that women would turn them into clothes and meals. Of course, slaveowners' assumptions of the work men and women performed often duplicated the assumptions of slaves themselves, as the responsibilities slaves allotted to husbands and wives suggests. Slaveowners, however, added these tasks to full-time labor elsewhere on the plantation, creating a double day for slave women long before twentieth-century feminists would invent the term.[28]

Slave women resented their masters' demands, but they took pride in the work itself. They saw their strength and skills as a positive affirmation of their womanhood. Remembering his childhood in slavery for an interviewer in the 1930s, Charlie Crump bragged about his mother's ability to plow with a particularly ornery donkey. "My mammy had more grit dan any gal I now knows of has in her craw," he declared with evident pride. Working another shift after a day in the fields—with or without an ornery donkey—was burdensome and exhausting, but slave women could take comfort in the fact that the domestic labor they performed was central to their families' survival. Women who were particularly skilled in cooking, weaving, sewing, healing, and spirituality were rewarded with positions of social prominence in their communities.[29]

Slave women, moreover, did not always acquiesce to the demands of their masters and mistresses. "One day my mother's temper ran wild," remembered Cornelia, a former slave. "For some reason Mistress Jennings struck her with a stick. Ma struck back and a fight followed. . . . For half hour they wrestled in the kitchen. Mistress, seeing that she could not get the better of ma, ran out in the road, with ma right on her heels." When they were finally separated, Cornelia's mother made her position clear: "I'll kill her dead if she ever strikes me again." Later, she told Cornelia the same, "I'll kill you, gal, if you don't stand up for yourself. Fight, and if you can't fight, kick; if you can't kick, then bite." Plantation records and slave reminiscences are filled with similar women. Their examples clearly inspired the younger generation, although slaves also knew that such brashness could carry a high price.[30]

When slave women did not fight back physically, they "misinterpreted" instructions, "accidentally" broke tools, "succumbed" to sudden and exotic female illnesses, "liberated" supplies from their masters' storehouses, and "left" to avoid punishment or to protest excessive demands on them. Women also worked with their communities to sabotage the system, slowing down the work pace, limiting the amount of work masters could require, and expanding their privileges to produce for their own use.[31]

Their efforts shaped work patterns in significant ways. In the rice-growing areas of coastal Georgia and South Carolina, for instance, masters assigned slaves specific tasks, expecting them to complete a given amount of work in each day. Turning the system to their advantage, slaves managed to keep the work allotment in their daily tasks down so that they could finish in the afternoon, well before sundown. Those who completed their tasks earlier would help those who were slower. That way, everyone could share in the benefits, and masters could not use faster workers to raise the standard for everyone else.

Slaves who worked cotton and tobacco in gangs did not have the option of leaving the fields early, but they insisted on moving through the fields much more slowly than their masters would have liked. Keeping this pace required the cooperation of all those in the gang, so that no one person worked faster than anyone else. Using similar tactics, they also managed to take Sundays and, on some plantations, Saturday afternoons off.

Slaves then devoted their reserved time and energy to hunting and fishing and to their own garden plots, flocks of chickens, and other livestock. While using these goods themselves, slaves also participated in well-developed trading networks, selling to one another, to neighboring whites, and even to their own masters. Technically, of course, slaves were not allowed to own property. Practically, however, masters found it a useful incentive that, once established, was impossible to take away. Of course, masters occasionally tried to increase their slaves' work load or restrict their extracurricular economic activities. But in so doing, they risked the wrath of their entire work force,

Slave quarters on a South Carolina plantation showing livestock, wagons, and various domestic articles that slaves "owned" themselves. (Photo by G. N. Barnard, circa 1865; courtesy of the Collection of the New-York Historical Society, neg. 48169)

whose foot-dragging and neglect could negate expected gains and even cause the plantation's productivity to decline.[32]

In the big house, where slave women and their mistresses worked together in closer quarters, relations often devolved into a complicated battle of wills. Such was the experience of Gertrude Clanton Thomas and Isabella, as we have already seen. This conflict, like so many other conflicts between slaves and their mistresses, comes filtered through the perspective of the mistress. Isabella confused and troubled Gertrude, who nonetheless valued Isabella's skills as a nurse and a seamstress. Gertrude also felt a deep sense of personal attachment to Isabella. But she found it impossible to control Isabella. Frustrated, Gertrude eventually banished her to an outlying plantation as a temporary punishment to encourage better behavior. The plan failed. When Isabella returned, she was ungrateful, unrepentant, and still unwilling to bend to her mistress's will. This time Isabella took matters into her own hands and ran away, eluding capture for six months before she was picked up and jailed. On her return, Gertrude admitted defeat and sold her. Dismissing Isabella as an unruly and ungovernable dependent, Gertrude refused to acknowledge the possibility that Isabella might have legitimate complaints of her own.[33]

We will never know what, exactly, Isabella's complaints were, but Jacobs left an account of her master and mistress that suggests there were other sides to stories of slave women's "disobedience." According to Jacobs, her second mistress, Mrs. Flint, "like many southern women was totally deficient in energy. She had not strength to superintend her household affairs; but her nerves were so strong, that she could sit in her easy chair and see a woman whipped, till the blood trickled from every stroke of the lash."[34]

Flint also managed to summon the energy to keep minute accounts of all the household supplies. "Provisions were weighed out by the pound and ounce, three times a day," Jacobs observed. "I can assure you she gave them no chance to eat wheat bread from her flour barrel. She knew how many biscuits a quart of flour would make, and exactly what size they ought to be." She could also be quite spiteful. "If dinner was not served at the exact time," Jacobs explained, Flint "would station herself in the kitchen, and wait till it was dished and then spit in all the kettles and pans that had been used for cooking. She did this to prevent her cook and her children from eking out their megre fare with the remains of the gravy and other scrapings. The slaves could get nothing to eat except what she chose to give them."[35]

Of course, Gertrude was not Mrs. Flint, and Isabella was not Jacobs. Even Flint's husband thought her a particularly bad housekeeper. But like Jacobs, Isabella and other female house slaves saw even efficient mistresses as lazy, spiteful, greedy, domineering, and arbitrary.[36]

Jacobs had even more troubles with her master, Mr. Flint. Slave women were particularly vulnerable to the advances of their white masters, many of whom demanded female slaves' sexual favors as a matter of course. Planter-class women preferred to look the other way. As we have already seen, Gertrude's husband, Jefferson Thomas, seems to have had a long-term relationship with one of the slave women on their plantation. Gertrude made only oblique references to it, registering her disapproval through increasingly angry diatribes against the sexual double standard. Mary Boykin Chesnut, a planter-class woman from South Carolina, was more blunt: "Like the patriarchs of old our men live all in one house with their wives and their concubines, and the mulattoes one sees in every family exactly resemble the white children—and every lady tells you who is the father of all the mulatto children in everybody's household." But, she continued with characteristic sarcasm, "those in her own she seems to think drop from the clouds."[37]

Slave women, however, were unable to turn their heads. "If God has bestowed beauty upon her," wrote Harriet Jacobs, "it will prove her greatest curse. That which commands admiration in the white woman only hastens the degradation of the female slave."[38]

Harriet Jacobs. (Photo by
Gilbert Studios, Washing-
ton, D.C.)

Jacobs crowds her account with examples of masters forcing their sexual attentions on enslaved women. The most dramatic is her own. At fifteen,
Flint "began to whisper foul words in my ear. Young as I was, I could not
remain ignorant of their import." She tried to ignore them, but "he was my
master—I was compelled to live under the same roof with him." Flint delivered the ultimate argument: "He told me I was his property; that I must
be subject to his will in all things." Jacobs refused to bend. Instead of sub-
mitting to Flint, she took another white man, Mr. Sands, as her lover. She
describes Sands as a kind man, but he was only the best of the bad choices
available to her.[39]

Even so, she reveled in this assertion of agency: "I knew that nothing
would enrage Dr. Flint so much as to know that I favored another and it
was something to triumph over my tyrant even in that small way." She also
knew that her connection with Sands, a prominent and respected man,
would protect her from Flint. Moreover, she hoped that Flint would sell her
and that her new master would buy her and free her. She was thinking of
not just herself but also the children she knew she would eventually have

by some man. Above all, she did not want Flint to be their father. "I shuddered to think of being the mother of children that should be owned by my old tyrant. I knew that as soon as a new fancy took him, his victims were sold far off to get rid of them; especially if they had children. . . . He never allowed his offspring by slaves to remain long in sight of himself and his wife."[40]

Jacobs thus avoided Flint for a while, but she realized she would never be completely free from his grasp until she and her children were free from slavery itself. Freedom proved elusive. Despite repeated efforts by Sands, Flint refused to sell either Jacobs or the two children she had by Sands. With Sands's influence, Jacobs and her children remained at her grandmother's. Sands proved an inconstant ally, though. There was only so much he could do while Flint retained ownership of Jacobs and her children, and he was never as interested in freeing his slave mistress and her children as Jacobs herself was. Worse, Jacobs's successful maneuvering had added to Flint's rage and his desire to make Jacobs submit. Knowing that her power rested on her ties to powerful whites and respected blacks in town, Flint decided to isolate her on a rural plantation. There, she could not resist his advances. Nor could she challenge his power over her children, whom he intended to put to work as field hands.

Jacobs therefore took matters into her own hands. She staged an escape and then went into hiding in a tiny unheated, unventilated crawl space above a lean-to attached to her grandmother's house. She stayed there for seven years, looking for a way to free her children before she would leave herself. After several costly expeditions north to look for Jacobs, Flint finally sold her children to Sands. Then Jacobs waited even longer for Sands to free them, as he had promised. Finally, when both her children were safely freed and living in the North, she left.

Jacobs's journey did not end there. As she discovered, the federal Fugitive Slave Act denied her freedom, making her liable to be captured and returned to slavery at any time. Only if she purchased her freedom from Flint's heirs could she be truly free. That, however, meant affirming the logic of slavery—the idea that a human being could be held and sold by another as property. Like so many other slaves, Jacobs rejected that premise, along with its overt denial of her humanity and her womanhood. She had rejected it in all the incidents of her life leading up to and including her escape, and she had no intention of capitulating now. Although hunted down by Flint's heirs, she refused her white friends' offers to pay her purchase price.

But even the willful Jacobs had only so many options in a society that sanctioned slavery and made purchase the only way to establish her freedom legally. Despite her objections, this was how Jacobs ultimately became a free person. As she learned, freedom while slavery still existed was precarious and bittersweet for all African Americans. When South Carolina fired on Fort Sumter, many free blacks in the North therefore hoped that these would be the opening shots in the war against slavery, not just the beginning of a conflict to keep the Confederate states in the Union, as Lincoln and other northern leaders insisted. Many slaves in the South felt the same way. Together, these two groups of African Americans, free and enslaved, would rivet the nation's attention on the institution of slavery and play a key role in making it the central issue of the war.

Part Two

DURING

Until recently, the history of the war years has been told from the battlefront, as if women were completely removed from the action. As new scholarship has emphasized, the war was actually fought on southern soil where women lived. When the storm approached, it sucked them up into the vortex, whether they wanted to be there or not. Kate Stone, for instance, could see the shells exploding and hear the stomp of Union troops as she and her family fled their plantation. They held their breath and their tongues, feeling their way through the swamp in the middle of the night and praying that they would not be stopped. In the rush, they could take only what they could carry. They left everything else behind at Brokenburn, the family plantation on the Louisiana side of the Mississippi River, across from Vicksburg. The Stones had planned to go much earlier, but the roads were impassable and the trains were delayed. They almost waited too long. A few days later, on July 3, 1863, Vicksburg surrendered and Union troops took control of the area.[1]

In April of that same year, Sophia Cole's husband was shot and killed by Confederate soldiers in Walker County, Alabama. A unionist, he had been conscripted into the service against his will in 1862, deserted at the first opportunity, and came home. Confederate conscript officers made two unsuccessful attempts to arrest him. The third proved fatal. Afterward Sophia continued to support, supply, and spy for the "ly outs"—men, like her husband, who hid in the woods in an effort to escape service in the Confederate army.[2]

Meanwhile, it was not the Yankees who overran Brokenburn, as the Stone family had feared. Rather, the Stones' former slaves tried to claim the plantation as their own. Lucy, the head house servant, joined the others in dividing all the items that Kate and her family left behind. Lucy took Kate's mother's clothes, among other things. Then she gave herself the title "mistress."[3]

The home front literally became the battlefront during the course of the war. Once it did, women's experiences diverged, as the stories of Kate, Sophia, and Lucy suggest. These differences are surprising, given the reigning image of the mythic Confederate woman, who patiently sat at home, willingly sacrificed all, and bravely cheered on "the cause" to the bitter end. Neither Kate, nor Sophia, nor Lucy fit this image—nor, for that matter, did most southern women.

Kate came the closest. She turned up her nose at all those who voiced doubts about the war and demanded sacrifice to the Confederacy as a matter of course. "How much better to burn our cities," Kate wrote of the Union advance that would eventually drive her from home, "than let them fall into the enemy's hands."[4] Other planter-class women, such as Gertrude Clanton Thomas, expressed similar sentiments.

A closer look, however, reveals chinks (and, in some instances, gaping holes) in the patriotic armor. Women of this class were better at noble pronouncements than personal hardship. Kate, for instance, could demand heroic sacrifice in the abstract while complaining continually about all the discomforts, both petty and profound, that the war brought to her own life. Similarly, Gertrude endorsed the war but opposed her husband's participation in it. Much to her relief, he hired a replacement after just one year of sporadic service. Poorer Confederate women, who shouldered a greater share of the economic burdens of the war than did wealthy women like Kate, did not suffer in silence either. They wrote continually to government officials, complaining of high prices, shortages, and all the problems visited on them while their menfolk were away from home.

Many southern women opposed the Confederacy. African American women made their loyalties known early in the conflict. Slaves first slowed their work pace and defied their masters and mistresses. Then they ran to Union lines and worked for the army. Some of those who stayed behind, like the Stones' former slaves, took over plantations abandoned by their masters.

Free blacks were in a different position, because they had more to lose. At the outset of the war, most Confederate states further restricted their rights and, in some cases, tried to enslave them. Many left while they still could. Those who remained found themselves caught betwixt and between: the war imperiled their free status, while support of the Confederacy brought them no reward. Some free blacks remained on the periphery, trying to steer clear of the conflict and keep their lives intact. Others eventually cast their lot with enslaved African Americans. They supported the Union side in hopes that the resulting changes would improve their lot—for, surely, it could be no worse.[5]

White southern men did not all line up enthusiastically behind the Confederacy either. The image of the solid Confederate South is as mythic and misguided as the image of the long-suffering, patriotic Confederate woman. The Confederacy was born amidst intense internal conflict. South Carolina seceded from the Union in December 1860, right after Abraham Lincoln was elected president. Other states in the Deep South, including

Georgia, Mississippi, Alabama, Louisiana, and Texas, followed early in 1861. But even here, in the very heart of the Confederacy, many whites opposed secession. In four of these states, at least 40 percent of the vote went against immediate secession.[6]

Among the dissenters were some prominent whites, who felt that secession was not the best way to promote either their own interests or those of their region. Many of the nay-sayers, however, were from yeoman and poor white families in the Piedmont and up-country, where slaves were few, farms were small, and distrust of large slaveholders ran deep. Long after the war ended, unionists in Walker County, Alabama, believed they had been railroaded into war by elite slaveholders because the secession ordinance was passed by delegates at the special convention and was never submitted to the people for their approval. Some unionists thought the elections that chose convention delegates were also rigged. "The voting," one self-described unionist from Mississippi claimed, "was done by a few on the sly."[7]

The upper South did not secede until 1861. Until then, white southerners in this region had hoped for a peaceful solution to the crisis. But then the federal army refused to surrender Fort Sumter and returned fire on the South Carolina militia. On April 15, Lincoln called for 75,000 troops to force the lower South back into the Union, making it clear that states in the upper South would have to fight the lower South unless they seceded.

Still, many wealthy slaveholders and their political representatives strongly opposed secession. They thought the best way to preserve slavery and maintain the South's economic and political interests was to stay in the Union. In February 1861, for instance, Zebulon B. Vance, the future Confederate governor of North Carolina, declared that it would be "deeply humiliating (or ought to be) to any citizen of a Border state if they will allow these august cotton olygarchys south of them to dragoon them into their service."[8] In that state, the first secession vote failed miserably. When the second vote was taken, after the firing on Fort Sumter, Union sentiment was still strong, and the measure barely passed. The outcome was so close that many believed secessionists obtained victory by subverting the democratic process and manipulating the results.

In Virginia, Tennessee, and Arkansas, secession votes were just as close and just as contested. Northwest Virginia refused to follow the rest of the state and remained in the Union as the new state of West Virginia. East Tennessee would have done the same, but its location, isolated deep within Confederate territory, made it strategically impossible.[9]

These differences continued to plague the Confederacy after its formation. In Richmond, the seat of the new national government, Confederate officials continually squabbled over policy and jockeyed for personal position. They, in turn, fought off attacks from state officials who jealously guarded their own jurisdiction and ignored or contested Confederate mandates. It was not an auspicious way to launch a new nation.[10]

Outside the Confederate capital, differences between unionists and secessionists continued to surface and shape political debate throughout the war. Although most whites accepted the decision to leave the Union once it had been made, a sizable minority of white southerners rejected the legitimacy of secession and remained loyal to the Union. Like Sophia Cole's husband, the men in these families stayed at home when the first volunteer companies were raised. After Confederate conscription laws mandated military service, they evaded capture or deserted at the first opportunity. Thousands of white southern men actually fought for the Union side; every Confederate state, save South Carolina, had white Union regiments.

That so many other white families ultimately supported the Confederacy does not necessarily signify their complete acceptance of its leaders or policies. Many were skeptical of the Confederate government for the same reasons they had been skeptical of the slaveholding elite before secession. As the war dragged on, their doubts increased.

If race, class, and politics shaped southern women's experiences and perspectives, so did their gender. Women did not always view the war in exactly the same terms as the men in their families and communities, because the war affected them in fundamentally different ways. African American women had to battle racial and class barriers that had kept them in slavery. They also faced the distinct challenge of claiming and defining their womanhood, not an easy task in a society that refused to recognize them as women. Planter-class women wrestled with a different contradiction: the war on which their social status and economic security depended could destroy both by taking away their husbands, their wealth, and their slaves.

Poorer white Confederate women faced a similar contradiction, but they had much less stake in the war. Not surprisingly, they began to see the war itself as their greatest threat. On the other side of the fence, poorer white Union women paid an extremely high price for their families' politics. Whether Confederate or Union, women of poor to modest means did double duty for four long years, working against the odds to keep both their homes and their farms intact. Where wealthy women like Kate Stone lived in reduced circumstances, these women did without basic necessities. Unable to extract themselves from dangerous situations as easily as their wealthier neighbors, some lived in the midst of small-scale guerrilla wars.

Despite all the evidence of women's engagement in the war, many historians—particularly those who focus on military and political history—have taken their cues from planter-class women like Kate Stone, who imagined herself far away from the center of the conflict. Kate's perception of her role on the home front was based on her misperceptions about the battlefront, though. She saw war as a heroic adventure, where it was possible for individuals to alter the entire course of history. She could not imagine that anyone presented with such an opportunity would forgo it. "I would eat my heart away," she wrote in 1861, "were I a man *at home* these troublous times."[11]

But Kate was wrong about the battlefront. There were few chances for individual valor in what became the first modern war—or, more accurately, a war with modern weapons, particularly on the Union side, but lacking in modern medical care and supply methods, particularly on the Confederate side. Soldiers were mowed down by an enemy whose face they never saw, and more died of disease, malnutrition, and exposure than in battle. It was hardly heroic.

Kate was equally wrong about the home front. Women did not sit out the war in domestic isolation. What she and later historians did not see or understand was that the war was fought on two fronts: at home and in the battlefields. Often, it was impossible to distinguish the two.

4　Embracing That Which Would Destroy Them

THE divisions that informed the secession debate were lost on many planter-class women, particularly those in the Deep South. Their enthusiasm for secession drowned out all else. "Never shall I forget the state of intense excitement which pervaded the city of Augusta when it was announced that the fight was going on down at Sumter," wrote Gertrude Clanton Thomas. Physically drawn to the action, Gertrude's father left for Charleston to join hundreds of others who watched the bombardment and cheered the South Carolina forces from the roofs of houses and hotels. Gertrude herself became so engrossed with the news of early battles and preparations for war that she neglected to record the birth of her son. She, like so many other white southerners of her class, believed that the war would be short. The "insolent" North, predicted Kate Stone, would be unable to wage war.[1]

Women of the planter class remained loyal to the Confederacy because they had much more invested in the existing social structure than other southerners did. In July 1861, Gertrude claimed that she had no wish to have her husband remain with her when everything that was important in their lives hung in the balance. "When Duty and Honour call him it would be strange if I would influence him to remain 'in the lap of inglorious ease' when so much is at stake. Our country is invaded—our homes are in danger— We are deprived or they are attempting to deprive us of that glorious liberty for which our Fathers fought and bled and shall we tamely submit to this? Never!"[2]

Duty, honor, liberty, and home were not hollow rhetoric. They were the cornerstones that grounded planter-class men's position and power in the southern social structure. White men's position at home, as heads of household, came with the duty to protect and provide for their legal dependents—wives, children, and slaves. That position also gave them liberty, in the form of legally recognized civil and political rights, to fulfill these duties. Wealthy white men's place at the head of large households, which included slaves as well as wives and children in the immediate white nuclear family, distinguished them from other men and magnified their private duties and their public power. Honor came from the performance of duty and the exercise of liberty. Conversely, the dereliction of duty or the surrender of liberty meant dishonor and shame.

From the outset, then, many elite white southern women saw the war in terms of their men's social, economic, and political position. By extension, their own place in the social hierarchy was also at issue, because these women's fortunes rose and fell with those of their menfolk. Indeed, Gertrude's identification with "liberty," "honor," and "duty" that were not her own suggests how completely many planter-class women merged their own interests with those of their husbands, fathers, and other male relatives. At the same time, however, these women defined their menfolk's responsibilities to their families and communities in their own way.[3]

⁓

At first, elite white women seemed certain that all southerners were as enthusiastic about the Confederacy as they were. These women's unwavering faith in Confederate unity stemmed from the assumption that their own interests represented those of all southerners. Gertrude, for instance, was completely oblivious to political differences among southerners. Until the very last months of the war, it did not occur to her that the slaves on her families' plantations might have a different stake in the outcome. Division among whites was even more unimaginable to her.[4]

Kate Stone did acknowledge divisions among southerners, but she, too, found ways to dismiss them. Kate concluded that the reluctance of poorer white men to join the army resulted from personal cowardice, not political principle. Having explained the problem in terms of deviant and dishonorable individuals, she was unable to see high desertion rates as evidence of legitimate political differences among southerners over the Confederate cause. Similarly, when slaves in her area began defying their masters and running away to Union lines, it never occurred to Kate that this, too, was southern opposition to the Confederacy.[5]

Peering at the war through a romantic haze, many planter-class Confederate women initially saw it as an exciting adventure that would affirm

Kate Stone. (Courtesy of the John Q. Anderson Papers, Louisiana and Lower Mississippi Valley Collections, LSU Libraries, Louisiana State University, Baton Rouge)

the mastery of their menfolk and, by extension, the virtue of slaveholding society. They encouraged enlistment, sewed uniforms, and puffed with pride as their husbands, brothers, and fathers left for battle. Gertrude was particularly gratified to hear the compliments her husband received from an admiring crowd, which had gathered to watch his company show off their uniforms and their horsemanship before leaving for the front.[6]

Kate made sure that the officers she knew looked the part, sewing decorative rosettes and other flourishes for their uniforms. The Confederate forces went off to war in a riot of color. Before the draft and more centralized control of recruitment and training, many companies were privately organized and outfitted. Like so many gaudy butterflies, wealthy men donned uniforms of bright yellows, reds, blues, and greens, with all the trimmings their womenfolk's imaginations could muster.[7]

At the beginning of the war, elite white women even encouraged militarism in children. Kate looked on approvingly when her younger brothers mimicked the bluff, bluster, and violence that she associated with soldiering. Gertrude did the same with her seven-year-old son Turner, bragging that he "shows great military spirit" and "expresses himself as being anxious to engage in the war." In these early months, neither woman questioned warlike behavior. Nor did it register that colorful uniforms, temperamental thoroughbreds, and arrogant self-assurance might be poor preparation for the bloodiest war in U.S. history. The ease and anonymity of death in modern warfare had not yet entered into their calculations.[8]

Although planter-class women supported the principles of Confederacy until the bitter end, they soon lost their enthusiasm for the business of
making war. The war did not remain at arm's length for long; it came into
their homes and forever altered their lives. One of the first casualties was
the attraction to military grandeur. Gertrude began dreading her husband's
impending departure less than two weeks after she had so categorically stated
that she did not want him to stay home. "When I think of it," she confided
to her diary, "I find the tears roll irresistibly down my cheeks." After he left,
her depression deepened. She missed her husband's presence, feared for his
life, and became increasingly anxious for her family's future.[9]

Thousands of Confederate women, rich and poor, experienced similar
emotions. Sending their menfolk off to war made them confront the limitations and vulnerability of their legally and culturally defined dependence.
Obviously, the well-being of poor white and yeoman women was the most
precarious. But for planter-class women, like Gertrude, the realization was
particularly terrifying because it was so new. Gertrude had seen destitution
and despair. She had even known women who sank into such conditions
through bad marriages and other misfortunes. But wrapped comfortably in
her privilege, Gertrude had never considered such things as personal threats
to her own life. Neither had many other women in her class. Now, as husbands, brothers, sons, and fathers left for the front, the possibility became
painfully and frighteningly clear.[10]

Shortages hit even before the first troops left. Cloth, shoes, food, paper,
ink, books, crockery, kitchen utensils, tools, building materials—everything
was in short supply. As the war ground on, stocks dwindled and prices sky-
rocketed. Even the wealthiest southerners cut back drastically.

Finding the resources to buy what was available proved just as difficult.
The same Union embargo that kept goods out of the South also made it
impossible to sell cotton and other staple crops. Rampant inflation ate away
at assets. Plantations slowed or ceased production altogether. Then, the
planter class's most valuable possessions literally walked away to freedom.

In 1862, Kate remarked that it was odd to have company and no "delicacies." They were on "war footing," with only corn bread, meal, milk, butter,
and tea. "A year ago we would have considered it impossible to get on for a
day without the things that we have been doing without for months." In
many areas, particularly toward the end of the war, even gold could no longer
purchase comfort, because there was nothing of comfort left to buy.[11]

Historians often discuss wartime poverty as if it hit all southerners equally, but deprivation was a relative state. Despite Kate's grumbling, most southerners would have considered the Stone household well supplied, even by

prewar standards. In addition to the basics Kate listed, the larders contained molasses, sugar, eggs, chicken, and pork. The main absence was wheat flour.[12]

Planter-class women's complaints about shortages reveal as much about their prewar expectations as their wartime deprivation. Although Gertrude complained each Christmas about the lack of presents and the bareness of the table, her children's presents were both numerous and expensive until the very last Christmas of the war. The festivities were elaborate by most southerners' standards even that year. Gertrude admitted as much herself, after considering the situation of a widowed woman living with her children in an unheated, abandoned railroad car. "The idea occurred to me," wrote Gertrude, "that next Christmas I might be unable to provide my children with Christmas gifts." Acting on impulse, she gave the woman five dollars "to buy some supplies for her children." Kate was more honest. "I doubt I was ever intended for a poor girl," she wrote in 1864, longing for a carriage. "Deprivations go hard with me."[13]

Of course, Kate's and Gertrude's families were particularly well off. They were also removed from the fighting and Union occupation. Many other formerly wealthy families found it increasingly difficult to scrape together the basic necessities. Still, white southerners all over the South's interior complained about elite refugees, who swept into town and annoyed long-time residents with their spending power and their material expectations. Kate's comments on local ill will toward planter-class refugees in Texas are particularly revealing. The Texans, she noted, were jealous because the refugees in her social circle were "nicer and more refined people." When Kate, her family, and others in her refugee community attended a local Masonic festival, they remained aloof and refused to eat the barbecue. "We went out, as Mamma said, 'to see the animals feed,'" she remarked. Other southerners complained about the local elite, who managed a level of comfort that had become impossible for others. "Poverty" obviously meant different things to different people.[14]

The scarcity of cloth was particularly difficult for women who had depended on clothing to mark their social status. Fashion is "obsolete," sulked Kate in 1862. Hoops, the staple of every good lady's wardrobe, were reduced or abandoned because the yards and yards of cloth required to drape over them were no longer available. Wealthy women, who had been accustomed to ordering wardrobes from New York and Paris, wore their clothes until they were threadbare, made new dresses from common varieties of cloth they never would have touched before the war, and began buying used clothes.[15]

Still, planter-class women did not forsake fashion. To the contrary, they made extraordinary efforts to keep up appearances. Kate's entire wartime diary, for instance, contains a running commentary on her efforts to maintain and update her own wardrobe and those of the other women in her social circle. Although she and other planter-class women did not dress as they had in the past, they still dressed well. In the fall of 1863, additions to Kate's wardrobe included a remade green silk dress and two new calico ones. That same month, her mother spent ninety-five dollars on a new dress for herself and purchased several bolts of calico and wool for other items.[16]

Kate also maintained a critical eye when judging other women's wardrobes. The aspiring women in the Texas backcountry failed to pass muster. She found their pretensions at fashion laughable. "Nothing looks funnier," she sniffed, "than a woman walking around with an immense hoop—bare footed." More shocking was the complete absence of fashion that she encountered at one poor household. "There are two women and a girl and not a scrap of ribbon or lace or any kind of adornment in the House. I never saw a woman before without a ribbon." Clothing—or the lack thereof—established both class standing and womanhood. Therein lay the source of planter-class women's obsession and anxieties. Without silk dresses, leather shoes, white linens, ribbons, and lace, what would visibly distinguish Kate from the common women she so loathed?[17]

Planter-class women did more than simply bemoan wartime shortages. They stepped up domestic production, organizing the making of cloth, food, and other basic items on their plantations. They also did crucial work for the Confederacy, which never developed the production and distribution network to supply its army that the Union did. Planter-class women formed sewing societies to outfit soldiers. They raised money to fund gunboats. They rolled bandages, set up convalescent homes for wounded soldiers, and worked in hospitals. Gertrude, a "directress" of the local Soldiers' Aid Society, engaged in a range of such activities. She not only sewed but also worked in the Confederate hospital that opened in Augusta. Kate also devoted considerable time to sewing and knitting for Confederate troops.[18]

Although women did much of the work on a volunteer basis, the Confederacy began hiring women for pay, giving piece rates for sewing and hiring well-connected white women as hospital matrons and government clerks. For some planter-class women in difficult circumstances, the income was what kept them alive. These jobs were also welcome opportunities for women who felt stifled in the restrictive gender roles of the planter class or who longed to do something meaningful for the "cause." As we will see, however, neither public duties nor wage work necessarily signaled a complete transformation in the way planter-class women saw themselves and their relationship to society.[19]

Johanna "Nannie" McKenzie Semple, a "treasury girl" hired to sign Confederate currency, was one of many well-connected women from the planter class who did clerical work for the Confederate government. (Courtesy of the Museum of the Confederacy)

Women also kept plantations running. Widowed before the war, Kate's mother was accustomed to acting as "deputy husband" and managing the family's economic interests. When the men left for the front, women stepped into this traditional female role and took over the difficult task of plantation management under particularly demanding circumstances. Husbands wrote lengthy letters full of agricultural advice about such things as planting, harvesting, milking, slaughtering, marketing, and negotiating relations with overseers and slaves. But an irregular mail service brought advice sporadically. Basically, women were on their own.[20]

Some, like Kate's mother, rose to the occasion. Seeing the inevitability of Union occupation, she sent most of the Stone family slaves to Texas before they could escape or be freed by federal troops. There, she had them hired out so her own family could live on their wages. Later, after the family escaped to Texas, Kate's mother hired an overseer, rented land, and worked it with some of the slaves. Throughout the war, she carefully supervised the family's investment in human property, making numerous difficult trips to check on the slaves' living and working conditions. It was her expert management that kept Kate in silk dresses throughout the war and preserved what remained of the family's estate.[21]

Other women, however, crumbled. Of all the plantation's many demands, it was slave management that defeated planter-class women. Mistresses did not command the same authority as masters—and slaves knew it. They disappeared, left work undone, ignored orders, and drove their mistresses to distraction. "Master's eye and voice are more potent than Mistress's," observed one South Carolina woman. A Georgia planter was blunter. The slaves "are very difficult to control," he wrote in 1864, because they have no "fear of the women." By 1864, however, even masters were having trouble. When masters could no longer hold slaves in place, mistresses had no hope. It was probably no coincidence that the slaves in Mrs. Hardison's care "behaved worse than anyone's" in Kate's neighborhood.[22]

It was not just slaveholding women who complained. The problem of slave management punctuated political debates, filled newspaper columns, and clogged Confederate officials' mailboxes. "In behalf of the women and children," wrote G. W. Gayle to the Confederate War Department, "I beg you to instruct the War Department to receive no more . . . troops" from Dallas County, Mississippi. Dallas was one of the largest slaveholding counties in the Confederacy, Gayle pointed out. It needed white men to "keep the slaves down." Otherwise, "anarchy will prevail and the slaves become one nation, if they can."[23]

Gayle was writing early in the war, before the Confederacy began tightening military service policies and scooping up every able-bodied white man to keep its armies in the field. Complaints multiplied thereafter. The Confederate government, however, privileged battles with the Union army over the battles on southern plantations. While sympathetic to the problem of unsupervised slaves, officials decided they needed all the manpower they could get for the military.[24]

Planter-class women found changes in their slaves and the institution of slavery difficult to grasp, let alone accept. Even Kate, a particularly honest and insightful observer, could not admit that slavery was crumbling, although she described its demise in vivid detail. She clung desperately to the belief that slavery really was in the best interests of slaves and that slaves really were the passive, faithful, helpless people that she imagined them to be.

In 1862, Kate believed that her family's slaves would remain, although slaves were deserting all the plantations around them. "Mamma had all the men on the place called up," Kate wrote, "and she told them if the Yankees came on the place each Negro must take care of himself and run away and hide. We think they will." She was, of course, mistaken. But Kate could not believe that slaves could ever live successfully as free people. Their desire for freedom proved their need for white guidance. If the Union won, Kate assured herself, slaves would only trade the "old allegiance" for "the new"— Confederate masters for Union ones.[25]

Occasionally, insight pierced through the denial. Kate could imagine that slaves might desire freedom. She could admit that some slaves might be rejecting their masters' authority. She could even wonder what her family would do if all the slaves left them. But Kate and other slaveholding women pushed such thoughts only so far because the conclusions were too disturbing. Denial was easier.[26]

That denial, combined with years of seeing slaves as extensions of themselves, left slaveholding women completely unprepared to deal with African Americans outside the institution of slavery. African Americans became the enemy, one more powerful and menacing than the hated Yankees. Kate, for instance, was certain that Jane, a particularly aggressive slave who had run away, would return for vengeance. Kate dreamed of Jane stabbing the Stone family in their beds. She even carried a gun for a while to protect herself.[27]

Fear also gripped Kate as she rode through the quarters, now filled with escaped slaves from other plantations. "There were numbers of strange Negro men standing around," she wrote. "They did not say anything but they looked at us and grinned and that terrified us more and more. It held such a promise of evil." By the end of the war, some elite white women saw signs of slave uprising in every black face.[28]

Fear and the frustration of managing slaves led other planter-class women to conclude that slavery was more trouble than it was worth. Slavery, Gertrude finally decided, was good for slaves but bad for slaveholders. "I have become convinced," she wrote in 1864, "the Negro *as a race* is better off with us as he has been than if he were made free, but I am by no means so sure that we would not gain by his having his freedom given him." At this point in the war, many other slaveholding women concurred.[29]

Planter-class women's willingness to question slavery suggests how disillusioned they had become with the war. Not all were as resourceful or resilient as Kate's mother, and the war tried even the strongest women in this class. In many cases, the war was literally waged on their doorsteps. Repeated battles left Virginia bathed in blood, as waves of troops washed back and forth over the civilian population. "Oh! Such a fearful day!" wrote Fannie Page Hume in July 1862 from her family's plantation in Orange, Virginia. "The Yankees are all around us—whilst I write,—the yard & porches are full of them, the Office occupied by three of their officers."[30]

They soon left, only to be replaced by Confederate soldiers a few days later. Once again, the yard was "filled with soldiers, lounging about in every direction. . . . the servants have done nothing but cook for them." Thereafter, the presence of soldiers became commonplace. One month later, Fannie and her family watched a skirmish from their house and gave over their yard to wounded Confederates again. "It was a sickening sight," wrote Fannie, "*blood* in every direction."[31]

Although stymied in Virginia, the Union army made deep inroads elsewhere in the South. Federal troops occupied the Sea Islands off the coast of Georgia and South Carolina in 1861 and then took Wilmington, New Bern, and other parts of the North Carolina coast in 1862. To the west, both New Orleans and Memphis fell in 1862. From these two points, the Union army moved north and south along the Mississippi, coming together to defeat Vicksburg in 1863. That same year, federal forces occupied Tennessee, Louisiana, and parts of South Carolina, Georgia, and Mississippi.

Wherever the Union army moved in, wealthy Confederates fled. Like Kate's family, they left their homes and everything they could not carry. They transported what slaves they could. They joined the growing refugee communities that took root in areas removed from the armies' paths.[32]

Often, however, it was the men who left and the women who stayed behind to endure Union occupation, economic deprivation, and guerrilla war. Planter-class women became renowned for their bold rejection and verbal taunts of Union soldiers. Such actions tied Union soldiers up in knots, for they had no socially acceptable way to respond to "ladies" who behaved in such "unladylike" ways. Grappling for a way to deal with the situation in New Orleans, General Benjamin Butler issued his famous "Woman Order," which threatened to treat as prostitutes all women who openly supported the Confederacy.[33]

Most women, however, dreaded the arrival of troops too much to muster such spunk. In 1864, the chaos of war reached even more households when Sherman defeated Atlanta and began his march toward the sea, burning and pillaging along the way. Gertrude, who lived in Sherman's path, waited anxiously for raiding parties to appear. She hid the valuables and packed so that she could flee at a moment's notice. Then she sat contemplating the destruction of her home and her life until she was so distraught that she hoped the troops would arrive and release her from emotional limbo. At this late date, there was nowhere "safe" for Gertrude to go. Even if she had found a quiet corner in which to hide, she could not escape the war completely. No matter where elite white women went, death and destruction followed them. The death toll was staggering. By the end of the war, close to 30 percent of all white southern men had died.[34]

With death and destruction came despair, anger, and, finally, opposition. Abandoning the militant pride of the war's early months, planter-class wom-

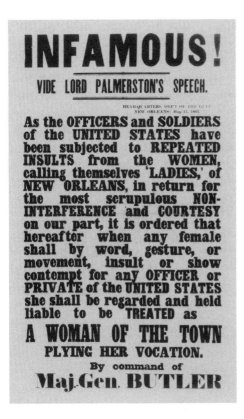

INFAMOUS!

VIDE LORD PALMERSTON'S SPEECH.

HEADQUARTERS, DEPT OF THE GULF
NEW ORLEANS, *May 15, 1862.*

As the OFFICERS and SOLDIERS of the UNITED STATES have been subjected to REPEATED INSULTS from the WOMEN, calling themselves 'LADIES,' of NEW ORLEANS, in return for the most scrupulous NON-INTERFERENCE and COURTESY on our part, it is ordered that hereafter when any female shall by word, gesture, or movement, insult or show contempt for any OFFICER or PRIVATE of the UNITED STATES she shall be regarded and held liable to be TREATED as

A WOMAN OF THE TOWN

PLYING HER VOCATION.

By command of

Maj.Gen. BUTLER

General Butler's notorious "Woman's Order," which provoked outrage among Confederates, who interpreted it as an invitation to sexually molest white women. (Courtesy of the Historic New Orleans Collection, accession no. 82-93-L)

en scrambled for ways to shield their menfolk, their property, and themselves from the ravages of war. Gertrude breathed a sigh of relief when her husband resigned from the service in 1862 and hired a substitute to avoid conscription. "I shall never regret the one year spent in service," she wrote. But one year was enough. "I say now that I would most heartily oppose his joining again unless the enemy were at our doors."[35]

Although Kate never went this far, she wholeheartedly supported her mother's efforts to get her favorite brother transferred away from the Virginia front in 1864. As the war dragged on, letters from white women to Confederate officials requesting exemptions or transfers for their male relatives grew from a trickle to a flood. Of course, women from prominent planter-class families had the advantage. At first, Confederate service policies openly favored the wealthy by permitting the hiring of substitutes and giving exemptions to men who owned twenty or more slaves. Later, when these loopholes closed, planter-class men and women used their social networks to obtain special consideration from Confederate officials.[36]

More than sentiment motivated Confederate women. To be sure, they loved their menfolk and missed their companionship, but they were also economically and socially dependent on their male relatives. They needed men at home to take care of business: to control the slaves and to manage the property. Kate's mother, for instance, went to greater lengths to keep her overseer out of the army than she did to get her son transferred. Decentralization and lack of coordination in the Confederate ranks meant that she had to make several personal appeals, securing an exemption from one officer, only to have the overseer forced into service by another one. Kate was furious. Don't they see, she asked, that "Mamma is forced to have someone to manage for her?"[37]

Agreeing with Kate, many other planter-class women made similar efforts to keep overseers at home. With their own menfolk gone, they thought it only right that they have some white man around to do for them. Toward the end of the war, when these women's racial fears began to get the best of them, they begged to keep any white man at all in their neighborhoods—even those who did not work on their plantations. "We would be practically helpless should the Negroes rise," wrote Kate, "since there are so few men left at home. It is only because the Negroes do not want to kill us that we are still alive."[38]

"The Negroes," wrote one North Carolina woman with much less optimism and a far looser grip on reality, "are making every effort in their power to murder the people." "Their plans are to kill all of the white men & old white women & Negroe women & have the young white Ladys for their companions." Then she laid the situation at the governor's feet, insisting that he come up with some "plan by which this can be broken up." In these women's minds, demands for military protection were completely justified because the home front had become a battlefront. Moreover, as dependent wives and daughters, women could demand protection as their due.[39]

Of course, elite Confederate women had expected to make material and personal sacrifices. They were willing to dress down, do without, run life on the home front, and even give up their menfolk. But they had not expected to do so indefinitely. They had supported the war to preserve what they had. Even women who took on untraditional jobs did not expect their employment to lead to permanent changes in women's roles or southern society. The sacrifice that even the most die-hard among them were the least willing to make was the surrender of their social standing—their place as women in the slaveholding class at the pinnacle of white southern society. As they saw it, that standing was what the war was about.

Ironically, it was the war itself that destroyed it. While the Union and

Confederate armies battled on, unable to resolve the issue with guns, slaves left, land became worthless, wealth disappeared, class distinctions crumbled, once-proud families were decimated, and formerly privileged women were reduced to poverty and hard labor. As planter-class women watched the slow, painful deterioration of life on the home front, the endless battles became increasingly meaningless. What was the point of continuing a war that had already been lost?[40]

In some ways, elite Confederate women's disillusionment with the war was the understandable outcome of despair and exhaustion. But even at their most militant, the basis of many elite white women's support had been fragile, because they so thoroughly conflated the Confederacy with their own families' interests. Nowhere was this more evident than in elite white women's efforts to secure promotions and appointments for their male relatives. They did so with the arrogance of those accustomed to privilege, certain that the business of war should accommodate their personal desires and their families' needs. As they saw it, the Confederate cause was *their* cause in a very literal sense. Not surprisingly, many of these women became disillusioned when they discovered that the correspondence between the two was not so exact. Some were willing to endure far more than others. But others had definite limits.[41]

Gertrude reached hers in 1862, when her husband was passed over for promotion. "While he was contented, and satisfied with camp life," she confided to her diary, "I never should have been the woman to have urged him to come home, however much I might have missed his society." But when his commanding officer "did him the great injustice" of promoting "several others over him," Gertrude agreed that "a due sense of self respect demanded his resignation." She had longed to have her husband safe at home before this, but now she felt that she could act on her desires. After all, how could she be expected to sacrifice her husband to a cause that did not treat him with the respect due a man of his social standing? Like so many other women of her class who were used to having things done for them, Gertrude saw no contradiction in her continued support of the war and her efforts to limit her own family's involvement in it.[42]

For other elite Confederate women, the war never completely lost its patriotic glow. Kate, for instance, did not voice the opposition that Gertrude did. Distance blunted the war's horrors for Kate, who as a refugee in Texas spent most of the time far from the centers of conflict. Moreover, the security of Kate's family did not depend on the life of a single man, as it did for other Confederate women. To be sure, the loss of brothers and other male family members and friends were enormous emotional blows for Kate. Still, their deaths did not spell economic disaster for her and her female relatives in the same way that other men's deaths did for their wives and daughters.

Even Kate began to voice doubts, however, when simmering hostilities between unionists and Confederates in Texas threatened to break into open conflict toward the end of the war. What disturbed her the most was the effect on the next generation. Her younger brother, she discovered, had been going to school armed. "How little we can know what is in the heart of a boy," wrote Kate, struggling with the realization that she was partly responsible for his behavior. "Here we are, so pleased with their innocent sports, thinking them absorbed in their marbles and horses and marching around, when every boy was expecting a deadly encounter and burning with hatred for his enemies." The war had finally come home, and Kate did not like what she saw.[43]

Yet even as planter-class women rejected the war, they did not want defeat. They never doubted the principles that led them to support the Confederacy in the first place. Even if they questioned slavery, they still believed in the innate inferiority of all African Americans. They still felt superior to poorer whites. They still thought that their interests represented "the South." They still felt entitled to a certain level of ease and material comfort in their lives. They still expected their menfolk to protect and provide for them in the style to which they had become accustomed.

As much as elite white women might have wanted to separate the war from their antebellum way of life, however, it was impossible to do. The two were of a piece: abandoning the war meant abandoning what they had been, which these women had no desire to do. These contradictions produced anger, bitterness, and hatred. At times, elite white women vented their ire on Confederate officials or Confederate policies. Occasionally, they even unleashed pent up frustrations on their own menfolk. But, ultimately, they could not turn their backs on either the Confederacy or their own male relatives without rejecting the basis of their own privilege. Unwilling to question that, elite white women directed their rage at the North and at African Americans, blaming them for everything they had lost.[44]

5   *Fighting Any Longer Is Fighting against God*

EVERYTHING about the Civil War was far worse for white women from yeoman and propertyless families than it was for their wealthier white neighbors. Instead of making do with less, they went without. Their clothes went to rags, their farms went to weeds, their livestock went to the Confederate army, and they went hungry. When their husbands and fathers were killed, they lost their land, were evicted from their homes, and were expected to make ends meet on their own.

By 1864, many could endure it no more. "Especlly for they sake of surfering women and children," one woman begged Governor Zebulon B. Vance of North Carolina, "do try and stop this cruel war." "Here I am without one mouthfull to eat for myself and five children and God only knows where I will get somthin, now you know . . . that it is imposible to whip they yankees, therefor I beg you for God sake to try and make peace on some terms and let they rest of they poor men come home and try to make somthing to eat, my husband has been kiled, and if they all stay till they are dead, what in they name of God will become of us poor women and children"? "I believe slavery is doomed to dy out," she concluded. "God is agoing to liberate neggars, and fighting any longer is fighting against God."[1]

This one letter, smudged and torn, written in a shaky, unpracticed hand, is the only documentation left by this woman. Even her name is unknown, for her signature is illegible. What did she think in 1861 when her state seceded? Did she support the Confederacy? Or did she have doubts? Had her husband volunteered or was he forced into military service through conscription? When had he been killed? Did she believe that it was in her interests for him to fight? Did he leave her with land and a house? Were her children old enough to help her make a living? What led her to write at this time?

The questions hang, unanswered and unanswerable. One thing seems certain: this woman was not a member of the planter class. Her use of "poor" did not necessarily place her on the lowest rungs of southern society. In letters of this kind, the term poor often meant "unfortunate" or "weak." But neither was this woman a member of Kate Stone's or Gertrude Thomas's social circle.

Her single outburst contrasts with the voluminous diaries left by Kate and Gertrude, but then Kate's and Gertrude's ability to document their thoughts about the war was one of their class privileges. "Instead of the perfect quiet, the delightful contentment arising from having little to do except read and make myself comfortable, I have been in a constant state of bustle and excitement," wrote Gertrude, complaining in 1862 of an increased work load because of illness among her house servants. Historians have used such complaints to counter the popular perception of planter-class women as pampered belles who did not perform important, productive labor. Work they did. But these women also expected to have time to themselves to "read" and be "comfortable," even if they were often disappointed in practice.[2]

Poorer women, however, could not even entertain such thoughts. They never had the time. For many, it was their families' need for labor that kept them from learning to read and write in the first place. That most common white women did not leave a written record of sustained reflection on the meaning of the war does not mean they were silent, though. They made their thoughts known in other ways. Like the unknown North Carolina woman, they put pen to paper in moments of crisis. At other times, their actions spoke louder than words. Throughout the war, they tried to keep their households together. As that became impossible, they began to withdraw their support and, then, openly challenge the war and their Confederate leaders. What they did was crucial to the war's outcome.

~

White women outside the planter class were a very diverse group, as we saw in the previous section. They included propertyless women who supported themselves as well as the wives of solid yeoman farmers who owned land and a handful of slaves. White women's positions on the war were equally varied and reflected the politics and social position of their families. The majority of these women sent their menfolk off to war with their blessings— at least at first. Why? One of the most frequently asked, most debated questions in the history of the Civil War is why so many ordinary white southerners were so willing to back the Confederacy. Of course, white families that owned a few slaves had a vested interest in the existing social and political structure, but even those without slaves identified with southern society enough to go to war. None of these white men and women had the same status as those in the planter class. Many southern whites actually viewed the planter class with deep suspicion, if not outright hostility.

Nonetheless, white men and women outside the planter class had good reason to take up the Confederacy's banner, particularly if they were from families with property. Ultimately, they benefited from the same social structure that supported the slaveholding class. Whether their households were large or small, all propertied white men derived their rights as "free men" from the same body of laws and social practices. All these men had authority over their households, along with the responsibility to provide for and protect their dependents. Their position as heads of households grounded their public standing as independent citizens: they needed full civil and political rights to fulfill their domestic obligations, or so the logic went.

Although women could not claim the rights of "free men" themselves, they did benefit as the mothers, wives, and daughters of "free men." If their menfolk lost their rights, they, too, would suffer. Viewing events in 1860 and 1861 from this perspective, many common white women and men felt personally threatened by northern policies. To question slavery, as the newly elected president had done, was to question the authority of all white household heads. For the federal government to impose its will on the South, as it tried to do by refusing to surrender Fort Sumter and calling for troops to hold seceded states in the Union, was to undermine the rights of every white southern man. By extension, such acts jeopardized the security of white women as well.[3]

The willingness to fight, however, did not imply unconditional support for either the war or the Confederacy. Many yeoman and propertyless whites entered the Confederacy with a deep distrust of slaveholders. The tendency to see the war in terms of their own families' interests placed limits on the time and resources white southerners were willing to give.

These limits were apparent from the very beginning of the war. Many men had to be cajoled into Confederate service. Some declined altogether. Even those who agreed had their terms. In 1861, for instance, the Confederate War Department received hundreds of letters from men who were willing to raise volunteer companies but only if they could serve less than the standard service requirement. As A. G. Hammock explained, "Many of us here is anxious to serve our country if needed," but "we are mostly men of famileys and cannot leave our families for so long a term as three years." "If a company . . . will be received for twelve months we will raise a company and be ready to report for service in five days." A company in Georgia had conditions about the place as well as the amount of time served. They wanted to remain "in our State & feel that twelve months will be best for us & our families." "Please let me know," their representative informed the governor, "if you will receive as above." After all, if this was a war to protect their rights as "free men," it made sense that it should be conducted on their terms.[4]

If anything, common white women's support for the war and the Confederacy was even more conditional. To be sure, many common white women supported the war with great enthusiasm at first. For every woman who thought that their husbands, fathers, brothers, and sons needed to fight to protect their rights as "free men," however, there were others who thought that war was not necessarily the best way to resolve the issue. In 1861, for instance, Elizabeth Sarol wrote to the Confederate War Department demanding the release of her husband from service. He "joined the regular army without my consent," she explained, "and has left me in a bad condition with my family to support and I will be obliged to suffer if you do not discharge him."[5]

Other women made similar requests, although they were far more likely to demand the return of minor sons, who were still legal wards of their parents. Nonetheless, the assertiveness of their demands is striking. These women not only thought they should have a say in deciding if their menfolk should go off to war but also assumed that the government should consider their needs in formulating military policy. White women felt comfortable in making such claims because they saw the abstract rights of "free men" as a means to an end. Legal rights and government institutions were what allowed men to fulfill their responsibilities to their families. When rights and institutions failed to produce that result, many white women withdrew their support.[6]

Common whites' long-held suspicions of the planter class were also well grounded. From the very beginning of the war, slaveholders made it clear that Confederate unity did not imply equality within its ranks. Far from it. Kate sniffed with distaste at "the aristocratic officers" in one of her brother's companies: "a liverystable keeper," "an overseer," and "a 'bold butcher boy.'" How, she wondered, could such obviously inferior men fill leadership positions? Gertrude, who came into regular contact with common white soldiers while working in the Augusta hospital, remained deeply ambivalent about these men. She worked hard to maintain her respect for those who were sacrificing their lives for the cause she supported, but, at times, she recoiled with disgust from their coarse habits and unkempt bodies.[7]

Although common whites felt the snubs that wealthy individuals like Kate tossed their way, they were far more disturbed by the ability of slave-holders to shield themselves from the war's hardships. Of all the conflicts among Confederates, military service was the most explosive. Friction began almost immediately, as poorer whites made it clear that they did not want to be left holding the bag, fighting and dying while the wealthy stayed comfortably at home. Kate, for instance, defended the decision of family friends to keep their own son out of the army in 1861. Others were not so sympathetic. "The overseers and that class of men," she noted, "are abusing him roundly among themselves—a rich man's son too good to fight the battles of the rich—let the rich men go who are most interested—they will stay at home."[8]

Military service rules that favored the wealthy confirmed suspicions of a rich man's war and a poor man's fight. The Confederate government passed its first conscription act in 1862, making all white men aged eighteen to thirty-five eligible for military service. The act produced a flurry of criticism from slaveholders, who insisted that white men were needed at home to control the slave population. A few months after the act was passed, the Confederate Congress acknowledged these complaints, allowing each plantation with twenty or more slaves to keep one white man—whether a family member or a hired overseer—at home.

If the policy seemed necessary to slaveholders, it smacked of arrogance and class privilege to other whites. The "Twenty-Nigger Law" came under such vocal attack that it was soon modified and slowly fazed out. Eventually, so was the hiring of substitutes, another way the wealthy slipped out of military service. Conscription became so unpopular that state officials began openly defying it to score political points with disgruntled whites.[9]

Still, the sense that the wealthy were not pulling their weight lingered. Many governors liberally granted exemptions to favored applicants. Some, like Governor Joseph Brown of Georgia, exempted a range of local officials, including justices of peace, constables, and officers of the state militia, who remained on call at home. Gertrude's husband, for instance, escaped active duty in the Confederate army after the repeal of the substitute law by serving as a state militia officer.[10]

The wealthy, complained a group of white women in Georgia, "dont care what becomes of the poor class of people" as long as "they can save there niggroes." An anonymous, undated letter to Governor Brown of Georgia summed up these sentiments: "old Mr. Stuard had 5 sons in the army. . . .

Stuard is a poor man. Lee is rich and his sons are all at home, and it is so with other familys. They want other people do all the fighting and let them ly at home. Such people ought to be drafted and made go."[11]

High prices and scarce supplies were other sore points. Confederate officials fielded endless complaints about speculators, profiteers, and merchants who kept jacking up their prices, while denying credit and refusing to accept the Confederate currency with which soldiers were paid. "Do for Gods sake put an end to this unrighteous war!" one Georgian begged Governor Brown. Otherwise "we shall be eaten up by Confederate office holders and speculators."[12]

Mary Carnes agreed. "If you cant help such poor women as me," she wrote, "I dont no what we will do to keep cloaths and something to eat for those old specalators will starv us too death." She had a solution (as well as a dry sense of humor). "[G]et them all in a [regiment] and send them to . . . the yankeys," she advised, "and I [know] they would stop the war for the yankeys could not stand their charges."[13]

Complaints escalated as the circumstances of poorer white women and their families deteriorated. Gertrude and Kate complained of shortages, but they were never hungry. Other women were. Shortages and inflation hit the poor, particularly poor women, the hardest. Women in cities, who were unable to produce food themselves, suffered the most.[14]

The loss of men to the military also had different meanings for common white women than it did for those in the planter class. While planter-class women struggled with slave management, common white women had to do the heavy farm labor themselves. Many found it impossible. Labor was already at a premium in these households, even with the men at home. Everyone worked, and everyone's labor was necessary to keep the family going. No matter how strong or determined the women in these families were, there was no way they could compensate for the lost labor of husbands and sons. "There are many others besides myself who have neither brother husband nor Father at home to cut our wheat & no slave labor to depend on in this part of the county," wrote Nancy Jordan to Governor Vance in 1864. "We see no prospect to get our wheat cut & without something . . . done to save the present crop we are a ruined & subjugated people without substainence."[15]

The Confederate army's voracious demand for supplies made matters worse. It took horses and mules, undermining women's ability to perform routine field work. It took livestock, eliminating an important food source. It foraged among its own citizens, taking what little supplies they were able to grow. Then it took a direct 10 percent tax-in-kind from all remaining produce. Life would have been difficult under these circumstances, even if the men had been at home.[16]

The war also left thousands of women homeless. As the Union army encroached on Confederate soil and homes and fields became battlegrounds, many white women had to leave. Unlike Kate Stone and her family, these refugees did not have the resources to set up new households behind Confederate lines. They wandered the countryside, trusting in the kindness of strangers for food and shelter. Sometimes they found it. Other times, they did not. Many of these women became so desperate that they finally settled in Union-occupied garrison towns. Only the enemy would support them.[17]

Some white southerners had foreseen these problems. In 1861, for instance, John Sale had urged the Confederate War Department to recognize that most soldiers were also family provisioners. It was all well and good for such men to serve their country, but they could not do so indefinitely. The damages of leaving behind businesses and families, he warned, would ultimately be as devastating as the war. He was right.[18]

When the Confederacy did address the problem, its response was inadequate. Initially, the task of poor relief was left to local officials and private charity. Individual planters stepped in, selling grain at reduced prices, grinding it for free, and distributing food and other supplies. A few elite white women organized societies to dispense aid for the poor. But such efforts were too small and too sporadic. The wealthy could not reach everyone who needed help, even if they had the resources, which they did not. When Gertrude helped the woman living in the boxcar, for instance, she gave her enough food to last a few days. But what would the woman do after that? What about the thousands of other women just like her?[19]

In response, local officials expanded existing poor relief programs that had traditionally provided food, clothing, and shelter to the destitute. These programs, however, had been designed to meet the needs of a handful of paupers and were soon overwhelmed. Some towns and cities improvised and experimented. City officials in Mobile, Augusta, New Orleans, and Vicksburg organized the distribution of relief through "free markets." They solicited donations from merchants and planters and then made the goods available to all needy people at reduced prices.

Eventually, the magnitude of the problem and the threat of social unrest forced state governments into the business of poor relief. Wary of direct assistance, states began employing poor women to sew for the army and to manufacture munitions. At times, the distinction between charity and the exploitation of a cheap labor supply blurred, particularly for women employed by the states. In 1864, for instance, three North Carolina women wrote the governor asking him to raise the piece rates for shirts and pants. As they reminded him, "[S]ome of us have children to feed and clothe." Other women led walkouts and impromptu strikes. Perhaps the most graphic examples of exploitation came in munition factories. In 1862, an explosion blew open a cartridge factory in Virginia, scattering workers like confetti, killing thirty-two women, and injuring thirty more. In Jackson, Mississippi, at least fifteen more women lost their lives in a similar accident.[20]

The ever-growing mountain of requests for exemptions and furloughs testifies to the inadequacy of relief programs. "I want to go home," wrote George Hancock, "to prepare some land for to sow some wheat for the use of my family that is my dependance." Parrott Hardee wanted to know if he could defer entry into the military "until I can fatten my Poark." Evey S. Jackson wondered if Governor Vance and "Mr. Davis" could "send home the poor solgers to cut the wheat." Although quaintly and colloquially stated, these issues were not trivial. If the soil was not properly prepared in the spring, there would be no planting that year. If the pork was not fattened and slaughtered, there would be no meat for the winter. If the wheat was left standing too long, it would rot. The results would be disastrous.[21]

Requests for furloughs and exemptions, however, were even less effective than Confederate relief measures because common whites were unable to work the system as the wealthy could. Mrs. Smith, the wife of the Stone family's overseer in Texas, experienced the disparity firsthand. When her husband was conscripted, she was unable to do anything to keep him out of military service. But Kate Stone's mother could and did: she put on her best dress, marched over to Confederate headquarters, and demanded a hearing with the general in charge. "Mamma's eloquence carried the day," Kate reported. The general "impressed it on us all, but especially Mr. Smith, that it was entirely on Mamma's account that he was granted leave. Mamma's lovely face and winning manner stand her in good stead these days." As Kate made abundantly clear on this and other occasions, Mrs. Smith did not possess the kind of face or manner that would impress a general.[22]

Mrs. Smith, however, did not like being reminded of her many failings or her relative insignificance. "Mrs. Smith," Kate noted, "does not like to think Mr. Smith's freedom is entirely due to Mamma, but he is a relieved and grateful man." At least Mrs. Smith got to keep her husband at home. To less fortunate white women, such incidents stung like a slap in the face and reinforced their resentment of the slaveholding class.[23]

Frustration with conditions on the home front fed frustration among the troops. "It is not in the power of Yankee armies to cause us to wish ourselves at home," wrote a group of North Carolina soldiers in General Lee's army. But "we cannot hear the cries of our little ones, and stand. We must say something, must make an effort to relieve *them*." Their petition issued a thinly veiled threat: they would cease fighting unless someone did something to relieve conditions on the home front. "Very many of our wives were dependent on our labor for support before the war when articles of food and clothing could be obtained easier than now. At this time they are alone, without a protector, and cannot by hard and honest labor, obtain enough money to purchase the necessaries of life."[24]

Rather than wait for permission, growing numbers of soldiers just left. Of these, a few asked to be reinstated, explaining that they had left only temporarily to look after their families. As the war dragged on, however, many remained unrepentant at home, where they believed their primary responsibilities lay. The head of the Confederacy's Bureau of Conscription reported that desertion had become so common "that it has, in popular estimation, lost the stigma that justly pertains to it, and therefore the criminals are everywhere shielded by their families and by the sympathies of many communities." Confederate officials may not have acted on the complaints of white women from propertyless and yeoman families, but their menfolk did.[25]

Some women took matters into their own hands. Having endured so much, they felt justified in taking action—even illegal action. Traffic in stolen goods reached epidemic proportions, as white women increasingly turned to illicit trade for affordable supplies. What had been underground trading networks of slaves, free blacks, and the poorest whites in the antebellum period swelled and burst into the open during the war.

Many impoverished white women were willing to do more than buy stolen goods. They began stealing themselves. Sometimes they burgled and pilfered, hoping to escape detection, but a powerful sense of injustice led others to make public raids. In 1863, women and men rioted in the streets of Richmond, smashing the windows of local stores and breaking into warehouses to take supplies. This scene was repeated in smaller, less publicized incidents that took place on a daily basis all over the South. In one North Carolina county, a group of women openly looted a local mill. In a neighboring county, a group of ten women and three men stole a hundred pounds of cotton while the owner stood by, helpless to stop them. Where planters fled and the Union army moved in, common white men and women raided plantations and even claimed abandoned lands as their own.[26]

White women also targeted Confederate officials. It was their government. It represented their interests. They had given up their menfolk for it. It should therefore answer their requests. When they were ignored, com-

An engraving published in *Frank Leslie's Illustrated* on May 25, 1863, depicting women rioters, who had grown increasingly desperate because of food shortages, inflation, destruction, and death. (Photo courtesy of the Newberry Library)

mon white women felt betrayed. Two North Carolina women, for instance, attacked one local Confederate official "while [he was] discharging [his] official duties." The man's son later trivialized the attack, boasting that he would have prevented it had he been there. He clearly overestimated his power. Elsewhere in the state, a Confederate official tried to stop a group of white women armed with axes from raiding a government grain depot. But the women left him "sitting on a log blowing like the March wind," while they commandeered ten barrels of flour. In these people's eyes, Confederate officials were now the enemy.[27]

Even to those women who remained within the bounds of the law, the Yankees began to look less sinister than the well-fed, well-housed white planter or merchant who lived next door and professed loyalty to the Confederacy. Gertrude, for instance, was stunned at the public criticism of the well-meaning, but ill-conceived offer of her father, Turner Clanton, to sell cornmeal at discounted prices to the wives of Confederate soldiers. As one soldier's wife pointed out, the offer was worthless because she and other women like her had no way to get to his plantation and cart the meal home. Grain, she declared, "would not be cheap at 10 cts pr bushel unless delivered." What really angered this woman, however, was that people like Turner and Gertrude had surplus grain while other families were going hungry.[28]

Turner Clanton got an earful, but it was nothing compared with the rage directed at those who tried to profit from others' misery. "The rich is all at home makeing great fortunes," wrote a group of white women to the governor of Georgia, and "care nothing for nobody but themselves." "They can speculate of soldiers wives [and] make fortunes [on] them. . . . Just look at ther women & children that are begging bread . . . they would see them pearish before they would give them one bushel of corn." To Eliza Evans, evicted from her home by a man who had kept his son out of the army and prospered during the war, the underlying inequities of the war were clear. The "pore" suffered, while the wealthy profited.[29]

That the poor suffered came as no surprise to many white unionists. Like their Confederate neighbors, they also believed in the rights of "free men," but they had opposed secession because they thought the Union, not the Confederacy, would best protect those rights. Many of these doubters had accepted the inevitable when their states seceded. But others, like the unionists in Alabama's hill country, opposed the Confederacy throughout the war. These people were neither abolitionists nor northern Republicans. They had voted for Stephen Douglas or John Bell, not Lincoln. Their opposition to secession came out of their concern over large slaveholders, not their sympathy for slaves. They had been fighting political battles against the slaveholding elite for decades before the war, and they saw secession as another, particularly disastrous example of the dangers this class posed to "free men" and their families.

Robert Guttery, Walker County's representative to the Alabama secession convention, described himself as an "old Jackson Democrat," a phrase that summed up his politics. Like other "Jackson Democrats," he frowned on large concentrations of power that limited participatory democracy and granted special privileges to the elite. Guttery also explicitly opposed "what was called the 'states rights policy.'" By this, he meant states' rights doctrine that dated back to South Carolina's threat to leave the Union in 1832–33, a crisis that some white southerners saw as the act of spoiled slaveholders unwilling to submit to the will of the people. In 1861, Guttery and others in his area feared that the slaveholding class had finally managed to impose its will and destroy their rights as "free men." Another unionist from a neighboring county was reported to have said that the war would "ruin" them all. "The secession leaders," he continued, "had played the trump and plunged us in to a civil war over the heads of good council and all opposition." Now, "they might fight it out themselves for . . . he had had no hand in bringing on the war, but was opposed to it in every shape and form."[30]

In such areas as Alabama's and Mississippi's hill country, eastern Tennessee, northeastern Georgia, and parts of North Carolina and Arkansas, unionists stood by their principles and encouraged anti-Confederate sentiments among those who wavered. In Walker County, for instance, men refused to volunteer, avoided conscription, and deserted when forced into the army. By 1863, the woods were crawling with "ly outs." Initially, these evaders and deserters were unionists who had opposed secession. Later, they were joined by converts, those who were not unionists at the beginning of the war but had grown so weary of it that they now opposed the Confederacy. Eventually, a sizable number of Walker County's "ly outs" stole through Confederate lines to join the Union army. According to one turncoat, he had absolutely no use for "this one horse barefooted naked famine stricken Southern Confederacy."[31]

Alabama's desertion rates reflect the persistence and growth of unionist and anti-Confederate sentiments. The state's head conscript officer reported that half of the 7,994 known deserters had been captured and returned

Like unionists who lived in Walker County, Alabama, this family on Lookout Mountain, Tennessee, remained loyal to the Union. (Courtesy of the National Archives)

to duty in the summer of 1864. But that fall 6,000 more left. Efforts to flush deserters out of the woods resulted in more conflict, as Confederate troops and vigilante bands clashed with unionists and locals determined to shield their own. The situation got so bad that some families left to wait out the war behind Union lines. In Alabama, the governor sent out the home guard to suppress the uprising. Confederate leaders dispatched the army to restore order in coastal North Carolina. It ended up slaughtering its own citizens at the battle at Plymouth. Nor could southern unionists necessarily depend on the Union army to come to their aid.[32]

Of course, the violence was not one-sided. In Union strongholds, Confederate families were subject to attacks and raids as well. Poorer Confederate women suffered more than the wealthy white ladies who spat at and verbally abused federal soldiers. Union troops, who had little respect for the common white women they encountered in the South, had far less difficulty responding to them with force. Confederate women also fell prey to opportunists, who took advantage of the vulnerable, regardless of their political loyalties. Still, unionists bore the brunt of the violence. Outnumbered, outlawed, and out of power, they took great risks to oppose the Confederacy.[33]

White women were as strong in their unionism as their menfolk, as the statements and actions of women in Walker County suggest. According to Nancy Faught, "myself & husband have conversed many times on the subject of the war & both of us came to the same conclusion . . . that we would cheerfully give up the last thing we possesed in the world to prevent the South from seceding from the Union." One of Catherine Bowen's neighbors reported that she "recommended her husband to join the Union Army": "I saw her crying and she said that she would rather keep her husband at home, but as she could not do so she rather he would go and join the Union Army."[34]

When federal troops came to Mary Guttery's house for supplies, she first tried to use her family's unionism to spare herself: "I said to them, that my Husband was in the Union Army, my sons and sons in law & grand son, that they ought not take all I had." But when the officer said they needed supplies "to smash up the Rebellion," she softened. I "told them to go ahead, take all they could find that they needed, that I was sorry I didn't have more for them to take, that the Rebbs had run off my husband and children, and had kept me rob[b]ed until I had nothing hardly for them to take."[35]

Union opposition to the Confederacy in areas like Walker County would have been impossible without women's consent and aid. Deserters and evaders depended on female relatives and female networks to support them and keep them hidden. Women kept the farms going. They kept their menfolk's whereabouts a secret. They kept them alive, with food and information. Elizabeth Alvis, for instance, "had a signal, which was a white cloth, that she hung out if there was any danger, and if the cloth was not at a certain place" then "ly outs" were safe to go "to the house and get something to eat and all the information she had." Sarah Keeton "would bear any earand" for unionists and Union troops that "they required her to do." Some women even put on men's clothes, picked up weapons, and joined the fight. Without female collaborators, the "ly outs" would not have survived.[36]

Women not only enabled the opposition but also endured the consequences. Their womanhood gave them some protection. Sarah Keeton was a successful spy, her brother-in-law explained, because she was a woman and therefore "would not be molested by the rebel cavalry."[37] Confederate chivalry extended only so far, though. In North Carolina, Confederate conscript officers reportedly abused and even tortured women in an effort to get to the "ly outs." In Walker County, Union women were continually tormented. "I was not personally injured," admitted Susan Madison, "but I was molested and threatened until I hardly knew what to do. I stood in fear all the time." Confederates taunted Sarah Boshel, promising to take her property and to burn down her farmhouse, barn, and outbuildings. "All we had," she was told, would be "destroyed . . . because we stood firm to the Union." The Confederates followed through on their threats to Nancy Beard. Making numerous raids, they took corn, bacon, wool, livestock, and other supplies. One time, in what seems like an act of pure maliciousness, they stole all her bedclothes. Another time, the militia locked her children in the house, put ropes around her boys' necks, and "threatened to hang them."[38]

To escape this kind of treatment, Thomas Files's wife decided to leave and join her husband, who had enlisted in the Union army. To do so, she navigated her way through Confederate lines alone, a perilous journey that many of the men in the area refused to do without an experienced guide. Evidently, the trip was preferable to staying in Walker County.[39]

Unlike women of the planter class, common white women were more likely to reject *both* the war and the Confederacy. During the war, their indignation and weariness fed peace movements in some southern states, including Georgia, North Carolina, and Alabama. After the war, some unionists aligned themselves with northern Republicans and even became outspoken proponents of racial equality. Most common whites, even white unionists, did not go this far, however. They stood by their original principles, which did not allow much room for free African Americans or white northerners. The mothers, wives, and daughters of Confederate soldiers continued to believe that their men had fought the good fight, even though many ultimately turned against Confederate leaders and the war.[40]

Their opposition to both was based on the conviction that the poor were being trampled by the wealthy. But in their minds, the poor people who had suffered during the war were white. The rights of "free men" belonged to white men and white men only. The beneficiaries of these rights were white women and white women only. These rights gave white southerners the right to run their own communities in the way they wanted. They did not want outsiders from the North coming in and telling them what to do any more than they had wanted slaveholders telling them what to do. They certainly did not want to be bossed by former slaves. Above all, they hoped that Confederate surrender would return their lives to what they had been before the Civil War. But that was not to be.

6   For the Freedom of the
Colored People

THE slaves, wrote Kate Stone in 1861, "have gotten a confused idea . . . of the war; they think it is all to help them." Kate was right in one respect. At the beginning of the war, there was nothing in the policies of the federal government, the rhetoric of U.S. officials, or the tone of northern public sentiment to support the idea that the Union was fighting to destroy slavery in the southern states.

She was dead wrong in other ways, however. The war involved slaves from the outset. They endured the worst material deprivations, their work load increased, their homes were destroyed, and their families were separated. The war was also about the institution of slavery; its protection lay at the center of the Confederacy. Although northern officials did not go into the war with the intention of abolishing slavery, they ended up doing just that. Enslaved women and men helped push the process along. Defying their owners' authority and freeing themselves, they undermined the institution and forced both the Union and the Confederacy to deal with the implications.

"The war," claimed Riley Tirey, a former slave, "was for the freedom of the colored people." Lucy, the Stones' head house servant who called herself mistress once Kate and her family left the plantation, thought so as well. Many African Americans did not wait for the Union "to help them." They helped themselves. In the process, they made the war about something other than slavery. They made it a war about freedom and equality. Black women were as crucial in this war as black men were.[1]

～

Wartime shortages hit African Americans the hardest. For many free blacks, life became one long struggle to stave off starvation. The situation was not much better for slaves. With the shortages and high prices, slaveholders gave low priority to their slaves' needs. In 1861, for instance, one South Carolina planter gave the men on his plantation pants but no coats. The women got nothing at all. Shoes were particularly hard to come by, because inexpensive factory-made shoes from the North were no longer available and existing stocks in the South were earmarked for the army. In the fall of 1862, Kate Stone wrote that her brother Jimmy had gone in search of leather to make shoes for the slaves. "Should he fail to get it," she observed, "the Negroes will certainly suffer in the cold." Fortunately for the Stones' slaves, Jimmy was successful.[2]

Other planters, however, were either unable or unwilling to make such purchases, even when supplies were available. It was not unusual to see barefooted, half-naked slaves working the fields during the war. Hunger was equally common. In 1862, several planters on the South Carolina coast eliminated everything but rice from their slaves' rations. Pocketing the savings, they thrust the actual cost onto slaves, many of whom eventually died of malnutrition. Conditions were just as bad or worse on smaller farms. Small slaveholders were not inclined to be generous with their slaves when they could barely scrape together enough to feed their own children. Under these circumstances, slaves were the first to do without. Even relatively affluent slaveholders, like the Stones, pinched pennies at their slaves' expense.[3]

Planters' economizing was penny-wise and pound-foolish. In the long run, it only undermined their authority and fueled unrest in the slave quarters. Reductions in basic necessities incensed hungry, ill-clad slaves who were still expected to labor as long and as hard as ever. In 1864, one South Carolina overseer complained that he could "hardley Get aney thing out of the hands for thay have no shoes and [are] quite Bare for cloths." Even if they had been physically able, they had no reason to make an effort.[4]

Elsewhere, slaves began taking what they needed without asking permission. Pilfering, for instance, increased on the Stone plantation. In the fall of 1861, the overseer "found a barrel of pork in the cotton field and another barrel that had been opened and the meat taken." "The stealing is trying," griped Kate, because pork had gone up to "$35 per barrel." Obviously, the slaves found the situation "trying" as well, although for different reasons.[5]

Shortages had particular implications for slave women. When planters began to produce more food and clothing, most of the extra labor fell to female slaves. Not only were many already skilled in these areas, but also planters considered the labor to be "women's work." To be sure, planter-class women took on more domestic production as well, but they supervised and delegated, just as they had done before the war. It was slave women who did the heavy labor.

Kate's mother, for instance, decided to make cloth on the plantation in 1862 when it became too rare and dear to purchase. Kate learned to weave. It was like going back to the Revolution, she wrote, with ladies producing and wearing homespun. The coarse, scratchy material was not for the "ladies," however. Nor was it the "ladies" who had to spin, card, and weave or go without clothes.[6]

To make matters worse, slaveholders often added new chores to existing responsibilities. They expected slave women to work a full day in the fields and then stay up late into the night to produce basic necessities that owners could not or would not purchase.[7]

On smaller plantations, enslaved women were also expected to fill the gaping hole in the labor force created by the departure of white men. Unlike white women from propertyless households and slaveless yeoman families, mistresses on small plantations never did field work and considered it inappropriate for women of their standing. Slave women took up the slack instead.

White southerners generally found this situation unremarkable, a distinct contrast to the amount of ink they spilled over white women's assuming "male" work and responsibilities. But then, white southerners were accustomed to seeing black women work in the fields. They expected it. They did not even seem to notice they had dumped the primary burden of feeding their families onto African American women. My son, wrote one white mistress on a small plantation with a handful of slaves, "is the only white male on my farm who is able to perform any labor and upon whose labor depends the larger portion of my family for support." But her son was not the household's only support. They actually depended on her son and "one (colored) woman."[8]

African American women on large plantations also spent more time in the fields because the Confederacy pressed black men as well as white men into service. Significantly, the Confederate government never considered impressing slave women. Although slaveholders had no trouble with black women doing "men's" work in the fields, they were unwilling to bend gender conventions so far as to assign them military work. The army began using slave men to build military fortifications almost immediately, though. Initially, planters in threatened areas volunteered their male slaves, but demand soon outstripped supply, prompting individual states and then the Confederate government to begin impressment. In coastal South Carolina, for instance, thousands of African American men had been either volunteered or forced into service in 1861.

Elsewhere, slave men were not impressed in large numbers until later, when the Union army advanced further on southern soil. In 1864, as Sherman neared Atlanta, Gertrude noted that the militia was "impressing Negroes to work on the fortifications" there. "At first the order came for one hundred thousand Negroes and then for one fifth of what each man owned between the age of seventeen and fifty." "The Negroes," she concluded, "have been greatly exercised thereby."[9]

They had good reason. Torn from their families and homes, conscripted men were forced to support their own enslavement under conditions so bad that active duty might have been safer. Many slaveholders were unwilling to put their property at such great risk, even when Union troops threatened their own neighborhoods. For slave men, the only possible advantage was that impressment moved freedom closer by putting them within proximity of Union lines.

Free blacks did not escape service in the Confederate army either. Amid mounting casualties and increasing complaints from whites, the Confederacy began conscripting free black men in 1863. It stopped short of arming slaves and free blacks, although the idea had strong supporters and was seriously considered toward the very end of the war.[10]

It was not just the Confederate government that separated enslaved women from their menfolk. Planters also broke up families when they moved slaves out of the path of the Union army. Some resettled on rented lands well behind Confederate lines. Others hired out slaves as individuals or in groups. The Stone family did both, dispersing their slaves across Louisiana and Texas. In Texas, as we have already seen, Kate's mother worked some slaves on rented lands and hired out others. Before that, she sent many slaves to the saltworks, near Winnfield, Louisiana.

Salt manufactories sprang up all over the South after the Union blockade stopped incoming supplies of this essential mineral. Slave men also worked in Confederate hospitals, on railroads, and in iron and munitions factories. Conditions in them were notorious. The largely male work force survived long hours and backbreaking labor only to face malnutrition, exposure, and disease. "Bad news from the Negroes at the salt works," reported Kate in 1863. One of the men had died, and the several others were near death. Three had tried to escape to rejoin their wives "but were caught." One week later, two more had "died of pneumonia and neglect." Although extreme, conditions in the saltworks were not unlike those facing hired and relocated slaves generally. The experience meant separation from their homes and their loved ones under extremely difficult circumstances.[11]

Despite all the hardship, slaves had reason for optimism as well. They knew far better than their masters and mistresses how the war was altering authority. Watching and waiting, they took every opportunity to turn the situation to their advantage. It was not just slaveholding women who had problems governing slaves during the war. As slaves saw it, the war put *both* their masters' and mistresses' power in question. After all, the Confederacy might well lose. Then what?

Kate noticed the difference in the slaves on her family's plantation as soon as the war began. "The excitement in the air has infected them," she wrote in June, 1861. Slave women were as unruly as the men. "Still trouble with the house servants," Kate reported a few days later. "Aunt Lucy, the head of them all, ran away this morning, but was back by dinner. . . . All of them are demoralized."[12]

Demoralization was hardly how Lucy and the other slaves would have described it. Quite the opposite. As far as they were concerned, their owners' authority diminished with each Confederate defeat. That slaveholders could no longer provide them basic support in exchange for their labor did not help matters. The institution collapsed completely as the Union army neared. In 1863, with federal troops swarming all over Kate's neighborhood, "demoralization" turned to open rebellion.[13]

One of the most common acts of resistance was leaving. During the antebellum period, slaves who ran away were usually single men. Now slaves fled in family groups. Women as well as men left, although women with young children were less likely to do so because of the difficulties of transporting and supporting them on their own. In 1863, just before the fall of Vicksburg, Kate reported that "there are only twenty Negroes left on Mrs. Tibbetts' five places, and Dr. Tibbetts has only one left." On Mr. Hardison's plantation, "six of the men with their children and clothes walked off in broad daylight. . . . Mr. Hardison expected to get home today and move them all to Monroe, but he has waited too long. The other Negroes declare they are free and will leave as soon as they get ready."[14]

When the slaves in Kate's neighborhood claimed their freedom in 1863, they had the full force of federal policy on their side. A few months earlier, on January 1, 1863, the Emancipation Proclamation, which freed all slaves living in states that remained loyal to the Confederacy, went into effect. Although the Emancipation Proclamation did not abolish slavery complete-

African Americans celebrating the Emancipation Proclamation, in southern Virginia, near Winchester, published in *Le Monde Illustre,* March 21, 1863. (Photo courtesy of the Newberry Library)

ly, it was a major turning point in the wartime policy. Only three years earlier, President Abraham Lincoln had promised not to interfere with slavery where it already existed.

What changed his mind? With the Confederacy hanging on longer than anticipated and support for the war withering in the North, Lincoln needed to do something to turn the tide. He and his advisers knew how important slave labor was to the Confederacy. They also knew how terrified white southerners were of slave rebellion. The Emancipation Proclamation capitalized on these weaknesses. By offering freedom to slaves and encouraging them to abandon their masters, Lincoln opened a second front in the very heart of the Confederacy. White southerners understood the Emancipation Proclamation in exactly those terms. Kate called it "diabolical," and her comments were restrained compared with others.[15]

It was Lincoln who elevated emancipation to the level of official policy, but it was enslaved women and men who first thought of the idea. They had been freeing themselves long before the Union promised to protect their freedom. They began doing so the moment Union troops set foot on southern soil—as early as January 1861, along the coast of Georgia and South Carolina. They took great risks for freedom. Runaways could be executed if caught. Family and friends left behind became vulnerable to punishment by angry planters. Moreover, freedom was not necessarily guaranteed behind Union lines. Initially, the Union army had no intention of attacking slavery. With thousands of African Americans crowding into Union camps and following federal troops, however, military officials were forced to adapt their policies. They were also quick to realize the strategic benefits of slaves' departure. Capitalizing on the opportunity to undermine the Confederacy's will power and its labor power, the Union army began encouraging and assisting escaped slaves.

Still, escaped slaves did not become full citizens once they made it to Union lines. In the army's terminology, they were "contraband": property seized as a consequence of war. Of course, contrabands were not really "seized." Moreover, they demanded freedom. Gradually, federal policy evolved toward legal recognition of refugees' free status. It was a slow process, though. The Emancipation Proclamation, for instance, freed only those slaves in the Confederacy. The status of refugees in Union-occupied areas was not entirely clear, and some military officials did not apply the proclamation to the refugees under their command.[16]

Despite all the risks, slaves kept coming. Between 1862 and 1864, the refugee population in Union-occupied areas of South Carolina swelled to around fifteen or sixteen thousand. As the war ground on and the Union cinched its noose tighter, slaves from the interior began leaving as well. The experience of Hannah and Henry Guy was typical. As Hannah later recalled, they left their owner when "the U.S. Army came through Alabama" in 1863. From there, they followed the troops to Union-occupied Corinth, Mississippi.[17]

As the numbers of refugees multiplied, the army organized permanent camps and put them to work. Refugees also congregated in Union-occupied towns and cities, where they lived without official oversight. By 1863, such enclaves circled the Confederacy's perimeter, from the Sea Islands up the Atlantic coast to New Bern and Roanoke Island in North Carolina and Fortress Monroe in Virginia, across the Confederacy's northern border to Nashville and Memphis, and then down the Mississippi River to Vicksburg and New Orleans.

Freedom in the Union-occupied South had its own problems. With the War Department, the Treasury Department, and northern missionaries continually battling for jurisdiction over the refugee camps, governance was erratic, and living conditions were worse. With few exceptions, the camps

An engraving of slaves moving behind Union lines, published in *Harper's Weekly,* January 31, 1863. (Photo courtesy of the Newberry Library)

were overcrowded and disease ridden. Conditions in towns and cities not officially under military supervision were no better. Makeshift housing let in wintry winds, driving rains, and sweltering heat, as well as swarms of feathered, furry, and scaly pests. Sometimes there were rations from missionary societies and other voluntary aid organizations in the North. More often, refugees were on their own.[18]

From the first, the Union army's official policy was that contrabands had to work to support themselves. The policy applied to both men and women. Before the fall of 1862 when the Union army began using African American soldiers, male refugees did a wide variety of paid labor in and around Union camps. Often, they had no choice. The military pressed them into service, whether they wanted to do the work or not.

Military wages rarely supported an entire family. But then, military laborers were lucky to get paid at all. Sometimes they were compensated in the form of food and clothing, which may or may not have been adequate for a family's needs. Sometimes the complications of their status and the military's policies meant they received nothing at all. Given the precariousness of the situation, everyone had to pitch in to make ends meet.[19]

The federal government also put black men and women back into the fields. That was the case on the plantations in the Mississippi Valley—although, as we have seen, the slaves saw the land as their own, a perspective distinctly different from that of the federal government. The same held true for land along the coast of South Carolina and Georgia, in southern Louisiana, and in parts of North Carolina and Virginia. In some areas, southern Louisiana prime among them, the federal government gave the land back to owners when they took a loyalty oath to the Union. Otherwise, plantations were leased out to northerners. Here, too, fugitive slaves were not always asked whether they wanted the work. The decision was often made for them by the army, which gathered up refugees and shipped them back to the plantations. There, black laborers were forced to sign year-long contracts, forfeited all their pay if they quit, and worked from dawn to dusk under white overseers. Understandably, neither women nor men were eager to return to the fields under circumstances so similar to slavery.[20]

For the most part, the federal government ignored African Americans' claims to the land. It gave land back to planters and auctioned it off to northern interests, despite the protests of slaves who were living and working there and who tried to obtain legal title themselves. The military did lease some plantations to slaves and set aside land for settlement by refugees. But this was the exception, not the rule. Women were denied even these limited benefits; only the families of soldiers and male household heads could make claims. It may have been just as well. As we will see in the next chapter, title to these lands was not absolute, and the U.S. government eventually returned them to their original, white owners.[21]

Once the army allowed it, African American men volunteered for military service. For many, it was a watershed that marked their passage from slavery into free manhood. Yet others were forced into it. They had good reason to drag their feet. Army life was bleak, particularly for black troops. Soldiers' pay was low to begin with, and, until 1864, black soldiers received much less than white soldiers. As one company of black Virginia troops described their time in service, "[N]ever was wee any more treated Like slaves than wee are now."[22]

Above all, it was their inability to look to "the pertection of our wifes" that made these Virginia soldiers feel enslaved. Even assuming soldiers managed to get their paychecks to their families, their low pay did not cover their families' needs. Enlisted men also worried about the safety of their loved ones. Violence against both slaves and free blacks had escalated during the war. Since John Brown's raid on Harpers Ferry, white southerners tried to nip uprisings (real and imagined) in the bud. If the families of black soldiers stayed put, they had to live among angry white Confederates whose worst nightmare was a black man in uniform and who did not hesitate in taking out their anger on black soldiers' families.[23]

Nor was the safety of soldiers' families guaranteed if they sought shelter in refugee camps or if they followed the troops. With notable exceptions, white Union soldiers were a racist lot. They had particularly negative conceptions of black women, believing them to be immoral and sexually promiscuous. Acting on these beliefs, they made rape and other forms of physical violence against African American women common both inside and outside the refugee camps.[24]

African American women never really fit in the federal government's official policies. The military based its decision to harbor refugees on the assumption that the military could use cheap labor: each slave the Confederacy lost meant one worker for the Union military. But army officials envisioned "workers" as single men whose labor they could deploy at will. They also saw the separation of families as part of military life. When soldiers went to war, they left their wives, children, and other kin at home. On top of all that, many federal officers assumed that slavery had destroyed families, which they defined as a nuclear unit composed of a legally married husband and wife and their biological children. As a result, they were completely unprepared for slaves in family groups, wholly baffled by the importance slaves placed on family ties, and totally dismissive of slaves' definitions of "family."[25]

Many northern officials were appalled when they realized that refugee couples were not legally married. Former slaves had celebrated their unions with a religious ceremony, lived in long-term unions defined as marriages in the slave quarters, or both. But their marriages were not recognized by law. Nor did the marriages automatically become legal once refugees were behind Union lines.

In the eyes of northern officials, legal marriage made all the difference in the status of families and the character of individuals. With it, there were families: men became responsible husbands and fathers, women were virtuous wives and caring mothers, and children were safe. Without it, families did not exist: men were lazy and irresponsible, women were little better than prostitutes, and their illegitimate children were doomed. Racism led some northern officials to conclude that African Americans could never manage "proper" marriages or families. Others, particularly army chaplains and missionaries, hoped to rescue black couples and their children from what they considered a moral and social crisis of catastrophic proportions. They proselytized and prodded. That failing, they pushed refugees into legalizing their unions.[26]

Of course, many African Americans sought legal marriage for their own reasons. For some, as we will see in the next chapter, marrying legally represented their new free status. But other refugees, like Hannah and Henry Guy, were satisfied with their domestic arrangements as they were. "After we had been at Corinth 2 or 3 months," explained Hannah, "orders came that everybody had to be married under the new laws, and a whole lot of us, including Henry and I were married by Mr. Pierson," the regimental chaplain. "He stood a whole lot of us up in line and married us. . . . I think he had a whole lot of papers in his hand, and he read all of our names out." To Mr. Pierson and the military officials who issued the order, the ceremony transformed Hannah and Henry Guy into a married couple. It meant little to them, though, because they already saw themselves as married.[27]

Legal marriage did not alter African Americans' ideas about family. Determined to keep their families together, black women refused to stay home like good soldiers' wives were supposed to do. After Henry Guy enlisted, for instance, Hannah followed his regiment to Memphis to be near him. Edith Reddick, who married while a refugee, moved constantly to remain with her husband. "The Regiment being under marching orders," she explained, "we were married on Sunday morning and left [the] same day at 11 o'clock for Augusta, Georgia. My Husband going with his Regiment and I with him. . . . I moved with my Husband in the Army from Augusta, Georgia to Edgefield, So. Carolina thence to Andersonville, thence to Walhalla and thence to Charleston So. Carolina where we remained until he was taken sick and . . . died at the Government Hospital."[28]

It was not just wives who followed husbands. Whether related by blood or through fictive kin ties, women tried to stay close to the men they loved. For that, they received nothing but contempt from army officers, who did everything they could to discourage black women from following the troops. The measures could be harsh. In 1864, for instance, the Union commander in South Carolina ordered all women who visited army camps to be arrested. Usually, however, officers made some concession to married couples, allowing wives to visit their husbands on occasion. But "unrelated" women and other female kin, whose ties to male soldiers did not fit into officer's middle-class conceptions of "family," remained on the outside.[29]

Northern officials believed that women belonged in male-headed family units. They had not expected large numbers of refugee women who were on their own, unattached to men. Nor did they make accommodations for these women after their arrival. Whether by the forced breakup of families or by individual preference, many black women had lived without men in slavery. Conscription, relocation, and the confusion of occupation multiplied their numbers. So did the rush to leave the plantations. Families often divided over the decision to leave, with some members going and others staying. Women were not always the ones left behind. Edith Reddick was around fifteen years old when she followed the Union army off her plantation in southern Georgia and arrived, parentless, in a refugee camp. Similarly, Jane, the slave Kate feared would stab her family in their beds, fled the Stone plantation with her three young children.[30]

Whether married or alone, with children or without, women had to struggle to survive in refugee camps and in Union-occupied towns and cities. Despite policies that directed women to support themselves, federal officials did not open many paid occupations to women. Besides field work, the only work they could imagine for black women was as cooks, laundresses, and prostitutes—although prostitution was officially discouraged. Options were not much better outside federal jurisdiction. Women were left to cobble together their own solutions. Like Hannah Guy, some women washed and cooked for the troops. Other women pieced together a subsistence,

The laundry staff at Hospital No. 3 in Nashville, Tennessee. Black women did much of the domestic labor required to keep Union armies going in the South and routine labor in Confederate hospitals. (Courtesy of the National Archives)

growing their own food, selling the surplus, peddling baked goods and other prepared foods, and taking paid work when they needed ready cash. This strategy was particularly attractive to some women because it allowed them to be free: to work for themselves, at their own pace, when and where they wanted.

If women's employment options were bad, their pay was worse. The same deeply ingrained ideas about gender roles that kept federal officials and civilians from hiring women to do "male" jobs also justified paying women less than men. Women could sometimes find work at higher wages on occupied lands that were being leased to white northerners, returned to "loyal" landowners, or run by the U.S. government. The labor force on many abandoned plantations in the Mississippi River Valley, for instance, was made up primarily of African American women. But, many women workers never actually received their wages, and working conditions were not what they had in mind after they had risked so much for their freedom.[31]

Drawing on the same extended family networks that supported them in slavery, women banded together and leaned on each other. Often, younger women found shelter with older women. When Edith Reddick met her future husband, for instance, she was living with an aunt. Then, after her husband died, she moved in with Mrs. Doc Williams, the company's cook. Similarly, when Henry Guy's regiment went down the Mississippi River where Hannah could not follow, she settled with her husband's mother in Cairo, Illinois.[32]

Most northern officials did not recognize women's survival strategies as such. "This getting a precarious livelihood by doing a little at this thing, & a little at that is the very curse of the people," complained one plantation superintendent in South Carolina. "So far as possible," he continued, "they should be compelled to *steady labor.*" Inconvenienced by women's presence, blind to their problems, and indifferent to their desires, northern officials could not see the inadequacy of the available economic options. Often, they blamed the women themselves: if they were cold and hungry, it was because they were lazy and irresponsible.[33]

Once they seized their freedom, African American women and men tried to make the most of it. They began the struggle as soon as they reached Union lines. There, in refugee camps and regimental units, free blacks and former slaves had to overcome their differences, work together to change conditions around them, and define what freedom would mean. African Americans, young and old, packed the schools run by northern missionaries. They established their own churches and mutual aid societies. They made homes and tried to piece together livelihoods that would allow them to live free of white supervision. They peppered federal officials with complaints, bristling with references to their rights as free people. They also began organizing around these concerns, defining their own political agendas centered on racial equality and economic justice.[34]

Not every slave, however, left the plantations. Many more stayed where they were. Some did so because they heard rumors of the Union army's abuse of escaped slaves. Some saw it as their best hope for survival. Others were reluctant to leave the homes they had built and the land they had tended. Some felt so strongly about it that they defied their masters' wishes to relocate them to safer places.[35]

The Stones' slaves resisted relocation for this reason. "Of course the Negroes do not want to go," Kate noted, when discussing the family's plans to move to Texas. More accurately, the slaves refused to go. "Mamma will have the Negro men taken to the back country tomorrow," Kate wrote a few days later, "if she can get them to go." Evidently, Kate's mother was unsuccessful, because many slaves stayed on the plantation when the Stone family escaped to Texas.[36]

Once Kate and her family were gone, the slaves declared themselves free and took over the plantation. They divided the property, moving some of the furniture into the quarters and some of the families into the big house. The infamous Lucy got not only Kate's mother's clothes but also enough household supplies and small luxuries to make her cabin more comfortable. When Kate's brother Jimmy came back to round up the rest of the slaves, he found Lucy and another woman drinking the coffee Kate's mother had carefully horded, while heaping scorn on their former owners.[37]

That surprised Jimmy, but he knew enough about the situation to expect resistance. He had come with several Confederate soldiers. The party kept its arrival a secret and then surprised the slaves at daybreak. "They surrounded the cabins," as Kate related the story, "calling the Negroes out and telling them it was useless to resist." Then Jimmy and the soldiers marched the slaves at gunpoint to Texas. Other slaves were more fortunate, living and working on abandoned lands until after the war.[38]

Jimmy Stone's victory, however, was too little, too late. The situation was too far gone for the Stones or any other slaveholder in the area to be able to reestablish control. Slavery had actually collapsed before the Stones left for Texas. By early spring of 1863, planters in the area had abandoned any hope of working their plantations. One neighbor complained to Kate that "his Negroes will not even pretend to work." They were also confronting their owners, threatening them physically, and taking their property. Mrs. Hardison's slaves, Kate reported, "have done everything but strike her and have used very abusive language." One owner, according to Kate, was beat up by his slaves. Another was held at gunpoint. Kate herself had a brush with danger, cowering in the corner as a raiding party of armed black men plundered a neighbor's house where she was visiting.[39]

The same scenes were repeated elsewhere in the South, as slavery's foundations crumbled and the institution caved in on itself. The complaints of S. R. Hawley, who lived in Blockersville, North Carolina, echoed those made by Kate and her neighbors over a year earlier. The slaves, he wrote in September 1864, have been "absenting themselves from the employment of their owners and some of them is going about in open daytime entering houses it matters not whether the familys are at Home or not and taking off just what ever they choose." "It is," he concluded, "Exceedingly a Bad State of things."[40]

What white commentators often missed was that slaves did not loot and destroy property for the same reasons or in the same way that white union soldiers did. To be sure, some African Americans took advantage of the chaos to enrich themselves. Hunger drove others to take what they could. But more than greed or desperation was involved when slaves stripped their owners' big houses as the Stones' slaves did, taking what they wanted and methodically destroying the rest. As they saw it, they were taking property that had been purchased with their sweat and that had always been theirs. What they could not use or did not value, they destroyed, taking revenge on the people who had appropriated their labor for so long.[41]

Many slaves were actually as disgusted with the Union army's indiscriminate destruction of property as their owners were. When the army marched through, they took or destroyed everything. Slaves watched with despair as the troops razed buildings, toppled fences, and demolished fields they had worked so hard to build. Many enslaved men and women, particularly those on larger plantations, saw the lands they had worked as the foundation of their future. Why would they want to destroy what they planned to use themselves? They were even more angry when Union soldiers took their own possessions: household items, livestock, chickens, and supplies that meant the difference between starvation and survival then and would mean the difference between poverty and plenty later.[42]

Slavery's demise was not always loud and dramatic. In the interior areas, far away from the Union army, it ended quietly. Many slaveholders there refused to acknowledge either the collapse of slavery elsewhere or even the fact of emancipation after Confederate surrender. Some, such as those in Texas, were kept in bondage months after the Confederacy's official demise. Slaves therefore stayed put, marking time and waiting to see what would happen.[43]

Their silence was disturbing to many owners, who suspected that the slaves around them knew more than they were letting on. "Not by one word or look can we detect any change in the demeanor of these Negro servants," wrote the South Carolina mistress Mary Chesnut during the bombing of Fort Sumter. "They carry it too far. . . . Are they stolidly stupid or wiser than we are, silent and strong, biding their time?"[44]

The waiting paid off. In May 1865, after Confederate surrender, planters across the South gathered their remaining slaves together and informed them of their new status. Gertrude described the scene at the Thomases' house in Augusta. "Mr Thomas" said "that it was extremely probable that the Yankees would free them . . . and advised them to wait quietly and see what would be done." As far as the U.S. government was concerned, the slaves were already free. Many of the Thomases' slaves probably either knew or suspected as much already.[45]

Still, their response was measured and guarded—so much so that Gertrude mistook it for no response at all. She relaxed when she saw "no evidence of insubordination." To the contrary, "they all worked very cheerfully." Cheerful indeed. Gertrude had allowed herself to be fooled. The very next day, the Thomases' house servants began drifting off. Unlike the slaves in Kate's neighborhood, they did not take property or confront Gertrude and her husband directly. They made their plans and packed their belongings. Then, when the time was right, they disappeared without a word. Leaving and moving around on their own were the first acts of freedom for slaves after the collapse of the Confederacy, just as they had been for other slaves during the war.[46]

Slavery in the United States officially died with Confederate surrender and the passage of the Thirteenth Amendment.[47] But it had collapsed long before, in no small measure because of the efforts of slaves. Destroying slavery, however, would prove far easier than establishing freedom. African American women and men began the struggle during the war, but this was only the beginning. It would continue for generations.

Part Three

After

Kate Stone refused to admit defeat. At first, she simply dismissed reports of Robert E. Lee's surrender. Given the unreliability of news during the war, her skepticism was understandable. But the persistence of her doubts and the interpretation she gave to the available information strained credulity. When Kate could no longer ignore the fact of surrender, she insisted that it did not mean defeat and clung to rumors that General Albert Sidney Johnston was preparing for a "gallant fight." In May 1865, she still viewed the state of the Confederacy as "unsettled."[1]

Denial was harder for Gertrude, because of the proximity of military. The contrast between the neatly outfitted Union troops that occupied Augusta in the spring of 1865 and the ragged Confederate soldiers who trudged through on their way home served as a daily reminder of the war's outcome. Even more symbolic was Jefferson Davis's capture. After the fall of Richmond and Lee's surrender, Davis fled south to avoid arrest. On May 10, 1865, federal troops tracked him down near the Florida border, dashing any lingering hopes that the Confederacy might survive. Seven days later, Davis was escorted through Augusta under heavy guard on his way to prison. "*Jeff Davis* in Augusta and a prisoner," wrote Gertrude, "This was indeed the crowning point, the climax of our downfall. I buried my face on the pillow and wept bitterly."[2]

Both Gertrude and Kate marked the Confederacy's collapse through the public actions of military leaders and government officials. Yet, as we saw in the last section, the home front became a battleground during the war. There, southerners faced the disintegration of slavery, economic collapse, tensions among white southerners, and the failure of the Confederacy's basic social and political principles. The resulting conflicts were crucial to the war's outcome. By 1865, there was nothing that Robert E. Lee, Jefferson Davis, or any of the Confederacy's other leaders could have done to turn back the clock. Even if they had managed to save the Confederacy, the antebellum South was already gone.

Confederate surrender did not resolve the battles that had ravaged the home front. Traditionally, historians have looked to party politics to explain the outcome of Reconstruction. Even as northerners celebrated their victory, they began to divide over how to bring the former Confederate states back into the Union. In 1865, after the assassination of Abraham Lincoln, Vice President Andrew Johnson assumed the presidency and implemented his Reconstruction plan without consulting Congress. He required Confederate states to void their ordinances of secession and adopt the Thirteenth Amendment, which abolished slavery. Confederate soldiers had to take loyalty oaths before they could vote. Higher military officers and government officials had to obtain pardons personally from Johnson to restore their political rights. All other matters, including the status of former slaves, were left to the states.

In the summer and fall of 1865, the former Confederate states reorganized in ways that belied the war's outcome. The delegates to these state constitutional conventions included many high-ranking Confederate officials, who debated the nullification of their secession ordinances and the abolition of slavery as if they still had a say in these matters. Then, delegates undercut the intent of these measures with the infamous Black Codes. Built around the laws that had constrained free blacks before emancipation, the Black Codes were intended to place all African Americans in a legal position substantively different from and institutionally inferior to that of white citizens. In general, the Black Codes did allow African Americans to contract and gave them access to the criminal and civil courts, but these rights meant little, since the other provisions in the codes denied them virtually all the rights of free citizens.

Howls of protest issued from the North. Confederates seemed unabashedly unrepentant. They walked directly into the nation's capitol by the frontdoor and sneaked slavery into their own states through the backdoor, as if nothing had happened. Most northerners expected more after four bloody years of war. The election of former Confederates to Congress and the enactment of the Black Codes had much the same effect as a red flag waved in the face of angry bull: they solidified popular support in the North for congressional Republicans and their more liberal plans for reconstructing the South. A tug of war ensued. Congress lobbed legislation at Johnson that established African Americans' rights and imposed harsher terms on defeated Confederates. Johnson struck back with vetoes. Congress returned fire by overriding the vetoes and initiating impeachment proceedings.

By 1867, Congress finally gained the upper hand. The congressional plan, with the Fourteenth and Fifteenth amendments as its centerpiece, eliminated racial distinctions in the law and thus guaranteed African American men and women the same civil and political rights that whites had—although the rights of men and women were, of course, different. The new, democratized state constitutions formed during Reconstruction then swept aside the other legal impediments that kept African Americans from participating in state and local institutions of governance.

After the passage of the various pieces of legislation that composed Reconstruction, many northerners thought that the federal government's duty had ended. Just as they began to pull back, however, conservative white Democrats organized to "redeem" state and local governments. They used violence, intimidation, and fraud, causing such terror that the results resembled guerrilla war in some areas. Democrats seized control of one southern state after another, beginning in the early 1870s. Local Republicans, black and white, pleaded for federal intervention but to no avail. In 1876, as part of the compromise that resolved the disputed presidential election in favor of the Republican candidate, the federal government officially abandoned the South. Behind the political euphemism "home rule," Democrats made a mockery of the Fourteenth and Fifteenth amendments. Not only were African Americans denied civil rights and political rights, but many poor whites were as well.

It is a dramatic story. Yet the focus on party politics misses as much as Kate's and Gertrude's military-centered view of the Confederacy's demise. Just as the wartime policies inevitably politicized the "home front," so Reconstruction-era policies politicized the household. Confederate surrender and emancipation resulted in the transformation of the central institution of antebellum southern society—the household. As a result, many of the Reconstruction era's key issues were played out in the region's fields and houses.[3]

We usually think of these arenas as separate from politics, but passing laws does not necessarily make them a reality in people's daily lives. Southerners battled over the meaning of Reconstruction policies at every point in the process—from the enactment of the Black Codes, to the conferral of full civil and political rights to African Americans and concurrent changes that gave poor whites greater access to the South's governing structures, to the Democratic party's efforts to "redeem" the South. Daily conflicts that contributed to the success and failure of these policies were played out on Reconstruction's "home front," making this arena as politically important as the ballot box or the statehouse.

Just as public policy transformed the home front, so changes there reached out to reshape the public order. In the antebellum South, men's and women's status within households determined their social status, legal rights, and political power. As we have seen, domestic dependency placed wives, slaves, and children under the authority of household heads. Domestic dependency then followed these people outside their households, where it translated into limits on where they could go, what they could do and say, and how others could treat them. Household heads, in turn, acquired their public privileges through their ability to provide economically for their dependents. The twin blows of war and emancipation shattered this structure, opening up questions about southerners' places both within and outside their households.

The centrality of the home front drew women into the work of Reconstruction, regardless of whether they wanted to participate. Different groups of southern women approached this task in very different ways. None, however, duplicated the experiences of Melanie and Scarlett in *Gone with the Wind.* Elite white women, like Kate and Gertrude, came the closest. Although many women of the planter class had longed for the war's end, they had never wanted Confederate defeat. With slavery went the material and ideological foundations of their class position. They lost the immediate comforts of their lives. Beyond that, the foundations that supported who they were and why they were important collapsed. More like Scarlett than Melanie, these women were dragged kicking and screaming into the postwar era.[4]

Kate and Gertrude were no exception. After slogging through days filled with frustration and disappointment, they poured out their despair in diary entries so raw and intense that they make for difficult reading. These two mourned a past that they were unable to bring back. Like so many other women of their class and race, they did not accept the situation with patient forbearance, as Melanie did. Nor did they embrace the new order with the self-interest and impatience that Scarlett did. Rather, they actively sought new ways to define their own and their menfolk's status in a world without slavery, while bringing their version of the past into the present through various efforts to honor the Confederacy and the plantation South. In the process, they redefined their own role in southern society.

White women of poor to modest means greeted Confederate surrender with deep ambivalence. They hoped that the end of the war would return their lives to what they had been. That would never be. In an economic structure centered on male-headed families, women had a particularly difficult time piecing together a living. Many never recovered from the loss of their menfolk's labor. The lives of women whose menfolk did return were still difficult. They started the 1865 planting season late. They faced fallow fields grown over after years of neglect. They had no draft animals, stock, or supplies to see them through to harvest. Most had to borrow heavily to purchase what they needed. All this meant more work and fewer rewards for women. The results eventually stripped many white families of their land and plunged them into a cycle of debt and dependency from which they never escaped.[5]

Yet Reconstruction also presented opportunities, some less obvious than others. To be sure, emancipation shot gaping holes through the personal identity and social status of many nonslaveholding whites. Although they had no love for either slaveholders or slaves, many were still deeply invested in the institution of slavery because it elevated them above black southerners. Nonetheless, emancipation ushered in political changes that also benefited many white southerners. White women of poor to modest means were among those who seized these openings to improve their families' lot and their status as women.

African American women welcomed the postwar era with open arms. As Gertrude buried her head in the pillow and wept, African Americans ran out in the streets to celebrate Jefferson Davis's capture. For them, the event symbolized victory, not defeat. More than that, Confederate surrender was about promise and hope. With it came emancipation, the jubilee for which they had waited so long.[6]

Free blacks were more ambivalent. They had been identified with slaves more than with free citizens in law and social practice. The postwar restrictions on African Americans ate away at their freedom, making it hollow and fragile. That did not mean that all free blacks were eager to throw their lot with former slaves, however. A few established, light-skinned black families, who had accumulated property and carved out a social niche for themselves in such cities as Charleston and New Orleans, feared the loss of their own privileged status. Still, many free blacks did ultimately work with former slaves to claim full civil and political rights.[7]

African American women immediately set about making their hopes and dreams for freedom a reality. They brought their families together and then worked to make them economically and socially independent of whites. They joined their menfolk in the fight to secure full civil rights by claiming them in daily social interactions and, occasionally, in court. They also spoke in their own voices, stretching the meaning of these new rights by articulating their specific concerns as women who were also poor and black. As educational and economic opportunities contributed to the emergence of a black middle class, women in this group became vocal advocates for reform. All these African American women poured their hearts and souls into the task of rebuilding the South. Many suffered great physical and emotional losses. Some even lost their lives. In fact, the results of their efforts can seem trifling compared with what remained undone. These women have therefore often been dismissed and forgotten. Their imprint on the process of Reconstruction is unmistakable, though. Even when they failed, their attempts kept hope alive and made future struggles for racial justice possible.

7 Talking for Her Rights

BELLA Newton, an African American woman, lived in Granville County, North Carolina. According to the 1870 census, she was forty years old and light-skinned. She lived with her daughter Rowen, worked as a cook, rented a house, and owned no property that the census taker thought valuable enough to enumerate. Rowen, aged fourteen, attended school and could read and write, neither of which her mother could do.[1]

These bare facts, listed without ceremony by the census taker, would be all we knew about Newton if it were not for a certain incident. The previous year, she had been involved in a court case. That year, her household was larger, for she had two more children, Susan and William, living with Her. Her responsibilities were also more complicated because Susan and William had been assaulted by Alexander Noblin, a white neighbor.

The trouble began in the spring of 1869, as the two children were walking home across Noblin's land. He saw them and ordered them off. Then he tried to assault Susan sexually. Although frustrated in his attempt by William, who hurled a rock at his head, Noblin fired a parting volley to reassert his authority. In William's words, he "shook his penis at us." After learning of the incident, Bella Newton's first response was in keeping with antebellum traditions. She publicized her complaint in the neighborhood and then made an informal bargain with Noblin, agreeing to drop the matter in exchange for one dollar and ten pounds of bacon. Noblin delivered the goods, but Newton did not fulfill her end of the deal. Instead of remaining quiet, she filed charges with the justice of the peace, an extremely bold move for this poor black woman. Much to his chagrin, Noblin learned that his actions carried much different consequences than they had before the war. He was indicted for assault during the spring term of the Superior Court. There is no further record of the case.[2]

The indictment, however, was a victory for Bella Newton. Legal action had been closed to her and other black women during slavery, when both formal and informal practices sanctioned violence against them. Still, the price for Newton and her children was high. The following year, Newton moved to another neighborhood. Neither William nor Susan lived with her anymore. Perhaps they chose to work elsewhere and lived with their employers or with other relatives who were closer to their place of employment. Perhaps they moved away for their own safety after what had happened. Perhaps they left for reasons entirely unrelated to Noblin and the resulting court case. We will never know. What is clear is that the lives of Bella Newton and her children changed forever after Noblin's attack.

Freedom was a daily struggle for Bella Newton and other African Americans. Bringing family members together, living in their own households, moving around, demanding control over their work and compensation for it, challenging physical violence and abuse—in all these ways African Americans tried to make freedom a reality. They had to fight for every inch of ground. They often had to fight for the same inch over and over again. Even the simplest acts, such as walking across a white landowner's property, met with resistance. Gestures as seemingly inconsequential as a muttered comment or a look directly returned could provoke violence. More assertive actions usually did.

None of this stopped African Americans intent on realizing their freedom. As Bella Newton's case indicates, black women played a central role in these struggles. Her court case was unusual, but her outspokenness was not. She and other women like her fought alongside the men in their families and communities, working toward shared goals and against shared oppression. But black women's lives during Reconstruction cannot be explained in exactly the same terms as the lives of black men. Like Bella Newton and her daughters, African American women faced their own challenges, had their own dreams, and acted on them in their own ways.

⌇

Bella Newton risked a great deal to protect her family. She was not alone. Establishing their own households and shielding family members from exploitation and abuse were among African Americans' highest priorities. The first act of freedom for many former slaves was reuniting their families. As we have seen, slaves often fled with their families to Union lines during the war. Once there, they defied indifferent federal policies and unsympathetic military officials to keep their families together. After emancipation, former slaves traveled long distances, searching for loved ones who had been sold during slavery. Even for those who had lived nearby or on the same plantation, the act of setting up their own households with their own family members was extremely important. Doing so meant repudiating the power masters had held over the most intimate relations in their lives.[3]

Bringing family members together was significant, but it was not enough. African Americans also wanted the power to preserve their family ties. Many embraced legal marriage during and after the war for this reason. Of course, conservative white lawmakers did legalize the existing unions of former slaves in the Black Codes, but the legislators who passed these measures were not particularly concerned about the rights or wishes of black couples and their families. Some states required African Americans to formalize their vows and fined them if they did not. Other states simply declared existing unions legal, without giving the couples involved any say at all. Conservative lawmakers' intent was to shed any economic responsibility for African Americans who were unable to support themselves. As they saw it, legal marriage would ensure that wives, children, the elderly, and the infirm would become the responsibility of individual household heads, not the state.[4]

African American men and women, however, valued legal marriage for very different reasons. As one black corporal in the Union army proclaimed to an audience of former slaves in Virginia, "The Marriage Covenant is at the foundation of all our rights. In slavery we could not have *legalised* marriage: *now* we have it . . . and we shall be established as a people." Legal marriage represented their new status as citizens. More than that, it promised security impossible under slavery, when their families could be broken up, their private lives disrupted, and their households entered at will.[5]

Marrying legally did not mean that African Americans accepted the law's definition of marriage, family, or households. Many freedpeople saw no reason to abandon their own customs. Some refused to marry legally at all. Even when they did, communities continued to play a significant role in defining and validating marriages, just as they had in slavery. Neighbors and kin had to recognize a couple as husband and wife for the marriage to be legitimate. Their standards could include legal registration, but the substance of the relationship often took precedence over the law. When women and men ceased to fulfill their responsibilities toward each other, neighbors and kin often considered the marriage over. Mary J. Moore's husband, for instance, beat her and ran around with other women on the sly. When he began to live openly with another woman, Mary considered the marriage

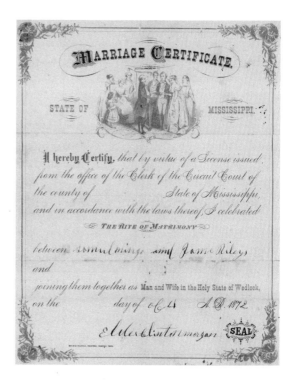

A marriage certificate for one of many African American couples married legally after emancipation. (Courtesy of the National Archives)

over, and her neighbors concurred. She went on to live with several other men in a series of monogamous relationships recognized as valid marriages in her neighborhood, although she never obtained a legal divorce.[6]

The families formed through these marriage practices were flexible and fluid, just as they had been in slavery. Many African Americans still did not define families only in terms of a male household head and his dependents or even people with biological connections to each other. The absence of a legally recognized father, for instance, did not spell disaster for unmarried women and their children. Children might eventually live in a household with their mothers and men who became their fathers even though they were not biologically related. They might continue to live with their mother in a household composed of related and fictive kin. Or they might live with a series of relatives.

That African Americans would assert legal claims to children who were either distantly related or no blood kin at all completely mystified federal officials in the South during Reconstruction. Most scoffed at freedpeople's ignorance, but it was they who were ignorant, incapable of comprehending kin ties that did not depend on legal marriage and did not revolve around a male-headed nuclear family.[7]

For African American women and their children, extended kin ties continued to be as important as they had been in slavery and during the war. The war left many black women widowed. Some never found spouses they had been separated from as slaves. Some did not want to locate them. Still others had no husbands to lose. Even those who had husbands could find themselves alone.

Making ends meet was difficult. Men often went in search of better paying work elsewhere, leaving their wives, children, and female relatives to fend for themselves. When Maria Hicks's husband went in search for work, she received no money for more than a year. Left to make do as best she could, Maria hired out her two daughters and "worked at anything I could get to do." She did not have much choice. Black women were confined to the lowest-paying work. In towns and cities, their only option was do-

A family of former slaves at Cumberland Landing, Virginia. (Courtesy of the Library of Congress)

mestic service. In rural areas, landowners often refused to rent them farmland and paid them about half what men received for agricultural labor.[8]

These women relied on kin and community as well as their own strength. Some of these networks, such as the schools, churches, charitable organizations, and mutual aid societies that flourished in cities and towns, were visible to outsiders. Others were not. They can be even more difficult to detect now. The census, for instance, gives the impression that Bella Newton and her daughter Rowen lived by themselves. But the ties that connected them to others were there, spreading out through the surrounding households and drawing them all together in a tight web that provided material and emotional support.[9]

After the war, white southerners ridiculed African Americans' efforts to establish and maintain their own households. By law, they could no longer compel blacks to live as dependents in their households, but that did not mean they accepted the idea that African Americans were capable of managing their own households. On the contrary, the idea that they could live independently disrupted white southerners' most basic notions of social order. In their minds, only propertied white men had the necessary qualities to head households of their own. African Americans, whose racial makeup made them naturally dependent, needed the guidance and discipline of whites. "White southerners," reported a *New York Tribune* correspondent, view "this eagerness among the darkeys to get married" a "good joke." "Whites laugh at the very idea of the thing," wrote a white southern minister. They "do not believe the negroes will respect those relations more than the brutes."[10]

As these comments suggest, white southerners were the ones with no respect for black families. Gertrude's indifference was typical. She was annoyed when Betsey, a young house slave, disappeared soon after the end of the war, but she was beside herself when she discovered that Betsey's mother had taken the girl home to live with her. "I felt interested in Betsey," wrote Gertrude. "She was a bright quick child and raised in our family would have become a good servant. As it is she will be under her mother's influence and run wild in the street." A little over a week later, Gertrude "succeeded in getting [a] little girl from the orphans' asylum" whose "mother and father are both dead." "I am glad," Gertrude concluded, that "she will have no outside influence exerted upon her."[11]

White southerners did not stop at indifference and derision. They broke up African Americans' households as well. As historians have pointed out, the Ku Klux Klan used terror to destroy the Republican party and to prevent black political organization. But the Klan and other vigilantes also routinely targeted black families and their homes, leaving them in ruins. As one black Georgian remembered, "Jus' as de Niggers was branchin' out and startin' to live lak free folks, dem nightriders com 'long beatin', cuttin' and slashin' 'em up."[12]

The way vigilantes carried out the violence is particularly revealing. During the 1865 Memphis race riot, for instance, whites raged through the black neighborhood and forced their way into individuals' homes. Once inside, they destroyed photos of male relatives in the Union army, clothes, china, and other personal possessions that represented the inhabitants' new status. Then they demanded services that symbolized the fragility of black families and the vulnerability of their members. The mob forced some women to cook for them. They raped others. Then, after white rioters had finished their destruction inside, they went outside and burned down the houses. These patterns were repeated across the South. The care that white vigilantes took in dismantling black households suggests both the depth of their contempt and the height of their fear.[13]

Violence was not the only means of destroying black households. The apprenticeship system in the Black Codes allowed white southerners to break them up legally as well. Under these laws, white southerners could rip African American children out of their homes and force them into unpaid labor until they reached adulthood. Former masters had first crack at custody, an option that many took. Between 1865 and 1867, while the Black Codes were in effect, southern courts apprenticed thousands of children, often without the consent of parents or other relatives.[14]

Those whites who received custody generally had their eyes on the labor of black children—some of whom were well beyond childhood. "In many instances," wrote a concerned Freedmen's Bureau officer, "boys of 12 and 14 years are taken from their parents, under the pretence that they (the parents) are incapable of supporting them, while the younger children are left to be maintained by the parents." "My office is visited every day by numbers of these poor creatures, asking for redress, which I have not the power to give," he continued. "They protest before the Court against binding their children to their former masters. . . . The law in all instances requires the child or the parents' consent, but it is not done. . . . justice has become a mockery."[15]

White planters disagreed. In their minds, black parents did not have the same rights to their children as white parents did to theirs. Jane Kamper's ex-master told her "that I was free but that my child Should be bound to" him. Then "he locked my Children up so that I could not find them." She did manage to steal them back and flee the area. Unwilling to let go, her former master followed her "to the Boat to get possession of my children," but she eluded him.[16]

Economic insecurity also threatened African Americans' efforts to establish independent households. For most freedpeople, the ideal solution was land. Former slaves linked land so closely with freedom that they often found it difficult to separate the two. For them, land was less a commodity than a means to an end. With land, African Americans could distance themselves from whites and gain control over their work and their lives. In this sense, freedom meant land.[17]

Many former slaves felt a sense of ownership because they had worked the land for so long. It was their sweat and blood that made it productive and valuable. That labor gave their claims precedence over those of their former owners, at least in their eyes. "This is our home," wrote a group of South Carolina slaves. "We have made these lands what they are." A Virginia freedman agreed, adding that the North had also gained from slave labor. The federal government therefore had an obligation to return the lands to those who had built up the nation. "We has a right to the land where we are located," he proclaimed. "For why? I tell you. Our wives, our children, our husbands, has been sold over and over again to purchase the lands we now locates upon; for that reason we have a divine right to the land. . . . And den didn't we clear the land, and raise de crops ob corn, ob cotton, ob tobacco, ob rice, ob sugar, ob everything. And den didn't dem large cities in de North grow up on de cotton and de sugars and de rice dat we made? . . . I say dey has grown rich, and my people is poor." As this freedman acknowledged, black women also worked the land and produced the wealth that others had enjoyed. They, too, were among those who asserted their claims to the land on this basis.[18]

Freedpeople who had lived on large plantations with stable populations felt strong connections to the plantations where they and their kin had lived and worked. These particular pieces of land were already so deeply enmeshed in their sense of family and community that they could not imagine freedom apart from it. Not only had the land maintained them for generations, but it connected them to their ancestors and future generations as well. They had cultivated, hunted, and fished it, and they had given their relatives back to the soil. "They cannot understand how it is," observed one South Carolina planter, "that they can have been born & raised on the soil & yet not inherit it upon becoming free."[19]

Freedpeople's expectations clashed with federal policy as well as the expectations of former slaveholders. After the war, plans to make land available to former slaves were scrapped. Instead, federal policy promoted a free labor system in which African Americans would become agricultural wage workers on land owned by white planters. For black workers, freedom would consist only of the right to contract their labor and receive compensation for it.

Racism tended to narrow this definition of freedom still further. Like so many northerners, many federal officials assumed that African Americans were unable to care for themselves and incapable of working unless compelled. If properly instructed, they might eventually internalize the values that made good workers. Until then, they needed to be kept in line—by force, if necessary. Many officials doubted that freedpeople would ever learn.[20]

In March 1865, Congress created the Bureau of Refugees, Freedmen, and Abandoned Lands to oversee the transition from slavery to freedom. Over the next year, bureau agents fanned out across the South, where they joined forces with the military officials who were already overseeing federal occupation. They stayed until 1868, when the former Confederate states reorganized under Reconstruction. The agents' specific goal was to get freedpeople to enter into year-long contracts as agricultural workers and to get white landowners to pay workers for their labor. Since cash and credit were scarce, the arrangement usually involved paying workers a share of the crops at harvest. The agents' larger mission was to win southerners over to their vision of freedom. They lectured African Americans on the joys of working for wages that barely covered the cost of food, clothing, and shelter. They lectured white southerners on the joys of paying their former slaves. Then they stood back, ready to admire the results.[21]

Instead, they were buried in a deluge of complaints. Neither freedpeople nor former slaveholders were particularly impressed with the bureau's didactic lectures: freedpeople saw no reason to sign away their freedom at year-long intervals, while former slaveholders saw no reason to pay for labor they used to command at will. Failure and frustration brought out the meaner side of many bureau agents. Unable to believe that African Americans were anything other than lazy and untruthful, many ignored workers' complaints of overwork, violence, and withheld wages. A few even beat and imprisoned black men and women to force them into contractual labor. Agents of this ilk clearly identified more closely with white employers than black workers. The hiring of white southerners to fill some bureau posts accentuated this bias in some areas. Still, there were many agents scattered across the South who were committed to defending freedpeople's interests. They could not do much to stop or to punish exploitative employers, but some did try to prevent the worst abuses.[22]

The deck was stacked in favor of white employers in other ways as well. Even when sympathetic bureau agents held employers to their labor con tracts, black workers came up short. The bureau's guidelines placed workers under the complete control of their employers while on the job. They had no say over what they did, how it was done, or when they did it. Nor could they break their contracts to find employment elsewhere without forfeiting their wages or risking prosecution. The bureau allowed limitations on their rights off the job as well. Agents permitted employers to enter workers' houses to search for stolen goods and approved clauses requiring them to maintain deference toward their employers and forbidding meetings, gatherings, or outside visitors. To close off economic alternatives that would allow freedpeople to avoid contract labor, federal officials in some areas worked closely with white landowners to abolish local trading networks as well as traditional rights to graze livestock on uncultivated land and to hunt, fish, or dig oysters.[23]

The Black Codes tilted the balance in favor of white landowners even more. Some states required African Americans to enter into year-long labor contracts and prohibited them from leaving before the end of the contract's term. In others, stiff vagrancy laws achieved similar results by criminalizing "idleness" and directing African Americans to show on demand proof of employment. Laws that encumbered their ability to buy and sell property foreclosed African Americans' hopes of acquiring land and working for themselves. Some states forbid African Americans from owning agricultural land at all.[24]

Congressional Republicans tempered the most blatant forms of inequality when they took control of the Reconstruction process in 1867. Most important, the Reconstruction Acts and the Fourteenth Amendment established African Americans' civil and political equality. The imbalance of power between freedpeople and their employers remained, however. Abstract equality in law did not mean equality in social and economic relations. Congress dashed African Americans' hopes for economic autonomy when it refused to include the redistribution of land in its Reconstruction plan. That decision left African Americans with no alternative but to work for their former masters. As propertyless laborers, they had little bargaining power. To be sure, they could challenge employers' violations of their contracts, but employers could write all sorts of unreasonable demands in those contracts and then hold their workers to them. If workers defied the terms, they were the ones at fault.[25]

African Americans, however, stubbornly clung to the belief that land and the freedom it represented would be theirs. Rumors about land redistribution circulated throughout the late 1860s. "I have been about the District," wrote one exasperated federal official in South Carolina, "and done all that is in my power to do away with the expectation, but I no sooner get back than there is another story started." African Americans peppered Congress, the president, and other federal officials with petitions asserting their rights to the land. Sometimes, they just took it, despite efforts to convince them that they were trespassing and stealing. As one Freedmen's Bureau agent explained, freedpeople had the "idea that they have a certain right to the property of their former masters, that they have earned it, and that if they can lay their hands on it, it is so much that belongs to them."[26]

Where they already had possession of land, they refused to give it back. Some African Americans had been living and working on plantations white owners had fled during the war. Others had moved onto land opened up by Union army officers for settlement. When former masters and federal officials arrived to reclaim these lands, they met resistance. Women, who felt as much claim and connection to the land as their menfolk did, were particularly vocal and visible. "I was beset by the women on this place in a very serious manner," a federal official reported after he tried to evict the African Americans living on a plantation in the Sea Islands. "After I had made known my errand and told them who I was, and what I came for, and being also in uniform, they absolutely refused to give me any information. . . . They said they would not make any arrangement whatever, for me or anybody else; that they cared for no United States officer: the Govt brought them to the island & 'they would burn down the house before they would move away' or 'farm it themselves until put out.'" Shovels and sharp tongues were no match against the array of weapons at the federal government's disposal, however. The land went back to its former owners.[27]

Forcing freedpeople off the land was one thing. Forcing them to abandon the freedom that land represented was quite another. As propertyless laborers, African Americans hung onto the essential elements of their vision of freedom. Moreover, they continued to act on these goals long after the Freedmen's Bureau packed its bags and left the South in 1868.

Black workers tried to push up their wages, while pushing down their hours and the amount of labor. In the decades following emancipation, agricultural workers, domestic servants, and common laborers in cities across the South struck for back wages, higher wages, and better working conditions. They also took their employers to the Freedmen's Bureau and local courts.[28]

They made use of evasion as well as confrontation. Gertrude's husband, Jeff, was surprised when two laborers refused "to put up some fencing which wanted repairing." They told him to "hire the labour and take it out of their portion of the crop." But Jeff "would not pay out money for their provision and hire men to do their work for he knew that when he settled with them they would be dissatisfied." So they left.[29]

These laborers' demands were common. Agricultural workers, women and men, would not do postharvest repair work, such as mending fences, repairing outbuildings, chopping wood, or ditching rice fields. As they saw it, they had been hired to cultivate crops. Labor to maintain the plantation was extra. They also tried to maintain traditional "rights" they had as slaves, such as access to provision grounds, the continuation of the task system in those areas where it had existed in slavery, and Sundays off.[30]

Women refused to do domestic labor in addition to their field work, as they had been required to do in slavery. Those who were hired as domestic servants would not "live in," where they would be on call and under supervision twenty-four hours a day. Many black women preferred laundry work because they could work at home at a defined task, away from the creeping demands and critical eyes of white women. Other women hired themselves out by the day to do specific agricultural or domestic chores, instead of being at the beck and call of one planter or one family for extended periods of time.[31]

This was clearly what a woman who was hired to wash clothes for Gertrude had in mind. Gertrude had hired the woman, whose name she did not record, for thirty cents. In her mind that meant that she had control of the woman's labor for the entire day, but the washerwoman saw it differ-

A depiction of women returning from the sugar cane fields, published in *Century*, November 1887. (Photo courtesy of the Newberry Library)

ently. That morning, Gertrude gave the woman a load of clothes to wash. "She was through by dinner time," Gertrude wrote, and "appeared to work steady. I gave her dinner and afterwards told her that I had a few more clothes I wished washed out." But the woman refused, saying "that she was tired." She had completed the assigned task, perhaps working harder than she otherwise would have to finish in a timely manner. Now she was ready to go. For thirty cents, she was unwilling to do more. Gertrude was furious. "If you suppose I engaged a woman to wash for me by the day and she stops by dinner time," Gertrude informed the woman through clenched teeth, "if you suppose I intend paying for the days work you are very much mistaken." Afterward, the woman stayed "and washed out a few other things." Gertrude told the story as if she were the victor, but that was not quite true. The washerwoman did not stay for the entire day.[32]

African Americans also limited the authority of white employers by refusing paid work altogether. Former slaveholders as well as Freedmen's Bureau agents wanted all African Americans—men, women, and children—to be working in the fields and houses of whites. African American families, however, had other plans. They set up collaborative household economies that mixed paid employment with other forms of productive labor. By keeping as many family members out of the paid labor force as possible, they distanced themselves from white employers and enhanced their ability to live on their own terms. When women and children stayed at home, they were also safe from sexual violence and other forms of physical abuse they often suffered on the job.[33]

Federal officials and white landowners completely misrepresented black women's withdrawal from paid work in the first few years following the Civil War. Bureau agents across the South complained constantly of black women "playing the lady." According to one influential agent, the "evil of female loaferism" now plagued the South. "Myriads of women who once earned their own living now have aspirations to be like white ladies," he wrote. "Instead of using the hoe, [they] pass the days in dawdling over their trivial housework, or gossiping among their neighbors." Southern planters were just as scornful. "Pete," sniffed one Virginia planter, "chooses to feed his wife out of his wages rather than to get her fed for her services."[34]

Taking these complaints at face value, some historians have concluded that black women quit work altogether. Black women did not, however, leave the employ of whites to enjoy a life of leisure. Their husbands' wages hardly made this a viable option. They just refused to work on the terms that white employers and federal officials preferred. Even the agent who coined the term "female loaferism" made it clear that it "did not mean that all

women were thus idle." "The larger proportion," he noted, "are still laboring afield, as of old; rigid necessity held them up to it." Instead of quitting
altogether, black women tried to place limits on the time spent doing wage
work. In the rice fields of South Carolina and Georgia, women negotiated
a two-day work week with planters. Others, like the woman who washed
clothes for Gertrude, continued to take on paid domestic and agricultural
work as needed. In the tobacco district, they hired out at certain times in
the growing cycle: to transplant delicate tobacco seedlings into the fields,
to pick worms off the plants, and to harvest. Elsewhere, they went into the
fields each fall to pick cotton.[35]

The notion that black women quit working when they were not working for wages also reflects northern observers' and current historians' devaluation of domestic labor. Far from "trivial," the labor African American
women did at home was as important to their families' well-being as waged
labor. They tended provision plots, raised poultry, made their families'
clothes, traded the surplus for items they were unable to make at home, and
took care of young children. Without women's labor, black families never
would have survived. Their domestic production was absolutely essential,
particularly since it took a long time to get paid. Most employers deferred
payment of agricultural laborers' and sharecroppers' wages, either in full or
in part, until the end of the growing season.[36]

Despite the difficulties, African Americans were remarkably successful
in one sense. White landowners, unable either to hire enough workers or
to control those they had, began renting land to African Americans for a
share of the crop. Not only did sharecropping allow black families to live
and work together, but it promised to free them from the direct control of
white employers, to satisfy their craving for land, and to facilitate upward
mobility as well. The arrangement made deep inroads by the 1870s, particularly in cotton- and tobacco-growing areas. These two crops, which could
be cultivated on small, individual plots of land, were well-suited to sharecropping. Rice and sugar, by contrast, continued to be grown on large plantations with hired hands.[37]

This toehold on economic autonomy soon gave way, however. During
the antebellum period, no southern state except North Carolina recognized
a difference between sharecroppers and renters. They were all tenants, who
were paid a specified amount to work the land for a given time and who
maintained control over their labor, their lives, and what they produced. As
soon as African Americans started becoming sharecroppers after the war, the
status of this position deteriorated. Southern law turned sharecroppers into
common laborers. The law gave employers complete control over the pro-

duction process and the crop. By law, workers could even be arrested for theft if they tried to sell any of the cotton or tobacco they had grown. To foreclose the possibility of economic independence, other laws prevented grazing, hunting, fishing, and trespassing on private lands.[38]

Without resources of their own, sharecroppers had to borrow to put in the crop and to make it through to harvest. They paid inflated interest rates and inflated prices, often at stores owned by the same men who rented them land. Powerlessness and poverty, combined with a cotton market that hit rock bottom soon after emancipation, threw many sharecroppers into a cycle of debt and despair from which they never escaped. By the last decades of the century, sharecropping had become synonymous with southern poverty.[39]

Worse, neither law nor cultural practice clearly limited the amount of power employers could assume over their sharecroppers' or laborers' private lives. An 1874 decision by the North Carolina State Supreme Court went so far as to equate all common laborers with domestic dependents. "There is a certain analogy among all the domestic relations," the presiding justice wrote "and it would be dangerous to the repose and happiness of families if the law permitted any man under whatever professions of philanthropy or charity, to sow discontent between the head of a family and its various members, wife, children and servants. Interference with such relations can only be justified under the most special circumstances." Of course, this decision did not mean that all employers tried to treat common laborers as if they were domestic dependents, but it did mean that sharecroppers and agricultural workers had no legal recourse if it happened.[40]

Some African Americans defied the odds. They successfully negotiated all the economic obstacles to emerge as merchants, professionals, skilled artisans, and farm owners. Given both the number and size of these obstacles, their successes are truly extraordinary. By the early twentieth century, 25 percent of all black families owned their own farms or homes, and that figure did not include those who owned businesses or other forms of property.[41]

These successful black families came to be known as the "better class." It was not wealth that gave them middle-class status. Economically, they were middle class only in comparison with other blacks. They usually fell below the white middle class by any monetary measure. The black middle class did, however, embrace education and middle-class cultural values. These families advocated temperance, respectability, religion, thrift, and hard work. They made great sacrifices to attend the newly opened black colleges that now dotted the South. Then they used their degrees to bring education to other African American children.[42]

Women worked hard for their families' economic independence and social status. Even many middle-class black women still had to work for wages, but black women took more pride in their work in freedom than they had in slavery. In Works Progress Administration interviews during the New Deal, black women bragged about their capacity for hard labor and their ability to keep up with the men in the fields. Mattie Curtis, for instance, insisted on talking about how she had carved out a farm from the forest, despite the interviewer's attempts to guide her away from the subject. Although married, Curtis performed the bulk of the work herself: "I cut down de big trees dat wus all over dese fields an' I mauled out de wood an' sold hit, den I plowed up de fields an' planted dem." "I done a heap of work at night too," she continued "all of my sewin' an' such an' de piece of lan' near de house over dar ain't never got no work 'cept at night." One of her proudest moments came when she sold her first bale of cotton, but most memorable of all was the day she "finally paid fer de land."[43]

African American women bragged about their ability to work like men, but that did not mean they considered themselves the same as or even equal to men. The fluidity in men's and women's gender roles coexisted with the assumption that men and women had different obligations to their families. Black women still assumed primary responsibility for reproductive labor, including childrearing, cooking, and housework, just as they had in slavery. Like Mattie Curtis, they took on "men's work," while still doing all their domestic chores. Many women had no choice because they headed their own families, but the pattern remained the same even when women were married or lived with a male household head.

The reverse was not true for African American men. They rarely expanded their role to help with "women's work" precisely because it was "women's work." Nor did black women expect them to do so. As they saw it, black men should work regularly, in some sort of paid employment or in their families' fields, to provide for their families. Catherine Massey, the wife of a Union soldier, held her husband to these standards. Asking his commander to send some of his pay to her, she explained, "I am his lawful wife and he has neglected to treat me as a husband should." Specifically, she had "not received a cent of money from him Since last March."[44]

Like other African American women, Massey did not expect that black men would be able to support their families by themselves, but she did expect her husband "to help me to support myself as I helped . . . support him." She needed his assistance now because of ill health and hard times. Another African American washerwoman remembered her dead husband with great fondness and the highest praise: "He was a good husband and father and provided for his family as best he could."[45]

Black women also worked hard to exercise and maintain the civil and political rights that had been granted to them and their menfolk. Until recently, scholars of the period assumed black women were politically insignificant because they were excluded from traditional political arenas—ballot boxes, campaign podiums, legislative floors, and even party rhetoric. New work has begun to revise this view. As some scholars have argued, many African Americans initially saw the vote as the possession of the entire community, not just individual men.

The actions of black women certainly support this conclusion. They were active and vocal participants at political meetings during Reconstruction. "The Negro women, if possible, were wilder than the men," reported a newspaper after an election riot in Macon, Georgia. "They were seen everywhere, talking in an excited manner, and urging the men on. Some of them were almost furious, showing it to be part of their religion to keep their husbands and brothers straight in politics."[46]

Educated black women, newly graduated from college, also promoted equal rights and social reform. For African American women, equal rights meant equality with white women. Ida B. Wells, a prominent reformer who

A depiction of African American men and women attending a political meeting, published in *Harper's Weekly,* July 25, 1868. (Photo courtesy of the Newberry Library)

would later be hounded out of the South for her opposition to lynching, brought several civil suits against southern railroads for refusing her access to the "woman's" car—as first-class cars were then known. To buttress such claims, women like Wells emphasized their similarities to elite white women. They, too, were well-dressed, well-mannered, modest, and educated. They, too, acted out of domestic concerns for their homes and children. They, too, advocated temperance, education, and reform in the Woman's Christian Temperance Union, church missionary groups, and other organizations. Why, then, were they treated differently from other women?[47]

Similarly, social reform meant racial justice. Instead of separating their interests from black men, educated black women tended to work with their menfolk politically. They had a direct stake in improving their families' and communities' access to economic resources, civil rights, and political power. They also had vested interests in preserving the rights of their menfolk. When conservative white southerners began reclaiming political control, these same women worked tirelessly to fend off disfranchisement. When their menfolk were pushed from the political arena after disfranchisement and when public action became dangerous for them, black women took up the political slack, initiating social reforms that would benefit the black community and working against segregation and other forms of racial inequality.[48]

Educated black women promoted not only racial equality but also education, material aid, and social uplift for other women of their race. They cooperated with reform-minded white women to advance their own efforts, even though these relationships were fraught with tensions and subjected black women to innumerable indignities. They also pressed for women's civil rights and even the vote, long before white southern women would come near these issues.[49]

Poor African American women also joined their menfolk in the fight for civil rights and political power. Their tactics were less subtle than their better-educated, more sophisticated counterparts': usually, they just stepped up and claimed what they thought should be theirs. After the Civil War, white observers constantly criticized African American women for being "uppity." They even found offense in the way black women dressed and carried themselves. "The chief ambition of a wench," scoffed one white southern woman in North Carolina, is "to wear a veil and carry a parasol." Gertrude also turned up her nose. "Yesterday," she sniffed in May 1865, "numbers of negro women some of them quite black were promenading up the streets with black lace veil shading them from the embrowning rays of a sun under whose influence they had worked all their life." Seeing three black women wearing brightly colored dresses and carrying parasols, another Georgia woman recoiled at their "swaggering air" and "unmistakably African appearance." The scene, she concluded, would "inspire the most casual observer with a feeling of contempt and rebellion."[50]

What white observers saw were assertive women. What they did not appreciate were African American women's efforts to exercise some of the most basic rights enjoyed by white people. Dressing as they wished, walking where they wanted, talking about what they wanted—all these things were essential to the kind of freedom that black women envisioned. All of these things were rights that white southerners had long enjoyed. None of these things would come easily to African American women, though. These freedoms were theirs only in theory. In practice, they continually had to assert their claims to them.[51]

Consider the case of Maria Mitchell. As Mitchell's son later testified, his "Mama was talking loud." Her target was B. D. Armstrong, a white man, probably her employer. When Armstrong asked her what all the "fuss" was about, Mitchell responded that "she was talking for her rights and would as much as she pleased and as loud as she pleased." Irritated, Armstrong threatened that "if she did not hush he would make her hush." Then he "struck her in the face five licks and broke out a piece of her tooth."[52]

Maria Mitchell's case had everything to do with the new rights of African Americans. She acted on her rights by talking "as much as she pleased and as loud as she pleased," even when it offended a prominent white man. With these words, Mitchell announced that she could express her own ideas, whenever, wherever, and to whomever she wanted. She was now her own person, not a legal extension of some white master's estate, and had the right to conduct herself and her life as she saw fit. B. D. Armstrong's reaction suggests why Mitchell's stand was so important. Ordering her to "hush" because her words irritated him, he rejected Mitchell's right to self-expression. Then Armstrong went one step further, denying her right to control her own body. With five blows to her mouth, he tried to obliterate the new boundaries Mitchell had drawn and to force her back into submission.[53]

Mitchell was not so easily silenced. African American men and women did not just assert their freedom in daily interactions. They also went to public forums, particularly the Freedmen's Bureau and local courts, where they hoped to gain a public, formal acknowledgment of their rights as free people. As many historians have noted, African Americans across the South were quick to claim access to institutions of governance. They filed legal complaints, fired off letters and petitions to congressmen and governors, and turned out en masse to hear candidates and debate issues. The ability to do so was extremely important to people who had formerly been subject to the personal whims of a single master. "We have no masters now," freed slaves in South Carolina were reported to have said. "We is come to the law now."[54]

Maria Mitchell did just that. She kept "talking for her rights," filed charges of assault against Armstrong, and succeeded in obtaining an indictment against him. In slavery, she would have been subject to a master's discipline for talking back. Now she was not. In slavery, she could not have charged her master or anyone else with assault. Now she could. And she did.

It was not an undertaking that African Americans took lightly. In some states in the Deep South, conservative whites retained control of the courts and blocked African Americans' access by ignoring or dismissing their complaints. Even when black litigants did get in the courthouse door, they were not guaranteed a fair trial. Depending on the local political climate, the process could be openly hostile or completely indifferent to their interests.

The routine arrest and conviction of African Americans actually became a cheap form of labor for southern states in the last decades of the nineteenth century. States leased out African American male prisoners to work on the railroads and in the mines. Many had been charged with minor offenses, such as petty theft, loitering, or vagrancy. Of those convicted, only a fraction received a fair, impartial trial. When public uproar brought an end to the convict-lease system at the turn of the twentieth century, black prisoners still labored on state roads or other public projects in chain gangs. Black women were also susceptible to arrest and conviction on flimsy grounds. Although they were not as visible to the public as male prisoners were, they endured brutal conditions and hard labor in the South's prisons.[55]

In areas with large black populations and a strong Republican party, however, African Americans could expect access to the courts. Even when they lost their cases, the process was still important. African Americans' civil rights would remain theoretical unless they were put into practice. Often, the only way to get recalcitrant white southerners to acknowledge those rights was to haul them into court.[56]

Black women faced legal hurdles that black men did not. Antebellum law had not recognized sexual violence against slave women as a crime, because it excluded enslaved women from the legal category "woman." In some states, even free black women were excluded. These laws matched the beliefs and practices of white southerners, as we have already seen in the life of Harriet Jacobs.

If anything, emancipation intensified violence against African American women, as white men like Alexander Noblin or the rioters in Memphis resorted to ritualized forms of sexual abuse to keep black women in their place. The legal bias against African American women also persisted, even

after the Reconstruction Acts and the Fourteenth Amendment had supposedly erased racial distinctions in the letter of the law. That was so because
class distinctions, which could be as easily turned against poor African
American women as they could against poor white women, remained. These
distinctions provided easy cover for legal officials unable or unwilling to
transcend their racial biases. Even white Republican officials who strongly
supported the goals of full civil and political equality for African Americans
balked when it came to black women. Many of these officials—southern
and northern—had come from privilege. It was difficult for them to put poor
white women in the same category as wealthy white women. They could
not even imagine putting poor black women there.[57]

If black women wanted to enjoy the respect and protection that were,
in theory, the rights of all women, they had to claim those rights themselves.
This is exactly what Bella Newton did when she decided to challenge Alexander Noblin's sexual assault of her daughter. First she went down to the
local store owned by Joseph Noblin, apparently a relative of Alexander
Noblin, and complained about the treatment of her daughter. Noblin and
several other white men organized a meeting to iron out the conflict. The
deal struck was that Alexander would pay Bella a dollar and ten pounds of
bacon in exchange for her silence. At first, Bella agreed. Then she changed
her mind. For whatever reason, settling the matter privately and keeping
silent was not enough. She needed to go to court. She needed to make a
public statement about her rights, her daughter's rights, and the limits of
Alexander Noblin's rights. Other African American women felt the same way.
They filed many complaints of sexual violence with the Freedmen's Bureau
while it was in operation. In those areas where local governments had opened
up to African Americans as a result of Republican rule, they also filed in the
local courts.[58]

Even as African American women tried to include themselves in the
existing system, they continually challenged the categories that defined their
rights as women. Southern law and the social conventions of elite whites
ranked the seriousness of assaults according to a woman's relationship with
her attacker. Only when an unrelated man attacked a woman was it considered an assault. By contrast, husbands and fathers could "discipline" their
wives and children. Most southern states did not consider wife-beating a
criminal offense until after the Civil War. Even then, it was treated as a crime
only under certain circumstances.[59]

African American women did not make the same distinctions. To them,
freedom meant freedom from abuse, regardless of who threw the punches.
Heedless of the law or the social conventions of elite whites, they publicly

charged male kin as well as outsiders with assault. These domestic disputes usually grew out of conflicts over wives' and husbands' respective roles. Whereas men claimed their wives neglected their household chores, children, and contributions to the family income, women charged their husbands with abandoning their economic duties and using excessive force to impose their will on other household members. Women who challenged their husbands did not necessarily question men's authority as heads of the household. What they questioned was how the power was exercised and what its limits were. When they felt that power had been abused, they sought the intervention of neighbors and kin. If informal mediation failed, some filed charges.[60]

In so doing, black women assumed a direct public presence as citizens in their own right. They questioned the notion that men could exercise broad disciplinary rights over them without being subject to public scrutiny and that they, as women, were without public recourse. Such claims provided a counterpoint to the political rhetoric of the Republican party, which emphasized citizenship and the vote as male prerogatives. They also stood in stark contrast to the position of Democratic white supremacists, who eliminated black women entirely from the category of womanhood and made complete domestic subordination the price of protection for white women.[61]

Once Democrats seized control of state and local governments and began dividing southern society into white and black, many of the public spaces in which black women had worked closed down. Some of the political implications are well known. Beginning in the 1870s and ending in Georgia in 1908, every southern state disfranchised black male voters through literacy tests, grandfather clauses, and poll taxes. Such laws violated the spirit of the Fourteenth and Fifteenth amendments, which forbid such discrimination on the basis of race or previous servitude. But, by the time Mississippi began the disfranchising process in 1871, northern Republicans had begun to lose interest in the South, and the federal courts were beginning to interpret the Reconstruction amendments narrowly. Ultimately, the courts upheld the laws because they did not make explicit racial references.[62]

Emboldened, Democrats began adding Jim Crow laws that rigidly segregated the region's public places. Race did appear in the letter of these laws. Here again, however, the federal government refused to intervene. In its landmark 1896 decision in *Plessy v. Ferguson,* the U.S. Supreme Court held that segregation was not inherently discriminatory. Separation of the races did not necessarily imply inequality, the court maintained. Thereafter, "separate but equal" became the legal fiction that governed social relations in the South.[63]

Democrats also encouraged white southerners to take the law into their own hands. Vigilante mobs were made up of whites from all walks of life. Even when the wealthy maintained a dignified distance from the actual violence, their silence and inaction still bloodied their hands. In the last decades of the century, white southerners increasingly justified lynching as retaliation for the rape and sexual assault of white women, but the terror extended to African Americans accused of other offenses as well. As the famous antilynching advocate Ida B. Wells argued in a series of pamphlets and speeches in the 1890s, rape charges were usually trumped up. They actually covered other transgressions in racial etiquette, such as the failure to show proper deference, the assertion of political rights, or simple economic success. Any African American who offended any white was susceptible to mob violence.[64]

The disfranchisement of black men, the expulsion of African Americans from the institutions of governance, the official sanction of lynching and other forms of extralegal violence, the advent of legal segregation, and other legislation designed to limit African Americans' civil rights and their economic opportunities all restricted the public arena in ways that affected black women as much as black men.

Democratic rule also reached into African Americans' homes. Throughout the late nineteenth century, the courts and other state institutions increased their power to oversee and regulate domestic relations. Government officials, who were usually white Democrats, now had the power to pass judgment on a wide range of family issues—divorce, child custody, adoption, domestic violence, and child abuse. But they did not chose to protect everyone. "The station in life, the temperament, state of health, habits and feelings of different persons are so unlike," claimed the North Carolina Supreme Court in an 1877 divorce case, "that treatment which would send the broken heart of one to the grave, would make no sensible impression upon another." Needless to say, Democratic officials rarely included black women among those so sensitive as to die of a broken heart.[65]

The same principles that deprived African Americans of legal protection and access to state aid also subjected them to indiscriminate governmental interference. After all, it was the prerogative of governmental officials to decide under what circumstances to intervene in citizens' private lives. "Delinquent" children were institutionalized. "Unfit" parents were deprived of their children. "Idle" adults were arrested and sentenced to hard labor for the state. "Mentally defective" men and women were forcibly sterilized. Medical "experimentation" was conducted without obtaining permission or even informing those involved. The cumulative effects not only violated individuals' civil rights but also threatened the integrity of black families. In some respects, these new policies were even more insidious than the Black Codes of the earlier generation because they were cast in the positive language of progressive reform instead of overtly racist, punitive strictures.[66]

Despite all this, black women continued the fight to achieve racial justice for all African Americans and to address the specific problems that they experienced as women who were also black and often poor. Many of women's political actions described in this chapter took place *after* the official end of Reconstruction. Even when they were unsuccessful, the very act of trying was important. By continually working to realize their rights in practice, they kept the promise of equality from dwindling into empty rhetoric or being forgotten altogether. In the process, they established a legacy of struggle that would support and inspire future movements for social justice.[67]

8   We Is Poor but We's Proud

THE Civil War had disastrous results for Sarah Guttery of Walker County, Alabama. As we learned in the first section, she had chosen to raise her two children on her own rather than marry their fathers or apprentice them to a landowning family. Although she remained on her father's farm, he had allowed her to do so with the understanding that she would work to earn her keep. She had held up her end of the bargain, doing hard labor in the fields while her children were small and unable to contribute economically. Right before the war started, her son reached the age where he could replace her in the fields. Her daughter also began to share the family's economic burdens. Had all gone well, they might have been able to rent their own land and set up their own household. For the first time in her life, Sarah Guttery looked forward to a life less difficult and more secure.

Then the Confederate government conscripted her son. When he was killed in action, Sarah Guttery's future changed. Sarah and her daughter did what they could to get by: field work, domestic labor, and sewing. But they never got out of poverty. By 1879, she had slid into complete destitution. When Guttery applied to the federal government for her son's pension benefits in that year, her broken body kept her from working, her daughter could no longer support her, and she relied on the charity of neighbors.[1]

Common white women are the most invisible of all southern women in the history of the post–Civil War South. Few books on the period make reference to them, and historians have only begun to chronicle their lives. To be sure, documentation on common white women is hard to find. Unlike elite white women, they did not leave diaries and letter collections. Unlike

African American women, they were not the subject of continual commentary by former slaveholders, northern observers, and federal employees.

The scarcity of sources does not completely explain their absence in the historical literature of this period, however. Political historians have focused on institutional party politics, a subject that tends to marginalize women. Social historians have focused on postwar economic change and emancipation. They have also assumed that women were unimportant to the story, because it was men who owned property and worked for wages. Studies of emancipation have recently expanded to include women, but they tend to center on the experiences of former slaves and former slaveholders. As a result, common white women have slipped through the historical cracks.

Just because historical frameworks have rendered them invisible does not mean these women were not there. On the contrary, they were everywhere. Nor did they just sit on their porches, watching and waiting. They were actively involved. The war had reached into their households and destroyed them. The process of rebuilding necessarily involved women as well as men. For many, it was a struggle that lasted a lifetime. In this sense, common white women's lives were not unlike those of African American women. But if both groups endured hardship and heartache, they did so under very different circumstances and in service to very different ends. Common white women hoped to rebuild the lives they had before the war. Beyond that, they hoped to make the New South more responsive to their interests—as women who were also members of yeoman and poor white families.

Their success was mixed. But, whether they survived these changes successfully or not, common white women played a crucial role in shaping their outcome. In their attempts to make sure their own interests and those of their families would be represented in the region's governing structures, they participated in the era's most wrenching political conflicts. In their efforts to put food on the table and to save their families' land, they helped move the South away from its traditional, agrarian economy. In the process, they ended up reshaping their own lives as well.

∾

Not all white women had as much to lose as Gertrude Thomas and Kate Stone. What they lost was just as dear, though. Many white households never recovered from the staggering loss of human life and the destruction of fields, stock, and implements. Sydney Andrews, a northern journalist who traveled through North Carolina, South Carolina, and Georgia after the war, described the devastation. "There is a scarcity of food everywhere," he wrote. "In many whole counties the merest necessaries of life are all any family have or can afford, while among the poorer classes there is great lack of even these."[2]

Although Andrews was referring specifically to Georgia, the same applied to other states as well. Conditions were worst in areas that had seen heavy fighting and Union occupation. There, the countryside had been completely drained by federal forces to supply their armies and subdue civilian resistance. Some areas, including parts of Tennessee, Arkansas, North Carolina, and Virginia, had descended into a state of civil disorder. Bandits roamed the countryside, preying on people and what little property remained.[3]

Without male laborers, women had to work that much harder. Many, like Sarah Guttery, could not compensate for what they had lost. Widows wandered the streets of every southern city and town, begging for work. There was little to be found. "There's hardly a day," wrote one North Carolinian, "when some poor females who used to earn their living by sewing for the rich comes round looking for work & can't get it because those for whom they used to work now have to do all their own work."[4]

It was not just widowed women or those from landless families who were looking for wage work. In 1865, few farmers had the resources to plant their crops. Those who managed did not have enough to feed themselves until harvest. John Richard Dennett, another northern journalist, listed specific examples from Virginia to convey the extent of the destruction. One farmer, who had a wife and nine children and owned six acres of land, had to borrow a horse and plow to cultivate his land. He had "no farming implements of his own." Another man "owns a hundred acres, and cultivates forty five." He, too, had to borrow a horse. "All the implements on his place [were] destroyed by General Butler's army; and he has nothing left but his farm." Edward Lee returned to his Tennessee farm to find "everything gone but the dirt." Bad weather, bad prices, and bad crop yields in years following the war magnified the problem, leaving many white southerners deeply in debt and on the verge of destitution.[5]

To many common whites, it made no sense that any society would sanction such a widespread loss of productive property. Creditors, they insisted, plunged households into permanent poverty. It was morally reprehensible to benefit themselves at the expense of others in this way. "I think it a hard case," wrote one man, "to take all a man has who is needy & give it to speculaters who has money plenty."[6]

More was at stake than temporary economic hardship. Land and productive property were what enabled common white men to fulfill their responsibilities as household heads—to protect and provide for their families. As households ceased to function economically, so did the social ties that held men, women, and children together. "[T]he worst feature" of the post-war years, claimed one newspaper, was not that many "found themselves reduced to poverty" but that men "thus reduced were surrounded by large and helpless families": "As he looked around upon his humble home . . . and thought of his relentless creditors . . . his brave heart, that had death un-daunted upon a hundred battlefields, sunk down in despair, as he saw in contemplation his shivering wife and helpless little ones turned out from the old homestead by the fiat of the law, and the clang of the sheriff's mal-liet, under the cry of *'Going—going—gone!'* Yes, gone!"[7]

Economic independence had secured common white men's social posi-tion and political power. The fear of dependency was what drew so many white southerners into the Confederacy in the first place. It was also what shaped many white southerners' opposition to it. Now, with the Confeder-acy's defeat, this nightmare was coming true.

As we have already seen, common white women had a vested interest in their menfolk's economic standing. They derived their own status—or lack thereof—through that of their male household heads. Those who lived in landowning families felt a strong sense of identification with the land and other property. Since they worked just as hard as their menfolk to secure their households' independence, they felt just as much stake in it.

An editorial written by one rural North Carolina woman reveals how strong their identification was. She, too, depicted an auction, but her ren-dering made the connection between land and men's roles as household heads much clearer, for it was the men themselves who were being auctioned. "'Here is a son for sale!'" she wrote. "'He was a mother's fondest, strongest only hope. He is a rare piece of property. What do we hear for him?' for so runs on the auctioneer; 'And here is a husband and father. He has an ami-able wife and lovely children as ever bounded the fireside circle. What do you hear for him?' Tears have been shed for him, but they'll not buy him back. Prayers have been offered, but prayers are not currency. Love has been pledged for his redemption, but he must be sold. Never mind his wife's fears and tears, they are not quoted in our price current. He is 'going, going.'" Denied the means to support their families and reduced to the position of slaves, these men were literally "gone." Beaten down by economic policies that supported the pursuit of profit over the integrity of the "fireside cir-cle," they were finally sold like slaves to the highest bidder. Their departure, of course, left women unnaturally and unforgivably exposed.[8]

Initially, no one did much to help. The Freedmen's Bureau did provide food and clothing to the indigent in the first few years following the war. But the notion that the federal government had a responsibility to jumpstart the lagging economy with massive infusions of direct aid awaited the next century, when the crisis of the Great Depression pushed the nation's governing structures in new directions. Nor was such action considered appropriate for state governments. In the constitutional conventions and legislatures convened in the South during 1865 and 1866, inaction was not just the result of oversight or lack of imagination, though. The conservative lawmakers who dominated these bodies took little notice of common whites' problems. Dominated by the former slaveholding elite, they focused on the control of freedpeople, with an eye on reestablishing their own plantations.[9]

Many of these conservative lawmakers viewed common whites, particularly those without property, with deep suspicion. Jonathan Worth, the principled but politically tone-deaf governor of North Carolina during Reconstruction under President Andrew Johnson's plan, stated the issue with characteristic bluntness. The "tendency" of democratic government, he wrote, "is to ignore virtue and property and intelligence—and to put the powers of government into the hands of mere *numbers*." He went on to explain that this was bad because the "majority in all times and in all countries" was "improvident and without property." Without the guidance of the better class, they would soon degenerate into "a great mob, ruled only by the will of the hour." He even used racial imagery to describe poor white men, referring to "the black and white negro" and "negroes and albinoes." Like so many white southern conservatives, Worth feared that whites and blacks would join together in this "great mob" and completely overwhelm them.[10]

Not surprisingly, elite conservatives cringed at the very thought of opening up state governments any more than they had to. At their constitutional conventions in 1865 and 1866, they opposed such measures as the direct election of judges and the abolition of property requirements for office. Many intended vagrancy laws and other labor restrictions to apply to poor whites as well as African Americans. They even reopened the question of universal white manhood suffrage. As one South Carolina conservative confided to Sydney Andrews, "It was a great mistake when we passed our free-suffrage law."[11]

Many of these political restrictions were aimed at propertyless people, not landed farmers. But debt now threatened to turn many yeomen into landless laborers. Elite conservatives opposed debt relief because, they argued, it took from the (deserving) rich and gave to the (undeserving) poor. Far from helping, debt relief would only encourage profligacy and immorality. Even those wealthy whites who favored debt relief often did so out of a desire to preserve existing social hierarchies. "If the sinking had been general," wrote one North Carolinian, "all would have still maintained their relative positions, but as it is the debtor sinks lower than those he once held in bondage." Like other white men of his class, this man was concerned with economic leveling that would reduce his own status.[12]

Sydney Andrews was appalled at the openness of elite white southerners' class bias. "It has been the purpose of the ruling class," he wrote in 1865, "to build new barriers between themselves and the common people rather than tear away any of those already existing." The barriers that already existed were considerable. "Any plan of reconstruction," he concluded, needed to ensure "the elevation of the common people. . . . Till civilization has been carried down into the homes and hearts of all classes, we shall have neither regard for humanity nor respect for the rights of the citizen."[13]

Andrews underestimated common white southerners. They were neither oblivious to nor accepting of the "barriers" that the "ruling class" had erected. The surveys of Tennessee's Civil War veterans, collected in the 1920s, are suggestive. Whereas those who had come from wealth remembered the past as a better, more harmonious time, poor veterans did not. Slaveholders, wrote William Babb, "always moved in [a] circle to themselves thinking themsevs on a hiar plane than the laboring man." Not only that, but slaveholders did not acknowledge his racial status. Instead, he "was looked by the slave holder as being down on a level with the slave or not as quit as good as the slave." Many of these veterans argued that unlike common white families, slaveholders did not value "honest labor" because they lived off the labor of others. "The comon class did work," wrote A. J. Childres, although "there were some that didnt work." "They had slaves to do their work" for them, he explained. As another veteran recalled, all were "on an equality" in his neighborhood precisely because there were no "slave kings" and "wealthy slave lords."[14]

The veterans' wives might have added some choice comments of their own had they been asked, but they were not. As we have seen, slaveholding women minced no words about common white women, when they deigned to acknowledge them at all. We know because slaveholders recorded their thoughts, but common white women did not usually record *their* thoughts about these encounters. One can only imagine what the Texas women with no hair ribbons thought of Kate Stone. We do know, however, what one woman thought when she informally apprenticed her daughter to Eliza Clitherall, a plantation mistress. The mother was furious when she learned that Clitherall had renamed the girl and dressed her in homespun, while clothing her own children in calico. This woman promptly took her daughter home. Clitherall recorded that the woman informed her that "her child was as good as mine."[15]

Common whites were also perfectly capable of taking political action. "I can tell you what," one man informed John Dennett in 1865, "we's done with them ar secessioners that brought this thing on, and they a'n't a-goin to git the upper hands agin." Then he went on to quiz Dennett "about the national debt, about Northern schools and railroads, about the wages of 'hirelin's,' the size of farms, the methods of cultivating corn and wheat, and especially about the feelings of the Northern people towards the rebellious States." This was no ignorant, downtrodden hayseed.[16]

Needless to say, the arrogance demonstrated by elite conservatives in the first few years following Confederate surrender did not sit well with many common whites. Conservatives seriously misjudged the extent to which their stock had fallen during the war. They faced significant opposition from whites in their own states, particularly in the upper South but even in the lower South. The unionists of Walker County, Alabama, for instance, were not eager to put Confederates back in power. Even white men who were not unionists were not sad to see the planter class fall. "Many people," reported one South Carolina planter, are "lighthearted at the ruin of the great slave owners." One man boasted that planters could "tyrannize now over only a small parcel of women and children, those only who are their very own family."[17]

Reconstruction gave common whites the opening they needed to act. Its terms disqualified Confederate officials from holding government office. It also enfranchised the one group of southerners—African American men— who were even less enthusiastic about slaveholders than they were. Common whites thus joined African Americans and a handful of forward-looking planters in building a biracial political coalition within the Republican party. To the extent that the Republican party was successful, it was because of white southerners. In no state except South Carolina could the votes of African Americans carry the party without the support of whites. "I have never voted for any person who was not a Union man during the war," claimed Claiborn C. Ballinger of Walker County in 1871, "and I never expect to vote for any man who was not . . . a good Republican."[18]

Being Republican was a decision that necessarily involved white women. They shared in the implications of their families' political affiliations, just as they had during the war. They, too, endured the snubs and social censure of their Democratic neighbors. They, too, became the targets of Klan terror. A circular posted on African American's homes by a vigilante group in Tennessee also threatened violence against whites who made common cause with blacks. "All white men found with negroes in secret places shall be dealt with," it promised ominously. Elsewhere, white mobs made good on such threats. When they did, women suffered along with their men.[19]

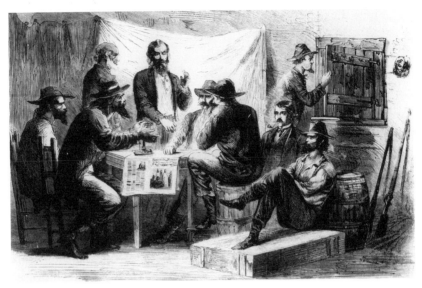

Depiction of southern Republicans holding a secret meeting in someone's home, published in *Harper's Weekly,* August 4, 1866. (Photo courtesy of the Newberry Library)

Racism, however, proved one of the biggest stumbling blocks to biracial politics in the South. Many whites had hated the slaveholders and the institution of slavery, but that did not mean they sympathized with slaves. On the contrary, they considered all African Americans lazy, promiscuous, untrustworthy, and a potential social threat. If anything, postwar economic and social dislocations tended to heighten racial prejudice. Before the war, explained one woman, "we poor folks was about ekil [equal] to the niggers, about bein' hard put to it to live, I mean, and now they's free they don't do nothin' but steal, and how we'll live I don't know. . . . I wish you'd tell me how poor folk is to live among these niggers."[20]

For this woman, as for so many white southerners, the recognition of commonalities with African Americans did not translate into a sense of social or political connection with them. Such attitudes not only continued but continually hardened over the following decades. Most white southerners could not bring themselves to join the Republicans because of the party's support of African Americans' civil and political rights. Some withdrew from politics, refusing to vote for either party. Some turned to the Democrats, certain that their interests would never be served by a party that also represented black southerners. Some acted out their hatred, donning hoods and white sheets in a attempt to physically eliminate African Americans and those politically allied with them.[21]

Even those common whites who voted Republican did not necessarily see African Americans as their equals. Yet if they failed to escape the racism of their time, they did not always act on it in the destructive ways that other white southerners did. Some white Republicans even supported full civil and political equality for blacks at considerable danger to themselves.[22]

White southerners may have divided over Republican rule, but it democratized state and local governments in ways that directly benefited them. Changes varied from state to state, but generally Republican legislatures enacted economic measures that appealed to common whites. Debt relief shielded their farms and homesteads from creditors, while other measures made it easier for skilled artisans and unskilled workers to collect their pay from tight-fisted or insolvent employers. Other inviting policies included more equitable taxation, abolition of property qualifications for officeholders, penal reform, and a public school system. Many states also made more offices elective, allowing common whites new power in state and local governments.[23]

Common white women participated in this democratizing process by claiming privileges that had long been withheld from them. Unlike African American women, they had theoretically enjoyed the same legal rights as wealthy white women in the antebellum period. In practice, however, they did not.

Poor white women, wrote a northern journalist who traveled through the South after the war, were "slatternly and utterly without any idea of decency or propriety." In the antebellum period, the slaveholding class concurred. It considered poor white women so degraded that they were less physically and emotionally sensitive than their social betters. Coarse, foul-mouthed, impervious to abuse or hardship, and unable to control themselves sexually, they did not need or deserve protection that wealthier white women did. The poorer the woman, the more vulnerable and less creditable she became. These attitudes were most obvious in cases involving sexual assault. Antebellum court officials had ignored poor women's complaints. Those who successfully pressed charges were hardly home free. The courts subjected their lives to intensive scrutiny. The process generally discredited poor women, who invariably fell short of the high moral standards required to establish feminine "virtue."[24]

Conservative politicians tried to rally white voters during Reconstruction with speeches about the sanctity of white womanhood, but the class bias against poor white women continued into the postemancipation period. They still found it difficult to prosecute cases of rape, sexual violence, or other physical abuse. Class distinctions among women were so commonly accepted that judges regularly invoked them to justify the differential treatment of women in legal matters. In an 1868 domestic violence case, the North Carolina Supreme Court drew on a standard legal distinction between women who lived in "hovels" and those of the "higher ranks." In the "hovel, where neither delicacy of sentiment nor refinement of manners is appreciated or known," the judge claimed, "the parties would be amazed if they were to be held responsible for rudeness or trifling violence. What do they care for insults and indignities?" By contrast, in "the higher ranks . . . education and culture have so refined nature, that a look cuts like a knife, and a word strikes like a hammer." Poor women, in other words, were used to abuse. Not only that, they often brought it on themselves through their own unwomanly actions.[25]

Consider the experience of Temple Cass. In 1869, this North Carolina woman charged William Somerville, a black man, with rape. After his conviction on the lesser charge of attempted rape, sixty men, white and black, petitioned the governor for Somerville's pardon. According to the petition, Cass was one of those women who cared nothing for insults and indignities. She had an illegitimate child. Recently, she had been abandoned by yet another man, who "after taking many indecent and improper liberties with her" had disappeared from the county. "[S]o great was the desire of the said prosecutrix [Cass] to get possession of money in order that she might have the means of pursuing and overtaking the young man Robertson who had wronged and deserted her," claimed the petitioners, "that she was influenced to a very great degree to submit to prostitution even at the hands of one of a different race and color."[26]

This account, of course, was the petitioners' interpretation of Cass's actions. Temple Cass, like Sarah Guttery, may have had no intention of pursuing her lover. We will never know. We will also never know whether she was actually raped. What we do know is that the male petitioners believed that Cass got what she deserved. As a woman with no virtue to steal, she was incapable of being raped. Cass, the petitioners maintained, had pressed charges only to make Somerville pay up. Why else would a prostitute claim to have been raped?[27]

Most common whites would have considered Temple Cass of low repute as well. Sarah Guttery, for instance, redeemed herself in her neighbors' eyes only after she gave up her wild ways and applied herself to raising her children, fulfilling her other familial responsibilities, and being a good neighbor. Temple Cass probably would have failed by these standards as well.

Nonetheless, the feminine standards of many white southerners were very different from those of their wealthier neighbors. Before the war, common whites had not automatically written off women who bore children outside of marriage, who lived with men as their husbands without the benefit of legal marriage, who separated from their husbands with or without legal sanction, or who otherwise lived unconventional lives. Nor did they do so afterward. Lola and Calvin, childhood sweethearts in Tennessee at the turn of the century, followed practices that white southerners had accepted for generations. First, Lola left their rural community to find work in a nearby city. Calvin followed soon after and asked her "keep house" for him. She agreed, and they moved in together. "I ain't noways ashamed that me and Calvin has never got around to the regular kind" of marriage, she insisted to an interviewer in the 1930s. "He's past fifty and I'm near to it and ain't neither of us ever trotted around loose like half the ones that blows about wedlock and such." They were respectable because of the way they had conducted themselves while living together. That was what mattered.[28]

But the class bias that worked against Temple Cass could ensnare white women like Lola and Sarah Guttery who *were* considered respectable in their own neighborhoods. Wealthier whites did not always honor or even recognize the fine distinctions that separated the respectable from the unrespectable poor. To them, poor women were just poor women. Poverty alone made their respectability questionable. Any deviation whatsoever from conventional sexual standards then disqualified them completely from the protections that were supposedly the right of all women. For wealthier white southerners, Sarah Guttery's two illegitimate children and Lola's common-law marriage placed them in the same category as Temple Cass.

Poor women felt otherwise. As Lola put it, "We is poor but we's decent." Sarah Guttery and her neighbors felt the same way. When she applied for a federal pension in 1879, her neighbors all insisted on her respectability, despite her poverty and her two illegitimate children. Although they had no doubts, the examiner did. He had to be convinced that her checkered past did not somehow disqualify her from receiving benefits. Acting on the same values that Sarah Guttery's neighbors had, women in North Carolina brought cases of sexual violence and other forms of physical assault to court in the years following emancipation. Like African American women who brought similar kinds of cases, poor white women insisted on public acknowledgement of their respectability. They also insisted that existing laws be extended to protect all white women, regardless of class position.[29]

Common white women also held men of their own class to their obligations to provide and protect. Many of these men insisted on the right to "discipline" women when they considered it necessary. Husbands regularly defended violence toward their wives by claiming they had been wronged or provoked in some way. So did men who inflicted violence on unrelated women. William Henry Nettles, for instance, admitted "that he did beat Mag Williams," but he insisted that "she gave him a cause to beat her." The "cause" was usually women's assertive words and actions.[30]

As Mag Williams's presence in court suggests, women were not always willing to submit. They did not reject the general principle of male authority, but they did question the abuse of that authority. Cynthia Oliver, for one, knew where to draw the line. On the day she filed criminal charges against her husband, Richard had come "home intoxicated in the morning after breakfast was over, got some raw bacon, said it had skippers and his old wife . . . would not clean it, sat down [and ate] a little, threw the coffee cup and coffee pot to the corner of the house, went out [and] cut two switches." If Richard disapproved of his wife's cooking, Cynthia disapproved of his staying out all night and coming home drunk when he should be out working in the fields. She also refused to accept his discipline for her alleged shortcomings as a housekeeper. When peace warrants and community intervention did nothing to alter his behavior, she left and filed criminal charges against him.[31]

In many ways, the claims of poor white women and African American women were similar. Both groups claimed the respect and rights that had been denied them before the war. Both groups also tried to place limits on the authority that all men—including those in their own families—could exercise over them.

If their claims to womanhood were similar, common white women did not necessarily intend to extend that status to black women. Instead, many made it very clear that the privileges of womanhood should be reserved only for *white* women. After hearing her sister-in-law's story of attempted rape in 1872, Ann Eakes went to her husband, demanding that he "kill the Black scoundrel." Many common white southerners considered all African Americans to be "scoundrels" who were unable to control their sexual desires. As they saw it, black men were prone to rape white women; black women were incapable of being raped because they had no virtue; and black women's lack of virtue made white women that much more attractive to black men. Moving black women down the scale moved white women up—or so it seemed to many whites. The courts agreed. Over the course of the nineteenth century, judges assumed that black men were guilty until proven innocent and bent the law to reflect their racial biases.[32]

The men in the Eakes family ended up prosecuting the "scoundrel" who allegedly attacked their kinswoman. Two decades later, the Eakes men might have organized a lynch mob instead. While the 1860s were known for brutal racial violence of all kinds, the lynching of black men for the alleged rape of white women developed later in the nineteenth century. Democratic political leaders encouraged this link by heightening the rhetoric of imperiled white womanhood in an effort to court white votes. Predatory black men, they claimed, posed a constant threat to white women. The only way to stop this threat, they insisted, was through extralegal violence so terrifying that it would literally scare African Americans into submission. "Whenever the constitution of my state steps between men and the defense of the virtue of the white woman," proclaimed Governor Coleman Blease of South Carolina in 1912, "then I say to hell with the Constitution!" "The pure-blooded Caucasian will always defend the virtue of our women no matter what the cost," he continued. "If rape is committed, death must follow!"[33]

Lynchings were done in the name of white women, but the elevation of white women had distinct limits. It reinforced their subordination to white men in ways such women as Cynthia Oliver would not have appreciated. It also silenced them politically. The Democratic party portrayed them as helpless victims who gratefully accepted the protection of their menfolk, instead of women with distinct opinions about their families and their position as women within them.[34]

Nor did the sanctity of white womanhood extend beyond the realm of political rhetoric. In practice, the elite Democratic officials who replaced Republicans from the 1870s through the 1890s remained as biased against poor white women as they had always been. "Among the lower classes [*sic*]," opined the North Carolina Supreme Court in 1877, "blows sometimes pass between married couples who in the main are very happy and have no desire to part; amidst very coarse habits such incidents occur almost as freely as rude or reproachful words."[35] In this particular case, the court sided with the woman because she was deemed "respectable." But such attitudes continued to obstruct poor white women's claims to their legal rights. Nor did they allow for political consideration of these women's particular social and political problems or even for common courtesy in daily social interactions.

This kind of entrenched class bias cast men and women in "lower classes" as coarse, ignorant, violent, and uncivilized people incapable of governing themselves. Not surprisingly, common whites also lost political power when Democrats "redeemed" the South. In most states, voting restrictions, such as literacy tests and poll taxes, disfranchised them as well as African

Americans. They, too, became the objects of both governmental and private "reforms" that encroached on their private lives in ways that were unheard of in the antebellum period.[36]

Democratic "redemption" of the South closed down meaningful political debate in party politics to some extent, but Democratic ascendancy did not happen over night. Nor did it unify all white southerners. Southern Democrats built a New South that was distinctly at odds with the one that common whites had hoped to build. This New South featured plantations worked by tenants and factories worked by wage laborers. Its boosters promised cheap, tractable labor so eager for work that they would give no trouble to their employers.[37]

It was as if the fractious, independent white men and women who had lived in the region for generations had suddenly disappeared. They did not fit into the New South rhetoric, but they were still there. They were still as fractious and independent as ever. Moreover, they continued to make their opinions known, even if they could not always do it through the formal channels of party politics.

The economic foundations of the New South were laid in the late antebellum period, when internal improvements, manufacturing, commercial agriculture, and other business activity began to increase. Federal policies that emphasized wage labor reinforced these changes. Southern Republicans then strengthened and expanded them during their tenure in power. To be sure, debt relief and Republican-sponsored legislation did help common white southerners hold onto their land and their way of life for a time. Political changes during this period also gave common whites greater political power and opened up government institutions to them. Many, however, never recovered from the economic devastation from the war. Changes set in motion by other factions in the Republican party made the task more difficult. As we have already seen, northern Republicans hoped to remake the southern economy in their own image. Their policies favored wage labor, commercialized farming, and continued economic expansion built around the manufacture and sale of consumer goods. Then, southern Democrats, among them business-minded members of the slaveholding elite, continued to promote the same kind of economic growth.[38]

This vision of the New South was not what most common whites had in mind. Although tempted by pretty things as much as the next person, they did not want to become commercial farmers or agricultural wage workers to obtain them. They wanted to return to a safety-first economic strategy that maximized their households' independence. The idea that anyone would want to work continually to satisfy ever-expanding desires for consumer items was as foreign to many white southerners as it had been to former slaves. Why work more if you already had enough?[39]

White southerners were not forced to confront the New South as soon or as suddenly as black southerners were. Many white southerners had land. They also escaped the kind of governmental supervision that freedpeople endured, since neither former slaveholders nor federal officials dared to legislate them into the status of wage workers in the same high-handed way that they did with African Americans. Politically, it was unthinkable. Of course, this is exactly what happened eventually, but economic change crept up on white southerners slowly. By the time they realized what was happening, the damage had already been done.

Immediately after the end of the war, white southerners busied themselves with the task of rebuilding their lives. Many northern observers could not tell they were doing much of anything at all. Assuming that all people were motivated by profit and accumulation, they saw only sloth, indolence, and immorality. "I am certain," wrote Sydney Andrews, "that there can be no lower class of people than the North Carolina 'clay-eaters,'—this being the local name for the poor whites": "They are always thinly clad, their habitations are mere hovels, they are entirely uneducated, and many of them are hardly above beasts in their habits. Very few families have fifty dollars' worth of property of any kind. . . . [T]hey cultivate a little corn, and sometimes a little patch of cow-peas, collards, or sweet potatotes. . . . They are lazy and thriftless, mostly choose to live by begging or pilfering, and are more unreliable as farm hands than the worst of the negroes."[40]

Andrews did acknowledge a difference between propertyless "clay-eaters" and landowning farmers, but landowning farmers did not fare much better in his estimation. As he quickly realized, the devastation he was seeing was not just the result of war. Some of this disorder was intended. Throwing up his hands at ramshackle houses with dirt floors and no linens, broken down fences and farm buildings, wiry stock that ran wild on unfenced common land, irregularly tended fields, men who spent more time idling and socializing than at work, and women who seemed completely unconcerned with housekeeping, he despaired for the entire state of South Carolina. The whole place, Andrews sniffed, needed a good scrubbing down with soap and water. "I am satisfied," he wrote, "that if the people of this State, with all their belongings and surroundings,—except such as would be damaged by water,— could be thoroughly washed at least once a week, a year would show a very material advance toward civilization." Cleanliness, he hoped, would be the first step toward the kind of social order that he favored.[41]

Andrews was disappointed in the 1860s. But change had already begun, and it continued after Democrats took control in the 1870s and 1880s. Although former slaveholders initially found it difficult to adjust to working with emancipated workers, they were not necessarily adverse to the kind of economic development favored by northern Republicans. Many, particularly in the upper South, had been involved in these kinds of business ventures before the war. Some even joined the Republican party in the late 1860s and early 1870s because of its support for economic growth. As the party's fortunes waned, these elite whites drifted back to the Democrats, who supported the economic projects—railroads, commerce, and manufacturing—so dear to their hearts.[42]

Nor did the Democrats do anything to stop the economic transformation of the countryside that slowly ate away at the foundations of common whites' households. They actively promoted it. In the immediate postwar years, many white farm families had to borrow money so that they could plant. To pay back the loans, they devoted more acreage to marketable crops—such as cotton or tobacco. Prices for these crops, however, either fell or remained stagnant. Tobacco farmers did well for a while because their crop was in high demand. But small farmers were selling their crops on a world market, where prices depended on what was happening halfway around the globe. They had little leverage. They could not wait for higher prices because they needed money right away. Nor did they have enough market share to be able to affect prices by withholding their crops. They had to take what was offered. If they were lucky, it was enough to break even. If not, they borrowed more.[43]

Grinding on unabated, year after year, this cycle transformed the rural South. Many white farm families watched helplessly as their land slipped out of their hands. Stubbornly clinging to the remnants of the life they knew, many remained, but not as owners. By 1880, one-third of all white southerners were tenants or sharecroppers.[44]

These changes made women's labor both less valuable and more essential. Cheap manufactured goods—such as cloth, ready-made clothes, and prepared foods—replaced items that white women had produced at home in the antebellum period. Of course, the same economic changes that made these new goods available also lowered prices for the crops their menfolk were still trying to produce. Women could therefore not quit work. Rural families expected daughters and wives to continue to pay their own way and contribute to their families' collective income, but how they did that changed.[45]

Many white women began spending less time on domestic production and more in the fields. The further their families moved down the economic ladder, the more their labor was needed to work cash crops to pay off that year's debts. Margaret Jarman Hagood's study of white tenant women in the 1930s is revealing. Expecting to find "Mothers of the South," Hagood was surprised to discover that the overwhelming majority of the white tenant women she interviewed spent most of their time in the fields. As one woman bragged, "[M]y papa said he lost his best hand when I got married." Others remembered when they were younger, stronger, and "used to work like a man."[46]

Of course, not all white southerners descended into poverty after the war. Many managed to keep their land but often at the cost of leaving the antebellum world behind. Abandoning the logic of the household economy, they became New South farmers. They adopted scientific farming techniques, maximized output, and produced marketable goods. Other farmers saw the handwriting on the wall and sold out completely. They became white-collar managers or professionals in the booming towns and cities.[47]

The women in the families of the New South's new middle class took a different path than did the women on tenant farms and in mill towns. Over time, they became more like the kind of housewives that white northerners had failed to find in the South before and immediately after the Civil War. Some rural women made this transformation as well, although they still continued to do farm labor in addition to housework. County newspapers and farm journals all boasted women's pages, with column after column devoted to a kind of domesticity that drew a sharp separation between the "home" and the "fields," "women's work" and "men's work." These articles encouraged women to maintain clean, inviting homes. They printed pictures of neat cottages, where workrooms were segregated from living areas. They urged women to become more involved with the morals and education of their children. They also directed women to contribute to the farm by performing such appropriately feminine chores as churning butter, gathering eggs, and preserving food.[48]

Reality, however, was often different from the ideal. Farm women, for instance, might move into their new cottages only to turn their parlors and bedrooms into work spaces. The demands of the farm life also meant few women could limit themselves only to "women's work" in the ways that domestic literature prescribed.[49]

As we will see in the next chapter, middle-class women, whether rural or urban, added their own touches to the gospel of domesticity. Nor did it completely isolate them within the home or release them from economic responsibility for their families. In general, the emphasis was on education, hard labor, and even wage work, if done in service to the interests of their families. Some took this advice to heart and eventually stepped out into the public realm to promote social reform in the name of protecting their own families and homes as well as those of other women.

Nonetheless, as the turn of the century approached, the cultural distance between the new middle class and poor white southerners grew. Where agricultural writers once promoted tenancy as a respectable position for hardworking young men, they began describing tenant families as lazy no-goods. Landowners who wrote to the North Carolina Bureau of Labor Statistics in the 1880s and 1890s criticized tenants for their farming practices, their work habits, and their morals. "Nearly all reliable white men," wrote one informant, "own their farms."[50]

A Georgia professor arrived at a similar conclusion, making it sound as if land were there for the taking and the only thing keeping tenants from it was their own ignorance. "Few rise to the top to take advantage of opportunities and secure homes," he wrote in 1900. Instead, "they live 'from hand to mouth' and are content at the end of the year to have a few dollars to spend for Christmas, and are willing to start out on a new year, and do so cheerfully, without having laid up a single dollar's worth of anything."[51]

White tenant women expressed their sense of the divide from a different perspective. The women that Margaret Hagood interviewed insisted on their preference for field work. "In the house," one woman explained, "you never get through." Another elaborated: "In the field there's just one thing and you can finish it up; but here in the house there's cooking, cleaning, washing, milking, churning, mending, sewing, canning, and always the children—and you don't know what to turn to next." Their insistence on this point puzzled Hagood. Unable to comprehend what she had heard, she attributed their lackadaisical housekeeping to ignorance, overwork, and poverty. What she missed were the ways that these women were distinguishing themselves and their work from their middle-class counterparts. They were telling Hagood that their domestic duties extended beyond the four walls of their houses and that their greatest domestic accomplishments could be found there. "No woman," snapped one informant, "really likes housework."[52]

In the late 1880s, those opposed to rural economic decline began taking matters into their own hands. White farmers across the South began joining together in the Farmers' Alliance. This cooperative organization built its own warehouses, factories, and purchasing cooperatives with the intent of cutting out the middlemen and keeping the profits for themselves. Women were actively involved, attending meetings and promoting the goals of the organization. The organization's platform primarily addressed the concerns of landowners who faced the loss of their land through mortgages and the crop-lien system.[53]

Tenants and agricultural wage workers, who did not legally own the crops they produced or control their own labor, could not fully participate in or benefit by the organization's cooperative schemes. The Farmers' Alliance's bias toward landowners had racial overtones as well, since the majority of African Americans were tenants and wage workers. The Farmers' Alliance did organize biracially, although it segregated white and black members. It also provided hope for the region's rural poor at a time when the Democrats and even Republicans offered none.

So did Populism, the political movement that grew out of the Farmers' Alliance in the 1890s. Addressing the problems of small growers across the country, the Populist platform included government regulation of the railroads, antitrust legislation, an inflationary monetary policy to boost stagnant farm prices, and an inventive scheme to stabilize volatile agricultural markets. Not only did Populism oppose the economic policies favored by Democratic leaders, but its politics and its popularity among voters threatened Democratic control as well.[54]

Populism stumbled at the national level in 1896. Allying with the Democratic party, watering down its platform, and supporting William Jennings Bryan for the presidency did nothing to catch its fall. Populist leaders in the South resolutely refused an alliance with the Democratic party because they saw that party as part of the problem. Yet southern Democrats managed to lure disgruntled whites away.

Appealing to racial supremacy as well as white southerners' notions of masculinity and femininity, Democratic leaders displaced economic concerns onto African Americans. If white southerners were experiencing difficulties, Democrats argued, it was because African Americans monopolized jobs, lowered wage levels, brought down property values, and slowed economic growth generally. Continual charges of black-on-white rape brought the argument home—literally. Declining economic fortunes meant that white men continued to lose the authority they once exercised over their wives and children as heads of household in the antebellum period. Democratic leaders capitalized on these fears and directed them in particular ways by playing on white men's sense of emasculation, on white women's sense of vulnerability, and on both men's and women's racial prejudices. It was not structural economic changes promoted by Democrats that were undermining white men's authority and making white women's lives harder. It was African Americans.[55]

The results were deadly. In North Carolina, where a biracial Populist-Republican "Fusion" ticket was strong enough to pose a real political threat in 1898, Democratic candidates and newspapers hurled accusations at African Americans. The force of these charges was particularly strong in the eastern part of the state, where a majority of the black population lived and where Fusion was strongest. It culminated with a violent race riot in Wilmington, consciously and carefully orchestrated by Democratic leaders in an attempt to take over that city. In other places, the rural uprising of the 1890s was neither so successful nor so dramatic in its defeat. Yet violence won the day in Wilmington and elsewhere in the South as well.[56]

The cost in black lives was obvious. The cost to white southerners was less so. Turning African Americans into the enemy, they lost the possibility of saving what was dearest to them. Many white southerners now saw every effort by African Americans to achieve respect, independence, and adequate compensation for their work as a dangerous threat to themselves. They then took out their frustrations on black men and women, using them to stand in for the complicated economic changes that were transforming white households. In their efforts to place themselves above the African American laborers, whites in Wilmington and elsewhere actually assisted in creating a future at odds with their own economic interests—a future where they, too, would be common laborers and where they, too, would endure the powerlessness that Democrats had built into the economy.

Although Democratic leaders fueled the fury, their tactics resonated because so many white southerners were already willing to listen. Had they only understood, whites had far more to learn from African Americans than from Democratic politicians. In the late nineteenth century and early twentieth, white southerners would be economically and politically marginalized. Labeled a problematic population in need of expert aid and occasional discipline, they would find it increasingly difficult to participate in the region's governing bodies or to shape public debate. Poor African Americans had been there already. They had been wage workers since emancipation, battling the same labor problems that whites were only now beginning to face. They had been struggling to obtain control over their private lives. And they had not let their political marginality keep them from making their voices and their concerns public. Instead of listening to African Americans, white southerners unleashed their frustration and rage on them. The ugly acts of violence supposedly marked their victory but really signaled their own defeat.[57]

After Populism's defeat, white women were as likely to be found working in factories as in the fields. As economic change continued to push white southerners off the land, cities ballooned with displaced rural people looking for "public work," as they called it. They found it in the New South's various industries—coal, lumber, iron, steel, furniture, textiles, and tobacco.

Some of these industries, particularly textiles, employed only whites. Others hired African Americans but only in the most subordinate, lowest paid positions. Factories were organized by sex as well as race. Most of the "best" jobs—although that is a relative term—were reserved for men. Still, southern industries, especially textiles, relied heavily on the inexpensive labor of white women. In cities and towns, factories hired women apart from their families. In textile mill villages, however, entire families labored together to earn a subsistence. They lived in houses provided by the company, attended churches and schools provided by the company, and shopped at a store provided by the company. They came, hoping to work a few years to get back on their feet and go back to farming. Some did, moving back and forth between farming and factory work. But most ended up staying a lifetime.

New South boosters and employers portrayed white southerners as docile, tractable, and grateful for whatever employers chose to dole out. But southern workers packed their pride and independence with them when they moved off the land. From the 1880s into the 1930s, waves of strikes and labor unrest hit southern industries. Women were active participants, even when they were not employed for wages. They demonstrated, stood firm behind labor's demands, and activated community networks to provide and distribute food and shelter. Many women saw such actions as an extension of their traditional roles as wives and mothers: they were tending to the interests of their families. Common white women often had had to take unconventional steps to do so in the past. Now was no different.[58]

For white women, these economic changes were bittersweet. They, too, mourned the loss of the land. Although they had never owned it in their own names, they felt the connection to it just as strongly as their menfolk. Many never recovered from that loss.[59] But the demise of the antebellum household economy also opened up new opportunities, by loosening the grip that husbands and fathers had over their wives and, especially, their daughters.[60]

At the turn of the century, women were overrepresented among urban migrants. Some financially strapped white families began encouraging daughters to find "public work" in nearby towns and cities. Some lived at home and commuted to nearby factories, while their husbands, fathers, and brothers tended the farms. Some lived with relatives who had already moved. Other young women simply picked up and left to make new lives for themselves on their own. Sarah Guttery was too old to participate in this transformation. But Lola, the woman who insisted on her respectability despite her common-law marriage, was not. She left her rural home while still a teenager to find work and adventure in the big city of Knoxville, Tennessee.[61]

Young women on a break from work in a Georgia cotton mill, 1909. (Photograph by Lewis Hine; courtesy of the Photography Collections, University of Maryland at Baltimore County)

She found both. Ultimately, Lola was glad to set up housekeeping with Calvin and escape the low pay and drudgery of wage work. Life was not all drab and dreary, however. Young working women in the early twentieth century announced their independence with fashionable clothes, stylish hair, and a penchant for movies, dating, and dance halls. This new defiant attitude carried over into labor organizing. Women not only participated in strikes with men in the late nineteenth and early twentieth centuries but also instigated their own labor actions and carried them out in their own distinctive ways. In a 1920s strike at a Tennessee hosiery mill, women workers dressed in their best to walk the picket line. Sashaying up and down, they taunted the National Guard troops sent to keep order. For all their playfulness, these were not giggly, empty-headed girls. They were dead serious about their demands for better wages and more autonomy on the job. These women and their demands were exactly what the New South middle class and conservative white Democrats had feared. And this is exactly what they reaped.[62]

9   *This Is New and Disagreeable Work to Us All*

THE Confederacy's official demise shocked Gertrude and Kate, but they were completely unprepared for changes in their daily lives. Gertrude brushed off emancipation at first. "As to the emancipation of the Negroes," she wrote in May, 1865, "while there is of course a natural dislike to the loss of so much property in my inmost soul I cannot regret it—I always felt that there was a great responsibility—It is in some degree a great relief to have this feeling removed." Kate Stone, always the realist, confronted what Gertrude could not. "If the Negroes are freed," she asked "we will have no income whatever, and what will we do?"[1]

To Kate and Gertrude in 1865, it seemed as if their world had been turned upside down. At least this was the metaphor that former slaveholders frequently used to describe the changes that followed in the wake of Confederate surrender and emancipation. The abolition of slavery marked an enormous watershed for them. It destroyed the foundations of slaveholding families' economic position, taking away material comforts and financial security. For the first time in their lives, Kate and Gertrude had to worry about money. More than money was at stake, though. The institution of slavery also had been a key anchor in their social status and their sense of individual identity. It had distinguished them from poorer white southerners and from African Americans. It had been a filter through which they understood their own place in the world. They had been the wives, daughters, and mothers of slaveholding men. Now what were they? *Who* were they? Without slavery, they might be the same as any other woman—the poor white women without hair ribbons whom Kate had met in Texas or the black woman who refused to stay all day to do Gertrude's laundry.

For women like Kate and Gertrude, the experience was disorienting and frightening. Gertrude fell into depression and remained there for more than two decades. Kate wrote sporadically, producing only a few journal pages before she quit altogether. "So this is the end," she concluded in 1868, "shall I ever care to write again?"[2]

Despite former slaveholders' complaints, however, the world was not turned completely upside down. To be sure, they sustained staggering losses. Many had poured all their resources into the Confederacy. What they did not give willingly was taken through inflation, taxes, and wartime destruction. Emancipation then drained them almost dry. The war and its aftermath, however, did not strip away everything. Kin and community, two pillars in slaveholding women's lives, emerged intact and upright, although sorely battered by the conflict. They still had land, although to make their land productive, they had to have labor to work it. Yet former slaveholders had more economic resources and power than other southerners had. Of course, they had less of both than they had before the Civil War, but they had enough of both to rebuild their status and to stop African Americans and common whites from taking over. In fact, the extent of change in their lives, as we will see, often seemed both more profound and more problematic to former slaveholders than it did to anyone else. Women like Kate and Gertrude played crucial roles in the process of rebuilding. They could not resurrect the Old South, but they did help create a New South very much at odds with the ones that African Americans and common whites envisioned.

⟨∾⟩

As Gertrude would soon discover, it was she who had been dependent on slaves.[3] Like many planter-class women, she could not cook at all. She was equally inexperienced with other unpleasant but necessary household chores, such as cleaning, washing, and ironing. In March 1865, she "made up the first cakes I ever accomplished. I remember trying once before to work up some flour without success." "The children stood around admiring 'Ma's performance' as I cut out men, thimble cakes and &c.—but my back ached when I was through and I have seen things I like to do better." One was studying French, which she did afterward. At this point, she still had a full complement of servants and could leave off housework when she wished. That soon changed. Two months later, she had to help one of her few remaining servants wash the breakfast dishes, "a thing I never remember to have done more than once or twice in my life." Thereafter, such chores became a regular feature of her life. By 1870, she "began seriously to think that it was in very bad taste to have three meals in one day" because it meant "more dishes to wash."[4]

It was not just that women like Gertrude were unskilled. Nor was it just the dirt and difficulty that made such labor so distasteful. These things did matter. According to Kate, the Stones "generally managed to keep a cook" after the war, because "this is new and disagreeable work to us all." More than that, sweating over a hot stove, heaving wet laundry from tub to tub, and getting down to scrub the floor had been reserved for enslaved woman and white women who were too poor to own slaves. Such labor symbolized these women's degraded position. Not doing it symbolized elite white women's superiority.[5]

As the wife of an Atlanta printer explained, "I could never look nice myself, keep my baby or my house clean" without domestic help. She had an ally in her husband, even during the war when money was tight. Despite—or perhaps because of—his occupation, he was sensitive to the way housework marked racial and class distinctions. He "dont want me to do kitchen drudgery," she continued, "says he will break up house keeping if I insist on doing without help." The point was obvious to a northern woman who resettled in Louisiana before the Civil War and enthusiastically embraced slaveholders' cultural standards. As she understood, the "fundamental premise of the southern ideal of womanhood" was that "women, to be ladies, had to have servants."[6]

Finding black women willing to do domestic work after emancipation was hard enough. Finding black women willing to work on elite white women's terms was virtually impossible. They wanted domestic servants to "live in," to do whatever they were told, and to be available seven days a week, twenty-four hours a day. They did not want their domestic servants' children around the house. And they wanted to pay when and if they wished, considering it more a gratuity than a wage. In 1865, Gertrude offered to pay one of her former slaves twenty-five cents a week. She was actually surprised when the woman left the next day without bothering to collect. On top of all that, elite white women wanted the work done with proper deference and good cheer. "Respect," insisted Gertrude, "is a quality I demand from servants even more than obedience. I can over look neglected work but cannot tolerate disrespect."[7]

Gertrude and other elite white women also wanted devotion. As Gertrude explained, what she really needed was a servant "who finds it to her interest to take an interest in pleasing me and interesting herself in my children." No wonder the cultural icon of "Mammy" became so popular in the years following the war. From the perspective of white southerners, Mammy was the ideal black woman. She was also the ideal domestic, one who identified completely with the interests of the white family she served. Mammy had no family or life of her own, at least not that her white employers needed to know about. White women like Gertrude longed to have Mammy work in their homes. They even convinced themselves that Mammy actually had worked there during slavery.[8]

But Mammy existed only in the imaginations of elite whites. As we have already seen, African American women wanted to work for their own families, not those of elite white women. Of course, many had no choice except to work for wages, but they were unwilling to let their employers' whims govern their lives.[9]

Elite white women, unaccustomed to having their desires pushed aside, spouted a steady stream of complaints about the irregular work habits and presumptuous conduct of African American domestics. Complaints continued throughout the late nineteenth century and into the twentieth, but the comments immediately following emancipation were the most acrid. "I am so vexed & tormented by freed women I can scarcely contain myself," one North Carolina woman fumed.[10]

Gertrude would have agreed, although she went to great lengths to emphasize her control in dealing with hired domestics. What seemed to unnerve her most was the realization that she had never really known those who had cooked, cleaned, and cared for her family for generations. She was particularly hurt when Daniel, a carriage driver and the first slave her husband had owned, attended a gathering at Gertrude's house but did not speak to her. "As I saw him leaving in company with some others I called him and said 'Why Daniel are you going away with out coming to see me?'" She reported that Daniel was "pleased" and "gratified" that she had acknowledged him. Perhaps. But Daniel was the first house slave to leave at the end of the war. He had returned only to obtain a recommendation so that he could find work elsewhere. Clearly, it was Gertrude who needed acknowledgment.[11]

By the 1870s, black domestics and their white employers had settled into an uneasy truce. Neither side gave up on their expectations. They just quit expecting the other side to meet them. White women tried to squeeze out as much work for the least amount of pay possible. There was little black women could do to alter this situation. They could, however, remove themselves from particularly annoying employers by walking out, which they often did. They quit so often that white women were surprised when domestics stayed on for any length of time. The results made the search for "better" domestics something of a full-time occupation for elite white women. Gertrude had a constant stream of workers in and out of her home. Most failed to meet her standards, but she failed to meet theirs as well. Usually, it was the domestics who left Gertrude, not the other way around.[12]

Elite women's dependence on slavery extended beyond their domestic servants. Their way of life rested on the labor of enslaved field hands. Without it, as Kate so acutely observed, they had "no income whatever." Gertrude also knew that emancipation would mean a loss of property. Like so many wealthy white women, however, she had no idea of the extent of her family's losses or what it had taken to maintain her previous standard of living. In May of 1865, she imagined that she could compensate for the loss of their slaves by teaching school. "I am not the person to permit pecuniary loss to afflict me," she chirped, "as long as I have health and energy."[13]

Gertrude's outlook had changed radically a few months later, as the magnitude of the situation finally settled in. "We owned more than 90 Negroes with a prospect of inheriting many more from Pa's estate," she wrote, with an air of stunned disbelief. "By the surrender of the Southern army slavery became a thing of the past and we were reduced from a state of affluence to comparative poverty—so far as I individually am concerned to utter beggary for the thirty thousand dollars Pa gave me when I married was invested in Negroes alone." "This view of the case," she continued, "I did not at first take and it is difficult now to realise it." It was so difficult that she lost her faith. "I did not know . . . how intimately my faith in revelations and my faith in the institution of slavery had been woven together—true I had seen the evil of the latter but if the *Bible* was right then slavery *must be*—Slavery was done away with and my faith in God's Holy Book was terribly shaken. For a time I doubted God."[14]

Even then, Gertrude did not completely understand. She was doubly dependent: she was financially dependent on her husband who, in turn, had been financially dependent on slavery. Women like Gertrude depended on their menfolk's ability to negotiate postwar economic changes successfully. Unfortunately, many were not up to the task.

Like their womenfolk, planter-class men found the concept of free labor baffling. Even those who were experienced in business interests besides agriculture found this particular economic concept difficult. That they should pay workers *before* the needs of their own families were satisfied seemed completely backwards. "What most distresses me," complained Kate of a short cotton crop in 1867, "is that none of that money went for our personal comfort. All of it went to the Negroes."[15]

That they could no longer compel African Americans to do as they wished also puzzled white men who had owned slaves. They did everything they could to retain their power over labor, as we have already seen. Although the law was on their side throughout the Reconstruction period, the law did not turn employers into masters or laborers into slaves. When Jeff Thomas received a summons to appear before the Freedmen's Bureau for nonpayment of wages, he was literally speechless. The charge itself must have been surprising, but it was the laborers' assertiveness in initiating suits that really left his mouth hanging open.[16]

Kate's brother Johnny discovered the limits of his power the hard way. He had a fight with a hired laborer while overseeing work on the Stone plantation in 1867. Unable to contain the conflict and unwilling to admit defeat, Johnny shot him. As Kate explained, Johnny "was mobbed in return." He "would have been killed," she continued, "but for the stand one of the Negroes made for him, and Uncle Bob's opportune arrival just as the Negroes brought him to the house—a howling, cursing mob with the women shrieking, 'Kill him!' and all brandishing pistols and guns." Johnny "had to be sent away" while passions cooled. After he returned, he never spoke of "killing people as he formerly had a habit of doing."[17]

Economic instability and stagnation compounded elite white families' financial problems. Emancipation and the wartime destruction of buildings, fields, and livestock put them in the hole. Then bad weather and low prices for many of the South's staple crops during the late 1860s dug them in deeper.

Mired in this economic muck, Kate's family sunk slowly into insolvency. Like so many others, the Stone family's crops failed in the late 1860s. They "spent $25,000," Kate reported in 1867 and produced only "20 bales of cotton." "Mamma would buy only bare necessaries for the table and plainest clothes for the family," she lamented. "Not a luxury, no furniture, carpets, or anything. We are worse off for those things than even in Texas [during the war] and such a sum spent. But Mamma said it was not honest to spend the money on anything but making the crop." That fall, her eldest brother's beau unceremoniously dropped him when the young woman's mother announced that her daughters "would marry only rich men." "By 1867," Kate noted wryly, "they have all done [so]." The following year, all three of her brothers were working in the fields themselves. One quit medical school to do so. He did not see the handwriting on the wall, but Kate did. She thought he was "throwing away the best chance of his life."[18]

Jeff Thomas was never particularly adept in economic matters even in the best of times. He had always relied on Gertrude's family to pick up after him, accepting gifts from her father and borrowing heavily on her inheritance. After the war, he seemed unable to produce anything but debt. He tried to run the family's plantations with free labor and failed. He opened a store in Augusta and failed in that as well. Creditors lined up to pick over the ruins. The property not sold at public auction was mortgaged to the hilt. Gertrude even signed over what she received in trust from her father's estate so that Jeff could use it as collateral to borrow more. The damage extended beyond the immediate family. When Jeff defaulted on loans, he also took down family members who had involved themselves in his affairs out of loyalty to Gertrude.[19]

For Gertrude, downward mobility was humiliating and terrifying. The humiliation came from Jeff's inability to fulfill his financial obligations and his squandering of the property that her own father had carefully accumulated over a lifetime. It also came from the public display of the family's reduced circumstances. She was ashamed to go to town when their property had been advertised for sale. She detested the clothes that she and her children had to wear. She was embarrassed that people knew how little she had. She was tortured by the damage done to her mother, brothers, and sisters. And she hated that her children would never have the advantages that she had known.[20]

The terror came from her husband's and her own inability to do anything about the situation. Gertrude had always assumed that men provided for their families. That was no longer true, at least in her case. "Oh my God!" she wrote, "My life, my glory, my honour have been so intimately blended with that of my husband and now to see him broken in fortune, health and spirits." Nor was she in a position to do much about it. She longed for her father to return from the grave to set matters right, but that was a fantasy. She tried to broach the subject with Jeff, but he refused to discuss financial matters with her, let alone listen to her advice. She racked her brain for ways to economize and to make money herself, but saving a bit here and there made little difference, and she could never earn enough to replace what her family had lost, no matter how hard she worked.[21]

Still, a little was better than nothing at all. Like many other elite white women in her position, Gertrude entered the ranks of the South's wage earners as a schoolteacher. She had expressed a desire to teach during the war, when she contemplated the implications of Confederate surrender for the family's finances. But Jeff would not allow it at first. To have his wife work for wages announced his own failure to provide for his family. It symbolized how far down in the world he had come. By 1878, however, with only debt coming in, he had no choice.

Gertrude went into the classroom because she wanted to, but she stayed because she had to. Although Gertrude took a genuine interest in her students, she found the work tiring, the students frustrating, the parents trying, and the results unsatisfying. By 1880, she dreaded the start of each term. "There has been no day during the time I have stopped teaching when the thought of beginning again was not extremely distasteful to me. I shrank from the idea with perfect aversion." That year, right before Christmas, she did quit. Jeff threw a wet blanket on her joy, though. "I have been thinking how we can get along if you give up this school," he informed her the very day she resigned her position. His conclusion was that they could not, for "we are dependent upon the salary you earn." So Gertrude returned to teaching.[22]

It is important to understand that downward mobility was not the same thing as abject or permanent impoverishment. Gertrude, Kate, and other former slaveholders thought it was, but their perceptions did not make it so. Former slaveholding families certainly had *less* than they did before the war. That was what stood out to them. Nonetheless, they still had *more* than most southerners. Housework, wage work, and penny pinching were all new to Gertrude. In her mind, that meant she was poor.

In fact, Gertrude always had more than enough. She and her children had new clothes every season. She had a carriage, furniture, china, and a nice house. Her children did not end up on tobacco road. They went to school, had dancing lessons, and attended social soirees. Although they never attained the wealth and preeminence of Gertrude's father, they did quite well by the standards of the New South. Turner (the eldest son Gertrude thought had been ruined forever because he had to do field labor like African Americans and poor whites) sold insurance and became a state senator. Her other children also weathered postwar hardships to become solid members of the postwar middle class.[23]

It is also important to realize that not all former slaveholders followed in the footsteps of Jeff Thomas. Some adapted to economic change better than others. Class status had always been for sale in the South, even in the antebellum period. Despite the myth of a stable, slaveholding aristocracy, the ranks of the planter class had been full of recent arrivals and self-made men. The economic rules did change after emancipation. Strategies that had worked before no longer produced the same results—something that many former slaveholders failed to understand. Jeff Thomas, never really successful under the old regime, floundered completely after its demise. Others, like Kate's brothers, refused to try.

While some men stubbornly continued their efforts to wring wealth out of the land, men-on-the-make passed them by with more profitable businesses and commercial ventures. Many antebellum planters had already branched out into new areas. That trend intensified in the postwar period: fortunes were made in railroads, coal, iron, steel, tobacco, textiles, and furniture, not plantations. As Gertrude noted in 1888, "I own land, much of it, and it does not support my family." As the urban centers of the Old South, such as Charleston, New Orleans, and Richmond, stagnated and decayed, power shifted to New South cities, such as Atlanta, Nashville, Durham, and Birmingham.[24]

Some of these men-on-the-make were newcomers. They were yeomen turned commercial farmers and entrepreneurs. The Dukes of North Carolina, for example, turned their family farm into a huge tobacco empire after the war. Other New South success stories were established members of the planter class, who had experience in business and commerce and adapted well to other postwar economic changes. One of the things that bothered Gertrude so much about Jeff's economic failure was that all the rest of her family was doing better. "My pride suffers," she wrote, "when I think of my children as the poor relations of the family."[25]

Recouping wealth was one thing. Recovering status and power was another. To be sure, wealth could buy political entrée and material goods, but these symbols had to be recognized by others to be transformed into power. That recognition did not necessarily have to be voluntary. African Americans, for instance, had not followed the rules of slavery out of admiration for their masters. They did so because of the way slaveholders' position had been institutionalized in the social and political structure.

Slavery had anchored slaveholding women's racial and class status as well as their own identities as women. In their minds, their own family members and their slaves had been inseparable pieces of a larger whole. Many slaveholding women so thoroughly mixed the two together in their letters and diaries that it is sometimes difficult for an outside reader to tell who is who. A rigid sense of hierarchy made this kind of slippage possible. In the antebellum period, elite white women did not need to use racial markers because slavery already located everyone on the plantation in a distinct place from which, at least in their minds, they could never stray.

The outlook of Sophronia Horner, the wife of a wealthy North Carolina slaveholder, suggests how slavery solidified racial difference. In 1861, as Horner awaited the arrival of her own child, a family slave named Susan delivered a very fair-skinned baby boy. Fascinated by the child's skin color, Horner's children puzzled over how to categorize the new arrival. "Ma," her daughter observed, "Susan's baby's hands are just as white as *us*." Her son finally concluded that the child was not really Susan's: "[A]h Suse you cant fool us, niggers dont be that white." Their mother, however, had no doubts. Although the child may have looked white, "[i]t is nevertheless a negroe."[26]

Horner probably had her own suspicions about how the child came by its light skin. Even if she never would have entertained the thought that her own male relatives might be responsible, she may have had suspicions in the back of her mind. Mary Chesnut summarized the conceit that many slave-holding women maintained in her famous remark, already quoted in a previous chapter, that "every lady tells you who is the father of all the mulatto children in everybody's household." But "those in her own she seems to think drop from the clouds." In fact, the Horner men may not have been responsible for Suse's child. If not, Horner may have had a good idea as to which white man in the neighborhood was.[27]

Horner's retelling of this incident, however, actually says more about the results than the origins of mixed race children. Regardless of her thoughts about the parentage of Susan's baby, she had no question about the child's status as long as slavery still existed. In Horner's mind, slavery fixed the child's identity. The status of Susan's child, in turn, helped establish Horner's own position.

Slavery also distinguished Kate Stone, Gertrude Thomas, and Sophronia Horner from other white women. In their eyes, the world fell out in ranked order according to class. They were superior to women who lived in families without slaves. They could tell because those women did their own housework, worked in the fields, wore clothes that allowed them to do such labor, and did not concern themselves with hair ribbons.

Being confused with these women was something that women like Kate, Gertrude, and Sophronia wanted to avoid at all costs. At worst, poor white women were fair game for other men. At best, they were invisible. "I do not think," wrote Gertrude, that Jeff is "the man to appreciate a wearied woman, wearing a faded calico until she can afford a better one, so much as a gay woman, fashionably dressed for which she is owing the money they cost."[28]

She had a point. War and emancipation reshuffled the deck, calling into question the markers that had distinguished elite white women. Women like Gertrude might not be destitute, but without the necessary material possessions, they were more easily confused with those who were. Racial boundaries were called into question as well. Sophronia Horner, for instance, could identify Susan's child as black because she knew Susan to be a slave. Without slavery, racial lines became much less certain. No longer a slave, the light-skinned child of Susan might be white. Or, if the racial categories operative in slavery ceased to be meaningful, the child's race might be of no consequence whatsoever.

Gertrude, as the historian Nell Painter has noted, worried about the interchangeability of women. She recoiled at the thought that another woman would take her place as wife and mother if she died. It was not just white women that concerned her. At the end of the war, she wrote an imaginary letter to the wife of General William T. Sherman, gloating that the general had replaced his wife with a black woman. Gertrude savored the image as revenge for the suffering Sherman had inflicted on her and other women like her. "Enquire of Gen Sherman when next you seem him," she wrote as if speaking to Mrs. Sherman, "who has been elevated to fill your place?" Tit for tat. Yet Gertrude's preoccupation with black women stealing away white husbands revealed less about actual circumstances than her own sense of insecurity at the blurring of racial and class lines, particularly regarding women.[29]

Elite white southerners did more than worry. They diligently policed racial boundaries. Of course, they had done so before the war as well. But afterward, such concerns acquired a new immediacy and stridency because the institution of slavery was no longer there to keep African Americans in their "place." Many white southerners saw racial blurring everywhere. As a conservative delegate to the 1865 constitutional convention in Arkansas insisted, giving African Americans "social and political equality" would be the "stepping stone to miscegenation." The logic, while tortured, was common. Wealthy whites across the South were convinced that civil and political rights meant that black men would take white men's place in the bedroom. African American men, snorted one Virginian, would only "vote themselves white wives." As we have seen, white southerners armed themselves with laws to prevent that possibility. Although the Black Codes were outlawed by the Fourteenth and Fifteenth amendments, conservative Democrats did manage to disfranchise African Americans and then enact Jim Crow laws that restricted their access to various public spaces.[30]

While the color line was being drawn, elite white women worked to rehabilitate the Confederacy. Guilt, inadequacy, and failure haunted Confederate supporters. Not only had they lost the war to the North, but also they had wreaked havoc at home. As other historians have shown, they exorcised the demons through "The Cult of the Lost Cause," a revision of the Civil War in which Confederate soldiers became brave warriors in an honorable but hopeless effort to defend a noble, harmonious society.

Elite white women were among the most active mythologizers. Through the United Daughters of the Confederacy and other organizations, they built monuments, made speeches, held commemorations, cared for wounded veterans and widows, and oversaw the writing of school textbooks. Their influence on public perceptions of the period was profound. They helped create the Old South of *Gone with Wind*, with its mint juleps, fine houses, beautiful belles, kind masters, and happy slaves. They contributed to the vilification of Reconstruction as an era of corruption, debauchery, and vio-

Mrs. W. W. Wadkins decorating the tombstone of Brigadier General Barnard E. Bee in Pendleton, South Carolina. (Courtesy of the Museum of the Confederacy)

lence. They also unflinchingly portrayed the violent overthrow of democratic reforms as honorable acts that were necessary to "redeem" the region.[31]

Elite white women also began rebuilding their own racial and class identity around a particular kind of domesticity. Information about domesticity was everywhere in the late-nineteenth-century South. Every local newspaper had advice columns, articles, or prescriptive fiction. Cookbooks, magazines, novels, and advice manuals picked up where the newspapers left off. White women of the former slaveholding elite joined those of the middle class in devouring this literature. They also produced much, if not most, of the domestic outpouring.[32]

Then they helped install domesticity as the new standard of elite womanhood. Devoting themselves to their husbands, overseeing their children's moral, physical, and mental development, putting well-prepared meals on the table, banishing dirt and dust, selecting tasteful interior decorations, and maintaining a cheerful, supportive atmosphere—all these things were the measure of a woman's worth and quality. All these things also separated worthy women from those who were not. Those who were not, of course, were the poor white and African American women who worked in other women's homes and in the region's fields and factories. Poverty prevented them from achieving the domestic standards of their social betters. As we have seen, however, many had no desire to do so even if they could have afforded it.[33]

Domesticity also acquired public overtones. Many of its devotees actually viewed it as a social mission. Creating and maintaining proper homes were what they could do to repair the damage done by war and emancipation and to put the South back on the right track. This is what Sarah A. Elliott, housewife-turned-domestic-expert, meant in the preface to her cookbook. "The change of times in the South," she wrote, "indicates to woman there a solemn duty." Far from powerless, "woman exerts a vast influence upon society as well as in the ordinary scenes of life, and to her is intrusted a moral power that hardly knows a limit." The best way to exercise her moral power and realize her social duty was through "a well regulated, systematic management of . . . household affairs."[34]

The rise of domesticity coexisted comfortably with increased educational and professional opportunities for middle-class white women. Not only did more colleges open up to women, but more families began sending their daughters to them. The curriculum and the communal setting of college life bred self-confidence and broadened young women's horizons. They left buoyed by a sense of social mission and the certainty that they could change the world.[35]

That is exactly what they set about doing after graduation. Some did so by entering professions, such as teaching and social work. They brought their ideals with them, trying to open up the world to other women and to all those less fortunate than they.

Paid employment, however, was not the only path to social reform. In the late nineteenth and early twentieth century, marriage and career were seen as mutually exclusive choices for white women. If a woman chose a career, it was thought that she could not marry because she could not devote herself wholly to her husband and children. But educated white women who did marry were often unwilling to drop their ideals or their desire to make a difference. They applied themselves to voluntary reform instead. Technically, they could argue that reform was not really "work" since it was unpaid. Far from threatening or new, it was really an extension of women's traditional charitable labor. Whether paid or not, reform-minded women continued to work together after graduation, collaborating on the same projects and working toward similar goals.

Domesticity was crucial to women's reform efforts. As women reformers argued, society as a whole would benefit from their particular insight, skills, and values. Such convictions had already drawn thousands of white middle-class women into church missionary organizations and the Woman's Christian Temperance Union (WCTU) by the 1880s. As the WCTU maintained, temperance was a woman's issue because chronic drunkenness destroyed the home and made it impossible for women to perform their domestic duties. From the 1880s into the early twentieth century, the WCTU and other women's reform groups extended the logic to other problems: unplanned urban growth, sanitation, rural poverty, education, and the vulnerability of women and children to the vagaries of the market. Their solutions included child-labor laws, literacy programs, better schools, changes in the legal status of married women, pure-food laws, as well as better housing, health care, and other social services. Domesticity thus launched white middle-class women into politics and public life.[36]

Eventually, domesticity also led many into woman suffrage. Frustrated with their inability to effect social change indirectly and insulted at their exclusion from formal politics, they demanded direct access. Here again, white women reformers couched their demands in the language of domesticity. *"We are told that the first duty of woman is as mother, and the highest sphere of woman is the home,"* announced one suffrage activist from North Carolina. "True," she agreed, "and it is that which places upon woman the obligation to enter into the life of her community, and nation, and help to make them a fit home for her child and her family." *"It is the right of woman,"* moreover, "to use not only the power of persuasion, but the power of the ballot, to protect herself and her children."[37]

Gertrude's life suggests the impact of these changes on elite white women. Her diary ends in 1889, with debt and despair. This was not the end of her life, however. What Gertrude lost financially, she gained in other ways. When she first thought about teaching in 1865, money was not the only motivation. Unstated, but implicit, was also her longing to do something more with her life—something creative and intellectually stimulating that would also bring public recognition. When schoolteaching failed to satisfy that craving, she began to look elsewhere. She wrote for publication, but she found her real calling in reform. In the years after her diary ended, she became a well-known women's rights activist. She first became involved in church missionary groups in the mid-1880s, moved on to serve as secretary and vice president of the Augusta WCTU, and then became president of the Georgia Woman Suffrage Association in 1899. She also wrote and spoke for the United Daughters of the Confederacy.[38]

Yet these changes did not extend unproblematically to other southern women. Like the domestic ideology that enabled elite white women's entrance into the public arena, elite white women's reform agenda established new racial and class hierarchies. While well-intentioned, reformers like Gertrude tended to impose their domestic values on other women, without asking for or obtaining consent. They assumed that all women should be just like them.

Of course, the goal of extending the privileges of womanhood to all women did allow for some new possibilities. African American women, in particular, used the language of domesticity and respectability in subversive ways to challenge racial restrictions. But few white reformers could get past their racial prejudice to even imagine a democracy among women. Deeply invested in limiting public power to those who were prosperous and white, most saw themselves as the proper representatives of women. Few white reformers questioned the idea that African Americans were childlike dependents or, as scientific racism took hold, unevolved barbarians. Their organizations regularly excluded black women and, at times, actively worked against them. Even so, racism did not preclude the possibility for biracial cooperation among southern women, although it did make such work much more difficult. These same reformers also kept poor white women on the margins, ignoring their critiques of capitalism and approaching them as unfortunate younger sisters in need of uplift.[39]

Ironically, it was postwar hardship that brought about Gertrude's transformation. Jeff's failure and its effects on her and the children altered Gertrude's view of the world. As he dragged her down economically and emotionally, she began to question not only his authority but also the authority of all men in ways that she never had before the war. She began to separate herself and her interests from Jeff and his concerns. She began to resent her dependence on him. Then she began to doubt the decisions of all men. Instead, she began to trust in her ability to control her own life. She began to believe that women needed to participate in the governance of society. She began to realize how the lack of civil and political rights reinforced her own dependence on Jeff and the dependence of women on men generally. By the late nineteenth century, she saw the solution in women's rights and the vote.[40]

Everything had changed, and nothing had changed. Working for woman suffrage and other women's causes, Gertrude found both the sense of purpose and the public recognition she had been seeking since before the war. Her experience with economic hardship did not erase her sense of racial and class hierarchy, though. Her reform work did not mean that she listened to women different from her or integrated their ideas into her social vision. She died in 1907, having achieved prominence in the New South, not the old. But her New South had much of the old still embedded in it.

Epilogue

'IN 1913, Judge Walter Clark, a progressive reformer, addressed the Federation of Women's Clubs in New Bern, North Carolina, on the political and legal status of women. Sympathetic to the cause of women's reform, he discussed the laws relating to married women's property rights, domestic violence, and suffrage. Judge Clark then attributed the recent changes in these laws to "progress." "Among savage tribes," he argued, "the club of the husband was logical. And under the common law so was the lash, because women being kept in ignorance and deprived of property rights could be thus governed. But when they were educated and given the right to own property these things became illogical and impossible."[1]

If "progress" made change for women inevitable, a small circle of educated, propertied men and women carried out its design. This assumption, widespread among progressive reformers in the South, tended to erase nineteenth-century women from history even as it elevated some women to positions of historical importance.

How? In this view, "ignorance" weighed down all women in the past. Because of this, they were unable to do much for themselves, let alone see the possibility of claiming rights and power. They could only wait for the turn of the twentieth century, when "progress" would open their eyes to their own potential. Then, they would form women's clubs and advocate reform that would be recognized as "women's issues." Then, they would become historical actors in their own right.

By extension, however, everything preceding that time became prologue. What nineteenth-century southern women did before they emerged in the formal political arena was important only insofar as it explained their later emergence. This framework presumes that women did not do much of anything with any wider social or political significance before the early twentieth century.

Judge Clark's analysis still carries a great deal of power today, where many people and even some historians still tend to see women's history as a slow march toward greater rights, political power, and historical agency. As we have seen, however, southern women in the nineteenth century were not simply objects of history. Members of the New Bern Women's Club and other late-nineteenth-century and twentieth-century women's organizations were not the first southern women to think they had rights or to act on them. To be sure, southern women in the nineteenth century did not think about women's rights and social reform in the same way that later activists did. Most did not see themselves pursuing "women's rights" at all. But they did have distinct conceptions of their rights as women, the rights of their families, and the shape of southern society. They acted on these ideas in ways that fundamentally shaped the course of southern history. To forget these women and to treat their actions as a prologue misconstrues the history of women *and* the history of southern society. Conversely, restoring the voices of nineteenth-century women—rich and poor, white and black—in the nineteenth century recasts our understanding of both the nineteenth century and the twentieth.

But including women and acknowledging their courage and their contributions constitute only part of the task. After all, Judge Clark's version of history did include women. At the same time, it left a lot of women out. It also left out conflict and differences among women. Neither Judge Clark nor the members of New Bern's Federation of Women's Clubs were particularly fond of assertive poor white and African American women intent on defining social and political issues in their own ways. Nor did these white reformers want to see their own role in creating the racial and class inequalities that had kept so many in poverty and out of power. In fact, they had a vested interest in portraying all poor whites and African Americans as people in need of aid and guidance.

Such a view legitimized elite white southerners' own claims to power. Even in the early twentieth century, according to Judge Clark, progress had not reached into the lives of poor white and black southerners. Unenlightened, they could only be the beneficiaries of reforms. They could never conceive of such measures or act in ways to better their own lives and society as a whole. If anything, he left the impression that all the bad things in poor women's lives came from the shroud of ignorance and poverty that hung over them.

Yet poor white and black southern women worked as hard to create the nineteenth-century South as their wealthier neighbors did. Judge Clark, for instance, made no mention of common white and African American efforts to build up their families and communities before the Civil War. He made no mention of African American women's opposition to the Confederacy or poor white women's opposition to the Civil War. He made no mention of all those women who struggled to keep their children, their wages, and their land and fought for the right to dress, talk, and gather as they pleased after the war. He certainly made no mention of the sexual abuse African American women experienced at the hands of white men or their efforts to stop it. These legacies are also part of southern history. They are valuable for they suggest new answers to old problems. Perhaps these legacies can replace the haze of moonlight and magnolias that now serves to soften the pain and violence of this region's past. Perhaps, then, we can begin using southern history in more productive ways.

Notes

Abbreviations

AC   Allowed Claims
CAP   Criminal Action Papers
DAC   Disallowed Claims
DU   Special Collections Library, Duke University, Durham, North Carolina
GDAH   Georgia Department of Archives and History, Atlanta, Georgia
GP   Governor's Papers
IC   Incoming Correspondence
LC   Library of Congress
LRCSW   Letters Received, Confederate Secretary of War
M   Microfilm collection
MR   Microfilm reel
NA   National Archives, Washington, D.C.
NCC   North Carolina Collection, University of North Carolina at Chapel Hill
NCDAH   North Carolina Department of Archives and History, Raleigh, North Carolina
RG   Record Group
RPB   Records of the United States Pension Bureau
SCDAH   South Carolina Department of Archives and History, Columbia, South Carolina
SCC   Southern Claims Commission
SCL   South Caroliniana Library, University of South Carolina, Columbia, South Carolina
USCT   United States Colored Troops

INTRODUCTION

1. Pioneering works in the field include Boatwright, *Status;* Gray, "Activities"; Spruill, *Women's Life;* and A. Taylor, *Short History.* For women and the Civil War, see Massey, *Bonnet Brigades;* Sterkx, *Partners;* and Wiley, *Confederate Women.* Scholarship in the area began a revival in the 1970s. See, for example, Hall, *Revolt;* Lerner, *Black Women;* Lerner, *Grimké Sisters;* Massey, "Making"; A. Scott, "'New Woman'"; and A. Scott, *Southern Lady.* The University of Missouri Press publishes selected essays from the Southern Association for Women Historians conference.

2. For discussions of the author of *Gone with the Wind,* Margaret Mitchell, and the differences between the movie and novel, see A. Jones, *Tomorrow;* and Pyron, *Southern Daughter.*

3. There is an emerging body of scholarship on these topics, although much of it is still unpublished. For notable exceptions, see S. Hill, *Weaving;* and Perdue, *Cherokee Women.*

PART 1 INTRODUCTION

1. Information on Marion Singleton Deveaux and her family is drawn from the Singleton Family Papers, LC, and the Singleton Family Papers and Singleton-Deveaux Family Papers, SCL. Information on Ella Gertrude Clanton Thomas (Gertrude went by her middle name) is drawn from her published diary, *Secret Eye;* the complete manuscript is at DU. See also Burr, "Woman"; and Painter, "Journal."

2. Information on Harriet Jacobs is drawn from Jacobs, *Incidents.*

3. Information on the women in Walker County is drawn from 1st Reg., Alabama Cavalry, RPB, RG 15, NA; and Walker County, Ala., AC, SCC, RG 217, NA. For a description of the area, see Flynt, *Poor,* 12–13.

4. For racial categories in law, see Bardaglio, *Reconstructing,* 48–64; Domínguez, *White by Definition;* and Haney-Lopez, *White.* For the difficulties of determining race in practice, see Bynum, "'White Negroes'"; Gross, "Litigating"; and Hodes, *White Women,* 19–122.

CHAPTER 1: PRIVILEGE AND ITS PRICE

1. *Converse v. Converse,* Sumter District, Equity Rolls, MR 227, 1854, SCDAH. See also the correspondence from Betty Coles to Marion, 1854–57, Singleton Family Papers, LC.

2. *Converse v. Converse.* For the legal and ideological connections between wives and slaves, see Bardaglio, *Reconstructing,* esp. 23–36; Bynum, *Unruly Women,* esp. 59–87; Edwards, *Gendered Strife,* esp. 25–31; Fox-Genovese, *Within the Plantation;* McCurry, *Masters,* esp. 208–38; McCurry, "Two Faces"; and Stanley, "Home Life."

3. Figures from Oakes, *Ruling Race,* 229; and Cooper and Terrill, *American South,* 207.

4. Singleton Family Papers, LC; Singleton Family Papers and Singleton-Deveaux Family Papers, SCL.

5. Fox-Genovese, *Within the Plantation,* 104–7; Vlach, *Back,* 18–31. For the mobility of planters, see Cashin, *Family Venture;* and Oakes, *Ruling Race.*

6. For the argument that shared ideological assumptions and the power to translate them into social structures, not material possessions alone, defined the planter class, see Fox-Genovese, *Within the Plantation,* esp. 37–99; and Genovese, *Roll.*

7. Painter, "Journal," 4; Fox-Genovese, *Within the Plantation,* 110–11, 113–14; Friedman, *Enclosed Garden,* 31–32; G. Thomas, *Secret Eye,* 75.

8. For Gertrude's fascination with clothes, see G. Thomas, *Secret Eye,* 71–92. Virtually every letter written by Angelica has some discussion of clothing. See Singleton Family Papers, LC. For slaveholding women's fascination with clothes, see Clinton, *Plantation Mistress,* 98–100; Fox-Genovese, *Within the Plantation,* 120–28, 111; and Stevenson, *Life,* 50–51.

9. Boatwright, *Status,* 5–24; Burr, "Woman," 216–17; Censer, *North Carolina Planters,* 42–46, 55–57; Clinton, *Plantation Mistress,* 123–38; Farnham, *Education,* 11–93; A. Scott, *Southern Lady,* 68–74; Stevenson, *Life,* 123–27.

10. Rebecca Singleton to Marion Singleton, February 10, 1829, and Rebecca Singleton to Marion and Angelica Singleton, [1827?], Singleton Family Papers, LC. For the ideal of the southern lady, see Clinton, *Plantation Mistress,* 87–103; A. Scott, *Southern Lady,* 3–21; and M. Weiner, *Mistresses and Slaves,* 53–71. For a comparison between the expectations of women and men, see Cashin, *Our Common Affairs,* 9–12. For schools' and parents' efforts to inculcate these qualities, see Censer, *North Carolina Planters,* 46–47, 48–50; Farnham, *Education,* 120–45; Rable, *Civil Wars,* 17–22; Stevenson, *Life,* 108–39; Stowe, *Intimacy,* 128–59, 164–249; and M. Weiner, *Mistresses and Slaves,* 61–66.

11. G. Thomas, *Secret Eye,* 82–92; Rebecca Singleton's letters to her daughters between 1827 and 1831, Singleton Family Papers, LC. For the indulgence of parents, see Censer, *North Carolina Planters,* 58–60. For particularly good discussions of the contradictions of submission and authority in slaveholding women's lives, see Fox-Genovese, *Within the Plantation;* and M. Weiner, *Mistresses and Slaves.*

12. G. Thomas, *Secret Eye,* 82–92; Painter, "Journal," 25–26.

13. Clinton, *Plantation Mistress,* 160–63; Friedman, *Enclosed Garden,* 11–20, 39–53; McCurry, *Masters,* 171–207; Rable, *Civil Wars,* 12–15; A. Scott, *Southern Lady,* 7–8, 10–16; Stevenson, *Life,* 120–22; M. Weiner, *Mistresses and Slaves,* 103–8. For discussions of religion and the southern social order from various perspectives, see Boles, *Great Revival;* Genovese and Fox-Genovese, "Divine Sanction"; Genovese and Fox-Genovese, "Social Thought"; Loveland, *Southern Evangelicals;* Maddex, "Proslavery Millennialism"; Maddex, "'Southern Apostasy'"; Matthews, *Religion;* and McCurry, *Masters,* 171–207. Southerners were overwhelmingly Protestant. For Catholicism, see Miller and Wakelyn, eds., *Catholics.*

14. For the importance of extended family ties to antebellum white southerners, see Cashin, *Family Venture,* 10–20, 29–30; Cashin, "Structure of Antebellum Families";

Clinton, *Plantation Mistress*, 36–58; Friedman, *Enclosed Garden*, 3–11; Kenzer, *Kinship*, 6–51; Reidy, *From Slavery*, 33–35; and Wyatt-Brown, "Ideal Typology." This theme also runs through Fox-Genovese, *Within the Plantation;* Stevenson, *Life*, 37–139 (although on 67–68 she notes the trend toward more privatized, nuclear families among southern professionals toward the end of the antebellum period); and Wyatt-Brown *Southern Honor.*

15. Rebecca Singleton to Marion and Angelica Singleton, July 21, [1828?], Singleton Family Papers, LC. For the importance of extended families in raising children, see Cashin, *Family Venture*, 21–22, 100–101; Clinton, *Plantation Mistress*, 50–54; and Stevenson, *Life*, 100–101. For letter writing, see Fox-Genovese, *Within the Plantation*, 111; and Stowe, *Intimacy.*

16. See note 35 in this chapter for the importance of kin ties to women.

17. For the experience of belles, see Clinton, *Plantation Mistress*, 61–62; and Fox-Genovese, *Within the Plantation*, 208–9.

18. For courtship and how romantic love and young people's desires mixed with financial concerns and the expectations of their parents, see Censer, *North Carolina Planters*, 65–95; Clinton, *Plantation Mistress*, 62–67; Fox-Genovese, *Within the Plantation*, 207–8; Lebsock, *Free Women*, 15–27; A. Scott, *Southern Lady*, 23–27; Stevenson, *Life*, 37–62; Stowe, *Intimacy*, 50–121; and Wyatt-Brown, *Southern Honor*, 195–225.

19. G. Thomas, *Secret Eye*, 122. For the stigma attached, see Stevenson, *Life*, 59–60. Other women were far less optimistic about marriage. See Cashin, "'Decidedly Opposed.'" Despite the pressure to marry, some women remained single. For diary excerpts of single women, see M. O'Brien, ed., *Evening.*

20. For planter-class women's lack of direct experience with housework, see M. Weiner, *Mistresses and Slaves*, 28–30. For analyses emphasizing the difficulty and importance of these women's work, see Boatwright, *Status*, 91–93; Clinton, *Plantation Mistress*, 16–29; Lebsock, *Free Women*, 148–64; Rable, *Civil Wars*, 8–10; and A. Scott, *Southern Lady*, 27–34. Recent studies, however, have emphasized its supervisory nature: Fox-Genovese, *Within the Plantation*, 114–29, 137–39; Friedman, *Enclosed Garden*, 26–31; Painter, "Journal," 51–52; Stevenson, *Life*, 72–77; and M. Weiner, *Mistresses and Slaves*, 23–49.

21. G. Thomas, *Secret Eye*, 119–20, 121. See also Burr, "Woman," 217–19.

22. Friedman, *Enclosed Garden*, 81–83; Fox-Genovese, *Within the Plantation*, 112–13, 142–45, 164–65, 205–7, 290–333; King, "Mistress"; A. Scott, *Southern Lady*, 36–37; Stevenson, *Life*, 196–99; M. Weiner, *Mistresses and Slaves*, 37–43; M. Weiner, "Mistresses, Morality, and the Dilemmas of Slaveholding." For the connection between sexual tensions and mistresses' cruelty, see Clinton, *Plantation Mistress*, 188; and J. Jones, *Labor*, 24–27.

23. G. Thomas, *Secret Eye*, 157, 158. For discussions of the complexity of mistress-slave relations, see Cashin, *Our Common Affairs*, 17–18; Fox-Genovese, *Within the Plantation*, 129–35; Painter, "Journal," 36–37; and M. Weiner, *Mistresses and Slaves*, 16, 72–88, 118–29.

24. Lerner, *Grimké Sisters.* For women in the Virginia Colonization Society, see Stevenson, *Life*, 278–85; and Varon, *We Mean*, 41–70. For an example of antislavery sentiment

after the Revolution and its limitations, see St. G. Tucker, "Dissertation." See also Doyle, "Lord"; and McCurry, *Masters,* 136–47.

25. Varon, *We Mean.* For antislavery southerners who remained, see Bynum, *Unruly Women,* 24–25, 52–54; and Stevenson, *Life,* 17.

26. For planter-class women's support for slavery, see Fox-Genovese, *Within the Plantation,* 197–98, 334–71; Friedman, *Enclosed Garden,* 87–91; Painter, "Journal," 63–65; Stevenson, *Life,* 199–205; M. Weiner, *Mistresses and Slaves,* 89–112; and M. Weiner, "Mistresses, Morality, and the Dilemmas of Slaveholding." Other scholars have taken mistresses' complaints about managing slaves and the comparisons they drew between themselves and slaves as evidence of their opposition to slavery: Clinton, *Plantation Mistress,* 180–98; and A. Scott, *Southern Lady,* 48–53.

27. See the correspondence between Marion and Robert, Singleton Family Papers, LC. For Gertrude, see Burr, "Woman," 219–20; Painter, "Journal," 33–42, 57–66; and G. Thomas, *Secret Eye,* 118–71. For discussions of interracial liaisons and marital discord, see Bynum, *Unruly Women,* 36–38; Cashin, "'Decidedly Opposed,'" 754–56; Cashin, *Our Common Affairs,* 13–14; Clinton, "'Southern Dishonor'"; Fox-Genovese, *Within the Plantation,* esp. 334–71; and Painter, "Of Lily." See also Johnston, *Race Relations;* and Williamson, *New People.* For interracial liaisons between white women and black men, see Hodes, *White Women;* and Sommerville, "Rape Myth." For the different forms that marriage and paternal power could take, see Cashin, "'Decidedly Opposed'"; Fox-Genovese, *Within the Plantation,* 239–41; Friedman, *Enclosed Garden,* 21–38; Lebsock, *Free Women,* 27–35; Stevenson, *Life,* 63–94; Stowe, *Intimacy,* 123–38, 164–249; and Wyatt-Brown, *Southern Honor,* 272–91.

28. *Converse v. Converse,* Sumter District, Equity Rolls, MR 227, 1854, SCDAH. See also the correspondence from Betty Coles to Marion, 1854–57, Singleton Family Papers, LC. For the court's refusal to handle domestic matters involving a husband's or father's abuse of his wife and children, see Bardaglio, "Outrage"; Bardaglio, *Reconstructing,* 34, 39–48; Bynum, *Unruly Women,* 59–87; McCurry, *Masters,* 85–91; and Wyatt-Brown, *Southern Honor,* 281–83.

29. Bardaglio, *Reconstructing,* 32–34, 80–97; Bynum, "Reshaping"; Bynum, *Unruly Women,* 57–87; Cashin, *Our Common Affairs,* 15; Censer, "'Smiling'"; Clinton, *Plantation Mistress,* 79–85; Goodheart, Harris, and Johnson, "Act"; Lebsock, *Free Women,* 67–72; Stevenson, *Life,* 140–56; Wyatt-Brown, *Southern Honor,* 242–47, 283–91, 300–307.

30. The classic statement of slaveholders' ethic of paternalism is Genovese, *Roll.* See also Bardaglio, "Outrage"; Bardaglio, *Reconstructing,* 25–26; Bynum, *Unruly Women,* 84–85; and McCurry, *Masters,* 176–79. The work on honor is also illustrative. See Greenberg, *Honor;* Greenberg, *Masters;* Stowe, *Intimacy;* and Wyatt-Brown, *Southern Honor.* For an opposing view, see Oakes, *Ruling Race.* Reidy, *From Slavery,* 31–57, synthesizes the two poles of the debate, noting that planters were marked by both participation in and resistance to capitalism and bourgeois values.

31. *Converse v. Converse,* Sumter District, Equity Rolls, MR 227, 1854, SCDAH. For divorce in South Carolina, see Hudson, "From Constitution."

32. Quote from the decision of Judge George M. Dargan, January 1856, from *Con-*

verse v. Converse, Sumter District, Equity Rolls, MR 227, 1854, SCDAH. For the conventions women had to fulfill to obtain a divorce, see Censer, "'Smiling.'" For results that served to reinforce patriarchal power, see Bardaglio, "Outrage"; Bardaglio, *Reconstructing,* 27–28; and Genovese, *Roll,* 3–112. In *Common Affairs,* 13, Cashin speculates that domestic violence was more common than previously thought.

33. G. Thomas, *Secret Eye,* 130, 141.

34. Mary Chesnut, who was childless, suffered acutely under the social pressure to have children. See Chesnut, *Civil War.* According to Lewis and Lockridge, "Sally," planter-class women also made efforts to limit childbearing. For the pressure to have children as well as the satisfaction women derived from motherhood, see Censer, *North Carolina Planters,* 20–41; Clinton, *Plantation Mistress,* 151–58; Fox-Genovese, *Within the Plantation,* 111–13, 276–81; McMillen, *Motherhood;* Painter, "Journal," 32–33; A. Scott, *Southern Lady,* 37–40; Stevenson, *Life,* 101–8; and Wyatt-Brown, *Southern Honor,* 236–47.

35. For the importance of extended family ties, particularly those among female kin, to women, see Cashin, "'Decidedly Opposed'"; Cashin, *Family Venture;* Cashin, *Our Common Affairs,* 12–26; Cashin, "Structure of Antebellum Families"; Clinton, *Plantation Mistress,* 37–38; Fox-Genovese, "Family"; Friedman, *Enclosed Garden;* Hoffschwelle, "Women's Sphere"; Smith-Rosenberg, "Female World"; Stevenson, *Life,* 70, 103, 135–36; and Wyatt-Brown, *Southern Honor,* 247–53. Cashin, *Family Venture,* 11–16, emphasizes that women—particularly in the East, where traveling was easier—used visiting as a means of maintaining these ties. For the importance of social visiting outside the circle of kin, see Fox-Genovese, *Within the Plantation,* 227–28. A brief survey of any slaveholding family's correspondence suggests that Clinton's emphasis on women's isolation in *Plantation Mistress,* 175–79, is overdrawn. Although writing about the colonial period, Ulrich, in *Goodwives* and *Midwife's Tale,* also notes the importance of the life cycle to women's mobility.

36. Cashin, *Family Venture;* Clinton, *Plantation Mistress,* 166–69.

37. Cashin, *Family Venture,* esp. 89–91, 108–12; Censer, *North Carolina Planters,* 96–118; Clinton, *Plantation Mistress,* 36–58.

38. Marion's petition in the separation suit reveals how she involved her family during her marriage. See *Converse v. Converse,* Sumter District, Equity Rolls, MR 227, 1854, SCDAH. See also Cashin, *Family Venture,* 111–12; and Wyatt-Brown, *Southern Honor,* 276.

39. *Converse v. Converse,* Sumter District, Equity Rolls, MR 227, 1854, SCDAH. For the final cash settlement with Augustus Converse, see Agreement, Feb. 20, 1857, Singleton-Deveaux Family Papers, SCL. See also Marion Converse to Matt Singleton, Dec. 20, 1853, and Dec. 25, 1853, Singleton Family Papers, SCL. For the extended family's and friends' responses, see, for instance, Betty Coles to Marion Deveaux, Feb. 19, 1854, Apr. 1, 1854, Apr. 11, 1854, May 16, 1854, July 31, 1854, Jan. 15, 1855, June 5, 1856, June 28, 1856, Sept. 17, 1856, and Jan. 11, 1857, Singleton Family Papers, LC; Sally W. Taylor to Marion Converse, Mar. 11, [1850–1855?], Singleton Family Papers, LC; J. Hamilton to Marion Converse, Nov. 22, 1853, Singleton-Deveaux Family Papers, SCL; [Illegible] to

Marion Deveaux Converse, Charlottesville, Jan. 11, 1858, Singleton-Deveaux Family Papers, SCL. The rest of the family correspondence, particularly the Singleton-Deveaux Family Papers, SCL, and the Singleton Family Papers, LC, indicates that Marion lived as if the marriage had never occurred.

Historians emphasizing honor have pointed out that the planter class preferred to resolve its domestic matters outside the legal system. While the negotiations were usually left to men, women could manipulate them and turn them to their advantage. For examples of patriarchs disciplining other patriarchs, see Bardaglio, *Reconstructing*, 3–5; and Stevenson, *Life*, 80.

40. Bynum, *Unruly Women*, 52–55; Gray, "Activities," 77–83; Lebsock, *Free Women*, 195–236; Matthews, *Religion*, 111–24; Varon, "'Ladies'"; Varon, "Tippecanoe"; Varon, *We Mean*; M. Weiner, *Mistresses and Slaves*, 68–69. For an interpretation of Whig women that differs from Varon's, see Isenberg, *Sex*, 19.

41. Angelica Singleton to Marion Singleton, Dec. 23, 1834, Singleton Family Papers, LC.

42. For the limits of women's organizations, see Bellows, "'My Children'"; Cashin, *Our Common Affairs*, 20–21; Fox-Genovese, *Within the Plantation*, 224–25, 231–35, 281–89; Friedman, *Enclosed Garden*, 3–53; McCurry, *Masters*, 110–11, 123–26; and M. Weiner, *Mistresses and Slaves*, 66–70, 89–112.

43. For Marion's engagement in plantation business, see, for instance, Richard Singleton to Marion Converse, July 31, 1849, and Aug. 8, 1849, Singleton Family Papers, LC. For discussions of this issue, see Clinton, *Plantation Mistress*, 29–33; and A. Scott, *Southern Lady*, 34–35.

44. *Converse v. Converse*, Sumter District, Equity Rolls, MR 227, 1854, SCDAH. Kate Stone's mother and Keziah Hopkins Brevard are examples of successful widows. See Stone, *Brokenburn;* and Brevard, *Plantation Mistress*. As the historian Suzanne Lebsock indicates in *Free Women*, 26–27, 48, 112–45, many widows who had the resources to live on their own chose not to remarry. See also see Friedman, *Enclosed Garden*, 31.

45. For separate estates and other legal mechanisms that protected married women's property rights, see Bardaglio, *Reconstructing*, 31–32; Bynum, *Unruly Women*, 64–68; Lebsock, *Free Women*, 54–86; Salmon, *Women and the Law*, 90–116, 168–72; and Salmon, "Women and Property."

46. Bardaglio, *Reconstructing*, 32; E. G. Brown, "Husband"; Chused, "Married"; Lebsock, "Radical Reconstruction"; Moncrief, "Mississippi"; Warbasse, *Changing Legal Rights*, 138–54.

47. Bardaglio, *Reconstructing*, 32; Bynum, *Unruly Women*, 64–65; Censer, *North Carolina Planters*, 115–17; Lebsock, *Free Women*, 35–48; Salmon, "Women and Property"; Wyatt-Brown, *Southern Honor*, 254–71.

48. Cashin, *Family Venture*, 109; Lebsock, "Radical Reconstruction."

49. Answer of Augustus L. Converse, from *Converse v. Converse*, Sumter District, Equity Rolls, MR 227, 1854, SCDAH.

50. Stevenson, *Life*, 78–80, 150, 151, notes that women's financial resources were often the source of marital conflict. See also Rosengarten, *Tombe*, 100–110. For the difficul-

ties women had managing property, see Clinton, *Plantation Mistress,* 33–35, 77–78; Fox-Genovese, *Within the Plantation,* 203–5; Lebsock, *Free Women,* 116–25; Stevenson, *Life,* 78–81; and Wyatt-Brown, *Southern Honor,* 256–71.

Chapter 2: The Myth of Male Independence

1. Olmsted, *Journey,* 169–70. For more on Olmsted, see Fox-Genovese, *Within the Plantation,* 98; and McCurry, *Masters,* 72–75. Such comments were common. See Flynt, *Poor,* 29–31.

2. For this point, see McCurry, *Masters.* Southern periodicals were kinder, emphasizing women's productive role. See Bynum, *Unruly Women,* 47–52, 55–56; and Hagler, "Ideal Woman."

3. Bolton, *Poor Whites,* 13 (figures). For declining economic opportunities, see Bolton, "Edward Isham"; Bolton, *Poor Whites,* 66–83; Reidy, *From Slavery,* 82–107; and Stevenson, *Life,* 25–28.

4. The migration patterns are evident in the testimony of Walker County, Ala., residents in AC, SCC, RG 217, NA.

5. Berlin, *Slaves;* Franklin, *Free Negro;* Johnson and Roark, *Black Masters,* esp. 153–94, 241–48; Stevenson, *Life,* 286–319. For economically successful free blacks, see V. Gould, ed., *Chained;* Johnson and Roark, *Black Masters;* Roark and Johnson, "Strategies"; and Schweninger, *Black Property Owners.*

6. For the class bias of elite white women, see Fox-Genovese, *Within the Plantation,* 223–25; and McCurry, *Masters,* 110–11, 121–29.

7. For differing discussions of the economic strategies of southern yeoman families, see Ash, *Middle Tennessee,* 13–22; R. Brown, "Southern Range," 1–98; Cecil-Fronsman, *Common Whites,* 9–30, 97–132; Escott, ed., *North Carolina Yeoman,* xliv–xlviii; Ford, *Origins,* 44–95; Hahn, *Roots,* 15–85; J. Harris, *Plain Folk;* McCurry, *Masters,* 37–91, 98–104; Owsley, *Plain Folk;* and Reidy, *From Slavery,* 14–30.

8. Edwards, *Gendered Strife,* 66–80; Edwards, "Problem." See also Forbath, "Ambiguities"; Stanley, *From Bondage;* and Steinfeld, *Invention.*

9. Berlin, *Slaves;* Franklin, *Free Negro;* Stevenson, *Life,* 258–85.

10. Lebsock, *Free Women,* 105–11, describes free black women's propensity to remain unmarried as a conscious choice to avoid the restraints of legal marriage. In contrast, Roark and Johnson, "Strategies," argue that free blacks valued marriage and entered into it whenever possible. Those free black women who remained unmarried did so because there were so few marriageable free black men. See also Burton, *In My Father's House,* 214–15; V. Gould, ed., *Chained,* xxii–xxvi, 3–38; Johnson and Roark, *Black Masters,* 209–10; and Stevenson, *Life,* 307–10.

11. For the precarious economic and legal position of propertyless whites, see Bolton, "Edward Isham"; Bolton, *Poor Whites;* Culclasure, "Edward Isham"; Edwards, "Problem"; Flynt, *Poor,* 3–25; and Kleit, "Stereoscopic." For women, in particular, see Bardaglio, "Rape"; Bardaglio, *Reconstructing,* 64–78, 102–6; Bynum, "Mothers"; Bynum, *Unruly Women,* 88–110; and Stevenson, *Life,* 29–30, 98–100.

12. Lebsock, *Free Women,* 103–11 (figures on 103–4); Burton, *In My Father's House,* 215. Even free black women who were married had to contribute economically to their families. See V. Gould, ed., *Chained,* xxiv–xxvi, xliv–xlviii, 3–38.

13. Lebsock, *Free Women,* 87–111 (87–88 for Eliza Gallie); Bynum, *Unruly Women,* 17, 39 (quote), 77–81, 87–110. See also A. Alexander, *Ambiguous Lives;* Bardaglio, *Reconstructing,* 104; V. Gould, ed., *Chained,* xxvi–xxxv, xxxviii–xli, 3–38; and Stevenson, *Life,* 291–319.

14. For the best statement of gender inequality in yeoman households, see McCurry, *Masters;* and McCurry, "Politics."

15. For the North, see Boydston, *Home;* Cott, *Bonds;* McMurry, *Families;* and Ryan, *Cradle.* For the South, see chapter 1.

16. For the association with decadence, see Escott, ed., *North Carolina Yeoman,* xlv–xlvi; and Stevenson, *Life,* 38, 40–41. Owsley, in his classic *Plain Folk,* played down class tensions in the South. So did Genovese, *Roll,* stressing the hegemony of the planter class. See also Genovese, *Political Economy;* Genovese, *World;* and Genovese and Fox-Genovese, *Fruits.* Oakes, *Ruling Race,* deemphasized class differences for different reasons, identifying yeomen as aspiring planters and characterizing planters in terms of individualistic, acquisitive values associated with liberal capitalism. Recent work has emphasized class differences, although giving them various meanings and levels of intensity. See Ash, *Middle Tennessee,* 39–51; Ash, *Yankees,* 3; Bolton, *Poor Whites;* R. Brown, "Southern Range"; Cecil-Fronsman, *Common Whites;* Escott, *Many Excellent People,* 3–31; Flynt, *Dixie's Forgotten People,* 1–32; Ford, *Origins;* Hahn, *Roots;* J. Harris, *Plain Folk;* Klein, *Unification;* McCurry, *Masters;* and Watson, "Conflict."

17. For the acknowledgment of women's labor, see McCurry, *Masters,* 77–78; and McCurry, "Politics." For the importance of women's labor to yeoman households, see McCurry, *Masters,* 37–91. See also Bynum, *Unruly Women,* 47–52, 55–56.

18. Friedman, *Enclosed Garden,* 21–26; Lebsock, *Free Women,* 164–94; McCurry, *Masters,* 56–61, 75–84, 101–2, 109; McCurry, "Politics"; Stevenson, *Life,* 44; M. Weiner, *Mistresses and Slaves,* 46–49. For the economic importance of women's domestic work generally, see Boydston, *Home;* Jensen, *Loosening;* and Stansell, *City.*

19. For class distinctions, see McCurry, *Masters,* 79–84. For women's field work, see Escott, ed., *North Carolina Yeoman,* xli; Friedman, *Enclosed Garden,* 22–23; Owsley, *Plain Folk,* 35; and Stevenson, *Life,* 102.

20. Quotes from Aramitta Guttery, in the file of Lucius C. Miller, #3143, and Rebecca Hisaw, in the file of William Hisaw, #10,505, both in Walker County, Ala., AC, SCC, RG 217, NA.

21. Nancy Beard, #2056, Sarah M. Boshell, #6483, and Catherine Bowen, #3352, all in Walker County, Ala., AC, SCC, RG 217, NA. For Sarah Guttery, see the file of Henry Guttery, 1st Reg., Co. L, Alabama Cavalry, RPB, RG 15, NA.

22. For these expectations in free black families, see Stevenson, *Life,* 295–96, 306–7.

23. Lebsock, *Free Women,* 185; Cooper and Terrill, *American South,* 1:284 (figures).

24. Harriet Ann (Moore Page Potter) Ames, Memoir, p. 1, LC.

25. Elizabeth Dare, Divorce Petition, 1826–27, General Assembly, Sessions Records,

NCDAH (quote); Henry Guttery, 1st Reg., Co. L, Alabama Cavalry, RPB, RG 15, NA. For women's occupations generally, see Boatwright, *Status,* 96–104; Bolton, *Poor Whites,* 15, 38–39; Escott, *Many Excellent People,* 62–63; Flynt, *Poor,* 23; Gray, "Activities," 85, 86–87; and Lebsock, *Free Women,* 97–99, 164–94.

26. Mary Guttery, in the file of Henry Guttery, 1st Reg., Co. L, Alabama Cavalry, RPB, RG 15, NA. For the general pattern, see McCurry, *Masters,* 81–84. Barton, "'Good Cooks,'" makes a similar point, although focusing on the importance of hired slaves to white women's work and status in Kentucky.

27. McMillen, *Motherhood,* 32–33 (birthrates), 195–96 (death rates among children). See also Cashin, *Our Common Affairs,* 14–15.

28. McCurry, *Masters,* 56–61.

29. Ibid., 82; Stevenson, *Life,* 102.

30. Mary Guttery, in the file of Henry Guttery, 1st Reg., Co. L, Alabama Cavalry, RPB, RG 15, NA.

31. McCurry, *Masters,* 84, 96–98, 121–23; Ownby, *Subduing,* 21–99; J. Taylor, *Eating.*

32. Escott, ed., *North Carolina Yeoman,* xiv–xx; Friedman, *Enclosed Garden,* 3–11; file of Henry Guttery, 1st Reg., Co. L, Alabama Cavalry, RPB, RG 15, NA; Kenzer, *Kinship,* 6–51; Kleit, "Stereoscopic"; McCurry, *Masters,* 121–23; Owsley, *Plain Folk.*

33. Ash, *Middle Tennessee,* 29–32; Bailey, "Caste"; Escott, ed., *North Carolina Yeoman,* xxviii–xxxii; Flynt, *Poor,* 26; Noble, *History.*

34. McCurry, *Masters,* 81–85. Little work has been done on this subject, but the process was likely similar to that described by Ulrich, *Midwife's Tale* and *Goodwives,* in the colonial Northeast.

35. Escott, ed., *North Carolina Yeoman,* xviii–xix; McCurry, *Masters,* 85. A similar approach to marriage is described in Ulrich, *Midwife's Tale,* 138–47.

36. Friedman, *Enclosed Garden,* 11–20; McCurry, *Masters,* 171–207. For religion and common whites generally, see Ash, *Middle Tennessee,* 32–38; Boles, *Great Revival;* Cecil-Fronsman, *Common Whites,* 169–202; Escott, ed., *North Carolina Yeoman,* xx–xxv; Flynt, *Dixie's Forgotten People,* 27–30; and Matthews, *Religion.*

37. Black Cree Primitive Baptist Church, Beaufort County, Church Book, 1828–1922, p. 1, SCL.

38. For church disciplinary hearings and women, see Friedman, *Enclosed Garden,* 14–18, 131–34; and McCurry, *Masters,* 181–91. For discussions of disciplinary actions for men, see Ash, *Middle Tennessee,* 35–37; Klein, *Unification,* 293–301; and Ownby, *Subduing,* 103–64.

39. Quoted in Friedman, *Enclosed Garden,* 16. For the South's oral culture, see Wyatt-Brown, *Southern Honor.* For the perceived danger of women's "gossip," see K. Brown, *Good Wives,* 140–49; Dayton, *Women,* 285–328; K. Fischer, "False"; and Kamensky, *Governing.*

40. For suggestive discussions, see McCurry, *Masters,* 89–90; and Stevenson, *Life,* 140–56. For one white yeoman who thought that women should use their moral influence publicly, see Escott, ed., *North Carolina Yeoman,* esp. xxxix–xl.

41. File of Henry Guttery, 1st Reg., Co. L, Alabama Cavalry, RPB, RG 15, NA.

42. Quoted in ibid.

43. Divorce Petitions, 1800–34, General Assembly, Sessions Records, NCDAH, support this point. So do the divorce cases that appeared before the local courts in North Carolina thereafter; see, for instance, those in Edgecombe, Granville, Haywood, and Randolph counties, NCDAH. Ash, *Yankees*, 5, makes the point that status in yeoman communities depended less on wealth or rank than on the ability to fulfill community standards of appropriate conduct. For the higher standard for planter-class women, see Wyatt-Brown, *Southern Honor*, 292–324.

44. The account of Westley Rhodes appears in Cecil-Fronsman, *Common Whites*, 133. For similar points, see Bolton, *Poor Whites*, 61–63; Cecil-Fronsman, *Common Whites*, 156–64; and Kenzer, *Kinship*, 20–22.

45. Bynum, *Unruly Women*, 73–74, 82–86; Cole, "Keeping"; Edwards, "Women." For suggestive discussion of community involvement in domestic life, see Stevenson, *Life*, 31–32, 140–56.

46. Bynum, *Unruly Women*, 74–76; Cole, "Keeping"; Edwards, "Women"; Stevenson, *Life*, 140–56. For similar patterns in domestic violence elsewhere, see Amussen, "'Being Stirred'"; del Mar, *What Trouble*, 9–46; Gordon, *Heroes;* Haag, "'Ill Use'"; McConville, "Rise"; and Stansell, *City*, 78–83

47. For this process, see Bynum, *Unruly Women*, 17, 88–89; and Stevenson, *Life*, 111–12.

48. Bynum, *Unruly Women*, 41–47, 88–110. See also Hodes, *White Women*, 19–95.

49. Biography of Edward Isham alias Hardaway Bone in the Notebook of David Schenck, David Schenck Papers, NCDAH. Isham's autobiography is published in Bolton and Culclasure, eds., *Confessions*. See the essays in that volume for more on Isham. See also Bolton, *Poor Whites*, 1–10; and Culclasure, "'I Have Killed.'" For Mary and poor white women like her, see Bynum, "Mothers."

CHAPTER 3: THE DILEMMAS OF WOMANHOOD IN SLAVERY

1. For the development of slavery, see Fields, "Ideology"; Fields, "Slavery, Race"; and Morgan, *American Slavery.* For accounts that make women central to the analysis, see Bardaglio, "'Shamefull Matches'"; K. Brown, *Good Wives;* K. Fischer, *Bodies;* and Hodes, *White Women*, 19–38. The Virginia slave code of 1705, for instance, codified and amplified a series of earlier statutes restricting the freedom of African servants and placing them in a position of perpetual servitude. See Hening, *Statutes.*

2. The most comprehensive recent study of the legal position of slaves is Morris, *Southern Slavery.* See also Bardaglio, "Rape"; Bardaglio, *Reconstructing*, 28–31; Gross, *Double Character;* Hindus, *Prison;* Schafer, *Slavery;* P. Schwartz, *Twice Condemned;* and Tushnet, *American Law.* For contemporary treatises, see T. Cobb, *Inquiry;* and O'Neall, *Negro Law.*

3. For the contradictions of defining slaves as both property and people, see Oakes, "Political Significance"; and Oakes, *Slavery.*

4. Cooper and Terrill, *American South*, 1:206–7. The association between field work and the ability to form communities runs throughout the recent literature on slavery. For an opposing view, see M. Weiner, *Mistresses and Slaves*, 118–23.

5. Examples of connections between free blacks and slaves are scattered throughout Jacobs, *Incidents*. See also Bynum, *Unruly Women*, 77–81, 87–110; and Gutman, *Black Family*, 101–84. For urban slavery, see Reidy, *From Slavery*, 73–78.

6. The classic statement on slaves' cultural accommodation to slavery is Genovese, *Roll*. For the ideological coherence and social power of daily resistance, although in a different context, see J. Scott, *Domination;* and J. Scott, *Weapons*.

7. G. Thomas, *Secret Eye*, 167. For slaveholders' power to break up slave families, see Stevenson, *Life*, 206–25.

8. G. Thomas, *Secret Eye*, 167–69, blamed "fancy girls," like Jacobs, for destroying white families. For the higher prices commanded by these beautiful, light-skinned women, see Stevenson, *Life*, 180–81.

9. Historians once accepted the conclusions of many abolitionists and northern observers at face value, measuring enslaved families by the rigid standards of the mid-twentieth century, overstating the power of slaveholders, and concluding that slavery destroyed families. See, for instance, Elkins, *Slavery;* Frazier, *Negro Family;* and Stampp, *Peculiar Institution*. These assumptions became embedded in public policy, as exemplified by the notorious Moynihan Report, which blamed African Americans' poverty on "dysfunctional" families, where women dominated men. The classic statement on the importance of marriage and nuclear families is Gutman, *Black Family*. See also Blassingame, *Slave Community;* and Malone, *Sweet Chariot*. Historians have begun to move away from this view. First, scholars pointed out the fallacy of attributing so much power to women who were so powerless. See, for instance, Farnham, "'Sapphire?'"; Lebsock, "Free Black Women"; and White, "Female Slaves." Then they began revising their view of slave families. The best summary of the new view is Stevenson, *Life*, 159–257. See also Friedman, *Enclosed Garden*, 85–87; J. Jones, *Labor*, 31–32; Schwalm, *Hard Fight*, 50, 54–55, 66–67 (although she notes on 50–51 and 52–54 the importance placed on two-parent households); and White, *Ar'n't I?* 142–51.

10. For slaves' insistence on defining marital practices in their own way, see Stevenson, *Life*, 226–57. For the emphasis on the substance of the relationship, see Frankel, *Freedom's Women*, 1, 8–14. See also Edwards, *Gendered Strife*, 54–65; and Edwards, "'Marriage Covenant.'" For expressions of these practices, see Schwalm, *Hard Fight*, 51–52; and White, *Ar'n't I?* 156–57.

11. For the importance of extended kin in childrearing, see Friedman, *Enclosed Garden*, 86; Stevenson, *Life*, 250–52; and White *Ar'n't I?* 127–28.

12. Gutman, *Black Family*, 61–86; White, *Ar'n't I?* 95–118.

13. For the prominent role of women in slave communities, see J. Jones, *Labor*, 40–41; Schwalm, *Hard Fight*, 67–71; Stevenson, *Life*, 221–23, 226–57; M. Weiner, *Mistresses and Slaves*, 19–20, 146–50; and White, *Ar'n't I?* 114–17.

14. Other slaves did so as well. See Bynum, *Unruly Women*, 38–39; and J. Jones, *Labor*, 37–38. For the attitudes of northerners, see Gutman, *Black Family*, 293–303. For white southerners, see Stevenson, *Life*, 244–45.

15. Schwalm, *Hard Fight*, 68; Stevenson, "Gender Convention"; Stevenson, *Life*, 241–

45; M. Weiner, *Mistresses and Slaves,* 103–8, 130–54. See also White, *Ar'n't I?* 151–53, 157–59, although she stresses egalitarianism.

16. The literature on slavery has generally emphasized the importance of slaves' families and communities. See, for instance, Blassingame, *Slave Community;* Genovese, *Roll,* 443–584; Gutman, *Black Family;* Joyner, *Down by the Riverside;* Levine, *Black Culture;* Rawick, *From Sundown;* Reidy, *From Slavery,* 63–65; Schwalm, *Hard Fight;* Stevenson, *Life;* M. Weiner, *Mistresses and Slaves,* esp. 130–54; and White, *Ar'n't I?*

17. Jacobs, *Incidents,* 68–69.

18. Genovese, *Roll,* 159–284; Joyner, *Down by the Riverside,* 141–71; Levine, *Black Culture,* 3–80, 136–89; Raboteau, *Slave Religion.* For women, in particular, see Friedman, *Enclosed Garden,* 65–91. For religion and the interactions between slaves and slaveholders, blacks and whites, see Boles, "Introduction"; Gallay, "Planters"; James, "Biracial Fellowship"; Klein, *Unification,* 269–302; and Touchstone, "Planters."

19. For childhood and slavery, see King, *Stolen Childhood.* In addition to note 23, below, see Fox-Genovese, *Within the Plantation,* 146–47; M. Weiner, *Mistresses and Slaves,* 8; and White, *Ar'n't I?* 92–94.

20. Jacobs, *Incidents,* 6. These sentiments are commonly expressed in the interviews in Rawick, *American Slave* (1972, 1977, and 1979).

21. See, for instance, Schwalm, *Hard Fight,* 54; and White, *Ar'n't I?* 105–18, 159–60.

22. Jacobs, *Incidents,* 86–7.

23. For the efforts that slave women made to squeeze in time for their children, to care for their needs, and to teach them how to get along in slavery, see Fox-Genovese, *Within the Plantation,* 148–49; Frankel, *Freedom's Women,* 7–8; Friedman, *Enclosed Garden,* 79–84; J. Jones, *Labor,* 35, 42; King, *Stolen Childhood;* King, "'Suffer'"; King, "Within the Professional Household"; M. Schwartz, "'At Noon'"; M. Weiner, *Mistresses and Slaves,* 21–22, 132–33, 143–46; and White, *Ar'n't I?* 122–23. For the power slaveholders had to disrupt their efforts, see Stevenson, *Life,* 249–50. As dramatized in Morrison's fictional account, *Beloved,* infanticide could be a desperate attempt to protect children from the slave system. For a historical account of the actual case that inspired Morrison's novel, see Weisenburger, *Modern Medea.*

24. For children's initiation into labor, see Fox-Genovese, *Within the Plantation,* 152–56; J. Jones, *Labor,* 23–24; Schwalm, *Hard Fight,* 29–30; Stevenson, *Life,* 187–88; M. Weiner, *Mistresses and Slaves,* 8–10; and White, *Ar'n't I?* 94–95.

25. J. Jones, *Labor,* 13–16; Pruneau, "All the Time"; Ramey, "'She Do'"; Robertson, "Africa"; Schwalm, *Hard Fight,* 19–28; Stevenson, *Life,* 187–92; Stevenson, "Slavery"; M. Weiner, *Mistresses and Slaves,* 12–13; Wood, *Women's Work,* 16–20. For the effect of heavy labor on women's health and reproduction, see Cody, "Cycles"; and Steckel, "Women."

26. For the gendered divisions of labor on plantations, see Fox-Genovese, *Within the Plantation,* 146–91; Frankel, *Freedom's Women,* 4–7; J. Jones, *Labor,* 16–18, 22–23; Joyner, *Down by the Riverside,* 41–89; Pruneau, "All the Time"; Ramey, "'She Do'"; Reidy, *From Slavery,* 71; Robertson, "Africa"; Schwalm, *Hard Fight,* 19–46; Stevenson, *Life,* 192; Stevenson, "Slavery"; M. Weiner, *Mistresses and Slaves,* 7–22; and White, *Ar'n't I?* 120–21, 129–30.

27. Ramey, "'She Do.'" See also J. Jones, *Labor,* 19–20; Stevenson, *Life,* 192; and White, *Ar'n't I?* 75–76.

28. For this interpretation, see Schwalm, *Hard Fight,* 47–72. See also Fox-Genovese, *Within the Plantation,* 177–78; Frankel, *Freedom's Women,* 1–2; Friedman, *Enclosed Garden,* 79, 84; J. Jones, *Labor,* 28, 30–31; M. Weiner, *Mistresses and Slaves,* 10–15; White, *Ar'n't I?* 122–23; and Wood, *Women's Work,* 31–52, although Wood downplays the differences in men's and women's labor. For the domestic lives of slaves generally, see Joyner, *Down by the Riverside,* 90–126.

29. Rawick, *American Slave* (1972), 14:214. For similar comments, see J. Jones, *Labor,* 42. For women's pride in their work, see Fox-Genovese, *Within the Plantation,* 176, 185–86; Stevenson, *Life,* 195; and White, *Ar'n't I?* 115–17.

30. Quoted in Friedman, *Enclosed Garden,* 82. Stevenson, *Life,* 235–37, notes that matrifocality placed responsibilities on black women to protect themselves and their children; such self-reliance was highly valued. For assertiveness in enslaved women, see Fox-Genovese, *Within the Plantation,* 186–89; J. Jones, *Labor,* 21; Stevenson, "Gender Convention"; M. Weiner, *Mistresses and Slaves,* 132–33; and White, *Ar'n't I?* 77–79.

31. For women's resistance, see Fox-Genovese, *Within the Plantation,* 112–13, 142–45, 164–65, 189–90, 205–7, 290–333; Friedman, *Enclosed Garden,* 81–83; J. Jones, *Labor,* 21–22; King, "Mistress"; Schwalm, *Hard Fight,* 37–45; Stevenson, *Life,* 192–93; White, *Ar'n't I?* 74–82; and the previous note.

32. Berlin and Morgan, "Introduction"; J. Campbell, "As 'A Kind'"; Genovese, *Roll,* 285–324, 535–40, 599–648; Joyner, *Down by the Riverside,* 52, 57–59, 127–30; McDonald, "Independent"; Penningroth, "Slavery"; Reidy, *From Slavery,* 60–63, 65–71; Saville, *Work,* 5–11; Schlotterbeck, "Internal Economy"; Schwalm, *Hard Fight,* 15, 60–63; Schweninger, *Black Property Owners,* 29–60; Stevenson, *Life,* 186; Walsh, "Work"; Wood, "'Never'"; Wood, *Women's Work.* For women's importance in market relations in the previous century, see Olwell, "'Loose.'"

33. G. Thomas, *Secret Eye,* 157, 158. See also M. Weiner, *Mistresses and Slaves,* 15–17.

34. Jacobs, *Incidents,* 12.

35. Ibid.

36. Fox-Genovese, *Within the Plantation,* 129–35; Painter, "Journal," 36–37; Stevenson, *Life,* 196–99; M. Weiner, *Mistresses and Slaves,* 126–29.

37. Chesnut, *Civil War,* 29.

38. Jacobs, *Incidents,* 28. Much has been written about enslaved and free black women's sexual vulnerability. See, for instance, Block, "Lines"; Bynum, *Unruly Women,* 109–10; Clinton, "Caught"; Clinton, "'Southern Dishonor'"; A. Davis, "Reflections"; Higginbotham, "African-American Women's History"; Hine, "Rape"; Jennings, "Us Colored Women"; J. Jones, *Labor,* 37–38; Lecaudey, "Behind"; McLaurin, *Celia;* C. Powell, "In Remembrance"; Stevenson, *Life,* 194, 239–41; M. Weiner, *Mistresses and Slaves,* 134–43; White, *Ar'n't I?* 152–53; and Wriggins, "Rape."

39. Jacobs, *Incidents,* 27.

40. Ibid., 55.

Part 2 Introduction

1. Stone, *Brokenburn*, 194–205. Chapter 4 follows the experiences of two planter-class women, Kate Stone and Gertrude Clanton Thomas. The discussion of Kate Stone is based on her published diary, *Brokenburn*. For material on Gertrude Thomas, see note 1 in the introduction to the first section.

2. Sophia Cole, #8150, Walker County, Ala., AC, SCC, RG 217, NA. This section continues to trace the experiences of poor white and yeoman women of Walker County, Alabama; for material on them, see note 3 in the introduction to the first section. The experiences of other white women of this class are included as well.

3. Stone, *Brokenburn*, 192–93, 209, 210. For similar acts by black women, see Edwards, *Gendered Strife*, 147–48; Hunter, *To 'Joy*, 4–5; and Schwalm, *Hard Fight*, 130–31. This section does not focus on the life of one enslaved woman, as the last section did. Instead, this section brings together the experiences of many different free black and enslaved women during the war.

4. Stone, *Brokenburn*, 101.

5. There is little work done on free blacks during the war; as a result, the chapter in this section on African Americans focuses primarily on the experience of slaves. For work that does address the issue, see Bynum, *Unruly Women;* Bynum, "War"; V. Gould, ed., *Chained,* xliii–xlvi; Johnson and Roark, *Black Masters,* 199–200, 200–206, 233–87, 288–310; Litwack, *Storm,* 16–17; and Mohr, *On the Threshold,* 14–19, 46–50, 70–71, 74, 237–38.

6. Potter, *Lincoln,* 208–15. Only in Texas was secession decided by popular vote. See also Barney, *Secession Impulse;* Bryant, *How Curious,* 55–70; R. Campbell, *Southern Community,* 147–97; Channing, *Crisis;* Coulter, *Confederate States,* 1–18; M. Holt, *Political Crisis,* 219–59; M. Johnson, *Toward a Patriarchal Republic;* McPherson, *Battle Cry,* 234–75; Roark, *Masters,* 1–32; and E. Thomas, *Confederate Nation,* 37–66.

7. James R. Scarbrough, Yazooo County, Miss., Report 7, Office 485, #2482, DAC, SCC, M1407, RG 233, NA. For complaints about the secession process in Walker County, see, for instance, Claiborn C. Ballinger, #3111, James M. Blackwell, #5787, and Lucius C. Miller, #3143, all in Walker County, Ala., AC, SCC, RG 217, NA.

8. Coulter, *Confederate States,* 33n1.

9. For the debate over secession in the upper South, see Ash, *Middle Tennessee,* 64–83; Coulter, *Confederate States,* 33–56; Crofts, *Reluctant Confederates;* Durrill, *War,* 19–39; M. Holt, *Political Crisis,* 219–59; Inscoe, *Mountain Masters,* 211–57; McPherson, *Battle Cry,* 276–307; Roark, *Masters,* 1–32; E. Thomas, *Confederate Nation,* 67–95; and Wright, *Secession Movement.*

10. For internal conflicts and the limits of Confederate nationalism, see Biles, *Brown,* 48–221; Coulter, *Confederate States,* 374–404; Escott, *After Secession;* Faust, *Creation;* Parks, *Brown,* 198–299; Potter, *Impending Crisis,* 462–78; Potter, *South,* 76–83; Rable, *Confederate Republic;* and E. Thomas, *Confederate Nation.*

11. Stone, *Brokenburn*, 87.

CHAPTER 4: EMBRACING THAT WHICH WOULD DESTROY THEM

1. G. Thomas, *Secret Eye,* 183, 186; Stone, *Brokenburn,* 39. The literature has traditionally emphasized white southern women's enthusiasm for and devotion to the Confederacy. See, for instance, Massey, *Bonnet Brigades;* Simkins and Patton, *Women;* Sterkx, *Partners;* E. Thomas, *Confederate Nation,* 225–29; and Wiley, *Confederate Women.* Besides Kate Stone's diary, see Edmondston, *Journal,* for another firsthand account of a particularly enthusiastic Confederate woman. Recent scholars have questioned white women's loyalty and complicated the analysis of the war. The best examples of this work for planter-class women are Cashin, *Our Common Affairs,* 22–26; Faust, "Alters"; Faust, *Mothers;* and Whites, *Civil War.*

2. G. Thomas, *Secret Eye,* 184.

3. For women's identification with their menfolk's rights and slavery at the war's outset, see Bercaw, "Politics," 25–87; Faust, *Mothers;* McCurry, *Masters,* 277–304; Rable, *Civil Wars,* 31–49; and Whites, *Civil War.*

4. G. Thomas, *Secret Eye,* 183–259.

5. Stone, *Brokenburn,* 60, 248–49 (for desertion), 125–98 (for slaves' opposition to the Confederacy).

6. G. Thomas, *Secret Eye,* 190.

7. Stone, *Brokenburn,* 38.

8. G. Thomas, *Secret Eye,* 187. For examples of white women's early support and enthusiasm for militarism and military display, see Coulter, *Confederate States,* 415–16; Simkins and Patton, *Women,* 1–13, 25–26; Sterkx, *Partners,* 17–53; and Wiley, *Confederate Women,* 140–42. Bercaw, "Politics," 36, notes that the romance of war appealed primarily to younger women.

9. G. Thomas, *Secret Eye,* 189–90. Recent work has emphasized the war's impact on planter-class women and households. See Bercaw, "Politics"; Faust, *Mothers;* Rable, *Civil Wars;* Roark, *Masters,* 35–67; and Whites, *Civil War.*

10. For women's ambivalence about sending away their male relatives, see Bercaw, "Politics," 34–38; Faust, "Altars"; Faust, *Mothers,* 9–29; and Whites, *Civil War,* 31–40.

11. Stone, *Brokenburn,* 109. For inflation and shortages, see Coulter, *Confederate States,* 219–39; Massey, *Ersatz;* Rable, *Civil Wars,* 91–111; Roark, *Masters,* 48–54; Simkins and Patton, *Women,* 129–37; and Sterkx, *Partners,* 134–35.

12. For this point, see Escott, *After Secession,* 114; Rable, *Confederate Republic,* 186; and Simkins and Patton, *Women,* 134–35. See the following two chapters for different levels of deprivation in the Confederacy.

13. G. Thomas, *Secret Eye,* 251 (the incident is also recounted in Whites, *Civil War,* 73–74); Stone, *Brokenburn,* 285. Rable, *Civil Wars,* 99–100, does note that Christmas was the one time that southerners saved to celebrate as lavishly as possible.

14. Stone, *Brokenburn,* 238, 292.

15. Ibid., 109.

16. Ibid., 240, 245–46.

17. Ibid., 225, 359. The importance of clothing is also evident in Solomon, *Civil War*

Diary. For discussions of this issue, see Faust, *Mothers,* 221–26; and Fox-Genovese, *Within the Plantation,* 212–16, 223–24. For other references to women's concern with clothes, see Sterkx, *Partners,* 135–36; and Wiley, *Confederate Women,* 168–69. For fears that poverty would diminish class differences, see Roark, *Masters,* 61.

18. G. Thomas, *Secret Eye,* 188, 191, 202, 229–30; Stone, *Brokenburn,* 47. For domestic production and women's voluntary organizations, see Bercaw, "Politics," 63–72; Bryant, *How Curious,* 78–80; Coulter, *Confederate States,* 209–10, 416–19; Faust, *Mothers,* 25–29, 45–51; Friedman, *Enclosed Garden,* 104–6; Rable, *Civil Wars,* 138–44; A. Scott, *Southern Lady,* 82–86; Simkins and Patton, *Women,* 18–24, 82–94, 138–39; Sterkx, *Partners,* 93–128, 137–41; E. Thomas, *Confederate Nation,* 225–26; M. Weiner, *Mistresses and Slaves,* 158–66; Whites, *Civil War,* 41–63; and Wiley, *Confederate Women,* 143–44, 145. As some historians point out, however, the bulk of domestic production fell to poor white women and enslaved women (see the subsequent chapters in this section).

19. For women's paid work, see Coulter, *Confederate States,* 419, 434; Faust, *Mothers,* 80–113; Friedman, *Enclosed Garden,* 105–6; Massey, *Bonnet Brigades,* esp. 3–24, 43–64, 131–52; Rable, *Civil Wars,* 121–35; Simkins and Patton, *Women,* 95–99, 116–18; E. Thomas, *Confederate Nation,* 227–28; and Wiley, *Confederate Women,* 144–45, 147. For firsthand accounts of elite white women who did such work, see Cumming, *Kate;* and Pember, *Southern Woman's Story.* For women who relished these new opportunities, see Bryant, *How Curious,* 80–81. For an excellent discussion of the limits and contradictions of planter-class women's public role, see Bercaw, "Politics," 60–87.

20. For irregular mail and the resulting sense of loneliness, see Faust, *Mothers,* 115–16.

21. Traditionally, historians emphasized elite white women's competence and willingness to take over "men's work" and other war-related work on the homefront. See, for instance, Massey, *Bonnet Brigades;* Simkins and Patton, *Women,* 111–14; Sterkx, *Partners,* 129–32; E. Thomas, *Confederate Nation,* 227–28; A. Scott, *Southern Lady,* 81–102 (although Scott points out that some women were not up to the task); and Wiley, *Confederate Women,* 148–49. Recent work that emphasizes women's competence in this area has taken a different direction, acknowledging both women's successes and failures. See Cashin, "Since the War"; Inscoe, "Civil War's Empowerment"; and Inscoe, "Coping."

22. M. Weiner, *Mistresses and Slaves,* 164; A Citizen, Aug. 12, 1864, box 22, Gov. Joseph Emerson Brown Papers, IC, GDAH; Stone, *Brokenburn,* 185. For the best recent analyses of women's difficulty with slave management and slavery, see Bercaw, "Politics," 31–60; Faust, *Mothers,* 62–70; and Faust, "'Trying.'" The issue is also discussed by Ash, *Yankees,* 199–200; R. Campbell, *Southern Community,* 221–41; Durrill, *War,* 84–85; Friedman, *Enclosed Garden,* 107; Inscoe, "Civil War's Empowerment"; Litwack, *Storm,* 11–14; Mohr, *On the Threshold,* 221–32; Roark, *Masters,* 48–49; Simkins and Patton, *Women,* 161–63; Sterkx, *Partners,* 132–34; and E. Thomas, *Confederate Nation,* 237–40.

23. G. W. Gayle, May 22, 1861, LRCSW, reel 3, M1106, RG 109, NA. For the collapse of masters' and mistresses' power over their slaves, see chapter 6.

24. For complaints, see Bercaw, "Politics," 50–53; Faust, "Altars"; and Litwack, *Storm,* 28. The point about the Confederate government's priorities is made by Faust, *Mothers,* 55–56.

25. Stone, *Brokenburn*, 125, 134.

26. These sentiments run through Kate's diary. For this issue generally, see Bercaw, "Politics," 88; Faust, *Mothers*, 74–79; M. Weiner, *Mistresses and Slaves*, 166–84. See also Ash, *Yankees*, 156–60; Litwack, *Storm*, 16–18, 149–63; and Roark, *Masters*, 83–85.

27. Stone, *Brokenburn*, 170–72. For slaveholders' racial fears, see Litwack, *Storm*, 27–30, 59–63.

28. Stone, *Brokenburn*, 197. For women's fears, see Ash, *Yankees*, 158; and Bercaw, "Politics," 51–53.

29. G. Thomas, *Secret Eye*, 236; Faust, *Mothers*, 56–62, 70–74; Roark, *Masters*, 85–94; M. Weiner, *Mistresses and Slaves*, 166–84. For an example of a slaveholding woman with particularly vivid racial fears, see Keziah Goodwyn Hopkins Brevard, Diary, SCL.

30. Fannie Page Hume, Diary, p. 61, LC.

31. Ibid., 63, 67.

32. For the disruption of elite white women's households and refugee communities, see Bercaw, "Politics," 49–50; Faust, *Mothers*, 30–52; Friedman, *Enclosed Garden*, 95–98; Massey, *Bonnet Brigades*, 291–316; Rable, *Civil Wars*, 50–72, 181–201; Simkins and Patton, *Women*, 100–110; and Wiley, *Confederate Women*, 151–52.

33. Faust, *Mothers*, 196–219. For a broader discussion based on this incident, see Ryan, *Women in Public*, 3–4, 130–71. For women's defiance of Union occupation, see Ash, *Middle Tennessee*, 42–43, 61–62; Bercaw, "Politics," 159–61; and Simkins and Patton, *Women*, 40–49.

34. G. Thomas, *Secret Eye*, 234–59. For women's dread of being alone in the midst of such uncertainties, see Bercaw, "Politics," 46–49. For women being more likely to stay, see Ash, *Yankees*, 18–20. For life in occupied areas for the well-to-do, see Simkins and Patton, *Women*, 50–69; and Sterkx, *Partners*, 168–77, 181–84.

35. G. Thomas, *Secret Eye*, 209. The best recent statement of the breakdown of Confederate women's enthusiasm is Faust, *Mothers*. Others have also noted the phenomena: Bryant, *How Curious*, 82–83; Simkins and Patton, *Women*, 206–27; Sterkx, *Partners*, 187–201; and Wiley, *Confederate Women*, 154–56.

36. Stone, *Brokenburn*, 273, 276. For attempts to get Kate's younger brother Jimmy exempted when the draft age was lowered to seventeen, see ibid., 282–83. For discussions of other women's attempts to get exemptions, see Faust, "Altars"; Faust, *Mothers*, 238–44; and Rable, *Civil Wars*, 73–90.

37. Stone, *Brokenburn*, 242. For the genuine affection between separated couples, see Wiley, *Confederate Women*, 170–72.

38. Stone, *Brokenburn*, 298.

39. [No name], Dec. 13, 1864, box 182, GP, Zebulon Vance, NCDAH. For efforts to keep white men and overseers at home, see also Bercaw, "Politics," 56; Faust, *Mothers*, 56–62; and McPherson, *Battle Cry*, 611. For planter-class women's sense of entitlement as dependents, see Bercaw, "Politics," 38–42.

40. For this point, see Bercaw, "Politics," 25–87; Faust, *Mothers*; Rable, *Civil Wars*, 202–20; and Whites, *Civil War*, 41–131.

41. For this point, see Bercaw, "Politics," esp. 161–62.

42. G. Thomas, *Secret Eye*, 209. For work emphasizing planter-class women's limits, see Faust, *Mothers;* and Rable, *Civil Wars.*

43. Stone, *Brokenburn*, 251.

44. For discussions of these issues, see Bercaw, "Politics," 42–45; and M. Weiner, *Mistresses and Slaves*, 228–33.

CHAPTER 5: FIGHTING ANY LONGER IS FIGHTING AGAINST GOD

1. [Illegible], Jan. 10, 1865, box 183, GP, Zebulon Vance, NCDAH.

2. G. Thomas, *Secret Eye*, 212. For elite women's interest in reading, see Faust, *Mothers*, 153–78.

3. This point is made by McCurry, *Masters*, esp. 277–304.

4. A. G. Hammock, June 1, 1861, LRCSW, reel 3, M1106, RG 109, NA; John R. Allen, Sept. 7, 1861, box 22, Gov. Joseph Emerson Brown Papers, IC, GDAH. For class tensions from the beginning of the Confederacy, see Durrill, *War*, 19–39, 40–67; Escott, *After Secession*, esp. 32–53, 94–98; Escott, *Many Excellent People*, 59–84; and Escott, ed., *North Carolina Yeoman*, xlviii–liv. For reluctance to serve, see Durrill, *War*, 36–38. Escott, *After Secession*, 114–16, explains the underlying issue in these letters. The Confederate government would only supply volunteers who signed up for three years; those who signed up for one year had to supply themselves. Many found the class bias inherent in these policies particularly unfair.

5. Elizabeth Sarol, May 17, 1861, LRCSW, reel 2, M1106, RG 109, NA. For examples of women's enthusiasm, see Simkins and Patton, *Women*, 17–18.

6. For other examples, see Bercaw, "Politics," 40–41; Mirandy and Margaret Cox, April 29, 1863, Adjutant General Papers, IC, box 6, GDAH; and Rable, *Civil Wars*, 71.

7. Stone, *Brokenburn*, 99; G. Thomas, *Secret Eye*, 229. For discussion of this issue, see Whites, *Civil War*, 93, 110–14, 166, 249n39.

8. Stone, *Brokenburn*, 95. McCurry, *Masters*, 126–27, notes that elite women's class biases seemed to increase during the course of the war. For class tensions in the army, see Escott, *After Secession*, 102–4.

9. For recruitment and conscription policies as well as opposition to them, see Coulter, *Confederate States*, 308–32; Escott, *After Secession*, 63–64, 70–71, 80–87, 116–21; Escott, *Many Excellent People*, 82; McPherson, *Battle Cry*, 611–13; Moore, *Conscription;* and E. Thomas, *Confederate Nation*, 152–55. Desertion rates and the armed bands of deserters that congregated in various areas of the South are also good indications of dissatisfaction with forced military service (see discussion in this chapter). McPherson, *Battle Cry*, 614–15, argues that the poor were not overrepresented in the Confederate army, but his conclusions are limited because the largest occupational category of soldiers (61.5 percent of the total) was undifferentiated by class and included planters, farmers, and farm laborers. For this point, see also Bryant, *How Curious*, 84–85.

10. G. Thomas, *Secret Eye*, 219–20. North Carolina officials also followed practices similar to Governor Brown's. See Coulter, *Confederate States*, 317–18; L. Hill, *Brown*, 48–193; and Parks, *Brown*, 198–252.

11. The Ladies of Spaulding County, June 25, 1864, and [Anonymous], no date, both in box 22, Gov. Joseph Emerson Brown Papers, IC, GDAH. For similar complaints, see Escott, *After Secession*, 121–22; and Escott, *Many Excellent People*, 74.

12. [Anonymous], no date, box 22, Gov. Joseph Emerson Brown Papers, IC, GDAH.

13. Mary C. Carnes, Mar. 21, 1863, box 26, Gov. Joseph Emerson Brown Papers, IC, GDAH.

14. For complaints and the desperate situation of many poor white women, see Bercaw, "Politics," 67–68; Bynum, *Unruly Women*, 111–29; Bynum "War"; Escott, *After Secession*, 104–5, 122–25, 128; Escott, *Many Excellent People*, 52–53, 54–55; Faust, *Creation*, 52–56; Flynt, *Poor*, 38–44; Rable, *Civil Wars*, 102–6; Schwalm, *Hard Fight*, 77–81; Sterkx, *Partners*, 142–43; Whites, *Civil War*, 64–70; and Wiley, *Confederate Women*, 176. For greater poverty in urban areas, see Ash, *Middle Tennessee*, 84–95; and E. Thomas, *Confederate Nation*, 210–2.

15. Nancy Jordan, June 12, 1864, box 178, GP, Zebulon Vance, NCDAH. For the loss of male laborers, see Escott, *After Secession*, 105–9; Escott, *Many Excellent People*, 53–54; Reidy, *From Slavery*, 114–15; and E. Thomas, *Confederate Nation*, 200–1. For women taking over heavy farm work, see Simkins and Patton, *Women*, 114–16; Sterkx, *Partners*, 142; E. Thomas, *Confederate Nation*, 226–27; and Wiley, *Confederate Women*, 147–48.

16. For Confederate policies and foraging, see Coulter, *Confederate States*, 178–82, 250–54; Escott, *After Secession*, 66–68, 72, 109–11; Escott, *Many Excellent People*, 53; Flynt, *Poor*, 39; McPherson, *Battle Cry*, 615–17; Simkins and Patton, *Women*, 114–15; Sterkx, *Partners*, 178; E. Thomas, *Confederate Nation*, 197–99, 201–2; and Wiley, *Confederate Women*, 149.

17. Ash, *Yankees*, 178–80, 202–3; Cashin, "Into the Trackless Wilderness"; Coulter, *Confederate States*, 427–28; Wiley, *Confederate Women*, 151–52.

18. John B. Sale, May 28, 1861, LRCSW, reel 3, M1106, RG 109, NA.

19. For private relief efforts, see Coulter, *Confederate States*, 424–26; Flynt, *Poor*, 40–41; Simkins and Patton, *Women*, 118–26; and Sterkx, *Partners*, 103–5.

20. Elizur Maxwell, Hannah Parker, and Sallie F. [last name illegible], Oct. 8, 1864, box 181, GP, Zebulon B. Vance, NCDAH. For the munitions factory explosions, see Rable, *Civil Wars*, 134. For women in strikes, see Coulter, *Confederate States*, 237–39; and Friedman, *Enclosed Garden*, 102–3. For southern women sewing and working in factories, see Bryant, *How Curious*, 78–79, 81; Massey, *Bonnet Brigades*, 131–52; Simkins and Patton, *Women*, 116–18; and Wiley, *Confederate Women*, 146. For Confederate relief efforts at the state and local level, see Coulter, *Confederate States*, 426–27; Escott, *After Secession*, 140–67; Escott, "'Cry'"; Escott, *Many Excellent People*, 55–58; Escott, "Poverty"; Flynt, *Poor*, 40; McPherson, *Battle Cry*, 615; Simkins and Patton, *Women*, 118–26; E. Thomas, *Confederate Nation*, 205–6; and Whites, *Civil War*, 64–95.

21. George L. Hancock, Sept. 25, 1864, box 180; Parrott Hardee, Oct. 16, 1864, box 181; and Evey S. Jackson, June 5, 1865, box 178, all in GP, Zebulon Vance, NCDAH. For similar requests, see Flynt, *Poor*, 38–39, 43.

22. Stone, *Brokenburn*, 231.

23. Ibid. For a discussion of favoritism and inconsistencies within the exemption system, see Rable, *Civil Wars*, 73–90.

24. North Carolina Soldiers of Lee's Army, Jan. 24, 1865, box 183, GP, Zebulon Vance, NCDAH. For similar letters, see Escott, *Many Excellent People*, 43–44. For increasing class divisions during the war, see Ash, *Yankees*, 170–94, 214–28; Escott, *After Secession;* Roark, *Masters*, 55–67; and E. Thomas, *Confederate Nation*, 232–35. For those among women in particular, see Bercaw, "Politics," 69–72.

25. Quoted in Catton, *Never Call*, 436. For women encouraging desertion, see Coulter, *Confederate States*, 422; Faust, "Alters"; Faust, *Mothers*, 243; and Wiley, *Confederate Women*, 176–77. For desertion generally, see Bardolph, "Inconstant Rebels"; Coulter, *Confederate States*, 463–68; Escott, *Many Excellent People*, 65; Flynt, *Poor*, 44–45; Lonn, *Desertion;* and McPherson, *Battle Cry*, 613–14.

26. For the cotton raid, see *State v. Henley and others*, 1865, CAP, Granville County, NCDAH. For the reference to the women plundering the mill, see Bynum, *Unruly Women*, 128; for the issues generally, see 112, 120–29, 145–46. See also Bercaw, "Politics," 165–66; Bryant, *How Curious*, 71; Bynum, "War"; Coulter, *Confederate States*, 422–24; Escott, *Many Excellent People*, 63, 65–67; Escott, "Moral Economy"; Faust, "Alters," 1224–27; Flynt, *Poor*, 42–43; Friedman, *Enclosed Garden*, 103; McPherson, *Battle Cry*, 617–19; Rable, *Civil Wars*, 106–11; Simkins and Patton, *Women*, 126–28; Sterkx, *Partners*, 144, 146; and E. Thomas, *Confederate Nation*, 202–5. For whites claiming land and other property, see Ash, *Yankees*, 180–81, 189–94; Bercaw, "Politics," 167; Durrill, *War*, 181–83; and Schwalm, *Hard Fight*, 132.

27. Bynum, *Unruly Women*, 128–29 (first quote on 128), 130–50; Yearns and Barrett, *North Carolina Civil War*, 220 (second quote). For common whites' expectation that their government would aid them, see Escott, *After Secession*, 137–40; and Escott, *Many Excellent People*, 55. In some cases, common whites informed on wealthier Confederates. See Ash, *Yankees*, 183–84.

28. G. Thomas, *Secret Eye*, 203–4. The incident is also recounted in Rable, *Civil Wars*, 107; and Whites, *Civil War*, 74–75.

29. The Ladies of Spaulding County, June 25, 1864, box 22, Gov. Joseph Emerson Brown Papers, IC, GDAH; Eliza Evans, Nov. 10, 1864, box 182, GP, Zebulon Vance, NCDAH. For inflation, complaints about speculators, and efforts to lower prices, see Bynum, *Unruly Women*, 111–29; Coulter, *Confederate States*, 219–39; Rable, *Confederate Republic*, 184–85; and Sterkx, *Partners*, 144–45. Bryant, *How Curious*, 71–77, and Whites, *Civil War*, 64–95, both point out that this issue was cast in terms of individual versus communal needs.

30. Robert Guttery, #3128, and Thomas A. Christian, #6089, both in Walker County, Ala., AC, SCC, RG 217, NA. For opposition in this area, see Escott, *After Secession*, 97–98. Some southern whites did express their class concerns in terms of opposition to slavery. See Escott, ed., *North Carolina Yeoman*, l–lii. That opposition did not, however, necessarily translate into support for equality for African Americans. For an example of such logic, see Hamilton, "Benjamin Sherwood Hedrick."

31. Coulter, *Confederate States*, 468–70 (quote on 469). For the Alabama regiment in particular, see Hoole, *Alabama Tories*. Flynt, *Poor*, 38, notes that the folklore about Alabama's unionists may be richer than their actual commitment to the Union; only 2,578 Alabama white men joined the Union army.

32. Statistics from Catton, *Never Call*, 403. For Alabama, see Flynt, *Poor*, 39, 45–46. For the North Carolina incident, see Durrill, *War*, 186–210; for social disorder generally see 166–85. See also Ash, *Middle Tennessee*, 108–31; Auman, "Neighbor"; Auman and Scarboro, "Heroes"; Bynum, "War"; Escott, *After Secession*, 129–34; Escott, *Many Excellent People*, 44–45, 64–65, 67–70, 73–81; Honey, "War"; Klingberg, *Southern Claims*; Sterkx, *Partners*, 178; and Tatum, *Disloyalty*.

33. For guerrilla conflict in Union-occupied areas and its effects on women, see Ash, *Yankees*, 38–75, 200–203, 203–13; Fellman, *Inside War*, esp. 193–230; Fellman, "Women"; Sterkx, *Partners*, 177–78; and E. Thomas, *Confederate Nation*, 247–50.

34. Nancy Faught, #2063, and Catherine Bowen, #3352, both in Walker County, Ala., AC, SCC, RG 217, NA.

35. Mary Guttery, in the file of Johnson Guttery, #20,130, Walker County, Ala., AC, SCC, RG 217, NA. Other women were well informed politically as well. See Bynum "Misshapen Identity"; Bynum, *Unruly Women*, 130–50; and Escott, *Many Excellent People*, 67.

36. Elizabeth Alvis, #2337, and Sarah F. Keeton, #11,636, both in Walker County, Ala., AC, SCC, RG 217, NA; Bynum, *Unruly Women*, 130–50. See also Fellman, *Inside War*, 195–98, 214–16.

37. Sarah F. Keeton, #11,636, Walker County, Ala., AC, SCC, RG 217, NA.

38. Sarah M. Boshell, #6483, Susan Madison, and Nancy Beard, #2056, all in Walker County, Ala., AC, SCC, RG 217, NA. For violence endured by women, see Bynum, *Unruly Women*, 130–50; Escott, *Many Excellent People*, 75; and Fellman, *Inside War*, 199–230.

39. Thomas B. Files, #7537, Walker County, Ala., AC, SCC, RG 217, NA.

40. For peace movements, see Coulter, *Confederate States*, 533–42; Escott, *Many Excellent People*, 45–49; L. Hill, *Brown*, 222–42; Honey, "War"; McPherson, *Battle Cry*, 692–98; Rable, *Confederate Republic*, 200–205, 245–48, 265–71; Raper, *Holden*, 4–58; and Roberts, "Peace Movement."

CHAPTER 6: FOR THE FREEDOM OF THE COLORED PEOPLE

1. Stone, *Brokenburn*, 37; Riley Tirey, in the claim of Robert Guttery, #3128, Walker County, Ala., AC, SCC, RG 217, NA. For the best recent works that discuss the importance of black women in the Civil War, see Bercaw, "Politics"; Clinton, *Tara*; Frankel, *Freedom's Women*; Schwalm, *Hard Fight*; and M. Weiner, *Mistresses and Slaves*, 157–84.

2. Schwalm, *Hard Fight*, 77; Stone, *Brokenburn*, 152.

3. For the South Carolina planters, see Schwalm, *Hard Fight*, 79.

4. Quoted in ibid., 78.

5. Stone, *Brokenburn*, 53. For a discussion of the effects of shortages on African

Americans, see Bynum, *Unruly Women,* 121–22; Litwack, *Storm,* 5–6; Mohr, *On the Threshold,* 211–15; Schwalm, *Hard Fight,* 77–81; and Wiley, *Southern Negroes,* chap 2.

6. Stone, *Brokenburn,* 146–47, 53. On 286, Kate noted that she was helping to sew the cloth the slaves had woven.

7. For the domestic labor of slave women during the war, see Frankel, *Freedom's Women,* 22–23; and Schwalm, *Hard Fight,* 78–81. Faust, *Mothers,* 45–51, notes the limits of elite white women's forays into domestic production. Fannie Page Hume's diary, LC, underscores the point.

8. Nancy Bird, Nov. 9, 1864, box 182, GP, Zebulon Vance, NCDAH.

9. G. Thomas, *Secret Eye,* 226, 242.

10. For the effect of impressment on enslaved women, see Frankel, *Freedom's Women,* 16–19; J. Jones, *Labor,* 48–49; and Schwalm, *Hard Fight,* 81–86. For impressment of slaves, see Cimprich, *Slavery's End,* 14–16; Coulter, *Confederate States,* 258–29; Escott, *After Secession,* 65–66; Litwack, *Storm,* 36–45; Mohr, *On the Threshold,* 120–28, 170–89; B. Nelson, "Confederate Slave Impressment"; Roark, *Masters,* 79–80; and E. Thomas, *Confederate Nation,* 240–41. For the Confederate government arming slaves, see Escott, *After Secession,* 239–55; Litwack, *Storm,* 42–44; and Mohr, *On the Threshold,* 272–93.

11. Stone, *Brokenburn,* 204, 207. For the work of hired slaves, see Mohr, *On the Threshold,* 128–59, 170–89. For relocation of slaves, see Durrill, *War,* 68–90, 145–65; Litwack, *Storm,* 30–36; Mohr, *On the Threshold,* 99–119; Schwalm, *Hard Fight,* 80–81, 88; and E. Thomas, *Confederate Nation,* 240.

12. Stone, *Brokenburn,* 33, 35.

13. For enslaved men's and women's covert and overt resistance and the collapse of their masters' and mistresses' authority, see Ash, *Middle Tennessee,* 106–42; Ash, *Yankees,* 153–54; Bercaw, "Politics," 95–100; Cimprich, *Slavery's End,* 19–32; Durrill, *War,* 72–74, 82–83, 85–90; Escott, *Many Excellent People,* 62–63; Frankel, *Freedom's Women,* 25–27; Glymph, "'This Species,'" 61; Hunter, *To 'Joy,* 4–20; Litwack, *Storm,* 104–17, 144–49; Mohr, *On the Threshold,* 223–32; Reidy, *From Slavery,* 116–35; Schwalm, *Hard Fight,* 75–144; and E. Thomas, *Confederate Nation,* 236–42. For the collapse of slavery, see note 38 in this chapter.

14. Stone, *Brokenburn,* 176, 183. For slaves fleeing, see Ash, *Middle Tennessee,* 112–13, 118–20; Ash, *Yankees,* 153; Bercaw, "Politics," 96–99, 101–3, 123–26; Du Bois, *Black Reconstruction,* 55–83; Escott, *Many Excellent People,* 42–43; Litwack, *Storm,* 52–59, 135–39; Mohr, *On the Threshold,* 70–75; and Saville, *Work,* 32–36. Women made up a significant part of this flight. See Frankel, *Freedom's Women,* 31–35; Glymph, "'Species'"; J. Jones, *Labor,* 49; Schwalm, *Hard Fight,* 88–97; and Wiley, *Confederate Women,* 163–64.

15. Stone, *Brokenburn,* 145.

16. The legal recognition of African Americans' freedom was a long, complicated process. See Ash, *Middle Tennessee,* 149–53; Bercaw, "Politics," 101–8; Berlin, Fields, Glymph, Reidy, and Rowland, eds., *Destruction,* 1–56; Cimprich, *Slavery's End,* 33–45, 98–117; Durrill, *War,* 119–44; Engs, *Freedom's First Generation,* 18–43; and Gerteis, *From Contraband,* 11–32. For white southerners' reactions to the Emancipation Proclamation, see Coulter, *Confederate States,* 264–65.

17. Henry Guy, 55th Reg., Co. A, USCT, RPG, RG 15, NA. For similar experiences, see Bercaw, "Politics," 88, 123; and Frankel, *Freedom's Women*, 32–33.

18. For conditions in refugee camps and urban areas, see Ash, *Middle Tennessee*, 134–38; Ash, *Yankees*, 155–56; Berlin, Glymph, Miller, Reidy, Rowland, and Saville, eds., *Wartime Genesis: Lower South;* Berlin, Miller, Reidy, and Rowland, eds., *Wartime Genesis: Upper South;* Cimprich, *Slavery's End*, 46–59; Engs, *Freedom's First Generation*, 18–45; and Frankel, *Freedom's Women*, 31–38. For firsthand accounts, see Botume, *First Days;* and S. Taylor, *Reminiscences.*

19. For the development of the army's policy, see Gerteis, *From Contraband,* 33–48. For military labor and other forms of wage work, see Ash, *Middle Tennessee*, 139–40; Berlin, Fields, Glymph, Reidy, and Rowland, eds., *Destruction;* Berlin, Glymph, Miller, Reidy, Rowland, and Saville, eds., *Wartime Genesis: Lower South;* Berlin, Miller, Reidy, and Rowland, eds., *Wartime Genesis: Upper South;* Berlin, Reidy, and Rowland, eds., *Black Military;* Cimprich, *Slavery's End,* 62–72; Roark, *Masters,* 112–20; Saville, *Work,* 36–38; and Schwalm, *Hard Fight,* 101–2. For black women's labor, see note 31 in this chapter.

20. For plantations in occupied areas during the war, see Bercaw, "Politics," 126–30; Berlin, Fields, Glymph, Reidy, and Rowland, eds., *Destruction,* 187–245; Berlin, Glymph, Miller, Reidy, Rowland, and Saville, eds., *Wartime Genesis: Lower South;* R. Davis, *Good and Faithful Labor,* 59–73; Frankel, *Freedom's Women,* 44–45; Gerteis, *From Contraband,* 49–62, 65–181; T. Holt, "Empire"; L. Powell, *New Masters;* Robinson, "'Worser'"; Rose, *Rehearsal;* and Saville, *Work,* 40–71.

21. Frankel, *Freedom's Women,* 53–54, and Schwalm, *Hard Fight,* 125, make the point about the exclusion of women from land policy. For the exclusion of African Americans from the federal government's land policies, see Berlin, Fields, Glymph, Reidy, and Rowland, eds., *Destruction;* Berlin, Glymph, Miller, Reidy, Rowland, and Saville, eds., *Wartime Genesis: Lower South;* Berlin, Miller, Reidy, and Rowland, eds., *Wartime Genesis: Upper South;* and Gerteis, *From Contraband.* For a more detailed discussion of former slaves' desire for land, see chapter 7.

22. Berlin, Reidy, and Rowland, eds., *Black Military,* 725. For the inequalities faced by black men in the military as well as the liberating nature of the experience, see ibid., 303–516. See also Bercaw, "Politics," 133–38; Cimprich, *Slavery's End,* 81–97; Cullen, "I's a Man"; Litwack, *Storm,* 64–103; and Mohr, *On the Threshold,* 75–96.

23. Berlin, Reidy, and Rowland, eds., *Black Military,* 727. For the experience of black soldiers' families, see ibid., 656–730. For black soldiers' concern for their families, see Bercaw, "Politics," 139; Glymph, "'This Species,'" 66–68, 69–70; J. Jones, *Labor,* 50; and Mohr, *On the Threshold,* 76–77. For violence against slaves, see Ash, *Middle Tennessee,* 66–67, 77–78; Ash, *Yankees,* 162–65; and Mohr, *On the Threshold,* 3–67, 215–20.

24. For white Union troop's negative perceptions and abuse of black women, see Bercaw, "Politics," 143–45; Fellman, *Inside War,* 211–14; Frankel, *Freedom's Women,* 39–40; Glymph, "'This Species,'" 64; Hunter, *To 'Joy,* 20; Litwack, *Storm,* 129; Schwalm, *Hard Fight,* 102–3, 119–21, 141–42; and Wiley, *Confederate Women,* 164–65. For slaves

generally, see Ash, *Middle Tennessee*, 106–8, 132–34; Bryant, *How Curious*, 20; and Litwack, *Storm*, 117–35.

25. For this point, see Bercaw, "Politics," 105–6, 139–40, 145–47; Frankel, *Freedom's Women*, 39–40; Glymph, "'This Species'"; and Schwalm, *Hard Fight*, 75–144.

26. For the ambivalence in federal policy about this issue, see Bercaw, "Politics," 105–6, 139–40; Frankel, *Freedom's Women*, 40–44; and Schwalm, *Hard Fight*, 239–48. For further discussion of this issue, see chapter 7.

27. Henry Guy, 55th Reg., Co. A, USCT, RPB, RG 15, NA. For further discussion of this issue, see chapter 7.

28. Henry Guy, 55th Reg., Co. A, and Taylor Reddick, 33d Reg., Co. D, both in USCT, RPB, RG 15, NA.

29. For the South Carolina commander's policy on camp followers, see Schwalm, *Hard Fight*, 142–43. For family and kin following soldiers and male military laborers, see Bercaw, "Politics," 106, 140–41; Berlin, Reidy, and Rowland, eds., *Black Military*, 656–60, 713–19; Frankel, *Freedom's Women*, 44–48; Glymph, "'This Species,'" 64–68; J. Jones, *Labor*, 50–51; and Schwalm, *Hard Fight*, 136–44.

30. Taylor Reddick, 33d Reg., Co. D, USCT, RPB, RG 15, NA; Stone, *Brokenburn*, 170–71. See also Berlin and Rowland, eds., *Families*, 21–53; Frankel, *Freedom's Women*, 31–35; and Schwalm, *Hard Fight*, 88–97.

31. For the work, pay, and survival strategies of black women refugees, see Bercaw, "Politics," 107, 141–42, 146–52; Frankel, *Freedom's Women*, 34–35, 44–55; Glymph, "'This Species,'" 61–62; and Schwalm, *Hard Fight*, 97–104.

32. Taylor Reddick, 33d Reg., Co. D, and Henry Guy, 55th Reg., Co. A, both in USCT, RPB, RG 15, NA. For women's support networks, see Schwalm, *Hard Fight*, 103–4, 120.

33. Quoted in Schwalm, *Hard Fight*, 100. See also Berlin, Glymph, Miller, Reidy, Rowland, and Saville, eds., *Wartime Genesis: Lower South*, 316–19.

34. For community building and political organizing, see Ash, *Middle Tennessee*, 138–42; Berlin, Fields, Glymph, Reidy, and Rowland, eds., *Destruction*; Berlin, Glymph, Miller, Reidy, Rowland, and Saville, eds., *Wartime Genesis: Lower South*; Berlin, Miller, Reidy, and Rowland, eds., *Wartime Genesis: Upper South*; Berlin, Reidy, and Rowland, eds., *Black Military*; Cimprich, *Slavery's End*, 72–80; Engs, *Freedom's First Generation*, 15–65, 67–79; and Schwalm, *Hard Fight*, 103–4.

35. For slaves' refusal to leave, see Bercaw, "Politics," 98–99; Berlin, Fields, Glymph, Reidy, and Rowland, eds., *Destruction*, 11, 41–42, 49, 104, 252; Durrill, *War*, 69–72; Escott, *Many Excellent People*, 42; Frankel, *Freedom's Women*, 19–25; Glymph, "'This Species,'" 63; Litwack, *Storm*, 113–14; Mohr, *On the Threshold*, 102–3; and Schwalm, *Hard Fight*, 108–14.

36. Stone, *Brokenburn*, 127, 128.

37. Ibid., 209.

38. Ibid. Other slaveowners used violence to keep their slaves from fleeing and to keep them in line if they did not. See Ash, *Middle Tennessee*, 122–28; and Litwack, *Storm*, 29–30, 113–14. For the motivations of slaves who stayed, see Berlin, Fields, Glymph, Reidy,

and Rowland, eds., *Destruction,* 154–55; Litwack, *Storm,* 185–86; and Saville, *Work,* 15. For slaves who stayed behind, declared themselves free, and lived as such, see Ash, *Middle Tennessee,* 114–18; Ash, *Yankees,* 153–54; Bercaw, "Politics," 100–101, 108–22, 126–30; Durrill, *War,* 139–44; Gerteis, *From Contraband,* 33–48, 55–58; Glymph, "'This Species,'" 63–64; J. Jones, *Labor,* 51; and Saville, *Work,* 15–16.

39. Stone, *Brokenburn,* 175, 185, 195–96. The first historian to argue for the functional collapse of slavery before the official end of the war and slaves' efforts in bringing it about is Du Bois, *Black Reconstruction,* esp. 55–127. For this point in more recent work as well as confrontations between former slaves and whites, see Ash, *Middle Tennessee,* 128–32; Ash, *Yankees,* 165–69; Berlin, Fields, Glymph, Reidy, and Rowland, eds., *Destruction;* Berlin, Glymph, Miller, Reidy, Rowland, and Saville, eds., *Wartime Genesis: Lower South;* Berlin, Miller, Reidy, and Rowland, eds., *Wartime Genesis: Upper South;* Litwack, *Storm,* 104–66; Mohr, *On the Threshold,* 235–71; Reidy, *From Slavery,* 108–35; Roark, *Masters,* 68–108; and Schwalm, *Hard Fight,* 116–44.

40. S. R. Hawly, Sept. 8, 1864, box 180, GP, Zebulon Vance, NCDAH.

41. Schwalm, *Hard Fight,* 127–32; Saville, *Work,* 34. For looting, see Litwack, *Storm,* 139–44; Saville, *Work,* 34; and Schwalm, *Hard Fight,* 122–26.

42. For slaves' claims to property, see Penningroth, "Slavery."

43. Bryant, *How Curious,* 86–89, 94–97; Litwack, *Storm,* 18–27. For an example of such attitudes, see E. Andrews, *War-Time Journal.* In Texas, emancipation did not take place until the summer of 1865.

44. Chesnut, *Civil War,* 48. Also quoted in Litwack, *Storm,* 4.

45. G. Thomas, *Secret Eye,* 267. The actions of other planters were similar. See Litwack, *Storm,* 179–93.

46. G. Thomas, *Secret Eye,* 267, 267–88. For the movement of slaves generally, see Litwack, *Storm,* 149–63, 292–335. For the reactions of planters as freed slaves finally left, see Friedman, *Enclosed Garden,* 107–8; Rable, *Civil Wars,* 253–54; M. Weiner, *Mistresses and Slaves,* 157–84; and Whites, *Civil War,* 128–31.

47. Slavery held on in the Indian territories until the 1870s.

PART 3 INTRODUCTION

1. Stone, *Brokenburn,* 335, 339.

2. G. Thomas, *Secret Eye,* 268.

3. For this argument, see Bardaglio, *Reconstructing,* esp. 115–36; Bercaw, "Politics"; Edwards, "Disappearance"; Edwards, *Gendered Strife;* Edwards, "Marriage Covenant"; Whites, *Civil War;* and Whites, "Civil War."

4. This chapter continues to follow the experiences of two planter-class women, Kate Stone and Gertrude Clanton Thomas. The discussion of Kate Stone is based on her published diary, *Brokenburn.* For material on Gertrude Thomas, see note 1 in the introduction to the first section.

5. This section continues to trace the experiences of poor white and yeoman women

of Walker County, Alabama; for material on them, see note 3 in the introduction to the first section. The experiences of other white women of this class are included as well.

6. G. Thomas, *Secret Eye*, 268–69. For a similar scene, see Litwack, *Storm*, 167–72. This section brings together the experiences of many different African American women after the war.

7. For tensions among free blacks and freed slaves, see T. Holt, *Black*. For the difficulties free blacks had adjusting to postemancipation society, see V. Gould, ed., *Chained*, xlvi–xlix, 41–91.

Chapter 7: Talking for Her Rights

1. U.S. Census, Manuscript Returns, Granville County, N.C., p. 335, M1139, NA.

2. *State v. Noblin*, 1870, CAP, Granville County, NCDAH; Edwards, "Sexual Violence."

3. Ash, *Middle Tennessee*, 210–11; Berlin, Miller, and Rowland, eds., "Afro-American Families"; Berlin and Rowland, eds., *Families;* Bryant, *How Curious*, 99–100; E. Foner, *Reconstruction*, 82–84; Frankel, *Freedom's Women*, esp. 123–45; Gutman, *Black Family*, 367–85; Hunter, *To 'Joy*, 35–37; Litwack, *Storm*, 229–47; Magdol, *Right*, 56–61; Saville, *Work*, 102–3, 105–10; Schwalm, *Hard Fight*, 151, 155–56.

4. Edwards, *Gendered Strife*, 31–45; Edwards, "Marriage Covenant"; Frankel, *Freedom's Women*, 79–122; Schwalm, *Hard Fight*, 249–50; M. Weiner, *Mistresses and Slaves*, 203.

5. Quoted in Berlin, Reidy, and Rowland, eds., *Black Military*, 672. For the classic statement on the importance of marriage to freedpeople during and after the Civil War, see Gutman, *Black Family*, 412–18, 425–30. Later work has revised this view in different ways. See Bardaglio, *Reconstructing*, 132–33; Berlin and Rowland, eds., *Families*, 155–91; Edwards, *Gendered Strife*, 45–54; Edwards, "Marriage Covenant"; Frankel, *Freedom's Women*, esp. 79–122; and Schwalm, *Hard Fight*, 239–44.

6. Jacob Moore, 14th Reg., Co. A, Heavy Artillery, USCT, RPB, RG 15, NA.

7. For the definition and operation of marital relations, see Frankel, *Freedom's Women*, 79–122. See also Bercaw, "Politics," 201, 210–15; Edwards, *Gendered Strife*, 54–65; Edwards, "Marriage Covenant"; and Schwalm, *Hard Fight*, 244–48. Gutman, *Black Family*, 418–25, is also suggestive. For examples of federal officials' confusion, see Edwards, *Gendered Strife*, 59; and Fields, *Slavery*, 156.

8. Hicks's testimony quoted in the file of Edward Lewis, alias Everett Lewis, 14th Reg., Co. A, Heavy Artillery, USCT, RPB, RG 15, NA. For men leaving to find seasonal wage work, see J. Jones, *Labor*, 92; Saville, *Work*, 135–41; and Schwalm, *Hard Fight*, 176–77, 257–60. For the continued importance of extended family ties, see Berlin and Rowland, eds., *Families*, 225–43; Burton, *In My Father's House*, 237–38, 263–64, 274–79; Edwards, *Gendered Strife*, 59–65; Fields, *Slavery*, 156; Gutman, *Black Family*, 185–229; Hunter, *To 'Joy*, 37–38; J. Jones, *Labor*, 65–66, 84–85; Magdol, *Right*, 59; and Schwalm, *Hard Fight*, 234–68. Some historians have noted that black households became more nuclear over time: R. Davis, *Good and Faithful Labor*, 169–86; and Kolchin, *First Freedom*, 56–78.

But such work generally views households in isolation and does not consider the ties that bound them to other households in the neighborhood. Bercaw, "Politics," 195–266, argues that federal policies and planters' practices forced a nuclear structure on African Americans to eliminate the extended community ties that allowed freedpeople to limit their involvement in waged labor.

9. For the importance of social networks to women, see Edwards, *Gendered Strife,* 152–53; Frankel, *Freedom's Women,* 146–54, 160–80; Hunter, *To 'Joy;* and Schwalm, *Hard Fight.* For charitable organizations and other community institutions, see Ash, *Middle Tennessee,* 201, 209–17, 219–20; Berkeley, "'Colored Ladies'"; E. B. Brown, "Womanist Consciousness"; E. Foner, *Reconstruction,* 88–102; Hunter, *To 'Joy,* 24–25, 68–73; Kolchin, *First Freedom,* 79–127; Litwack, *Storm,* 450–501; Magdol, *Right,* 35–108; Rachleff, *Black Labor,* 13–33; Reidy, *From Slavery,* 165–76; and Robinson, "Plans."

10. *New York Tribune,* Sept. 8, 1865 (first quote); Gutman, *Black Family,* 620n35 (remaining quotes). For similar comments, see S. Andrews, *South,* 178–79; and Dennett, *South,* 164–65. Many white northerners were not much more optimistic. See Berlin, Reidy, and Rowland, eds., *Black Military,* 604, 709, 713–15; and Schwalm, *Hard Fight,* 239–48.

11. G. Thomas, *Secret Eye,* 268, 271. See also Berlin, Miller, and Rowland, eds., "Afro-American Families"; Berlin and Rowland, eds., *Families,* 193–224; and Hunter, *To 'Joy,* 35–37.

12. Quoted in Bryant, *How Curious,* 130. Virtually every book on the Reconstruction era notes the extent and importance of Klan violence. For work focusing on the Klan, see Olsen, "Ku Klux Klan"; Rable, *But There Was No Peace;* and Trelease, *White Terror.* The many volumes of congressional testimony on the Ku Klux Klan provide the best firsthand accounts of vigilante violence during Reconstruction. See U.S. Congress, *Report* (KKK testimony). See also Tourgée, *Fool's Errand;* and Tourgée, *Invisible Empire.*

13. U.S. Congress, House of Representatives, *Memphis Riots;* Rosen, "'Not That Sort.'" See also Bercaw, "Politics," 181–89; Berlin and Rowland, eds., *Families,* 188–89; Clinton, "Reconstructing," 316–17; Edwards, *Gendered Strife,* 197; and Hunter, *To 'Joy,* 33–34. Hodes, in "Sexualization" and *White Women,* 125–212, argues that such acts were intended to "unman" black men and push them out of the political arena.

14. R. Alexander, *North Carolina,* 112–19; Ash, *Middle Tennessee,* 199; Berlin and Rowland, eds., *Families,* 193–224; Engs, *Freedom's First Generation,* 122–24; Escott, *Many Excellent People,* 113–14, 123–24; Evans, *Ballots,* 74–75; Fields, *Slavery,* 139–42; E. Foner, *Reconstruction,* 201–2; Frankel, *Freedom's Women,* 135–45; Gutman, *Black Family,* 402–12; Kolchin, *First Freedom,* 64–67; Reidy, *From Slavery,* 153–55; R. Scott, "Battle." For work that emphasizes planters' unwillingness to recognize black families, see Bercaw, "Politics," 235–38; Edwards, *Gendered Strife,* 45–65, 92–106; Edwards, "Marriage Covenant"; and Schwalm, *Hard Fight,* 250–54.

15. Berlin and Rowland, eds., *Families,* 212, 213.

16. Ibid., 214.

17. Pointing to the experiences of emancipated slaves and serfs elsewhere, E. Foner,

Nothing, 8–38, maintains that land, in and of itself, would not necessarily have resolved all freedpeople's problems. See also Edwards, *Gendered Strife.*

18. E. Foner, *Reconstruction,* 105 (South Carolina slaves' quote); Vlach, *Back,* ix (Virginia freedman's quote).

19. Quoted in Schwalm, *Hard Fight,* 161. For slaves' and former slaves' sense of ownership and connection to the land, see E. Foner, *Nothing, But,* 55–56, 81–84; E. Foner, *Reconstruction,* 102–10; Joyner, *Down by the Riverside,* 42–43; Litwack, *Storm,* 399–408; Magdol, *Right,* 55–56, 139–223; Reidy, *From Slavery,* 61; Saville, *Work,* 18–20; Schwalm, *Hard Fight,* 154–58; and Vlach, *Back.*

20. E. Foner, *Nothing,* 8–38; T. Holt, "Empire"; Montgomery, *Beyond Equality,* 72–89. See also Bryant, *How Curious,* 97–99; and Gerteis, *From Contraband.*

21. For the federal government's vision of free labor, see E. Foner, *Reconstruction,* 142–70; Gerteis, *From Contraband;* T. Holt, "Empire"; Litwack, *Storm,* 374–79; Montgomery, *Beyond Equality,* 45–89; and Roark, *Masters,* 112–20.

22. The record of the bureau was mixed. See Bryant, *How Curious,* 103–4, 110–11, 114–16; Cohen, *At Freedom's Edge,* 44–77; Edwards, *Gendered Strife,* 49–50, 63–64, 92–94; Engs, *Freedom's First Generation,* 99–136; Fields, *Slavery,* 156–66; T. Holt, "Empire"; Litwack, *Storm,* 379–86; Rapport, "Freedmen's Bureau"; Saville, *Work,* 25–28, 102–41; and Schwalm, *Hard Fight,* 167–73. For institutional histories, see Abbott, *Freedmen's Bureau;* Bentley, *History;* Cimprich, *Slavery's End,* 118–31; and Nieman, *To Set.* See also McFeely, *Yankee Stepfather.*

23. Bercaw, "Politics," 195–266; R. Brown, "Southern Range," 164–222; Bryant, *How Curious,* 115–16; R. Davis, *Good and Faithful Labor,* 73–88; Engs, *Freedom's First Generation,* 99–121; Fields, *Slavery,* 167–93; E. Foner, *Reconstruction,* 128–42; Litwack, *Storm,* 408–25; Reidy, *From Slavery,* 136–60; Saville, *Work,* 78–79, 110–21, 128–35; Schwalm, *Hard Fight,* 147–233.

24. For the Black Codes and state government under that phase of Reconstruction, see W. Harris, *Presidential Reconstruction;* Maddex, *Virginia Conservatives,* 35–45; and C. B. Wilson, *Black Codes.* Carter, *When the War Was Over,* points out that the political leaders who passed the Black Codes were not the most conservative or reactionary southerners and actually were trying to accommodate the end of the slavery. His point underscores the overlap between northern and southern policies that other scholars have also noted. For the Black Codes' effects on labor relations, see Ash, *Middle Tennessee,* 198–200; Bryant, *How Curious,* 102, 109–10, 116; Cohen, *At Freedom's Edge,* 23–43; E. Foner, *Nothing,* 49–52; E. Foner, *Reconstruction,* 198–216; and Litwack, *Storm,* 364–74.

25. Edwards, "Problem"; E. Foner, *Reconstruction,* 228–80, 364–79; and Woodman, *New South.* See also Tomlins, *Law;* and Stanley, "Beggars."

26. Saville, *Work,* 20 (first quote); C. B. Wilson, *Black Codes,* 49 (second quote).

27. Quoted in Saville, *Work,* 99, 72–101. See also Allen, "Struggle"; Engs, *Freedom's First Generation,* 102–4; Evans, *Ballots,* 69–70; and Magdol, *Right,* 153–73. Schwalm, *Hard Fight,* 156–61, 190–94, emphasizes women's prominence in these efforts.

28. For strikes, see Arneson, *Waterfront Workers;* Bryant, *How Curious,* 106–8, 110; E.

Foner, *Nothing*, 74–110; P. Foner, *Organized Labor*, 17–22; J. Gould, "Strike of 1887"; Hunter, *To 'Joy*, 74–97; J. Jones, *Labor*, 56–57; and Rachleff, *Black Labor*. For court cases, see Edwards, *Gendered Strife*, 92–106; and J. Jones, *Labor*, 53–55.

29. G. Thomas, *Secret Eye*, 300–301.

30. R. Davis, *Good and Faithful Labor*, 89–120; Fields, "Advent"; Flynn, *White Land*, 1–28, 67–70; T. Holt, "Empire"; Jaynes, *Branches;* Litwack, *Storm*, 387–99, 414–25, 431–49; Magdol, *Right*, 46–52; Saville, *Work*, 102–41; Strickland, "Traditional Culture." For work that discusses the centrality of women in this process, see Bercaw, "Politics," 195–266, 283–89; Frankel, *Freedom's Women*, 56–78; and Schwalm, *Hard Fight*, 161–67, 173–76, 183–86, 194–204. See also note 28 in this chapter; at issue were the same underlying issues that led to strikes.

31. Frankel, *Freedom's Women*, 62–64; Hunter, "Domination"; Hunter, *To 'Joy*, 7–65, 526–31; J. Jones, *Labor*, 127–34; Schwalm, *Hard Fight*, 177–79, 207–10; M. Weiner, *Mistresses and Slaves*, 198–99, 201–3, 209–12.

32. G. Thomas, *Secret Eye*, 272.

33. Bercaw, "Politics," 202–10; Berlin and Rowland, eds., *Families*, 190–91; Edwards, *Gendered Strife*, 92–106; Flynn, *White Land*, 60–64; Frankel, *Freedom's Women*, 70–78; Reidy, *From Slavery*, 155–56; Schwalm, *Hard Fight*, 204–7; M. Weiner, *Mistresses and Slaves*, 203–4. For concerns about sexual exploitation in particular, see J. Jones, *Labor*, 60.

34. Schwalm, *Hard Fight*, 205 (first quote); C. B. Wilson, *Black Codes*, 52 (second quote).

35. Schwalm, *Hard Fight*, 204–7 (quote on 206). See also Edwards, *Gendered Strife*, 151–52; E. Foner, *Reconstruction*, 84–87, Frankel, *Freedom's Women*, 70–78; Hunter, *To 'Joy;* J. Jones, *Labor*, 74–75, 94–95, 127–42; Litwack, *Storm*, 244–45; and M. Weiner, *Mistresses and Slaves*, 204–6.

36. For the economic importance of black women's nonwaged labor, see Bercaw, "Politics," 207–9; Edwards, *Gendered Strife*, 148–51; Frankel, *Freedom's Women*, 70–78; S. Holt, "Making Freedom"; Jaynes, *Branches*, 229–32; J. Jones, *Labor*, 58–64, 84–91; Schwalm, *Hard Fight*, 147–233; and M. Weiner, *Mistresses and Slaves*, 209.

37. For the effects of sharecropping on black women, see note 45 in this chapter. Sharecropping emerged at different times in different areas. For its development, see Ash, *Middle Tennessee*, 187–88; R. Davis, *Good and Faithful Labor;* Edwards, *Gendered Strife*, 80–92; Flynn, *White Land*, esp. 70–83; E. Foner, *Reconstruction*, 170–75, 400–409; Glymph, "Freedpeople"; Kolchin, *First Freedom*, 30–55; McKenzie, "Postbellum Tenancy"; Ransom and Sutch, *One Kind;* J. Weiner, "AHR Forum"; and Woodman, "Sequel." For the demands of different crop cultures, see Daniel, *Breaking;* and Sitterson, *Sugar Country.*

38. Bryant, *How Curious*, 147–65; Cohen, *At Freedom's Edge*, 201–311; Flynn, *White Land*, 84–149; Reidy, *From Slavery*, 215–41; Saville, *Work*, 125–30; Woodman, *New South;* Woodman, "Post–Civil War Southern Agriculture."

39. For the economic problems of sharecropping, see discussion in the next chapter.

40. *Haskins* v. Royster 70 N.C. 601 (1874). See also Edwards, *Gendered Strife*, 68–80;

Edwards, "Problem." Sometimes black workers were literally forced into peonage, see Daniel, *Shadow.*

41. Schweninger, *Black Property Owners,* 184. See also Ash, *Middle Tennessee,* 217–18; Ayers, *Promise,* 208–10; Engs, *Freedom's First Generation,* 161–82; Gilmore, "Gender"; Kenzer, *Enterprising Southerners;* and Schultz, "Dream."

42. Engs, *Freedom's First Generation,* 137–60, 183–95; Gatewood, *Aristocrats;* Gilmore, *Gender and Jim Crow;* Greenwood, *Bittersweet Legacy;* Higginbotham, *Righteous Discontent;* Kolchin, *First Freedom,* 128–50; Smith, "Ties." For the economic limits this group faced, see E. Foner, *Reconstruction,* 396–99.

43. Rawick, *American Slave* (1972), 14:220, 221. See also Bradley and Williamson, *Rural Children,* 35; Edwards, *Gendered Strife,* 150–51; and Janiewski, *Sisterhood,* 30–32. For the wage work of middle-class black women, see J. Jones, *Labor,* 142–46.

44. Berlin, Reidy, and Rowland, eds., *Black Military,* 667.

45. Ibid., 402–03, 664–65, 667 (first quote), 675, 678–80, 682, 686–87, 698–700; Hunter, *To 'Joy,* 50 (second quote). For family economy, see Berlin and Rowland, eds., *Families,* 177–87; Saville, *Work;* and Schwalm, *Hard Fight,* 147–268. Mann, "Slavery," has argued that, after emancipation, particularly with the development of sharecropping, black women came under the patriarchal power of individual male heads of household in the same way as white women. This argument, however, ignores the racial and class barriers that kept black men from exercising the social power that white men did. Other work, however, emphasizes the importance of the division of labor in black families, while still acknowledging the racial and class hierarchies that affected men as well as women. See Bercaw, "Politics," 195–266; Edwards, *Gendered Strife,* 145–83; Frankel, *Freedom's Women,* esp. 92–104, 123, 126–35; J. Jones, *Labor,* 62–64, 85–86, 79–109; M. Weiner, *Mistresses and Slaves,* 207–12; and White, *Ar'n't I?* 121–32.

46. Quoted in Drago, "Militancy," 841. See also E. B. Brown, "Negotiating"; T. Holt, *Black,* 34–35; Hunter, *To 'Joy,* 32–33, 87–88; Reidy, *From Slavery,* 192; Saville, *Work,* 167–70; and Schwalm, *Hard Fight,* 232–33. However, Bercaw, "Politics," 290–92, and Frankel, *Freedom's Women,* 174–77, note gendered differences within the political activities of black men and women.

47. Bederman, "'Civilization'"; Carby, *Reconstructing Womanhood;* Gilmore, *Gender and Jim Crow;* Hewitt, "Politicizing Domesticity"; Higginbotham, *Righteous Discontent;* Sterling, *We Are;* Tate, *Domestic Allegories.* For a more critical portrayal of the political uses of respectability, see Gaines, *Uplifting.*

48. Ayers, *Promise,* 15–16; Berkeley, "'Colored Ladies'"; E. B. Brown, "Womanist Consciousness"; Giddings, *When and Where;* Gilmore, *Gender and Jim Crow;* Rouse, "Atlanta's African-American Women's Attack"; Rouse, *Lugenia Burns Hope;* Terborg-Penn, "African-American Women's Networks." See also Collins, *Black Feminist Thought;* and hooks, *Feminist Theory.*

49. A. Alexander, "Adella Hunt Logan"; Giddings, *When and Where;* Gilmore, *Gender and Jim Crow,* esp. 147–202; Gilmore, "'Melting Time'"; Gordon, "Black"; Hine, "'We Specialize'"; Rouse, *Lugenia Burns Hope;* Salem, *To Better;* A. Scott, "Most Invisible"; A. Scott, *Natural Allies;* Shaw, "Black Club Women"; Smith, "Ties"; Terborg-Penn,

"African American Women"; Terborg-Penn, "Discontented Black Feminists"; Turner, *Women,* 261–86; White, "Cost."

50. S. Andrews, *South,* 186 (first quote); G. Thomas, *Secret Eye,* 274 (second quote); Hunter, *To 'Joy,* 2 (final quotes). For complaints among whites in North Carolina about black women dressing out of their station, see E. Foner, *Reconstruction,* 85–87; J. Jones, *Labor,* 69–70; and Litwack, *Storm,* 244–47. See also Schwalm, *Hard Fight,* 174.

51. For African Americans' assertion of their rights in daily social interactions, see Ash, *Middle Tennessee,* 221–22; Clinton, "Reconstructing"; Dailey, *Before Jim Crow;* Dailey, "Deference"; Edwards, "Captives"; Edwards, *Gendered Strife,* 154–55; Gilmore, *Gender and Jim Crow,* 99–105; Hunter, "Domination"; Hunter, *To 'Joy;* J. Jones, *Labor,* 68–72; Kelley, *Race Rebels,* 17–75; Litwack, *Storm,* 247–67, 274–91; and Schwalm, *Hard Fight,* 147–268.

52. *State v. Armstrong,* 1870, CAP, Edgecombe County, NCDAH.

53. Ibid.

54. Quoted in Saville, *Work,* 92. For African Americans' embrace of the political arena, see Ash, *Middle Tennessee,* 218–19; Bryant, "'We Have No Chance'"; Cimprich, *Slavery's End,* 110–13; Engs, *Freedom's First Generation,* 91–92; E. Foner, *Reconstruction,* 110–19, 281–91; Kolchin, *First Freedom,* 151–54; Litwack, *Storm,* 502–56; Magdol, *Right,* 40–46; and Saville, *Work,* 91–93, 143–95. The documents authored by African Americans in the various volumes of the series *Freedom,* edited by Ira Berlin et al., also suggest the importance of basic civil rights to African Americans and their eagerness to participate in institutions' governance.

55. For forced labor through the justice system, see Lichtenstein, *Twice;* and Novak, *Wheel.* For female prisoners, see Curtin, "'Human World'"; and Kerber, *No Constitutional Right,* 47–80.

56. For African Americans' use of the local courts as well as their difficulties, see Ash, *Middle Tennessee,* 220–21; Ayers, *Vengeance,* 141–222; Bryant, "'We Have No Chance'"; Edwards, "Captives"; Edwards, *Gendered Strife;* E. Foner, *Reconstruction,* 262–64; Nieman, "Political Power"; Waldrep, *Roots;* and Waldrep, "Substituting Law."

57. For black women's vulnerability after emancipation, see Bercaw, "Politics," 244–46; Clinton, "Bloody Terrain"; and Rosen, "'Not That Sort.'" For the legal bias against African American women after emancipation, see Bardaglio, *Reconstructing,* 190–91, 195–97; Edwards, *Gendered Strife,* 198–217; and Edwards, "Sexual Violence."

58. For women's challenges, see Clinton, "Bloody Terrain"; Edwards, *Gendered Strife,* 198–210; Edwards, "Sexual Violence"; Rosen, "'Not That Sort'"; and Gutman, *Black Family,* 385–99.

59. Georgia and Tennessee criminalized wife-beating before the war, but the statutes were irregularly enforced. For domestic violence in the antebellum South, see Bardaglio, *Reconstructing,* 33–34, 103–5, 157–65; Bynum, *Unruly Women,* 68–77; McCurry, *Masters,* 85–91; and Wyatt-Brown, *Southern Honor,* 281–83. For changes in the handling of domestic violence after the war, see Edwards, *Gendered Strife,* 177–83, 215; and Edwards, "Women."

60. Edwards, *Gendered Strife,* 177–83; Edwards, "Women." See also Bercaw, "Poli-

tics," 198, 240–44, 259–64; E. Foner, *Reconstruction*, 88; Frankel, *Freedom's Women;* Hunter, *To 'Joy*, 39–40; Schwalm, *Hard Fight*, 260–68; and M. Weiner, *Mistresses and Slaves*, 220–24.

61. Edwards, *Gendered Strife*, 177–83, 198–210; Edwards, "Women."

62. Although Mississippi did not pass its disfranchising constitution until 1890, it began the process in 1871, when the Democrats redeemed the state. The classic statements are Key, *Southern Politics;* and Kousser, *Shaping*. See also Anderson, *Race;* Ayers, *Promise*, 146–49, 304–9; Gilmore, *Gender and Jim Crow*, 91–146; and Maddex, *Virginia Conservatives*, 194–99.

63. The origins, timing, and meaning of segregation have been the subject of much debate. Woodward, *Strange Career*, argued that segregation was new to the late nineteenth century; other scholars, notably Rabinowitz in *Race Relations*, maintained that Jim Crow laws simply legalized social practices long in existence and were, in part, a response to African Americans' claims to new rights. Although influenced by this debate, recent work has tended to take a less polarized view of the issue. See Ayers, *Promise*, 136–46; Cell, *Highest Stage;* Hodes, *White Women;* and Welke, "When All." For the historical significance of *Plessy v. Ferguson*, see Lofgren, *Plessy Case;* and Olsen, ed., *Thin Disguise*. For the course of segregation in various states, see R. Fischer, *Segregation;* and Maddex, *Virginia Conservatives*, 188–93.

64. Wells, *Red Record;* Wells, *Southern Horrors*. For Wells, see Bederman, "'Civilization.'" For the connection between white southerners' reaction to sexual violence and racial hierarchies, see Bardaglio, *Reconstructing*, 189–201; Hall, "Mind"; and Hall, *Revolt*. For the literature on lynching, see note 33 in chapter 8. For the link between lynching and interracial sexual relations, see note 30 in chapter 9.

65. *Taylor v. Taylor*, 76 N.C. 433 (1877). See also Bardaglio, *Reconstructing*, 115–228; Edwards, *Gendered Strife*, esp. 210–54; and Grossberg, *Governing*.

66. Bardaglio, *Reconstructing*, 137–75.

67. For the continuation of black political struggles after Reconstruction and disfranchisement, see Dailey, *Before Jim Crow;* Dailey, "Deference"; Gilmore, *Gender and Jim Crow;* Higginbotham, *Righteous Discontent;* Kelley, "Not What We Seem"; and Kelley, *Race Rebels*.

Chapter 8: We Is Poor but We's Proud

1. Henry Guttery, 1st Reg., Co. L, Alabama Cavalry, RPB, RG 15, NA.

2. S. Andrews, *South*, 377.

3. T. Alexander, *Political Reconstruction*, 49–68; Ash, *Middle Tennessee*, 84–95, 143–74, 175, 190–91; Ash, *Yankees*, 76–107; Flynt, *Poor*, 46–48.

4. Doug Lacy to Susan Bullock, Mar. 9, 1866, John Bullock Papers, DU.

5. Dennett, *South*, 24 (first quote); Bailey, *Class*, 103 (remaining quotes). For the particular difficulties of poor white farmers getting back on their feet, see Ash, *Middle Tennessee*, 232–50.

6. Smith H. Powell, Jan. 27, 1873, box 234, GP, Todd R. Caldwell, NCDAH.

7. *Raleigh Gazette,* Feb. 4, 1871. For discussions of debt relief, see Escott, *Many Excellent People,* 40, 96–97, 100, 140–42; E. Foner, *Reconstruction,* 212, 326–27; Hahn, *Roots,* 193–203; and Reidy, *From Slavery,* 164–65.

8. *Oxford Torchlight,* Oct. 13, 1874. For white women's expectations, see Edwards, *Gendered Strife,* 162–66.

9. For Freedmen's Bureau's aid, see Flynt, *Poor,* 51–54. For the state level, see E. Foner, *Reconstruction,* 176–216.

10. Hamilton, ed., *Correspondence,* 2:1156 (first and second quotes), 2:860 (third quote), 2:1004 (fourth quote), 2:1048 (fifth quote). Later, the expression *white negro* was also used to describe white and black families that had intermarried and their mixed race offspring. See Bynum, "'White Negroes.'"

11. S. Andrews, *South,* 41.

12. L. J. Horner, Jan. 15, 1869, box 215, GP, William W. Holden, NCDAH. For the class bias evident in the South during Reconstruction generally, see Escott, *Many Excellent People,* 85–112; E. Foner, *Reconstruction,* 192–95; and Perman, *Reunion.*

13. S. Andrews, *South,* 387. Many white northerners saw common whites as politically ignorant and inept. See Ash, *Yankees,* 35, 171–77.

14. Dyer and Moore, comps., *Tennessee Veterans,* 1:8, 503, 595. See also Ash, *Middle Tennessee,* 39–51; and Bailey, *Class.*

15. Quoted in Fox-Genovese, *Within the Plantation,* 224. See also Bercaw, "Politics," 168; Fox-Genovese, *Within the Plantation,* 223–25; and McCurry, *Masters,* 110–11, 121–29.

16. Quoted in Dennett, *South,* 142–43.

17. Quoted in Escott, *After Secession,* 251.

18. Claiborn C. Ballinger, #3111, Walker County, Ala., AC, SCC, RG 217, NA. As Olsen notes in "An Incongruous Presence," 164, white Republicans "were likely to have been Whigs or Douglas Democrats, opponents of secession, outspoken critics of the Confederacy, leaders in the peace movement, and/or advocates of democratic reform." See also Coulter, *William G. Brownlow;* Escott, *Many Excellent People,* 136–70; E. Foner, *Reconstruction,* 297–302; Goodwyn, "Populist Dreams"; Moneyhon, *Republicanism;* Pereyra, *Alcorn;* Perman, *Road;* and Robinson, "Beyond the Realm."

19. Berlin and Rowland, eds., *Families,* 189. See also U.S. Congress, *Report* (KKK testimony); Tourgée, *Fool's Errand;* and Tourgée, *Invisible Empire.*

20. Quoted in Dennett, *South,* 146. See also Escott, *Many Excellent People,* 116–19.

21. For an interesting discussion of race relations among poor southerners, see J. Jones, "Political Economy."

22. For white Republicans' waffling on racial equality, see T. Alexander, *Political Reconstruction,* 98–112, 122–40; Coulter, *William G. Brownlow,* 289–93, 328–31; 333–40; E. Foner, *Reconstruction,* 302–3, 346–64; L. Hill, *Brown,* 266–90; McKinney, *Southern Mountain Republicans;* Parks, *Brown,* 373–474; and Perman, *Road.* For those who supported it, see Duncan, "Georgia Governor"; Nathans, *Losing;* Olsen, *Carpetbagger's Crusade;* and Rogers, *Black Belt Scalawag.* For others who first supported racial equal-

ity and then abandoned it later in the nineteenth century, see Pereyra, *Alcorn,* esp. 73–206; and Raper, *Holden.*

23. For the appeal of Republican policies to many whites, see R. Campbell, *Southern Community,* 305–35; Escott, *Many Excellent People,* 136–70; and E. Foner, *Reconstruction,* 346–79.

24. Quoted in S. Andrews, *South,* 177. For the unequal treatment of women in the antebellum period, see Bardaglio, "Rape"; Bardaglio, *Reconstructing,* 64–78; Bynum, *Unruly Women,* 117–18; and G. Johnson, *Ante-bellum,* 508–10. See also Block, "Lines."

25. *State v. Rhodes,* 61 N.C. 453 (1868). See also Bardaglio, *Reconstructing,* 198–99; Edwards, "Disappearance"; Edwards, *Gendered Strife,* 198–217; and Edwards, "Sexual Violence."

26. Petition for Clemency for William Somerville, May 5–10, 1869, box 218, GP, Holden, NCDAH.

27. Ibid.

28. Quoted in Terrill and Hirsch, eds., *Such as Us,* 124. See also Edwards, *Gendered Strife,* 54–65; Edwards, "Women"; Flynt, "Folks."

29. Edwards, *Gendered Strife,* 198–210; Edwards, "Sexual Violence."

30. *State v. William Henry Nettles,* 1873, CAP, Edgecombe County, NCDAH.

31. *State v. Oliver,* #10,815, Supreme Court Original Cases, 1800–1900; and *State v. Oliver,* 1873, CAP, Alexander County, both in NCDAH. See also Edwards, *Gendered Strife,* 177–83; and Edwards, "Women."

32. *State v. Baird,* 1872, CAP, Granville County, NCDAH. For the classic statement of white southerners' stake in the racialization of rape, see Hall, "Mind"; and Hall, *Revolt.* For the legal developments, see Bardaglio, *Reconstructing,* 189–201; and Sommerville, "Rape Myth."

33. Quoted in Simon, *Fabric,* 32. For political uses of rape and lynching in the late nineteenth century and early twentieth century, see Gilmore, *Gender and Jim Crow,* 82–99; Kantrowitz, *Ben Tillman;* Simon, "Appeal"; and Simon, *Fabric,* 11–89. For lynching in this period, see Ayers, *Vengeance,* 223–65; Bardaglio, *Reconstructing,* 214–22; Brundage, *Lynching;* and Flynt, *Poor,* 212–16. For the increasing connection between rape and lynching, see Edwards, *Gendered Strife,* 245–54; Hodes, *White Women;* and Sommerville, "Rape Myth."

34. The best statements of the effects of the rape-lynching connection for white women are Hall, "Mind"; and Hall, *Revolt.*

35. *Taylor v. Taylor,* 76 N.C. 433 (1877).

36. For the development of the patriarchal state in the South, see Bardaglio, *Reconstructing,* 115–228; and Edwards, *Gendered Strife,* esp. 210–54. For the disfranchisement of whites, see Key, *Southern Politics;* and Kousser, *Shaping.*

37. Ayers, *Promise,* 34–54; Edwards, *Gendered Strife,* 218–54; Escott, *Many Excellent People,* 171–95; Flynt, *Poor,* 244–50; E. Foner, *Reconstruction,* 564–601; Hair, *Bourbonism;* Hyman, *Anti-Redeemers;* Maddex, *Virginia Conservatives;* Reidy, *From Slavery,* 161–241; Rogers, *One-Gallused Rebellion.*

38. For antebellum economic change, see Coclanis, *Shadow;* Hahn, *Roots,* 137–289; Reidy, *From Slavery,* 14–107; and Thornton, *Politics,* esp. 163–342. For white southerners' failure to recover from wartime losses, see Flynt, *Poor,* 48–55. For southern Republicans' promotion of commercial development, see R. Campbell, *Southern Community,* 323–28; E. Foner, *Reconstruction,* 303–5, 379–409; Perman, *Road;* Summers, *Railroads;* and Trelease, *North Carolina Railroad.*

39. For the resistance of many white southerners to capitalist economic change, see Durrill, *War,* 184–85; Ford, "Rednecks"; Goodwyn, *Democratic Promise;* Hahn, *Roots,* 137–289; and McMath, "Sandy Land."

40. S. Andrews, *South,* 177.

41. Ibid., 222. Such observations were common among white northerners, who often reserved their harshest comments for common white women. For more on this point, see Ash, *Yankees,* 35, 171–77; Davidson, "Post-Bellum Poor-White"; Edwards, *Gendered Strife,* 12; Fellman, *Inside War,* 216–18; and Flynt, "Folks," 225. R. Campbell, *Southern Community,* 21–22, notes that even prosperous southern farms did not look neat and tidy.

42. For Democratic promotion of commercial agriculture, business, and industry, see Durrill, "Producing"; Escott, *Many Excellent People,* 171–219, 241–62; E. Foner, *Reconstruction,* 209–14; Hair, *Bourbonism;* Hyman, *Anti-Redeemers;* Maddex, *Virginia Conservatives,* 143–83; Perman, *Road,* 244–50; and Reidy, *From Slavery,* 215–41. For Republican leaders who became Democrats, see L. Hill, *Brown,* 291–327; and Parks, *Brown,* 475–506.

43. Flynt, *White Land,* 84–183, argues that all the restrictions meant to coerce blacks into working for white landowners ultimately extended to whites as well, although they remained slightly above blacks on the rural economic ladder. For the commercialization of southern agriculture and its negative effects on rural southerners, see Ayers, *Promise,* 187–213; Daniel, *Breaking;* Escott, *Many Excellent People,* 174–79, 220–21; Flynt, *Poor,* 59–91, 162–70, 173–89; E. Foner, *Reconstruction,* 392–409; Goodwyn, *Democratic Promise;* Hahn, *Roots,* 137–289; and Reidy, *From Slavery,* 215–41. Others have argued that the lack of commercialization lay at the root of rural poverty. See, for instance, Fite, *Cotton Fields.* Most historians, however, agree that the rural South stagnated economically. See, for instance, Ash, *Middle Tennessee,* 185–89; McKenzie, "Postbellum Tenancy"; and Ransom and Sutch, *One Kind.*

44. E. Foner, *Reconstruction,* 394.

45. For the growth of consumer culture in the South, see Ayers, *Promise,* 81–103. For expectation of women and children working, see Flynt, *Poor,* 191–92, 202–4.

46. Quoted in Hagood, *Mothers,* 89, 91. See also Ayers, *Promise,* 204–6; Edwards, *Gendered Strife,* 148–51; and Janiewski, *Sisterhood,* 30–31.

47. The *Progressive Farmer,* the newspaper of the North Carolina Farmers' Alliance, provides an excellent illustration of this trend. It can also be seen in local newspapers. See also Edwards, *Gendered Strife,* 121–29; Escott, *Many Excellent People,* 173–74; and Fite, *Cotton Fields,* 3–29. Hahn's account in *Roots,* 137–289, is also full of such farmers.

48. Edwards, *Gendered Strife,* 129–44.

49. Williams, *Homeplace*. For changes in southern architecture that emphasized privacy and separate work areas, see Bishir, *North Carolina Architecture*.

50. North Carolina Bureau of Labor Statistics, *First Annual Report*, 108. The bureau's annual reports (1887–1900) are filled with similar comments. This same bias was evident in the *Progressive Farmer*.

51. Quoted in J. Jones, "Political Economy," 201. For the hardening of class distinctions around the difference between landowners and tenants, see Ayers, *Promise*, 206–8; and Flynt, *Dixie's Forgotten People*, 38–46.

52. Quoted in Hagood, *Mothers*, 90, 89, 100. For the general point, see Edwards, *Gendered Strife*, 156–57; Hagood, *Mothers*, 77–107; and Janiewski, *Sisterhood*, 31–33. For rural white southerners' pride and resistance to the condescension of wealthier whites, see Ash, *Middle Tennessee*, 237–38; Flynt, *Dixie's Forgotten People*, 15–32; and Flynt, *Poor*, 76–91.

53. For women's role in the movement, see Jeffrey, "Women." For the literature on the Farmers' Alliance and Populism, see the following two notes.

54. The classic statement of the Farmers' Alliance's "movement culture" that drew thousands of white southerners into its fold and motivated them to action is Goodwyn, *Democratic Promise*. See also Ayers, *Promise*, 214–82; Escott, *Many Excellent People*, 241–53; Flynt, *Dixie's Forgotten People*, 52–54; Flynt, *Poor*, 250–56; Ford, "Rednecks"; Hahn, *Roots*, 204–89; McMath, "Sandy Land"; Rogers, *One-Gallused Rebellion*; Woodward, *Origins*; and Woodward, *Tom Watson*. Much of the work on the Farmers' Alliance and Populism in the South has emphasized the potential of forming a biracial alliance and then decried the movement's fragmentation along racial lines. This literature assumes that tenants were simply poorer versions of landowners and that the problems of both groups were the same. For existing racial and class tensions within the structure of the Farmers' Alliance and Populism, see McMath, "Southern White Farmers."

55. The classic statement of the failure of biracial coalitions centered on Populism and the racial demagoguery that emerged is Woodward, *Tom Watson*. See also Anderson, *Race*; Ayers, *Promise*, 283–309; Edmonds, *Negro*; Escott, *Many Excellent People*, 253–62; Flynt, *Dixie's Forgotten People*, 54–56; Gilmore, *Gender and Jim Crow*, 91–146; and Woodward, *Origins*.

56. For the Wilmington race riot, see Cecelski and Tyson, eds., *Democracy Betrayed*; and Prather, *We Have Taken*.

57. The classic statement of this argument is Du Bois, *Black Reconstruction*. See also Edwards, "Captives"; and Roediger, *Wages*.

58. For work on urbanization and the growth of southern industry, see the discussion in the following chapter. For industrial laborers in the New South and labor unrest, see Carlton, *Mill*; Eller, *Miners*; Escott, *Many Excellent People*, 220–40; Flynt, *Dixie's Forgotten People*, 46–51; Flynt, *Poor*, 92–162, 256–77; and Simon, *Fabric*. For work that includes or focuses on women's participation in these events, see Frederickson, "I Know"; Hall, "O. Delight Smith"; Hall et al., *Like a Family*; Hewitt, "In Pursuit"; Hewitt, "Politicizing Domesticity"; Hewitt, "Voice"; and Janiewski, *Sisterhood*.

59. For the deep attachment to and the loss of rural culture, see Daniel, *Breaking;* and Kirby, *Rural Worlds.*

60. In addition to the following two notes, see Flynt, *Poor,* 195–98, 204–5, for this point.

61. Terrill and Hirsch, eds., *Such as Us,* 124. For white women's lack of economic opportunities in rural areas and their urban migration in the South, see Ayers, *Promise,* 69, 77, 204. This also held true for black women. See Goldin, "Female Labor"; Hunter, *To 'Joy;* and J. Jones, *Labor,* 73–74. This pattern was repeated elsewhere in the country at different times. See Dublin, *Women;* Faue, *Community;* Meyerowitz, *Women;* and Stansell, *City.*

62. The story of the strike is from Hall, "Disorderly Women." These changes were also disturbing to many working-class men. See MacLean, *Behind the Mask;* MacLean, "Leo Frank"; Simon, "Appeal"; and Simon, *Fabric,* 11–35.

CHAPTER 9: THIS IS NEW AND DISAGREEABLE WORK TO US ALL

1. G. Thomas, *Secret Eye,* 265; Stone, *Brokenburn,* 335. Gertrude's reaction was common. See Litwack, *Storm,* 149–63; and Rable, *Civil Wars,* 253–54.

2. Stone, *Brokenburn,* 378.

3. The point about wealthy whites' dependence on black labor is made by Litwack, *Storm,* 358–63; and Roark, *Masters,* 120–55.

4. G. Thomas, *Secret Eye,* 259, 272, 349. For her continuing trials with housework, see ibid., 260–446. See also Censer, "Changing World"; Friedman, *Enclosed Garden,* 108–9; Litwack, *Storm,* 354–58; Rable, *Civil Wars,* 254–56; M. Weiner, *Mistresses and Slaves,* 196–203; and Whites, *Civil War,* 129–30, 145–48.

5. Stone, *Brokenburn,* 373. This point also runs throughout Fox-Genovese, *Within the Plantation.*

6. Hunter, *To 'Joy,* 11; King, "Mistress," 85.

7. G. Thomas, *Secret Eye,* 367. For her expectations and conflicts with domestic laborers, see ibid., 260–446. For the literature on domestic service, see note 12 of this chapter.

8. G. Thomas, *Secret Eye,* 370. For the image of Mammy, see White, *Ar'n't I?* 46–61.

9. In "The Present Becomes the Past," Oakes argues that elite whites' reminiscences of devoted black slaves actually projected their current desires for mastery backward in time.

10. Lucy [last name unknown] to Susan Bullock, June 11, 1867, John Bullock Papers, DU.

11. G. Thomas, *Secret Eye,* 284. For Gertrude's reserve in talking about domestics, see Burr, "Woman," 226. For planters' difficulties in dealing with changes in their relations with former slaves, see Litwack, *Storm,* 205–12, 292–96, 301–4.

12. The best analysis of relations between white women and black domestics in the late nineteenth century is Hunter, *To 'Joy.* For firsthand accounts, see S. Tucker, *Telling Memories.* See also Edwards, *Gendered Strife,* 117–18; Hunter, "Domination"; J. Jones,

Labor, 127–34; King, "Mistress"; Litwack, *Storm,* 346–51; Painter, "Journal," 51–55; Rable, *Civil Wars,* 250–64; M. Weiner, *Mistresses and Slaves,* 198–99, 201–3; 209–12, 224–28; and Whites, *Civil War,* 128–31.

13. G. Thomas, *Secret Eye,* 265.

14. Ibid., 276–77.

15. Stone, *Brokenburn,* 369.

16. G. Thomas, *Secret Eye,* 275–76.

17. Stone, *Brokenburn,* 368, 369. For planters' difficulties in adapting to the new system, see also Ash, *Middle Tennessee,* 193–95; Cimprich, *Slavery's End,* 118–31; Litwack, *Storm,* 193–99, 336–46; and Roark, *Masters,* 120–55.

18. Stone, *Brokenburn,* 369, 371, 375.

19. Burr, "Woman," 222–28.

20. Ibid.

21. G. Thomas, *Secret Eye,* 310. For the Thomases' relationship after the war, see ibid., 151–57. For the postwar transformation of elite white men's and women's gender roles in general, see S. Nelson, "Livestock"; M. Weiner, *Mistresses and Slaves,* 212–20; and Whites, *Civil War,* 132–59. For the confusion attached to these changes in the immediate postemancipation period, see Bercaw, "Politics," 153–94.

22. G. Thomas, *Secret Eye,* 407, 419. See also Bercaw, "Politics," 175–76; Burr, "Woman," 227; and G. Thomas, *Secret Eye,* 14–15, 265, 377–94.

23. G. Thomas, *Secret Eye,* 443. See also Edwards, *Gendered Strife,* 116–17. R. Campbell, *Southern Community,* 385–95, makes the point that the planter class in one Texas community lost wealth in absolute terms, but compared with others in the county, they did quite well and recouped their losses quickly.

24. G. Thomas, *Secret Eye,* 443. Roark, *Masters,* 134, explains, "The small knot of planters who refused to recognize the new order were enraged by the majority who had." The classic statement of planters leaving the land and a new generation embracing a different economic regime is Woodward, *Origins.* For the resulting historiographical debate about persistence of the planter elite, see note 25 in this chapter. Other scholars, however, have emphasized the roots of economic change in the antebellum period. See note 38 in chapter 8. See also Ayers, *Promise,* 24–28, 200–204; Escott, *Many Excellent People,* 196–219; E. Foner, *Reconstruction,* 399–404; and Roark, *Masters,* 131–209. For urbanization and industrialization, see Ash, *Middle Tennessee,* 182–84; Ayers, *Promise,* 20–22, 55–80, 104–31; Carlton, *Mill;* Chesson, *Richmond;* J. Cobb, *Industrialization;* and Gaston, *New South Creed.*

25. Quoted in Burr, "Woman," 225. Woodward's thesis of the New South's transformation in *Origins* produced a lively debate about persistence and change in the postwar ruling elite. Reflecting the terms of Woodward's thesis, scholars initially balanced individuals' retention of wealth and status against larger economic and social changes. See Ash, *Middle Tennessee,* 227–32; Billings, *Planters;* R. Campbell, *Southern Community,* 385–95; G. O'Brien, *Legal Fraternity;* and J. Weiner, *Social Origins.* More recent work has moved from individuals to structural changes in the economy and ideological changes in the construction of social status, allowing for a combination of persis-

tence and change. While certain individuals, ideas, and social practices carried over, they coexisted with larger social changes. See Ayers, *Promise;* Coclanis, *Shadow;* Edwards, *Gendered Strife,* 121–29; Escott, *Many Excellent People,* 171–267; Gilmore, *Gender and Jim Crow,* esp. 31–146; and J. Weiner, "AHR Forum."

26. Sophronia Horner to James H. Horner, Aug. 18, 1861, James H. Horner Papers, DU.

27. Chesnut, *Civil War,* 29. For the literature on elite whites and interracial mixing, see chapter 1, note 27.

28. G. Thomas, *Secret Eye,* 323. For such attitudes, see Bynum, *Unruly Women;* Fox-Genovese, *Within the Plantation,* 192–241; and McCurry, *Masters,* 121–28. For similar attitudes in the North, see Stansell, *City.*

29. G. Thomas, *Secret Eye,* 254; Painter, "Journal," 34–42. See also Painter, "Of *Lily.*"

30. Bardaglio, *Reconstructing,* 176 (quotes); Dennett, *South,* 31. Some recent historians have argued that whites' fears of racial blurring were new to the postwar South. See Hodes, "Sexualization"; Hodes, *White Women;* Sommerville, "Rape Myth"; and Sommerville, "Rape, Race, and Castration." For work that emphasizes changes between the antebellum and postbellum eras without casting the argument in such dichotomous terms, see Bardaglio, *Reconstructing,* 48–78, 176–89; Bardaglio, "'Shamefull Matches'"; Bercaw, "Politics," 189–93; Bynum, "Misshapen Identity"; Bynum, "'White Negroes'"; Gross, "Litigating"; S. Nelson, "Livestock"; and Painter, "'Social Equality.'" The classic statement of the development of racial categories is Jordan, *White.* See also K. Brown, *Good Wives;* and K. Fischer, *Bodies.*

31. Bailey, "Free Speech"; Bailey, "Textbooks"; Foster, *Ghosts;* Parrott, "Love"; Whites, *Civil War,* 160–224. While other scholars of the "Lost Cause" have not emphasized gender, it is often implicit in their analyses. See Ayers, *Promise,* 334–38; Connelly and Bellows, *God;* Osterweis, *Myth;* and C. R. Wilson, *Baptized.* For a fascinating study of the cultural reconstruction of the elite's postwar status that brings together issues of racial status, class standing, and antebellum mythologizing, see Leathem, "Carnival." These efforts dovetailed with the Democratic party's rhetoric and strategies to reclaim political power. See Dailey, *Before Jim Crow;* Edwards, *Gendered Strife;* Gilmore, *Gender and Jim Crow;* Kantrowitz, *Ben Tillman;* and Simon, "Appeal."

32. For this literature, see Edwards, *Gendered Strife,* 107–44; and Grubb, "House." For elite women's embrace of these domestic standards, see Censer, "Changing World."

33. Edwards, *Gendered Strife,* 120–21, 129–44. See also M. Weiner, *Mistresses and Slaves,* 228–33; and Whites, *Civil War,* esp. 132–59.

34. Elliott, *Mrs. Elliott's Housewife,* v, vi. For the public ramifications, see Edwards, *Gendered Strife,* 107–33, 218–54.

35. Dean, "Learning"; McCandless, "Progressivism"; A. Scott, *Southern Lady,* 110–14.

36. The classic statements of this argument are A. Scott, "'New Woman'"; and A. Scott, *Southern Lady,* 106–231, although she attributes the changes to a collapse in the southern patriarchy during and after the war. More recent work has emphasized middle-class and elite white women's new roles without positing such a sharp break with the past. See Ayers, *Promise,* 77–79, 320–22; Berkeley, "'Ladies'"; Friedman, *Enclosed*

Garden, 110–20; Hewitt, "Politicizing Domesticity"; Leloudis, "School Reform"; Mc-Dowell, *Social Gospel;* Sims, "'Sword'"; M. Thomas, *New Woman;* Turner, *Women;* Turner, "Women"; and Wedell, *Elite Women.* For similar changes in the North, see Cott, *Bonds;* Epstein, *Politics;* and Ryan, *Cradle.*

37. Quoted in McGenee, "Woman's Place," 638. See also Ayers, *Promise,* 316–20; Berkeley, "Elizabeth Avery Meriwether"; Friedman, *Enclosed Garden,* 120–22; A. Scott, *Southern Lady,* 165–84; A. Taylor, *Short History;* M. Thomas, "Ideology"; M. Thomas, *New Woman,;* Turner, *Women,* 261–86; Wheeler, *New Women;* and Wheeler, *VOTES FOR WOMEN!* For antisuffrage women, see Green, *Southern Strategies.*

38. Burr, "Woman," 230–31; Massey, "Making"; Painter, "Journal," 16–19.

39. For racial tensions, see Friedman, *Enclosed Garden,* 122–27; Hewitt, "In Pursuit"; Terborg-Penn, "African American Women"; Terborg-Penn, "Discontented Black Feminists"; Wheeler, *New Women;* Whites, *Civil War,* 132–98; and Whites, "Rebecca Latimer Felton." For evidence of interracial cooperation, even if fraught with tensions, see Frederickson, "'Each One'"; Gilmore, *Gender and Jim Crow,* 177–202; Gilmore, "'Melting Time'"; Hall, *Revolt;* Lebsock, "Woman Suffrage"; Roydhouse, "Bridging Chasms"; and White, "Cost." For different views of cross-class alliances, see Turner, *Women,* 287–94; and Whites, "Charitable."

40. Burr, "Woman"; Painter, "Journal."

Epilogue

1. Walter Clark, "The Legal Status of Women in North Carolina: Past, Present, and Prospective," New Bern, North Carolina, May 8, 1913, NCC.

BIBLIOGRAPHY

Abbott, Martin. *The Freedmen's Bureau in South Carolina, 1865–1872.* Chapel Hill: University of North Carolina Press, 1967.

Alexander, Adele Logan. "Adella Hunt Logan and the Tuskegee Women's Clubs: Building a Foundation for Suffrage." In *Stepping out of the Shadows: Alabama Women, 1819–1990,* edited by Mary Martha Thomas, 96–113. Tuscaloosa: University of Alabama Press, 1995.

———. *Ambiguous Lives: Free Women of Color in Rural Georgia, 1789–1879.* Fayetteville: University of Arkansas Press, 1991.

Alexander, Roberta Sue. *North Carolina Faces the Freedmen: Race Relations during Presidential Reconstruction, 1865–67.* Durham, N.C.: Duke University Press, 1985.

Alexander, Thomas B. *Political Reconstruction in Tennessee.* Nashville, Tenn.: Vanderbilt University Press, 1950.

Allen, James S. "The Struggle for Land during the Reconstruction Period." *Science and Society* 1 (Spring 1937): 378–401.

Amussen, Susan Dwyer. "'Being Stirred to Much Unquietness': Violence and Domestic Violence in Early Modern England." *Journal of Women's History* 6 (Summer 1994): 70–89.

Anderson, Eric. *Race and Politics in North Carolina, 1872–1901.* Baton Rouge: Louisiana State University Press, 1981.

Andrews, Eliza Frances. *The War-Time Journal of a Georgia Girl, 1864–1865.* Lincoln: University of Nebraska Press, 1997.

Andrews, Sidney. *The South since the War: As Shown by Fourteen Weeks of Travel and Observation in Georgia and the Carolinas.* Boston: Ticknor and Fields, 1866.

Arneson, Eric. *Waterfront Workers of New Orleans: Race, Class, and Politics, 1863–1923.* New York: Oxford University Press, 1991.

Ash, Stephen V. *Middle Tennessee Society Transformed, 1860–1870: War and Peace in the Upper South.* Baton Rouge: Louisiana State University Press, 1987.

———. *When the Yankees Came: Conflict and Chaos in the Occupied South, 1861–65.* Chapel Hill: University of North Carolina Press, 1995.

Auman, William T. "Neighbor against Neighbor: The Inner Civil War in the Randolph County Area of Confederate North Carolina." *North Carolina Historical Review* 61 (January 1984): 60–90.

Auman, William T., and David D. Scarboro. "The Heroes of America in Civil War North Carolina." *North Carolina Historical Review* 58 (October 1981): 327–63.

Ayers, Edward L. *The Promise of the New South: Life after Reconstruction.* New York: Oxford University Press, 1992.

———. *Vengeance and Justice: Crime and Punishment in the Nineteenth-Century American South.* New York: Oxford University Press, 1984.

Bailey, Fred Arthur. "Caste and Classroom in Antebellum Tennessee." *Maryland Historian* 13 (Spring/Summer 1982): 39–54.

———. *Class and Tennessee's Confederate Generation.* Chapel Hill: University of North Carolina Press, 1986.

———. "Free Speech and the Lost Cause in the Old Dominion." *Virginia Magazine of History and Biography* 103 (April 1995): 237–66.

———. "The Textbooks of the 'Lost Cause': Censorship and the Creation of Southern State Histories." *Georgia Historical Quarterly* 75 (Fall 1991): 507–33.

Bardaglio, Peter. "'An Outrage upon Nature': Incest and the Law in the Nineteenth-Century South." In *In Joy and in Sorrow: Women, Family, and Marriage in the Victorian South, 1830–1900,* edited by Carol Bleser, 32–51. New York: Oxford University Press, 1991.

———. "Rape and the Law in the Old South: 'Calculated to Excite Indignation in Every Heart.'" *Journal of Southern History* 60 (November 1994): 749–72.

———. *Reconstructing the Household: Families, Sex, and the Law in the Nineteenth-Century South.* Chapel Hill: University of North Carolina Press, 1995.

———. "'Shamefull Matches': The Regulation of Interracial Sex and Marriage in the South before 1900." In *Sex, Love, Race: Crossing Boundaries in North American History,* edited by Martha Hodes, 112–38. New York: New York University Press, 1999.

Bardolph, Richard. "Inconstant Rebels: Desertion of North Carolina Troops in the Civil War." *North Carolina Historical Review* 41 (April 1964): 163–89.

Barney, William L., *The Secession Impulse: Alabama and Mississippi in 1860.* Princeton, N.J.: Princeton University Press, 1963.

Barton, Keith C. "'Good Cooks and Washers': Slave Hiring, Domestic Labor, and the Market in Bourbon County, Kentucky." *Journal of American History* 84 (September 1997): 436–60.

Bederman, Gail. "'Civilization,' the Decline of Middle-Class Manliness, and Ida B. Wells's Antilynching Campaign (1892–94)." *Radical History Review* 52 (1992): 6–30.

Bellows, Barbara L. "'My Children, Gentlemen, Are My Own': Poor Women, the Urban Elite, and the Bonds of Obligation in Antebellum Charleston." In *The Web of*

Southern Social Relations: Women, Family, and Education, edited by Walter J. Fraser Jr., R. Frank Saunders Jr., and Jon L. Wakelyn, 52–71. Athens: University of Georgia Press, 1985.

Bentley, George R. *A History of the Freedmen's Bureau.* Philadelphia: University of Pennsylvania Press, 1955.

Bercaw, Nancy Dunlap. "Politics of Household during the Transition from Slavery to Freedom in the Yazoo-Mississippi Delta, 1861–1876." Ph.D. diss., University of Pennsylvania, 1996.

Berkeley, Kathleen. "'Colored Ladies Also Contributed': Black Women Activities from Benevolence to Social Welfare, 1866–1896." In *The Web of Southern Social Relations: Women, Family, and Education,* edited by Walter J. Fraser Jr., R. Frank Saunders Jr., and Jon L. Wakelyn, 181–203. Athens: University of Georgia Press, 1985.

———. "Elizabeth Avery Meriwether, 'An Advocate for Her Sex': Feminism and Conservatism in the Post–Civil War South." *Tennessee Historical Quarterly* 43 (Winter 1984): 390–406.

———. "'The Ladies Want to Bring about Reform in the Public Schools': Public Education and Women's Rights in the Post–Civil War South." *History of Educational Quarterly* 24 (Spring 1984): 45–58.

Berlin, Ira. *Slaves without Masters: The Free Negro in the Antebellum South.* New York: Pantheon Books, 1974.

Berlin, Ira, and Philip D. Morgan. "Introduction." In *Slaves' Economy: Independent Production by Slaves in the Americas,* edited by Ira Berlin and Philip D. Morgan, 1–27. London: Frank Cass, 1991.

Berlin, Ira, Barbara J. Fields, Thavolia Glymph, Joseph P. Reidy, and Leslie S. Rowland, eds. *The Destruction of Slavery.* Series 1, vol. 1 of *Freedom: A Documentary History of Emancipation, 1861–1867.* New York: Cambridge University Press, 1985.

Berlin, Ira, Thavolia Glymph, Steven F. Miller, Joseph P. Reidy, Leslie S. Rowland, and Julie Saville, eds. *The Wartime Genesis of Free Labor: The Lower South.* Series 1, vol. 3 of *Freedom: A Documentary History of Emancipation, 1861–1867.* New York: Cambridge University Press, 1991.

Berlin, Ira, Steven F. Miller, Joseph P. Reidy, and Leslie S. Rowland, eds. *The Wartime Genesis of Free Labor: The Upper South.* Series 1, vol. 2 of *Freedom: A Documentary History of Emancipation, 1861–1867.* New York: Cambridge University Press, 1993.

Berlin, Ira, Stephen F. Miller, Leslie S. Rowland, eds. "Afro-American Families in the Transition from Slavery to Freedom." *Radical History Review* 42 (1988): 89–121.

Berlin, Ira, Joseph P. Reidy, and Leslie S. Rowland, eds. *The Black Military Experience.* Series 2 of *Freedom: A Documentary History of Emancipation, 1861–1867.* New York: Cambridge University Press, 1982.

Berlin, Ira, and Leslie Rowland, eds. *Families and Freedom: A Documentary History of African-American Kinship in the Civil War Era.* New York: New Press, 1997.

Billings, Dwight B., Jr. *Planters and the Making of a "New South": Class, Politics, and Development in North Carolina, 1865–1900.* Chapel Hill: University of North Carolina Press, 1979.

Bishir, Catherine W. *North Carolina Architecture.* Chapel Hill: University of North Carolina Press for the Historic Preservation Foundation of North Carolina, 1990.

Blassingame, John. *The Slave Community: Plantation Life in the Antebellum South.* New York: Oxford University Press, 1972.

Block, Sharon. "Lines of Color, Sex, and Service: Comparative Sexual Coercion in Early America." In *Sex, Love, Race: Crossing Boundaries in North American History,* edited by Martha Hodes, 141–63. New York: New York University Press, 1999.

Boatwright, Eleanor Miot. *Status of Women in Georgia, 1783–1860.* New York: Carlson, 1994.

Boles, John B. *The Great Revival, 1787–1805: The Origins of the Southern Evangelical Mind.* Lexington: University Press of Kentucky, 1972.

———. "Introduction." In *Masters and Slaves in the House of the Lord: Race and Religion in the American South, 1740–1870,* edited by John B. Boles, 1–18. Lexington: University Press of Kentucky, 1988.

Bolton, Charles C. "Edward Isham and Poor White Labor in the Old South." In *The Confessions of Edward Isham: A Poor White Life of the Old South,* edited by Charles C. Bolton and Scott P. Culclasure, 19–31. Athens: University of Georgia Press, 1998.

———. *Poor Whites of the Antebellum South: Tenants and Laborers in Central North Carolina and Northeast Mississippi.* Durham, N.C.: Duke University Press, 1994.

Bolton, Charles C., and Scott P. Culclasure, eds. *The Confessions of Edward Isham: A Poor White Life of the Old South.* Athens: University of Georgia Press, 1998.

Botume, Elizabeth Hyde. *First Days amongst the Contrabands.* Boston: Lee and Shepard, 1893; reprint, New York: Arno, 1968.

Boydston, Jeanne. *Home and Work: Housework, Wages, and the Ideology of Labor in the Early Republic.* New York: Oxford University Press, 1990.

Bradley, Frances Sage, and Margetta A. Williamson. *Rural Children in Selected Counties of North Carolina.* Washington, D.C.: U.S. Children's Bureau, 1918; reprint, New York: Negro Universities Press, 1969.

Brevard, Keziah Goodwyn Hopkins. *A Plantation Mistress on the Eve of the Civil War: The Diary of Keziah Goodwyn Hopkins Brevard, 1860–61.* Edited by John Hammond Moore. Columbia: University of South Carolina Press, 1993.

Brown, Elizabeth G. "Husband and Wife—Memorandum on the Mississippi Woman's Law of 1839." *Michigan Law Review* 42 (April 1944): 110–21.

Brown, Elsa Barkely. "Negotiating and Transforming the Public Sphere: African American Political Life in the Transition from Slavery to Freedom." *Public Culture* 7 (Fall 1994): 107–26.

———. "Womanist Consciousness: Maggie Lena Walker and the Independent Order of Saint Luke." *Signs* 14 (Spring 1989): 610–33.

Brown, Kathleen M. *Good Wives, "Nasty Wenches," and Anxious Patriarchs: Gender, Race, and Power in Colonial Virginia.* Chapel Hill: University of North Carolina Press, 1996.

Brown, R. Ben. "The Southern Range: A Study in Nineteenth Century Law and Society." Ph.D. diss., University of Michigan, 1993.

Brundage, W. Fitzhugh. *Lynching in the New South: Georgia and Virginia, 1880–1930.* Urbana: University of Illinois Press, 1993.

Bryant, Jonathan M. *How Curious a Land: Conflict and Change in Greene County, Georgia, 1850–1885.* Chapel Hill: University of North Carolina Press, 1996.

———. "'We Have No Chance of Justice before the Courts': The Freedmen's Struggle for Power in Greene County, Georgia, 1865–1874." In *Georgia in Black and White: Explorations in the Race Relations of a Southern State, 1865–1950,* edited by John C. Inscoe, 13–37. Athens: University of Georgia Press, 1994.

Burr, Virginia Ingraham. "A Woman Made to Suffer and Be Strong: Ella Gertrude Clanton Thomas, 1834–1907." In *In Joy and in Sorrow: Women, Family, and Marriage in the Victorian South, 1830–1900,* edited by Carol Bleser, 215–32. New York: Oxford University Press, 1991.

Burton, Orville Vernon. *In My Father's House Are Many Mansions: Family and Community in Edgefield, South Carolina.* Chapel Hill: University of North Carolina Press, 1985.

Bynum, Victoria. "Misshapen Identity: Memory, Folklore, and the Legend of Rachel Knight." In *Discovering the Women in Slavery: Emancipating Perspectives on the American Past,* edited by Patricia Morton, 29–46. Athens: University of Georgia Press, 1996.

———. "Mothers, Lovers, and Wives: Images of Poor White Women in Edward Isham's Autobiography." In *The Confessions of Edward Isham: A Poor White Life of the Old South,* edited by Charles C. Bolton and Scott P. Culclasure, 85–100. Athens: University of Georgia Press, 1998.

———. "Reshaping the Bonds of Womanhood: Divorce in Reconstruction North Carolina." In *Divided Houses: Gender and the Civil War,* edited by Catherine Clinton and Nina Silber, 320–33. New York: Oxford University Press, 1992.

———. *Unruly Women: The Politics of Social and Sexual Control in the Old South.* Chapel Hill: University of North Carolina Press, 1992.

———. "'War within a War': Women's Participation in the Revolt of the North Carolina Piedmont, 1863–1865." *Frontiers* 9, no. 3 (1987): 43–49.

———. "'White Negroes' in Segregated Mississippi: Miscegenation, Racial Identity, and the Law." *Journal of Southern History* 64 (May 1998): 247–76.

Campbell, John. "As 'A Kind of Freeman'? Slaves' Market-Related Activities in the South Carolina Upcountry, 1800–1860." In *Slaves' Economy: Independent Production by Slaves in the Americas,* edited by Ira Berlin and Philip D. Morgan, 131–69. London: Frank Cass, 1991.

Campbell, Randolph B. *A Southern Community in Crisis: Harrison County, Texas, 1850–1880.* Austin: Texas State Historical Association, 1983.

Carby, Hazel. *Reconstructing Womanhood: The Emergence of the Afro-American Woman Novelist.* New York: Oxford University Press, 1987.

Carlton, David. *Mill and Town in South Carolina, 1880–1920.* Baton Rouge: Louisiana State University Press, 1982.

Carter, Dan T. *When the War Was Over: The Failure of Self-Reconstruction in the South, 1865–1867.* Baton Rouge: Louisiana State University Press, 1985.

Cashin, Joan E. "'Decidedly Opposed to *the Union*': Women's Culture, Marriage, and Politics in Antebellum South Carolina." *Georgia Historical Quarterly* 77 (Winter 1994): 735–59.

————. *A Family Venture: Men and Women on the Southern Frontier.* New York: Oxford University Press, 1991.

————. "Into the Trackless Wilderness: The Refugee Experience in the Civil War." In *A Woman's War: Southern Women, Civil War, and the Confederate Legacy,* edited by Edward D. C. Campbell Jr. and Kym S. Rice, 29–53. Charlottesville: University Press of Virginia for the Museum of the Confederacy, 1996.

————. *Our Common Affairs: Texts from Women in the Old South.* Baltimore: Johns Hopkins University Press, 1996.

————. "'Since the War Broke Out': The Marriage of Kate and William McLure." In *Divided Houses: Gender and the Civil War,* edited by Catherine Clinton and Nina Silber, 200–212. New York: Oxford University Press, 1992.

————. "The Structure of Antebellum Families: 'The Ties That Bound Us Was Strong.'" *Journal of Southern History* 56 (February 1990): 55–70.

Catton, Bruce. *Never Call Retreat.* New York: Doubleday, 1965.

Cecelski, David S., and Timothy B. Tyson, eds. *Democracy Betrayed: The Wilmington Race Riot of 1898 and Its Legacy.* Chapel Hill: University of North Carolina Press, 1998.

Cecil-Fronsman, Bill. *Common Whites: Class and Culture in Antebellum North Carolina.* Lexington: University Press of Kentucky, 1992.

Cell, John W. *The Highest Stage of White Supremacy: The Origins of Segregation in South Africa and the American South.* Cambridge: Cambridge University Press, 1982.

Censer, Jane Turner. "A Changing World of Work: North Carolina Elite Women, 1865–1895." *North Carolina Historical Review* 73 (January 1996): 28–55.

————. *North Carolina Planters and Their Children, 1800–1860.* Baton Rouge: Louisiana State University Press, 1984.

————. "'Smiling through Her Tears': Ante-Bellum Southern Women and Divorce." *American Journal of Legal History* 25 (January 1982): 114–34.

Channing, Steven A. *Crisis of Fear: Secession in South Carolina.* New York: Simon and Schuster, 1970.

Chesnut, Mary. *Mary Chesnut's Civil War.* Edited by C. Vann Woodward. New Haven, Conn.: Yale University Press, 1981.

Chesson, Michael B. *Richmond after the War, 1865–1890.* Richmond: Virginia State Library, 1981.

Chused, Richard H. "Married Women's Property Law: 1800–1850." *Georgetown Law Journal* 71 (June 1983): 1359–1425.

Cimprich, John. *Slavery's End in Tennessee.* University: University of Alabama Press, 1986.

Clinton, Catherine. "Bloody Terrain: Freedwomen, Sexuality, and Violence during Reconstruction." *Georgia Historical Quarterly* 76 (Summer 1992): 310–32.

————. "Caught in the Web of the Big House: Women and Slavery." In *The Web of Southern Social Relations: Women, Family, and Education,* edited by Walter J. Fraser

Jr., R. Frank Saunders Jr., and Jon L. Wakelyn, 19–34. Athens: University of Georgia Press, 1985.

———. *The Plantation Mistress: Woman's World in the Old South.* New York: Pantheon Books, 1982.

———. "Reconstructing Freedwomen." In *Divided Houses: Gender and the Civil War,* edited by Catherine Clinton and Nina Silber, 306–19. New York: Oxford University Press, 1992.

———. "'Southern Dishonor': Flesh, Blood, Race, and Bondage." In *In Joy and in Sorrow: Women, Family, and Marriage in the Victorian South, 1830–1900,* edited by Carol Bleser, 52–68. New York: Oxford University Press, 1991.

———. *Tara Revisited: Women, War, and the Plantation Legend.* New York: Abbeville, 1995.

Cobb, James C. *Industrialization and Southern Society, 1877–1984.* Lexington: University Press of Kentucky, 1984.

Cobb, Thomas R. R. *An Inquiry into the Law of Negro Slavery in the United States of America.* Philadelphia: T. & J. W. Johnson; Savannah: W. T. Williams, 1858.

Coclanis, Peter A. *The Shadow of a Dream: Economic Life and Death in the South Carolina Low Country, 1670–1920.* New York: Oxford University Press, 1989.

Cody, Cheryll Ann. "Cycles of Work and of Childbearing: Seasonality in Women's lives on Low Country Plantations." In *More than Chattel: Black Women and Slavery in the Americas,* edited by David Barry Gaspar and Darlene Clark Hine, 61–78. Bloomington: Indiana University Press, 1996.

Cohen, William. *At Freedom's Edge: Black Mobility and the Southern White Quest for Racial Control, 1861–1915.* Baton Rouge: Louisiana State University Press, 1991.

Cole, Stephanie. "Keeping the Peace: Domestic Assault and Private Prosecution in Antebellum Baltimore." In *Over the Threshold: Intimate Violence in Early America,* edited by Christine Daniels and Michael V. Kennedy, 148–69. New York: Routledge, 1999.

Collins, Patricia Hill. *Black Feminist Thought: Knowledge, Consciousness, and the Politics of Empowerment.* Boston: Unwin Hyman, 1990.

Connelly, Thomas L., and Barbara L. Bellows. *God and General Longstreet: The Lost Cause and the Southern Mind.* Baton Rouge: Louisiana State University Press, 1982.

Cooper, William J., Jr., and Thomas E. Terrill. *The American South: A History.* 2 vols. New York: McGraw-Hill, 1991.

Cott, Nancy. *The Bonds of Womanhood: "Woman's Sphere" in New England, 1790–1835.* New Haven, Conn.: Yale University Press, 1978.

Coulter, E. Merton. *The Confederate States of America, 1861–65.* Baton Rouge: Louisiana State University Press, 1950.

———. *William G. Brownlow, Fighting Parson of the Southern Highlands.* Chapel Hill: University of North Carolina Press, 1937.

Crofts, Daniel W. *Reluctant Confederates: Upper South Unionists in the Secession Crisis.* Chapel Hill: University of North Carolina Press, 1989.

Culclasure, Scott P. "Edward Isham and Criminal Justice for the Poor White in Antebellum North Carolina." In *The Confessions of Edward Isham: A Poor White Life of the Old South,* edited by Charles C. Bolton and Scott P. Culclasure, 71–84. Athens: University of Georgia Press, 1998.

————. "'I Have Killed a Damned Dog': Murder by a Poor White in the Antebellum South." *North Carolina Historical Review* 70 (January 1993): 13–39.

Cullen, Jim. "'I's a Man Now': Gender and African American Men." In *Divided Houses: Gender and the Civil War,* edited by Catherine Clinton and Nina Silber, 76–91. New York: Oxford University Press, 1992.

Cumming, Kate. *Kate: The Journal of a Confederate Nurse.* Edited by Richard Barksdale Harwell. Baton Rouge: Louisiana State University Press, 1959.

Curtin, Mary Ellen. "The 'Human World' of Black Women in Alabama Prisons, 1879–1900." In *Hidden Histories of Women in the New South,* edited by Virginia Bernhard, Betty Brandon, Elizabeth Fox-Genovese, and Theda Perdue, 11–30. Columbia: University of Missouri Press, 1994.

Dailey, Jane. *Before Jim Crow: The Politics of Race in Post-Emancipation Virginia.* Chapel Hill: University of North Carolina Press, forthcoming.

————. "Deference and Violence in the Postbellum Urban South: Manners and Massacres in Danville, Virginia." *Journal of Southern History* 63 (August 1997): 553–90.

Daniel, Pete. *Breaking the Land: The Transformation of Cotton, Tobacco, and Rice Cultures since 1880.* Urbana: University of Illinois Press, 1985.

————. *The Shadow of Slavery: Peonage in the South, 1901–1969.* Lexington: University Press of Kentucky, 1978.

Davidson, James. "The Post-Bellum Poor-White as Seen by J. W. DeForest." *Southern Folklore Quarterly* 24 (June 1960): 102–7.

Davis, Angela. "Reflections on the Black Woman's Role in the Community of Slaves." *Black Scholar* 3 (December 1981): 3–15.

Davis, Ronald L. F. *Good and Faithful Labor: From Slavery to Sharecropping in the Natchez District, 1860–1890.* Westport, Conn.: Greenwood, 1982.

Dayton, Cornelia Hughes. *Women before the Bar: Gender, Law, and Society in Connecticut, 1639–1789.* Chapel Hill: University of North Carolina Press, 1995

Dean, Pamela. "Learning to Be New Women: Campus Culture at the North Carolina Normal and Industrial College." *North Carolina Historical Review* 67 (July 1991): 286–306.

del Mar, David Peterson. *What Trouble I Have Seen: A History of Violence against Wives.* Cambridge, Mass.: Harvard University Press, 1996.

Dennett, John Richard. *The South as It Is, 1865–1866.* New York: Viking, 1965; reprint, Athens: University of Georgia Press, 1986.

Domínguez, Virginia R. *White by Definition: Social Classification in Creole Louisiana.* New Brunswick, N.J.: Rutgers University Press, 1986.

Doyle, Christopher Leonard. "Lord, Master, and Patriot: St. George Tucker and Patriarchy in Republican Virginia, 1772–1851." Ph.D. diss., University of Connecticut, 1996.

Drago, Edmund. "Militancy and Black Women in Reconstruction Georgia." *Journal of American Culture* 1 (Winter 1978): 838–44.

Dublin, Thomas. *Women at Work: The Transformation of Work and Community in Lowell, Massachusetts, 1826–1860.* New York: Columbia University Press, 1979.

Du Bois, W. E. B. *Black Reconstruction: An Essay toward a History of the Part Which Black Folk Played in the Attempt to Reconstruct Democracy in America, 1860–1880.* New York: Russell and Russell, 1935.

Duncan, Russell. "A Georgia Governor Battles Racism: Rufus Bullock and the Fight for Black Legislators." In *Georgia in Black and White: Explorations in the Race Relations of a Southern State, 1865–1950,* edited by John C. Inscoe, 38–64. Athens: University of Georgia Press, 1994.

Durrill, Wayne K. "Producing Poverty: Local Government and Economic Development in a New South County, 1874–1884." *Journal of American History* 71 (March 1985): 764–81.

———. *War of Another Kind: A Southern Community in the Great Rebellion.* New York: Oxford University Press, 1990.

Dyer, Gustavus W., and John Trotwood Moore, comps. *The Tennessee Civil War Veterans Questionnaires.* 5 vols. Easley, S.C.: Southern Historical Press, 1985.

Edmonds, Helen G. *The Negro and Fusion Politics in North Carolina, 1894–1901.* Chapel Hill: University of North Carolina Press, 1951.

Edmondston, Catherine Ann Devereux. *Journal of a Secesh Lady: The Diary of Catherine Ann Devereux Edmondston, 1860–1866.* Edited by Beth G. Crabtree and James W. Patton. Raleigh, N.C.: Division of Archives and History, 1979.

Edwards, Laura F. "Captives of Wilmington: The Riot and Historical Memories of Political Conflict, 1865–1898." In *Democracy Betrayed: The Wilmington Race Riot of 1898 and Its Legacy,* edited by Timothy B. Tyson and David S. Cecelski, 113–41. Chapel Hill: University of North Carolina Press, 1998.

———. "The Disappearance of Susan Daniel and Henderson Cooper: Gender and Narratives of Political Conflict in the Reconstruction-Era U.S. South." *Feminist Studies* 22 (Summer 1996): 113–41.

———. *Gendered Strife and Confusion: The Political Culture of Reconstruction.* Urbana: University of Illinois Press, 1997.

———. "'The Marriage Covenant Is at the Foundation of All Our Rights': The Legal and Political Implications of Marriage in Postemancipation North Carolina." *Law and History Review* 14 (Spring 1996): 81–124

———. "The Problem of Dependency: African Americans, Labor Relations, and the Law in the Nineteenth-Century South." *Agricultural History* 72 (Spring 1998): 313–40.

———. "Sexual Violence, Gender, Reconstruction, and the Extension of Patriarchy in Granville County, North Carolina." *North Carolina Historical Review* 68 (July 1991): 237–60.

———. "Women and Domestic Violence in Nineteenth-Century North Carolina." In *Lethal Imagination: Violence and Brutality in American History,* edited by Michael Bellesiles, 115–36. New York: New York University Press, 1998.

Elkins, Stanley M. *Slavery: A Problem in American Institutional and Intellectual Life.* Chicago: University of Chicago Press, 1959.

Eller, Ronald D. *Miners, Millhands, and Mountaineers: Industrialization of the Appalachian South, 1880–1930.* Knoxville: University of Tennessee Press, 1982.

Elliott, Sarah. *Mrs. Elliott's Housewife, Containing Practical Receipts on Cookery.* Raleigh: Uzzell and Wiley, 1881.

Engs, Robert F. *Freedom's First Generation: Black Hampton, Virginia, 1861–1890.* Philadelphia: University of Pennsylvania Press, 1979.

Epstein, Barbara L. *The Politics of Domesticity: Women, Evangelism, and Temperance in Nineteenth-Century America.* Middletown, Conn.: Wesleyan University Press, 1981.

Escott, Paul D. *After Secession: Jefferson Davis and the Failure of Confederate Nationalism.* Baton Rouge: Louisiana State University Press, 1978.

———. "'The Cry of the Sufferers': The Problem of Welfare in the Confederacy." *Civil War History* 23 (September 1977): 228–40.

———. *Many Excellent People: Power and Privilege in North Carolina, 1850–1900.* Chapel Hill: University of North Carolina Press, 1985.

———. "The Moral Economy of the Crowd in Confederate North Carolina." *Maryland Historian* 13 (Spring/Summer 1982): 1–18.

———. "Poverty and Governmental Aid for the Poor in Confederate North Carolina." *North Carolina Historical Review* 61 (October 1984): 462–80.

———, ed. *North Carolina Yeoman: The Diary of Basil Armstrong Thomasson, 1853–1862.* Athens: University of Georgia Press, 1996.

Evans, William McKee. *Ballots and Fence Rails: Reconstruction on the Lower Cape Fear.* Chapel Hill: University of North Carolina Press, 1966.

Farnham, Christie. *The Education of the Southern Belle: Higher Education and Student Socialization in the Antebellum South.* New York: New York University Press, 1994.

———. "'Sapphire?': The Issue of Dominance in the Slave Family, 1830–1865." In *"To Toil the Livelong Day": America's Women at Work, 1780–1980,* edited by Carol Groneman and Mary Beth Norton, 68–83. Ithaca, N.Y.: Cornell University Press, 1987.

Faue, Elizabeth. *Community of Suffering and Struggle: Women, Men, and the Labor Movement in Minneapolis, 1915–1945.* Chapel Hill: University of North Carolina Press, 1991.

Faust, Drew Gilpin. "Altars of Sacrifice: Confederate Women and Narratives of War." *Journal of American History* 76 (March 1990): 1200–1228.

———. *The Creation of Confederate Nationalism: Ideology and Identity in the Civil War South.* Baton Rouge: Louisiana State University Press, 1988.

———. *Mothers of Invention: Women of the Slaveholding South in the American Civil War.* Chapel Hill: University of North Carolina Press, 1996.

———. "'Trying to Do a Man's Business': Slavery, Violence, and Gender in the American Civil War." *Gender and History* 4 (Summer 1992): 197–214.

Fellman, Michael. *Inside War: The Guerrilla Conflict in Missouri during the American Civil War.* New York: Oxford University Press, 1989.

———. "Women and Guerilla Warfare." In *Divided Houses: Gender and the Civil War,* edited by Catherine Clinton and Nina Silber, 147–65. New York: Oxford University Press, 1992.

Fields, Barbara J. "The Advent of Capitalist Agriculture: The New South in a Bourgeois World." In *Essays on the Postbellum Southern Economy,* edited by Thavolia Glymph and John J. Kushma, 73–94. College Station: Texas A&M Press for the University of Texas at Arlington, 1985.

———. "Ideology and Race in American History." In *Region, Race, and Reconstruction: Essays in Honor of C. Vann Woodward,* edited by J. Morgan Kousser and James McPherson, 143–77. New York: Oxford University Press, 1982.

———. *Slavery and Freedom on the Middle Ground: Maryland during the Nineteenth Century.* New Haven, Conn.: Yale University Press, 1985.

———. "Slavery, Race and Ideology in the United States of America." *New Left Review,* no. 181 (May–June 1990): 95–118.

Fischer, Kirsten. *Bodies of Evidence: The Racial Politics of Illicit Sex in Colonial North Carolina.* Ithaca, N.Y.: Cornell University Press, forthcoming.

———. "'False, Feigned, and Scandalous Words': Sexual Slander and Racial Ideology among Whites in Colonial North Carolina." In *The Devil's Lane: Sex and Race in the Early South,* edited by Catherine Clinton and Michele Gillespie, 139–53. New York: Oxford University Press, 1997.

Fischer, Roger A. *The Segregation Struggle in Louisiana, 1862–77.* Urbana: University of Illinois Press, 1974.

Fite, Gilbert C. *Cotton Fields No More: Southern Agriculture, 1865–1980.* Lexington: University Press of Kentucky, 1984.

Flynn, Charles L., Jr. *White Land, Black Labor: Caste and Class in Late Nineteenth-Century Georgia.* Baton Rouge: Louisiana State University Press, 1970.

Flynt, J. Wayne. *Dixie's Forgotten People: The South's Poor Whites.* Bloomington: Indiana University Press, 1979.

———. "Folks like Us: The Southern Poor White Family, 1865–1935." In *The Web of Southern Social Relations: Women, Family, and Education,* edited by Walter J. Fraser Jr., R. Frank Saunders Jr., and Jon L. Wakelyn, 225–44. Athens: University of Georgia Press, 1985.

———. *Poor but Proud: Alabama's Poor Whites.* Tuscaloosa: University of Alabama Press, 1989.

Foner, Eric. *Nothing but Freedom: Emancipation and Its Legacy.* Baton Rouge: Louisiana State University Press, 1983.

———. *Reconstruction: America's Unfinished Revolution.* New York: Harper and Row, 1988.

Foner, Philip S. *Organized Labor and the Black Worker, 1619–1973.* New York: International Publishers, 1974.

Forbath, William E. "The Ambiguities of Free Labor: Labor and the Law in the Gilded Age." *Wisconsin Law Review* 4 (July 1985): 767–817.

Ford, Lacy K., Jr. *Origins of Southern Radicalism: The South Carolina Upcountry, 1800–1860.* New York: Oxford University Press, 1988.

———. "Rednecks and Merchants: Economic Development and Social Tensions in the South Carolina Upcountry, 1865–1900." *Journal of American History* 71 (September 1984): 294–318.

Foster, Gaines M. *Ghosts of the Confederacy: Defeat, the Lost Cause, and the Emergence of the New South, 1865–1913.* New York: Oxford University Press, 1987.

Fox-Genovese, Elizabeth. "Family and Female Identity in the Antebellum South: Sarah Gayle and Her Family." In *In Joy and in Sorrow: Women, Family, and Marriage in the Victorian South, 1830–1900,* edited by Carol Bleser, 15–31. New York: Oxford University Press, 1991.

———. *Within the Plantation Household: Women in the Old South.* Chapel Hill: University of North Carolina Press, 1988.

Frankel, Noralee. *Freedom's Women: Black Women and Families in Civil War Era Mississippi.* Bloomington: Indiana University Press, 1999.

Franklin, John Hope. *The Free Negro in North Carolina, 1790–1860.* Chapel Hill: University of North Carolina Press, 1943; reprint, New York: Russell and Russell, 1969.

Frazier, E. Franklin. *The Negro Family in the United States.* Chicago: University of Chicago Press, 1939.

Frederickson, Mary. "'Each One Is Dependent on the Other': Southern Churchwomen, Racial Reform, and the Process of Transformation, 1880–1940." In *Visible Women: New Essays in American Activism,* edited by Nancy A. Hewitt and Suzanne Lebsock, 296–324. Urbana: University of Illinois Press, 1993.

———. "'I Know Which Side I'm On': Southern Women in the Labor Movement in the Twentieth Century." In *Women, Work, and Protest: A Century of U.S. Women's Labor History,* edited by Ruth Milkman, 156–80. Boston: Routledge and Kegan Paul, 1985.

Friedman, Jean E. *The Enclosed Garden: Women and Community in the Evangelical South, 1830–1900.* Chapel Hill: University of North Carolina Press, 1985.

Gaines, Kevin. *Uplifting the Race: Black Leadership, Politics, and Culture in the Twentieth Century.* Chapel Hill: University of North Carolina Press, 1996.

Gallay, Alan. "Planters and Slaves in the Great Awakening." In *Masters and Slaves in the House of the Lord: Race and Religion in the American South, 1740–1870,* edited by John B. Boles, 19–36. Lexington: University Press of Kentucky, 1988.

Gaston, Paul Morton. *The New South Creed: A Study in Southern Mythmaking.* New York: Knopf, 1970.

Gatewood, William B. *Aristocrats of Color: The Black Elite, 1880–1920.* Bloomington: Indiana University Press, 1990.

Genovese, Eugene D. *The Political Economy of Slavery: Studies in the Economy and Society of the Slave South.* New York: Pantheon Books, 1965.

———. *Roll, Jordan, Roll: The World the Slaves Made.* New York: Vintage Books, 1976.

———. *The World the Slaveholders Made: Two Essays in Interpretation.* New York: Pantheon Books, 1969.

Genovese, Eugene D., and Elizabeth Fox-Genovese. "The Divine Sanction of Social

Order: Religious Foundations of the Southern Slaveholders' World View." *Journal of the American Academy of Religion* 55 (Summer 1987): 211–33.

———. *Fruits of Merchant Capital: Slavery and Bourgeois Property in the Rise and Expansion of Capitalism.* New York: Oxford University Press, 1983.

———. "The Social Thought of the Antebellum Southern Divines." In *Looking South: Chapters in the Story of an American Region,* edited by Winifred B. Moore Jr. and Joseph F. Tripp, 31–40. New York: Greenwood, 1989.

Gerteis, Louis S. *From Contraband to Freedman: Federal Policy toward Southern Blacks, 1861–1865.* Westport, Conn.: Greenwood, 1973.

Giddings, Paula. *When and Where I Enter: The Impact of Black Women on Race and Sex in America.* New York: Bantam, 1984.

Gilmore, Glenda. "Gender and Jim Crow: Sarah Dudley Pettey's Vision of the New South." *North Carolina Historical Review* 58 (July 1991): 261–85.

———. *Gender and Jim Crow: Women and the Politics of White Supremacy in North Carolina, 1896–1920.* Chapel Hill: University of North Carolina Press, 1996.

———. "'A Melting Time': Black Women, White Women, and the WCTU in North Carolina, 1880–1900." In *Hidden Histories of Women in the New South,* edited by Virginia Bernhard, Betty Brandon, Elizabeth Fox-Genovese, and Theda Perdue, 153–72. Columbia: University of Missouri Press, 1994.

Glymph, Thavolia. "Freedpeople and Ex-Masters: Shaping a New Order in the Postbellum South, 1865–1868." In *Essays on the Postbellum Southern Economy,* edited by Thavolia Glymph and John J. Kushma, 48–72. College Station: Texas A&M Press for the University of Texas at Arlington, 1985.

———. "'This Species of Property': Female Slave Contrabands in the Civil War." In *A Woman's War: Southern Women, Civil War, and the Confederate Legacy,* edited by Edwards D. C. Campbell Jr. and Kym S. Rice, 55–71. Charlottesville: University Press of Virginia for the Museum of the Confederacy, 1996.

Goldin, Claudia. "Female Labor Force Participation: The Origin of Black and White Differences, 1870 and 1880." *Journal of Economic History* 37 (March 1977): 87–108.

Goodheart, Lawrence B., Nell Harris, and Elizabeth Johnson, "'An Act for the Relief of Females . . . ': Divorce and the Changing Legal Status of Women in Tennessee, 1796–1860, Parts I and II." *Tennessee Historical Quarterly* 44 (Fall–Winter 1985): 318–19, 402–16.

Goodwyn, Lawrence C. *The Democratic Promise.* New York: Oxford University Press, 1976.

———. "Populist Dreams and Negro Rights: East Texas as a Case Study." *American Historical Review* 76 (December 1971): 1435–56.

Gordon, Linda. "Black and White Visions of Welfare Reform: Women's Welfare Activism, 1890–1945." *Journal of American History* 78 (September 1991): 539–50.

———. *Heroes of Their Own Lives: The Politics and History of Family Violence.* New York: Viking, 1988.

Gould, Jeffrey. "The Strike of 1887: Louisiana Sugar War." *Southern Exposure* 12 (November–December 1984): 45–55.

Gould, Virginia Meacham, ed. *Chained to the Rock of Adversity: To Be Free, Black, and Female in the Old South.* Athens: University of Georgia Press, 1998.

Gray, Virginia Gearhart. "Activities of Southern Women, 1840–1860." In *Unheard Voices: The First Historians of Southern Women,* edited by Anne Scott, 76–91. Charlottesville: University Press of Virginia, 1993.

Green, Elna C. *Southern Strategies: Southern Women and the Woman Suffrage Question.* Chapel Hill: University of North Carolina Press, 1997.

Greenberg, Kenneth. *Honor and Slavery: Lies, Duels, Noses, Masks, Dressing as a Woman, Gifts, Strangers, Humanitarianism, Death, Slave Rebellions, the Proslavery Argument, Baseball, Hunting, and Gambling in the Old South.* Princeton, N.J.: Princeton University Press, 1996.

———. *Masters and Statesmen: The Political Culture of American Slavery.* Baltimore: Johns Hopkins University Press, 1985.

Greenwood, Janette Thomas. *Bittersweet Legacy: The Black and White "Better Classes" in Charlotte, 1850–1910.* Chapel Hill: University of North Carolina Press, 1994.

Gross, Ariela. *Double Character: Slavery and Mastery in the Southern Courtroom, 1800–1860.* Princeton, N.J.: Princeton University Press, forthcoming.

———. "Litigating Whiteness: Trials of Racial Determination in the Nineteenth-Century South." *Yale Law Journal* 108 (October 1998): 109–88.

Grossberg, Michael. *Governing the Hearth: Law and Family in Nineteenth-Century America.* Chapel Hill: University of North Carolina Press, 1985.

Grubb, Alan. "House and Home in the Victorian South: The Cookbook as Guide." In *In Joy and in Sorrow: Women, Family, and Marriage in the Victorian South, 1830–1900,* edited by Carol Bleser, 154–75. New York: Oxford University Press, 1991.

Gutman, Herbert G. *The Black Family in Slavery and Freedom, 1750–1925.* New York: Pantheon Books, 1976.

Haag, Pamela. "The 'Ill-Use of a Wife': Patterns of Working-Class Violence in Domestic and Public New York City, 1860–1880." *Journal of Social History* 25 (Spring 1992): 447–77.

Hagler, D. Harland. "The Ideal Woman in the Antebellum South: Lady or Farmwife?" *Journal of Southern History* 66 (August 1980): 405–18.

Hahn, Steven. *The Roots of Southern Populism: Yeoman Farmers and the Transformation of the Georgia Upcountry, 1850–1890.* New York: Oxford University Press, 1983.

Hair, William I. *Bourbonism and Agrarian Protest: Louisiana Politics, 1877–1900.* Baton Rouge: Louisiana State University Press, 1981.

Hall, Jacquelyn Dowd. "Disorderly Women: Gender and Labor Militancy in the Appalachian South." *Journal of American History* 73 (September 1986): 354–82.

———. "'The Mind That Burns in Each Body': Women, Rape, and Racial Violence." In *Powers of Desire: The Politics of Sexuality,* edited by Ann Snitow, Christine Stansell, and Sharon Thompson, 328–49. New York: Monthly Review Press, 1983.

———. "O. Delight Smith's Progressive Era: Labor, Feminism, and Reform in the Urban South." In *Visible Women: New Essays on American Activism,* edited by Nancy A. Hewitt and Suzanne Lebsock, 166–98. Urbana: University of Illinois Press, 1993.

————. *Revolt against Chivalry: Jessie Daniel Ames and the Women's Campaign against Lynching.* Rev. ed. New York: Columbia University Press, 1993.

Hall, Jacquelyn Dowd, James Leloudis, Robert Korstad, Mary Murphy, LuAnn Jones, and Christopher Daly. *Like a Family: The Making of a Southern Cotton Mill World.* Chapel Hill: University of North Carolina Press, 1987.

Hamilton, J. G. DeRoulhac. "Benjamin Sherwood Hedrick." *James Sprunt Historical Publications* 10, no. 1 (1910): 5–42.

————, ed. *The Correspondence of Jonathan Worth.* 2 vols. Raleigh: Edwards Broughton Printing for the North Carolina Historical Commission, 1909.

Haney-Lopez, Ian F. *White by Law: The Legal Construction of Race.* New York: New York University Press, 1996.

Harris, J. William. *Plain Folk and Gentry in a Slave Society: White Liberty and Black Slavery in Augusta's Hinterlands.* Middletown, Conn.: Wesleyan University Press, 1985.

Harris, William C. *Presidential Reconstruction in Mississippi.* Baton Rouge: Louisiana State University Press, 1967.

Hening, William W. *The Statutes at Large: Being a Collection of All the Laws of Virginia.* 13 vols. Richmond: Samuel Pleasants Jr., printer to the Commonwealth, 1809–23.

Hewitt, Nancy A. "In Pursuit of Power: The Political Economy of Women's Activism in Twentieth-Century Tampa." In *Visible Women: New Essays in American Activism,* edited by Nancy A. Hewitt and Suzanne Lebsock, 199–222. Urbana: University of Illinois Press, 1993.

————. "Politicizing Domesticity: Anglo, Black, and Latin Women in Tampa's Progressive Movements." In *Gender, Class, Race, and Reform in the Progressive Era,* edited by Noralee Frankel and Nancy S. Dye, 42–41. Lexington: University Press of Kentucky, 1991.

————. "'The Voice of Virile Labor': Labor Militancy, Community Solidarity, and Gender Identity among Tampa's Latin Workers, 1880–1921." In *Work Engendered: Toward a New History of American Labor,* edited by Ava Baron, 142–67. Ithaca, N.Y.: Cornell University Press, 1991.

Higginbotham, Evelyn Brooks. "African-American Women's History and the Metalanguage of Race." *Signs* 17 (Winter 1992): 251–74.

————. *Righteous Discontent: The Women's Movement in the Black Baptist Church, 1880–1920.* Cambridge, Mass.: Harvard University Press, 1993.

Hill, Louise Biles. *Joseph E. Brown and the Confederacy.* Chapel Hill: University of North Carolina Press, 1939.

Hill, Sarah H. *Weaving New Worlds: Southeastern Cherokee Women and Their Basketry.* Chapel Hill: University of North Carolina Press, 1997.

Hindus, Michael S. *Prison and Plantation: Crime, Justice, and Authority in Massachusetts and South Carolina, 1767–1878.* Chapel Hill: University of North Carolina Press, 1980.

Hine, Darlene Clark. "Rape and the Inner Lives of Black Women in the Middle West." *Signs* 14 (Summer 1989): 912–20.

————. "'We Specialize in the Wholly Impossible': The Philanthropic Work of Black

Women." In *Lady Bountiful Revisited: Women, Philanthropy, and Power*, edited by Kathleen McCarthy, 70–93. New Brunswick, N.J.: Rutgers University Press, 1990.

Hodes, Martha. "The Sexualization of Reconstruction Politics: White Women and Black Men in the South after the Civil War." *Journal of the History of Sexuality* 3, no. 3 (1993): 402–17.

———. *White Women, Black Men: Illicit Sex in the Nineteenth-Century South.* New Haven, Conn.: Yale University Press, 1997.

Hoffschwelle, Mary S. "Women's Sphere and the Creation of Female Community in the Antebellum South: Three Tennessee Slaveholding Women." *Tennessee Historical Quarterly* 50 (Summer 1991): 80–89.

Holt, Michael F. *The Political Crisis of the 1850s.* New York: Wiley, 1978.

Holt, Sharon Ann. "Making Freedom Pay: Freedpeople Working for Themselves, North Carolina, 1865–1900." *Journal of Southern History* 60 (May 1994): 229–62.

Holt, Thomas C. *Black over White: Negro Political Leadership in South Carolina during Reconstruction.* Urbana: University of Illinois Press, 1977.

———. "'An Empire over the Mind': Emancipation, Race, and Ideology in the British West Indies and the American South." In *Region, Race, and Reconstruction: Essays in Honor of C. Vann Woodward,* edited by J. Morgan Kousser and James M. McPherson, 283–313. New York: Oxford University Press, 1982.

Honey, Michael K. "The War within the Confederacy: White Unionists of North Carolina." *Prologue* 18 (Summer 1986): 74–93.

hooks, bell. *Feminist Theory from Margin to Center.* Boston: South End, 1984.

Hoole, William Stanley. *Alabama Tories: The First Alabama Cavalry, U.S.A., 1862–1865.* Tuscaloosa, Ala.: Confederate Printing, 1960.

Hudson, Janet. "From Constitution to Constitution, 1868–1895: South Carolina's Unique Stance on Divorce." *South Carolina Historical Magazine* 98 (January 1997): 75–96.

Hunter, Tera W. "Domination and Resistance: The Politics of Wage Household Labor in New South Atlanta." *Labor History* 34 (Spring/Summer 1993): 205–20.

———. *To 'Joy My Freedom: Southern Black Women's Lives and Labors after the Civil War.* Cambridge, Mass.: Harvard University Press, 1997.

Hyman, Michael R. *The Anti-Redeemers: Hill-Country Political Dissenters in the Lower South from Redemption to Populism.* Baton Rouge: Louisiana State University Press, 1990.

Inscoe, John. "The Civil War's Empowerment of an Appalachian Woman: The 1864 Slave Purchases of Mary Bell." In *Discovering the Women in Slavery: Emancipating Perspectives on the American Past,* edited by Patricia Morton, 61–81. Athens: University of Georgia Press, 1996.

———. "Coping in Confederate Appalachia: A Portrait of a Mountain Woman and Her Community at War." *North Carolina Historical Review* 69 (October 1992): 388–413.

———. *Mountain Masters, Slavery, and the Sectional Crisis in Western North Carolina.* Knoxville: University of Tennessee Press, 1989.

Isenberg, Nancy. *Sex and Citizenship in Antebellum America*. Chapel Hill: University of North Carolina Press, 1998.

Jacobs, Harriet. *Incidents in the Life of a Slave Girl: Written by Herself*. Edited by Jean Fagan Yellin. Cambridge, Mass.: Harvard University Press, 1987.

James, Larry M. "Biracial Fellowship in Antebellum Baptist Churches." In *Masters and Slaves in the House of the Lord: Race and Religion in the American South, 1740–1870*, edited by John B. Boles, 37–57. Lexington: University Press of Kentucky, 1988.

Janiewski, Dolores E. *Sisterhood Denied: Race, Gender, and Class in a New South Community*. Philadelphia: Temple University Press, 1985.

Jaynes, Gerald David. *Branches without Roots: Genesis of the Black Working Class in the American South, 1862–1882*. New York: Oxford University Press, 1986.

Jeffrey, Julie Roy. "Women in the Southern Farmers' Alliance: A Reconstruction of the Role and Status of Women in the Late Nineteenth-Century South. *Feminist Studies* 3 (Fall 1975): 72–91.

Jennings, Thelma. "'Us Colored Women Had to Go through a Plenty': Sexual Exploitation of African American Slave Women." *Journal of Women's History* 1 (Winter 1990): 45–74.

Jensen, Joan. *Loosening the Bonds: Mid-Atlantic Farm Women, 1750–1850*. New Haven, Conn.: Yale University Press, 1986.

Johnson, Guion Griffis. *Ante-bellum North Carolina: A Social History*. Chapel Hill: University of North Carolina Press, 1937.

Johnson, Michael P. *Toward a Patriarchal Republic: The Secession of Georgia*. Baton Rouge: Louisiana State University Press, 1977.

Johnson, Michael P., and James L. Roark. *Black Masters: A Free Family of Color in the Old South*. New York: Norton, 1984.

Johnston, James Hugo. *Race Relations in Virginia and Miscegenation in the South, 1776–1860*. Amherst: University of Massachusetts Press, 1970; reprint, New York: Free Press, 1980.

Jones, Anne Goodwyn. *Tomorrow Is Another Day: The Woman Writer in the South, 1859–1936*. Baton Rouge: Louisiana State University Press, 1981.

Jones, Jacqueline. *Labor of Love, Labor of Sorrow: Black Women, Work, and the Family from Slavery to the Present*. New York: Basic Books, 1985.

———. "The Political Economy of Sharecropping Families: Blacks and Poor Whites in the Rural South, 1865–1915." In *In Joy and in Sorrow: Women, Family, and Marriage in the Victorian South, 1830–1900*, edited by Carol Bleser, 196–214. New York: Oxford University Press, 1991.

Jordan, Winthrop. *White over Black: American Attitudes toward the Negro, 1580–1812*. Chapel Hill: University of North Carolina Press, 1968.

Joyner, Charles. *Down by the Riverside: A South Carolina Slave Community*. Urbana: University of Illinois Press, 1984.

Kamensky, Jane. *Governing the Tongue: The Politics of Speech in Early New England*. New York: Oxford University Press, 1997.

Kantrowitz, Steve. *Ben Tillman and the Reconstruction of White Supremacy.* Chapel Hill: University of North Carolina Press, forthcoming.

Kelley, Robin D. G. *Race Rebels: Culture, Politics, and the Black Working Class.* New York: Free Press, 1994.

———. "'We Are Not What We Seem': Rethinking Black Working-Class Opposition in the Jim Crow South." *Journal of American History* 80 (June 1993): 75–112.

Kenzer, Robert C. *Enterprising Southerners: Black Economic Success in North Carolina, 1865–1915.* Charlottesville: University Press of Virginia, 1997.

———. *Kinship and Neighborhood in a Southern Community: Orange County, North Carolina, 1849–1881.* Knoxville: University of Tennessee Press, 1987.

Kerber, Linda K. *No Constitutional Right to Be Ladies: Women and the Obligations of Citizenship.* New York: Hill and Wang, 1998.

Key, V. O. *Southern Politics in State and Nation.* New York: Knopf, 1949.

King, Wilma. "The Mistress and Her Maids: White and Black Women in a Louisiana Household, 1858–1868." In *Discovering the Women in Slavery: Emancipating Perspectives on the American Past,* edited by Patricia Morton, 82–106. Athens: University of Georgia Press, 1996.

———. *Stolen Childhood: Slave Youth in Nineteenth-Century America.* Bloomington: Indiana University Press, 1995.

———. "'Suffer with Them till Death': Slave Women and Their Children in Nineteenth-Century America." In *More than Chattel: Black Women and Slavery in the Americas,* edited by David Barry Gaspar and Darlene Clark Hine, 147–68. Bloomington: Indiana University Press, 1996.

———. "Within the Professional Household: Slave Children in the Antebellum South." *Historian* 59 (Spring 1997): 523–40.

Kirby, Jack Temple. *Rural Worlds Lost: The American South, 1920–1960.* Baton Rouge: Louisiana State University Press, 1987.

Klein, Rachel N. *Unification of a Slave State: The Rise of the Planter Class in the South Carolina Backcountry, 1760–1808.* Chapel Hill: University of North Carolina Press, 1990.

Kleit, David H. "A Stereoscopic View of the Frontier: George Swain, Edward Isham, and the Resettlement of the Cherokee Country." In *The Confessions of Edward Isham: A Poor White Life of the Old South,* edited by Charles C. Bolton and Scott P. Culclasure, 32–44. Athens: University of Georgia Press, 1998.

Klingberg, Frank W. *The Southern Claims Commission.* Berkeley: University of California Press, 1955.

Kolchin, Peter. *First Freedom: The Responses of Alabama's Blacks to Emancipation and Reconstruction.* Westport, Conn.: Greenwood, 1982.

Kousser, J. Morgan. *The Shaping of Southern Politics and the Establishment of the One-Party South, 1880–1910.* New Haven, Conn.: Yale University Press, 1974.

Leathem, Karen Trahan. "A Carnival according to Their Own Desires: Gender and Carnival in New Orleans, 1870–1941." Ph.D. diss., University of North Carolina at Chapel Hill, 1994.

Lebsock, Suzanne. "Free Black Women and the Question of Matriarchy: Petersburg, Virginia, 1784–1820." *Feminist Studies* 8 (Summer 1982): 271–92.

———. *The Free Women of Petersburg: Status and Culture in a Southern Town, 1784–1860.* New York: Norton, 1984.

———. "Radical Reconstruction and the Property Rights of Southern Women." *Journal of Southern History* 43 (May 1977): 195–216.

———. "Woman Suffrage and White Supremacy: A Virginia Case Study." In *Visible Women: New Essays on American Activism,* edited by Nancy A. Hewitt and Suzanne Lebsock, 62–100. Urbana: University of Illinois Press, 1993.

Lecaudey, Hélène. "Behind the Mask: Ex-slave Women and Interracial Sexual Relations." In *Discovering the Women in Slavery: Emancipating Perspectives on the American Past,* edited by Patricia Morton, 260–77. Athens: University of Georgia Press, 1996.

Leloudis, James. "School Reform in the New South: The Woman's Association for the Betterment of Public School Houses in North Carolina." *Journal of American History* 69 (March 1983): 886–909.

Lerner, Gerda. *Black Women in White America: A Documentary History.* New York: Pantheon Books, 1972.

———. *The Grimké Sisters from South Carolina: Pioneers for Woman's Rights and Abolition.* Boston: Houghton Mifflin, 1967.

Levine, Lawrence W. *Black Culture and Black Consciousness: Afro-American Folk Thought from Slavery to Freedom.* New York: Oxford University Press, 1997.

Lewis, Jan, and Kenneth Lockridge. "'Sally Has Been Sick': Pregnancy and Family Limitation among Virginia Gentry Women, 1780–1830." *Journal of Social History* 22 (Fall 1988): 5–19.

Lichtenstein, Alex. *Twice the Work of Free Labor: The Political Economy of Convict Labor in the New South.* New York: Verso, 1996.

Litwack, Leon. *Been in the Storm So Long: The Aftermath of Slavery.* New York: Knopf, 1979.

Lofgren, Charles A. *The Plessy Case: A Legal-Historical Interpretation.* New York: Oxford University Press, 1987.

Lonn, Ella. *Desertion during the Civil War.* New York: Century, 1928.

Loveland, Anne C. *Southern Evangelicals and the Social Order, 1800–1860.* Baton Rouge: Louisiana State University Press, 1980.

MacLean, Nancy. *Behind the Mask of Chivalry: The Making of the Second Ku Klux Klan.* New York: Oxford University Press, 1994.

———. "The Leo Frank Case Reconsidered: Gender and Sexual Politics in the Making of Reactionary Populism." *Journal of American History* 78 (December 1991): 917–48.

Maddex, Jack P., Jr. "Proslavery Millennialism: Social Eschatology in Antebellum Southern Calvinism." *American Quarterly* 31 (Spring 1979): 46–48.

———. "'The Southern Apostasy' Revisited: The Significance of Proslavery Christianity." *Marxist Perspectives,* no. 7 (1979): 132–41.

————. *The Virginia Conservatives, 1867–1879.* Chapel Hill: University of North Carolina Press, 1970.

Magdol, Edward. *A Right to the Land: Essays on the Freedmen's Community.* Westport, Conn.: Greenwood, 1977.

Malone, Ann Patton. *Sweet Chariot: Slave Family and Household Structure in Nineteenth-Century Louisiana.* Chapel Hill: University of North Carolina Press, 1992.

Mann, Susan A. "Slavery, Sharecropping, and Sexual Inequality." *Signs* 14 (Summer 1989): 774–99.

Massey, Mary Elizabeth. *Bonnet Brigades.* New York: Knopf, 1966.

————. *Ersatz in the Confederacy: Shortages and Substitutes on the Southern Homefront.* Columbia: University of South Carolina Press, 1952; reprint, Columbia: University of South Carolina Press, 1993.

————. "The Making of a Feminist." *Journal of Southern History* 39 (February 1973): 3–22.

Matthews, Donald. *Religion in the Old South.* Chicago: University of Chicago Press, 1977.

McCandless, Amy Thompson. "Progressivism and the Higher Education of Southern Women." *North Carolina Historical Review* 70 (July 1993): 302–25.

McConville, Brendan. "The Rise of Rough Music: Reflections on an Ancient New Custom in Eighteen-Century New Jersey." In *Festive Culture and Public Ritual in Early America,* edited by Simon Newman and William Pencak. University Park: Pennsylvania State University Press, forthcoming.

McCurry, Stephanie. *Masters of Small Worlds: Yeoman Households, Gender Relations, and the Political Culture of the Antebellum South Carolina Low Country.* New York: Oxford University Press, 1995.

————. "The Politics of Yeoman Households in South Carolina." In *Divided Houses: Gender and the Civil War,* edited by Catherine Clinton and Nina Silber, 22–38. New York: Oxford University Press, 1992.

————. "The Two Faces of Republicanism: Gender and Proslavery Politics in Antebellum South Carolina." *Journal of American History* 78 (March 1992): 1245–64.

McDonald, Roderick A. "Independent Economic Production by Slaves on Antebellum Louisiana Sugar Plantations." In *Slaves' Economy: Independent Production by Slaves in the Americas,* edited by Ira Berlin and Philip D. Morgan, 182–208. London: Frank Cass, 1991.

McDowell, John Patrick. *The Social Gospel in the South: The Woman's Home Mission Movement in the Methodist Episcopal Church, South, 1886–1939.* Baton Rouge: Louisiana State University Press, 1982.

McFeely, William S. *Yankee Stepfather: General O. O. Howard and the Freedmen.* New Haven, Conn.: Yale University Press, 1968.

McGenee, Eliza Skinner. "Woman's Place Is in Her Home, as Exemplified by Mrs. Archibald Henderson, President of Equal Suffrage League of North Carolina." *Sky-Land Magazine* 1 (September 1914): 635–42.

McKenzie, Robert Tracy. "Postbellum Tenancy in Fayette County, Tennessee: Its Implications for Economic Development and Persistent Black Poverty." *Agricultural History* 61 (Spring 1987): 16–33.

McKinney, Gordon B. *Southern Mountain Republicans, 1865–1900*. Chapel Hill: University of North Carolina Press, 1978.

McLaurin, Melton. *Celia, a Slave*. Athens: University of Georgia Press, 1991.

McMath, Robert C., Jr. "Sandy Land and Hogs in the Timber: (Agri)cultural Origins of the Farmers' Alliance in Texas." In *The Countryside in the Age of Capitalist Transformation: Essays in the Social History of Rural America*, edited by Steven Hahn and Jonathan Prude, 205–29. Chapel Hill: University of North Carolina Press, 1985.

———. "Southern White Farmers and the Organization of Black Farm Workers: A North Carolina Document." *Labor History* 18 (Winter 1977): 115–19.

McMillen, Sally G. *Motherhood in the Old South: Pregnancy, Childbirth, and Infant Rearing*. Baton Rouge: Louisiana State University Press, 1990.

McMurry, Sally. *Families and Farmhouses in Nineteenth-Century America: Vernacular Design and Social Change*. New York: Oxford University Press, 1988.

McPherson, James M. *Battle Cry of Freedom: The Civil War Era*. New York: Oxford University Press, 1988.

Meyerowitz, Joanne J. *Women Adrift: Independent Wage Earners in Chicago, 1880–1930*. Chicago: University of Chicago Press, 1988.

Miller, Randall A., and Jon L. Wakelyn, eds. *Catholics in the Old South: Essays on Church and Culture*. Macon, Ga.: Mercer University Press, 1983.

Mohr, Clarence. *On the Threshold of Freedom: Masters and Slaves in Civil War Georgia*. Athens: University of Georgia Press, 1986.

Moncrief, Sandra. "The Mississippi Married-Women's Property Act of 1839." *Journal of Mississippi History* 17 (May 1985): 110–25.

Moneyhon, Carl H. *Republicanism in Reconstruction Texas*. Austin: University of Texas Press, 1980.

Montgomery, David. *Beyond Equality: Labor and the Radical Republicans, 1862–1872*. New York: Knopf, 1967.

Moore, Albert Burton. *Conscription and Conflict in the Confederacy*. New York: Macmillan, 1924.

Morgan, Edmund. *American Slavery, American Freedom: The Ordeal of Colonial Virginia*. New York: Norton, 1975.

Morris, Thomas D. *Southern Slavery and the Law, 1619–1860*. Chapel Hill: University of North Carolina Press, 1996.

Morrison, Toni. *Beloved: A Novel*. New York: Knopf, 1987.

Moynihan, Daniel P. *The Negro Family: The Case for National Action*. Washington, D.C.: Office of Policy Planning and Research, United States Department of Labor, 1965.

Nathans, Elizabeth S. *Losing the Peace: Georgia Republicans and Reconstruction, 1865–1871*. Baton Rouge: Louisiana State University Press, 1968.

Nelson, Bernard H. "Confederate Slave Impressment Legislation, 1861–65." *Journal of Negro History* 31, no. 4 (1946): 392–410.

Nelson, Scott. "Livestock, Boundaries, and Public Space in Spartanburg: African American Men, Elite White Women, and the Spectacle of Conjugal Relations." In *Sex, Love, Race: Crossing Boundaries in North American History,* edited by Martha Hodes, 313–27. New York: New York University Press, 1999.

Nieman, Donald G. "Political Power and Criminal Justice: Washington County, Texas, 1868–1884." *Journal of Southern History* 55 (August 1989): 391–420.

———. *To Set the Law in Motion: The Freedmen's Bureau and the Legal Rights of Blacks, 1865–1868.* Millwood, N.Y.: KTO, 1979.

Noble, M. C. S. *A History of the Public Schools of North Carolina.* Chapel Hill: University of North Carolina Press, 1930.

North Carolina Bureau of Labor Statistics. *First Annual Report.* Raleigh: North Carolina Bureau of Labor Statistics, 1887.

Novak, Daniel A. *Wheel of Servitude: Black Forced Labor after Slavery.* Lexington: University Press of Kentucky, 1978.

Oakes, James. "The Political Significance of Slave Resistance." *History Workshop* 22 (Autumn 1986): 89–107.

———. "The Present Becomes the Past: The Planter Class in the Postbellum South." In *New Perspectives on Race and Slavery in America,* edited by Robert H. Abzug and Stephen E. Maizlish, 149–63. Lexington: University Press of Kentucky, 1986.

———. *The Ruling Race: A History of American Slaveholders.* New York: Knopf, 1982.

———. *Slavery and Freedom: An Interpretation of the Old South.* New York: Knopf, 1990.

O'Brien, Gail. *The Legal Fraternity and the Making of a New South Community.* Athens: University of Georgia Press, 1986.

O'Brien, Michael, ed. *An Evening When Alone: Four Journals of Single Women in the South, 1827–67.* Charlottesville: University Press of Virginia for the Southern Texts Society, 1993.

Olmsted, Frederick Law. *A Journey in the Back Country in the Winter of 1853–54.* New York: G. P. Putnam's Sons, 1860; reprint, New York: Knickerbocker, 1907.

Olsen, Otto H. *Carpetbagger's Crusade: The Life of Albion Winegar Tourgée.* Baltimore: Johns Hopkins University Press, 1965.

———. "The Ku Klux Klan: A Study in Reconstruction Politics and Propaganda." *North Carolina Historical Review* 39 (Summer 1962): 340–62.

———, ed. *The Thin Disguise: Turning Point in Negro History—Plessy v. Ferguson: A Documentary Presentation (1864–1896).* New York: Humanities, 1967.

Olwell, Robert. "'Loose, Idle and Disorderly': Slave Women in the Eighteenth-Century Charleston Marketplace." In *More than Chattel: Black Women and Slavery in the Americas,* edited by David Barry Gaspar and Darlene Clark Hine, 97–110. Bloomington: Indiana University Press, 1996.

O'Neall, John Belton. *The Negro Law of South Carolina.* Columbia, S.C.: J. G. Bowman, 1848.

Osterweis, Rollin G. *The Myth of the Lost Cause, 1865–1900.* Hamden, Conn.: Archon Books, 1973.

Ownby, Ted. *Subduing Satan: Religion, Recreation, and Manhood in the Rural South, 1865–1920*. Chapel Hill: University of North Carolina Press, 1990.

Owsley, Frank Lawrence. *Plain Folk of the Old South*. Baton Rouge: Louisiana State University Press, 1982.

Painter, Nell Irvin. "The Journal of Gertrude Clanton Thomas: An Educated White Woman in the Eras of Slavery, War, and Reconstruction." Introduction to *The Secret Eye: The Journal of Gertrude Clanton Thomas, 1848–1889*, edited by Virginia Ingraham Burr, 1–67. Chapel Hill: University of North Carolina Press, 1990.

———. "Of *Lily*, Linda Brent, and Freud: A Non-Exceptionalist Approach to Race, Class, and Gender in the Slaveholding South." *Georgia Historical Quarterly* 76 (Summer 1992): 241–59.

———. "'Social Equality,' Miscegenation, and the Maintenance of Power." In *The Evolution of Southern Culture*, edited by Numan B. Bartley, 47–67. Athens: University of Georgia Press, 1988.

Parks, Joseph H. *Joseph Brown of Georgia*. Baton Rouge: Louisiana State University Press, 1977.

Parrott, Angie. "'Love Makes Memory Eternal': The United Daughters of the Confederacy in Richmond, Virginia, 1897–1920." In *The Edge of the South: Life in Nineteenth-Century Virginia*, edited by Edward Ayers and John Willis, 219–38. Charlottesville: University Press of Virginia, 1991.

Pember, Phoebe Yates. *A Southern Woman's Story: Life in Confederate Richmond*. Edited by Bell Irvin Wiley. Jackson, Tenn.: McCowat-Mercer, 1959; reprint, Saint Simons Island, Ga.: Mockingbird Books, 1974; reprint, Troutdale, Oreg.: New Sage, 1995.

Penningroth, Dylan. "Slavery, Freedom, and Social Claims to Property among African Americans in Liberty County, Georgia, 1850–1880." *Journal of American History* 84 (September 1997): 405–35.

Perdue, Theda. *Cherokee Women: Gender and Culture Change, 1700–1835*. Lincoln: University of Nebraska Press, 1998.

Pereyra, Lillian A. *James Lusk Alcorn: Persistent Whig*. Baton Rouge: Louisiana State University Press, 1966.

Perman, Michael. *Reunion without Compromise: The South and Reconstruction, 1865–1868*. New York: Cambridge University Press, 1973.

———. *The Road to Redemption: Southern Politics, 1869–1879*. Chapel Hill: University of North Carolina Press, 1984.

Potter, David. *The Impending Crisis, 1848–1861*. Completed and edited by Don E. Fehrenbacher. New York: Harper and Row, 1976.

———. *Lincoln and His Party in the Secession Crisis*. New Haven, Conn.: Yale University Press, 1962.

———. *The South and Sectional Conflict*. Baton Rouge: Louisiana State University Press, 1968.

Powell, Carolyn J. "In Remembrance of Mira: Reflections on the Death of a Slave Woman." In *Discovering the Women in Slavery: Emancipating Perspectives on the*

American Past, edited by Patricia Morton, 47–60. Athens: University of Georgia Press, 1996.

Powell, Lawrence N. *New Masters: Northern Planters during the Civil War and Reconstruction.* New Haven, Conn.: Yale University Press, 1980.

Prather, H. Leon, Sr. *We Have Taken a City: Wilmington Massacre and Coup of 1898.* Cranbury, N.J.: Associated University Presses, 1984.

Pruneau, Leigh A. "All the Time Is Work Time: Gender and the Task System on Antebellum Lowcountry Rice Plantations." Ph.D. diss., University of Arizona, 1997.

Pyron, Darden Asbury. *Southern Daughter: The Life of Margaret Mitchell.* New York: Oxford University Press, 1991.

Rabinowitz, Howard N. *Race Relations in the Urban South, 1865–1890.* New York: Oxford University Press, 1978.

Rable, George C. *But There Was No Peace: The Role of Violence in the Politics of Reconstruction.* Athens: University of Georgia Press, 1984.

———. *Civil Wars: Women and the Crisis of Southern Nationalism.* Urbana: University of Illinois Press, 1989.

———. *Confederate Republic: A Revolution against Politics.* Chapel Hill: University of North Carolina Press, 1944.

Raboteau, Albert J. *Slave Religion: The "Invisible Institution" in the Antebellum South.* New York: Oxford University Press, 1978.

Rachleff, Peter J. *Black Labor in the South: Richmond, Virginia, 1865–1890.* Philadelphia: Temple University Press, 1984.

Ramey, Daina. "'She Do a Heap of Work': An Analysis of Female Slave Labor on Glynn County Rice and Cotton Plantations." *Georgia Historical Quarterly* 82 (Winter 1998): 707–34.

Ransom, Roger L., and Richard Sutch. *One Kind of Freedom: The Economic Consequences of Emancipation.* Cambridge: Cambridge University Press, 1977.

Raper, Horace W. *William W. Holden: North Carolina's Political Enigma.* Chapel Hill: University of North Carolina Press, 1985.

Rapport, Sara. "The Freedmen's Bureau as a Legal Agent for Black Men and Women in Georgia: 1865–1868." *Georgia Historical Quarterly* 73 (Spring 1989): 26–53.

Rawick, George P. *From Sundown to Sunup: The Making of the Black Community.* Westport, Conn.: Greenwood, 1972.

———, ed. *The American Slave: A Composite Autobiography.* 19 vols. Westport, Conn.: Greenwood, 1972.

———. *The American Slave: A Composite Autobiography, Supplement.* Series 1, 12 vols. Westport, Conn.: Greenwood, 1977.

———. *The American Slave: A Composite Autobiography, Supplement.* Series 2, 10 vols. Westport, Conn.: Greenwood, 1979.

Reidy, Joseph P. *From Slavery to Agrarian Capitalism in the Cotton Plantation South: Central Georgia, 1800–1880.* Chapel Hill: University of North Carolina Press, 1992.

Roark, James L. *Masters without Slaves: Southern Planters in the Civil War and Reconstruction.* New York: Norton, 1977.

Roark, James, and Michael Johnson. "Strategies of Survival: Free Negro Families and the Problem of Slavery." In *In Joy and in Sorrow: Women, Family, and Marriage in the Victorian South, 1830–1900,* edited by Carol Bleser, 88–102. New York: Oxford University Press, 1991.

Roberts, A. Sellew. "The Peace Movement in North Carolina." *Mississippi Valley Historical Review* 9 (June 1924): 190–99.

Robertson, Claire. "Africa into the Americas? Slavery and Women, the Family, and the Gender Division of Labor." In *More than Chattel: Black Women and Slavery in the Americas,* edited by David Barry Gaspar and Darlene Clark Hine, 3–40. Bloomington: Indiana University Press, 1996.

Robinson, Armstead. "Beyond the Realm of Social Consensus: New Meanings of Reconstruction for American History." *Journal of American History* 68 (May 1981): 276–97.

————. "Plans Dat Comed from God: Institution Building and the Emergence of Black Leadership in Reconstruction Memphis." In *Toward a New South? Studies in Post–Civil War Southern Communities,* edited by Robert McMath and Orville Vernon Burton, 71–102. Westport, Conn.: Greenwood, 1982.

————. "'Worser dan Jeff Davis': The Coming of Free Labor during the Civil War and Reconstruction." In *Essays of the Postbellum Southern Economy,* edited by Thavolia Glymph and John J. Kushma, 11–47. College Station: Texas A&M Press for the University of Texas at Arlington, 1985.

Roediger, David R. *The Wages of Whiteness: Race and the Making of the American Working Class.* New York: Verso, 1991.

Rogers, William Warren, Jr. *Black Belt Scalawag: Charles Hays and the Southern Republicans in the Era of Reconstruction.* Athens: University of Georgia Press, 1993.

————. *The One-Gallused Rebellion: Agrarianism in Alabama, 1865–1896.* Baton Rouge: Louisiana State University Press, 1970.

Rose, Willie Lee. *Rehearsal for Reconstruction: The Port Royal Experiment.* New York: Knopf, 1964.

Rosen, Hannah. "'Not That Sort of Women': Race, Gender, and Sexual Violence during the Memphis Riot of 1866." In *Sex, Love, Race: Crossing Boundaries in North American History,* edited by Martha Hodes, 267–93. New York: New York University Press, 1999.

Rosengarten, Theodore. *Tombee: Portrait of a Cotton Planter.* New York: Morrow, 1987.

Rouse, Jacqueline Anne. "Atlanta's African-American Women's Attack on Segregation, 1900–1920." In *Gender, Class, Race, and Reform in the Progressive Era,* edited by Noralee Frankel and Nancy S. Dye, 10–23. Lexington: University Press of Kentucky, 1991.

————. *Lugenia Burns Hope: Black Southern Reformer.* Athens: University of Georgia Press, 1989.

Roydhouse, Marion W. "Bridging Chasms: Community and the Southern YWCA." In *Visible Women: New Essays on American Activism,* edited by Nancy A. Hewitt and Suzanne Lebsock, 270–95. Urbana: University of Illinois Press, 1993.

Ryan, Mary P. *Cradle of the Middle Class: The Family in Oneida County, New York, 1790–1865.* Cambridge: Cambridge University Press, 1981.

————. *Women in Public: Between Banners and Ballots, 1825–1880.* Baltimore: Johns Hopkins University Press, 1990.

Salem, Dorothy. *To Better Our World: Black Women in Organized Reform, 1890–1920.* New York: Carlson, 1990.

Salmon, Marylynn. *Women and the Law of Property in Early America.* Chapel Hill: University of North Carolina Press, 1986.

————. "Women and Property in South Carolina: The Evidence from Marriage Settlements, 1730–1830." *William and Mary Quarterly* 39 (October 1982): 655–85.

Saville, Julie. *The Work of Reconstruction: From Slave to Wage Laborer in South Carolina, 1860–1870.* New York: Cambridge University Press, 1994.

Schafer, Judith Kelleher. *Slavery, Civil Law, and the Supreme Court of Louisiana.* Baton Rouge: Louisiana State University Press, 1994.

Schlotterbeck, John T. "The Internal Economy of Slavery in Rural Piedmont Virginia." In *Slaves' Economy: Independent Production by Slaves in the Americas,* edited by Ira Berlin and Philip D. Morgan, 170–81. London: Frank Cass, 1991.

Schultz, Mark R. "The Dream Realized? African American Landownership in Central Georgia between Reconstruction and World War Two." *Agricultural History* 72 (Spring 1998): 298–312.

Schwalm, Leslie A. *A Hard Fight for We: Women's Transition from Slavery to Freedom in South Carolina.* Urbana: University of Illinois Press, 1997.

Schwartz, Marie Jenkins. "'At Noon, Oh How I Ran': Breastfeeding and Weaning on Plantation and Farm in Antebellum Virginia and Alabama. In *Discovering the Women in Slavery: Emancipating Perspectives on the American Past,* edited by Patricia Morton, 241–59. Athens: University of Georgia Press, 1996.

Schwartz, Philip J. *Twice Condemned: Slaves and the Criminal Laws of Virginia, 1705–1865.* Baton Rouge: Louisiana State University Press, 1988.

Schweninger, Loren. *Black Property Owners in the South, 1790–1915.* Urbana: University of Illinois Press, 1990.

Scott, Anne Firor. *Natural Allies: Women's Associations in American History.* Urbana: University of Illinois Press, 1991.

————. "The 'New Woman' in the New South." *South Atlantic Quarterly* 61 (August 1962): 473–83.

————. "Most Invisible of All: Black Women's Voluntary Associations." *Journal of Southern History* 56 (February 1990): 3–22.

————. *The Southern Lady: From Pedestal to Politics, 1830–1930.* Chicago: University of Chicago Press, 1970.

Scott, James C. *Domination and the Arts of Resistance: Hidden Transcripts.* New Haven, Conn.: Yale University Press, 1990.

————. *Weapons of the Weak: Everyday Forms of Peasant Resistance.* New Haven, Conn.: Yale University Press, 1985.

Scott, Rebecca. "The Battle over the Child: Child Apprenticeship and the Freedmen's Bureau in North Carolina." *Prologue* 10 (Summer 1978): 101–13.

Shaw, Stephanie. "Black Club Women and the Creation of the National Association of Colored Women." *Journal of Women's History* 3 (Fall 1991): 10–25.

Simkins, Francis Butler, and James Welch Patton. *The Women of the Confederacy.* Richmond, N.Y.: Garrett and Massie, 1936.

Simon, Bryant. "The Appeal of Cole Blease of South Carolina: Race, Class, and Sex in the New South." *Journal of Southern History* 62 (February 1996): 57–86.

———. *A Fabric of Defeat: The Politics of South Carolina Millhands, 1910–1948.* Chapel Hill: University of North Carolina Press, 1998.

Sims, Anastasia. "'The Sword of the Spirit': The WCTU and Moral Reform in North Carolina, 1883–1933." *North Carolina Historical Review* 64 (October 1987): 394–415.

Sitterson, J. Carlyle. *Sugar Country.* Lexington: University of Kentucky Press, 1953.

Smith, Jennifer Lund. "The Ties That Bind: Educated African-American Women in Post-Emancipation Atlanta." In *Georgia in Black and White: Explorations in the Race Relations of a Southern State, 1865–1950,* edited by John C. Inscoe, 91–105. Athens: University of Georgia Press, 1994.

Smith-Rosenberg, Carroll. "The Female World of Love and Ritual: Relations between Women in Nineteenth-Century America." *Signs* 1 (Autumn 1975): 1–29.

Solomon, Clara. *The Civil War Diary of Clara Solomon: Growing Up in New Orleans, 1861–1862.* Edited by Elliott Ashkenazi. Baton Rouge: Louisiana State University Press, 1995.

Sommerville, Diane Miller. "The Rape Myth in the Old South Reconsidered." *Journal of Southern History* 61 (August 1995): 481–518.

———. "Rape, Race, and Castration in Slave Law in the Colonial and Early South." In *The Devil's Lane: Sex and Race in the Early South,* edited by Catherine Clinton and Michele Gillespie, 74–89. New York: Oxford University Press, 1997.

Spruill, Julia Cherry. *Women's Life and Work in the Southern Colonies.* Chapel Hill: University of North Carolina Press, 1938.

Stampp, Kenneth. *The Peculiar Institution: Slavery in the Antebellum South.* New York: Knopf, 1956.

Stanley, Amy Dru. "Beggars Can't Be Choosers: Compulsion and Contract in Postbellum America." *Journal of American History* 78 (March 1992): 1265–93.

———. *From Bondage to Contract: Wage Labor, Marriage, and the Market in the Age of Slave Emancipation.* New York: Cambridge University Press, 1998.

———. "Home Life and the Morality of the Market." In *The Market Revolution in America: Social, Political, and Religious Expression, 1800–1880,* edited by Melvyn Stokes and Stephen Conway, 74–96. Charlottesville: University Press of Virginia, 1996.

Stansell, Christine. *City of Women: Sex and Class in New York, 1789–1860.* Urbana: University of Illinois Press, 1987.

Steckel, Richard H. "Women, Work, and Health under Plantation Slavery in the United States." In *More than Chattel: Black Women and Slavery in the Americas,* edited by David Barry Gaspar and Darlene Clark Hine, 43–60. Bloomington: Indiana University Press, 1996.

Steinfeld, Robert J. *The Invention of Free Labor: The Employment Relation in English and American Law and Culture, 1350–1870.* Chapel Hill: University of North Carolina Press, 1991.

Sterkx, H. E. *Partners in Rebellion: Alabama Women in the Civil War.* Rutherford, N.J.: Fairleigh Dickinson University Press, 1970.

Sterling, Dorothy. *We Are Your Sisters: Black Women in the Nineteenth Century.* New York: Norton, 1984.

Stevenson, Brenda E. "Gender Convention, Ideals, and Identity among Antebellum Virginia Slave Women." In *More than Chattel: Black Women and Slavery in the Americas,* edited by David Barry Gaspar and Darlene Clark Hine, 169–90. Bloomington: Indiana University Press, 1996.

———. *Life in Black and White: Family and Community in the Slave South.* New York: Oxford University Press, 1996.

———. "Slavery." In *Black Women in America: An Historical Encyclopedia,* edited by Darlene Clark Hine et al., 1045–70. Bloomington: Indiana University Press, 1994.

Stone [Holmes], Sarah Katherine. *Brokenburn: The Journal of Kate Stone, 1861–1868.* Edited by John Q. Anderson. Baton Rouge: Louisiana State University Press, 1955.

Stowe, Steven M. *Intimacy and Power in the Old South: Ritual in the Lives of the Planters.* Baltimore: Johns Hopkins University Press, 1987.

Strickland, John Scott. "Traditional Culture and Moral Economy: Social and Economic Change in the South Carolina Low Country, 1865–1900." In *The Countryside in the Age of Capitalist Transformation: Essays on the Social History of Rural America,* edited by Steven Hahn and Jonathan Prude, 141–78. Chapel Hill: University of North Carolina Press, 1985.

Summers, Mark W. *Railroads, Reconstruction, and the Gospel of Prosperity: Aid under the Radical Republicans, 1865–1877.* Princeton, N.J.: Princeton University Press, 1984.

Tate, Claudia. *Domestic Allegories of Political Desire: The Black Heroine's Text at the Turn of the Century.* New York: Oxford University Press, 1992.

Tatum, Georgia Lee. *Disloyalty in the Confederacy.* Chapel Hill: University of North Carolina Press, 1934.

Taylor, A. Elizabeth. *A Short History of the Woman Suffrage Movement in Tennessee.* Nashville, Tenn.: Joint University Libraries, 1943.

Taylor, Joe Gray. *Eating, Drinking, and Visiting in the South: An Informal History.* Baton Rouge: Louisiana State University Press, 1982.

Taylor, Susie King. *Reminiscences of My Life in Camp with the 33rd U.S. Colored Troops, Late 1st South Carolina Volunteers: A Black Woman's Civil War Memoirs.* Edited by Patricia W. Romero and Willie Lee Rose. Boston: By the author, 1902; reprint, New York: Marcus Wiener, 1988.

Terborg-Penn, Rosalyn. "African American Women and the Woman Suffrage Movement." In *One Woman, One Vote: Rediscovering the Woman Suffrage Movement,* edited by Marjorie Spruill Wheeler, 135–55. Troutdale, Oreg.: New Sage, 1995.

————. "African-American Women's Networks in the Anti-Lynching Crusade." In *Gender, Class, Race, and Reform in the Progressive Era,* edited by Noralee Frankel and Nancy S. Dye, 148–61. Lexington: University Press of Kentucky, 1991.

————. "Discontented Black Feminists: Prelude and Postscript to the Passage of the Nineteenth Amendment." In *Decades of Discontent: The Women's Movement, 1920–1949,* edited by Lois Sharf and Joan M. Jensen, 261–78. Westport, Conn.: Greenwood, 1983.

Terrill, Tom E., and Jerrold Hirsch, eds. *Such as Us: Southern Voices of the Thirties.* Chapel Hill: University of North Carolina Press, 1978.

Thomas, Emory M. *The Confederate Nation: 1861–1865.* New York: Harper and Row, 1979.

Thomas, Gertrude Clanton. *The Secret Eye: The Journal of Gertrude Clanton Thomas, 1848–1889.* Edited by Virginia Ingraham Burr. Chapel Hill: University of North Carolina Press, 1990.

Thomas, Mary Martha. "The Ideology of the Alabama Woman Suffrage Movement, 1890–1920." In *Southern Women: Histories and Identities,* edited by Virginia Bernhard, Betty Brandon, Elizabeth Fox-Genovese, and Theda Perdue, 109–28. Columbia: University of Missouri Press, 1992.

————. *The New Woman in Alabama: Social Reforms and Suffrage, 1890–1920.* Tuscaloosa: University of Alabama Press, 1992.

Thornton, J. Mills. *Power and Politics in a Slave Society: Alabama, 1800–1860.* Baton Rouge: Louisiana State University Press, 1978.

Tomlins, Christopher L. *Law, Labor, and Ideology in the Early American Republic.* New York: Cambridge University Press, 1993.

Touchstone, Blake. "Planters and Slave Religion in the Deep South." In *Masters and Slaves in the House of the Lord: Race and Religion in the American South, 1740–1870,* edited by John B. Boles, 99–126. Lexington: University Press of Kentucky, 1988.

Tourgée, Albion W. *A Fool's Errand.* New York: Fords, Howard, and Hulbert, 1879; reprint, New York: Harper and Row, 1966.

————. *The Invisible Empire.* New York: Fords, Howard, and Hulbert, 1880; reprint, Baton Rouge: Louisiana State University Press, 1989.

Trelease, Allen W. *The North Carolina Railroad, 1849–1871, and the Modernization of North Carolina.* Chapel Hill: University of North Carolina Press, 1991.

————. *White Terror: The Ku Klux Klan Conspiracy and Southern Reconstruction.* New York: Harper and Row, 1971.

Tucker, St. George. "A Dissertation on Slavery: With a Proposal for the Gradual Abolition of It, in the State of Virginia." Philadelphia, 1796.

Tucker, Susan. *Telling Memories among Southern Women: Domestic Workers and Their Employers in the Segregated South.* Baton Rouge: Louisiana State University Press, 1988.

Turner, Elizabeth Hayes. *Women, Culture, and Community: Religion and Reform in Galveston, 1880–1920.* New York: Oxford University Press, 1997.

————. "Women, Religion, and Reform in Galveston, 1880–1920." In *Urban Texas: Politics and Development,* edited by Charles Miller and Heywood T. Sanders, 75–95. College Station: Texas A&M Press, 1990.

Tushnet, Mark V. *The American Law of Slavery, 1810–1860: Considerations of Humanity and Interest.* Princeton, N.J.: Princeton University Press, 1981.

Ulrich, Laurel Thatcher. *Good Wives: Image and Reality in the Lives of Women in Northern New England, 1650–1750.* New York: Oxford University Press, 1983.

———. *A Midwife's Tale: The Life of Martha Ballard, Based on Her Diary, 1785–1812.* New York: Knopf, 1990.

U.S. Congress. *Report of the Joint Select Committee to Inquire into the Condition of Affairs in the Late Insurrectionary States.* 13 vols. 42d Cong., 2d sess., 1872, S. Rept. 41, pt. 1.

U.S. Congress, House of Representatives. *Memphis Riots and Massacres.* 39th Cong., 1st sess., 1866, H. Rept. 101.

Varon, Elizabeth R. "'The Ladies Are Whigs': Lucy Barbour, Henry Clay, and Nineteenth-Century Virginia Politics." *Virginia Cavalcade* 42 (Autumn 1992): 73–83.

———. "Tippecanoe and the Ladies, Too: White Women and Party Politics in Antebellum Virginia." *Journal of American History* 82 (September 1995): 494–521.

———. *We Mean to Be Counted: White Women and Politics in Antebellum Virginia.* Chapel Hill: University of North Carolina Press, 1998.

Vlach, John Michael. *Back of the Big House: The Architecture of Plantation Slavery.* Chapel Hill: University of North Carolina Press, 1993.

Waldrep, Christopher. *Roots of Disorder: Race and Criminal Justice in the American South, 1817–80.* Urbana: University of Illinois Press, 1998.

———. "Substituting Law for the Lash: Emancipation and Legal Formalism in a Mississippi County Court." *Journal of American History* 82 (March 1996): 1425–51.

Walsh, Lorena S. "Work and Resistance in the New Republic: The Case of the Chesapeake, 1770–1820." In *From Chattel Slaves to Wage Slaves: The Dynamics of Labour Bargaining in the Americas,* edited by Mary Turner, 97–122. Bloomington: Indiana University Press, 1995.

Warbasse, Elizabeth Bowles. *The Changing Legal Rights of Married Women, 1800–1861.* New York: Garland, 1987.

Watson, Harry L. "Conflict and Collaboration: Yeomen, Slaveholders, and Politics in the Antebellum South." *Social History* 10 (October 1985): 273–98.

Wedell, Marsha. *Elite Women and the Reform Impulse in Memphis, 1875–1915.* Knoxville: University of Tennessee Press, 1991.

Weiner, Jonathan. "AHR Forum: Class Structure and Economic Development in the American South, 1865–1955." *American Historical Review* 84 (October 1979): 970–1006.

———. *Social Origins of the New South, 1860–1885.* Baton Rouge: Louisiana State University Press, 1978.

Weiner, Marli Frances. "Mistresses, Morality, and the Dilemmas of Slaveholding: The Ideology and Behavior of Elite Antebellum Women." In *Discovering the Women in Slavery: Emancipating Perspectives on the American Past,* edited by Patricia Morton, 199–312. Athens: University of Georgia Press, 1996.

————. *Mistresses and Slaves: Plantation Women in South Carolina, 1830–1880.* Urbana: University of Illinois Press, 1997.

Weisenburger, Steven. *Modern Medea: A Family Story of Slavery and Child-Murder from the Old South.* New York: Hill and Wang, 1998.

Welke, Barbara. "When All the Women Were White, and All the Blacks Were Men: Gender, Class, Race, and the Road to *Plessy,* 1855–1914." *Law and History Review* 13 (Fall 1995): 261–316.

Wells, Ida B. *A Red Record: Tabulated Statistics and Alleged Causes of Lynchings in the United States, 1892–1893–1894.* Chicago: n.p., 1894.

————. *Southern Horrors: Lynch Law in All Its Phases.* New York: New York Age Print, 1892.

Wheeler, Marjorie, Spruill. *New Women of the New South: The Leaders of the Woman Suffrage Movement in the Southern States.* New York: Oxford University Press, 1993.

————. *VOTES FOR WOMEN! The Suffrage Movement in Tennessee, the South, and the Nation.* Knoxville: University of Tennessee Press, 1995.

White, Deborah Gray. *Ar'n't I a Woman? Female Slaves in the Plantation South.* New York: Norton, 1985.

————. "The Cost of Club Work, the Price of Black Feminism." In *Visible Women: New Essays on American Activism,* edited by Nancy A. Hewitt and Suzanne Lebsock, 247–69. Urbana: University of Illinois Press, 1993.

————. "Female Slaves: Sex Roles and Status in the Antebellum Plantation South." *Journal of Family History* 8 (Fall 1983): 248–61.

Whites, LeeAnn. "The Charitable and the Poor: The Emergence of Domestic Politics in Augusta, Georgia, 1860–1880." *Journal of Social History* 17 (Summer 1984): 601–15.

————. "The Civil War as a Crisis in Gender." In *Divided Houses: Gender and the Civil War,* edited by Catherine Clinton and Nina Silber, 3–12. New York: Oxford University Press, 1992.

————. *The Civil War as a Crisis in Gender: Augusta, Georgia, 1860–1890.* Athens: University of Georgia Press, 1995.

————. "Rebecca Latimer Felton and the Problem of 'Protection' in the New South." In *Visible Women: New Essays in American Activism,* edited by Nancy A. Hewitt and Suzanne Lebsock, 41–61. Urbana: University of Illinois Press, 1993.

Wiley, Bell Irvin. *Confederate Women.* Westport, Conn.: Greenwood, 1975.

————. *Southern Negroes, 1861–1865.* New Haven, Conn.: Yale University Press, 1938.

Williams, Michael Ann. *Homeplace: The Social Use and Meaning of the Folk Dwelling in Southwestern North Carolina.* Athens: University of Georgia Press, 1991.

Williamson, Joel. *New People: Miscegenation and Mulattoes in the United States.* New York: Free Press, 1980.

Wilson, Charles Brantner. *The Black Codes of the South.* University: University of Alabama Press, 1965.

Wilson, Charles Reagan. *Baptized in Blood: The Religion of the Lost Cause, 1865–1920.* Athens: University of Georgia Press, 1980.

Wood, Betty. "'Never on a Sunday': Slavery and the Sabbath in Lowcountry Georgia, 1750–1830." In *From Chattel Slaves to Wage Slaves: The Dynamics of Labour Bargaining in the Americas,* edited by Mary Turner, 79–96. Bloomington: Indiana University Press, 1995.

———. *Women's Work, Men's Work: The Informal Slave Economies of Lowcountry Georgia.* Athens: University of Georgia Press, 1995.

Woodman, Harold D. *New South, New Law: The Legal Foundations of Credit and Labor Relations in the Postbellum Agricultural South.* Baton Rouge: Louisiana State University Press, 1995.

———. "Post–Civil War Southern Agriculture and the Law." *Agricultural History* 53 (January 1979): 319–37.

———. "Sequel to Slavery: The New History Views the Postbellum South." *Journal of Southern History* 48 (November 1977): 523–54.

Woodward, C. Vann. *Origins of the New South, 1877–1913.* Baton Rouge: Louisiana State University Press, 1951.

———. *The Strange Career of Jim Crow.* 3d rev. ed. New York: Oxford University Press, 1974.

———. *Tom Watson: Agrarian Rebel.* New York: Macmillan, 1938.

Wriggins, Jennifer. "Rape, Racism, and the Law." *Harvard Women's Law Journal* 6 (Spring 1983): 103–41.

Wright, William C. *The Secession Movement in the Middle Atlantic States.* Rutherford, N.J.: Fairleigh Dickinson University Press, 1982.

Wyatt-Brown, Bertram. "The Ideal Typology and Antebellum Southern History: A Testing of a New Approach." *Societas* 5 (Winter 1975): 1–29.

———. *Southern Honor: Ethics and Behavior in the Old South.* New York: Oxford University Press, 1982.

Yearns, Buck W., and John G. Barrett. *North Carolina Civil War Documentary.* Chapel Hill: University of North Carolina Press, 1980.

INDEX

Abolitionism, 22–23

Absalom, Absalom (Faulkner), 11

Adultery, 52–53, 127–28

African Americans: statistics on, as slaves, 16, 51; legal position of, as slaves, 49–50; and communities, 50–51, 55; and religion, 55–56; and childhood, 56, 57; efforts to define freedom of, during Civil War, 78–79, 104–6, 113–15; as refugees during Civil War, 103–4, 106–8, 113; claims to land, 108, 132–33, 134–35; claims to rights, 112–13; claims to property, 114; and families, 126–29; and marriage, 127–28; and mutual benefit societies, 130; and vigilante violence, 130–31, 147; and apprenticeship system, 131–32; and waged labor, 133–34, 135–36; and sharecropping, 138–39; middle-class status of, 139; political rights of, 146; civil rights of, 146, 147–48. *See also* Free blacks

—men: authority of, as slaves, 54–55; and Confederate service, 102–3; as Union soldiers, 108–9; views of labor, 140

—women: lack of historical studies on, 6; status of, as slaves, 11, 48–49; legal position of, 12; and conflicts with slaveholders, 21–22, 58–59, 60–61; and families, 51, 53–54, 110, 130; and marriage, 51–53, 109–10; relations to men, 54–55; and motherhood, 56–57; labor of, 57–58, 59, 101–3, 111–12; and property ownership, 59–60, 66; sexual assault of, 61–63; attempts to escape slavery, 63–64, 110–11; views of Civil War, 64, 67, 69, 100; and wartime shortages, 101; claims to land, 108, 135; vulnerability of, during Civil War, 108–9; as refugees, 111–12; views of Confederate surrender, 122–23; efforts to obtain civil and political rights, 125–25, 141–42, 142–44, 146; postwar economic position of, 129; and vigilante violence, 131, 147; and waged labor, 136–37, 137–38; views of labor, 139–40; and social reform, 142; and sexual violence, 144–45; and domestic violence, 145–46; similarities to common white women, 160; and conflicts with employers, 173–75

Alabama, 11, 32, 68, 95, 96, 97, 98

Alvis, Elizabeth, 98

American Colonization Society, 22

Andersonville, Ga., 110

Andrews, Sydney, 150, 151, 153, 154, 163

Antebellum South: geography of, 10–11. *See also* African Americans; Common whites; Slavery; Wealthy whites

Appalachian Mountains, 11

Apprenticeship system, 131–32

Arkansas, 11, 68, 96, 150, 181

Armstrong, B. D., 143–44

Atlanta, Ga., 80, 103, 173, 179

Augusta, Ga., 17, 91, 110, 115, 118, 177

LAURA F. EDWARDS is an associate professor in the History Department at UCLA. She is the author of *Gendered Strife and Confusion: The Political Culture of Reconstruction* (1997) and articles on women, gender, and the law in the nineteenth-century South.

Typeset in 11/13 Adobe Garamond
with Minion display
Designed by Paula Newcomb
Composed by Jim Proefrock
at the University of Illinois Press
Manufactured by Thomson-Shore, Inc.

University of Illinois Press
1325 South Oak Street
Champaign, IL 61820-6903
www.press.uillinois.edu